Revelation the Fair God

Pierre-Louis Ours

Published by NR3International, 2024.

REVELATION THE FAIR GOD

First edition. January 1, 2024.

Copyright © 2024 Pierre-Louis Ours.

ISBN: 979-8224856220

Written by Pierre-Louis Ours.

Also by Pierre-Louis Ours

The Rock Breaks the Globalists Empire
Revelation the Fair God
Le Rocher Brise L'Empire (Des Globalistes)

Revelation the Fair God
By Pierre-Louis Ours
Draft2Digital Edition
Published originally in 2013, Revelation the Fair God is revised and updated periodically.
Thank you for purchasing Revelation the Fair God. Even if you have downloaded a free copy, this book remains the copyrighted property of the author, and may not be reproduced, copied and distributed for commercial or non-commercial purposes. If you enjoyed this book, please encourage your friends to download their own copy; it is free on most platforms. Also, being an e-book allows corrections and annotations to be made continuously to improve readability; so do not hesitate to download the current version at anytime—it is free.

***

****

Table of Contents

****

Introduction

Fools will die because they refuse to listen; they will be destroyed because they do not care. But those who listen to me will live in safety and be at peace, without fear of injury.
(Proverbs 1:32 – 33 NCV)

Apocalypse, the Great Tribulation, the *antichrist* and other terms associated with the end times used to conjure vague images of dread for me. Revelation was intimidating and I seldom took the time to consider its message. Not anymore, a few years ago I was led to study it intensely and came through deeply encouraged. *Revelation, the Fair God* documents how the understanding of Revelation has enhanced the hope that is within me.

This book includes the entire text of Revelation from the Holman Christian Standard Bible. I also used the New Century Version, La Bible du Semeur and the EASY-TO-READ VERSION for balance and perspective. I did not use commentaries as I believe the biblical text should speak by itself. My "observations" and "thoughts to ponder" on specific subjects came about as the result of the study, and they are my own. Likewise any errors found in this book are mine.

Revelation the Fair God was first published in June 2013. Because it is in an electronic format; it could be treated as a working document. This gave me the advantage of improving and updating its text in two ways: for clarification, where needed, I provided appropriate backgrounds into the thought processes. I knew what I meant, so to speak, but the reader could not be expected to "read my mind". Lately, the unwieldy format requirements for Smashwords made it necessary to republish on another platform.

Second, history is being made every day: events that have taken place since 2013 have corroborated the content of this book. So, where pertinent, I have referenced those recent events. The reader can download the most current edition of *Revelation the Fair God* at anytime, for free from www.smashwords.com[1] or from most publishing platforms, domestic or international (some platforms like Kindle charge a modicum fee). A paper version now exists as well.

Understanding the terms

The beast

The book of Revelation uses the terms *beast*, *first beast* and *antichrist* to refer to the same person; wherever practical I will use the term *antichrist* for this person. The text of Revelation also refers to another beast as the *second beast* or the *false prophet*; I will use *false prophet* whenever possible to enhance clarity. (A prophet puts forth the truth; the *false prophet* will put forth lies—ergo the name.) Finally, the text also uses the term *beast* for the political empire that the *antichrist* will set up to extend his control over the populations; I will try to keep this distinction clear in my presentation.

Is the *testing time* of the end a confrontation between God and Satan?

No, it is not a time of confrontation between God and Satan. It is the time for the testing of men, orchestrated by God and managed by God. Satan does only what God strictly allows him to do.

We will see that Satan will never battle God directly. He will use his proxy, the *antichrist* to speak against God and to drive a human army against Jesus and His heavenly army. But Satan himself will never face off directly with God. He never has in the past and he never will.

---

1.   http://www.smashwords.com

Satan will not rule because he won the upper hand and thus can impose his will; it is God who makes it possible for him to come to power over the losers of this earth once the Almighty has removed His winners.

The book of Revelation reveals God's fairness and His goodness. Revelation describes how God will make absolutely certain that every last person who would have chosen Him can do so. We will see this process in the three and one-half years after the rapture of the saints of this age, when the choice will be imposed with absolute immediacy: choose Jesus or Satan (and his *antichrist*) now! From that point on, those who choose Jesus will be decapitated but will be permanently safe at His side and will be spared God's punishing calamities that will follow immediately these three and one-half years.

(Return to Table of Contents)

****

Chapter 1 - The Setting, Ephesus

Revelation 1:1 – 2:7

The setting of the book of Revelation

1:1 – 20

^{1}*The revelation of Jesus Christ that God gave Him to show His slaves what must quickly take place. He sent it and signified it through His angel to His slave John, ^{2}who testified to God's word and to the testimony about Jesus Christ, in all he saw. ^{3}The one who reads this is blessed, and those who hear the words of this prophecy and keep what is written in it are blessed, because the time is near! ^{4}John: To the seven churches in Asia. Grace and peace to you from the One who is, who was, and who is coming; from the seven spirits, before His throne; ^{5}and from Jesus Christ, the faithful witness, the firstborn from the dead and the ruler of the kings of the earth. To Him who loves us and has set us free from our sins by His blood, ^{6}and made us a kingdom, priests, to His God and Father—the glory and dominion are His forever and ever. Amen. ^{7}Look! He is coming with the clouds, and every eye will see Him, including those who pierced Him. And all the families of the earth will mourn over Him. This is certain. Amen. ^{8}"I am the Alpha and the Omega," says the Lord God, "the One who is, who was, and who is coming, the Almighty." ^{9}I, John, your brother and partner in the tribulation, kingdom, and endurance that are in Jesus, was on the island called Patmos because of God's word and the testimony about Jesus. ^{10}I was in the Spirit, on the Lord's day, and I heard a loud voice behind me like a trumpet ^{11}saying, "Write on a scroll what you see and send it to the seven churches:*

Ephesus, Smyrna, Pergamum, Thyatira, Sardis, Philadelphia, and Laodicea." [12] I turned to see whose voice it was that spoke to me. When I turned I saw seven gold lampstands, [13] and among the lampstands was One like the Son of Man, dressed in a long robe and with a gold sash wrapped around His chest. [14] His head and hair were white like wool—white as snow—and His eyes like a fiery flame. [15] His feet were like fine bronze as it is fired in a furnace, and His voice like the sound of cascading waters. [16] He had seven stars in His right hand; a sharp double-edged sword came from His mouth, and His face was shining like the sun at midday. [17] When I saw Him, I fell at His feet like a dead man. He laid His right hand on me and said, "Don't be afraid! I am the First and the Last, [18] and the Living One. I was dead, but look—I am alive forever and ever, and I hold the keys of death and Hades." [19] Therefore write what you have seen, what is, and what will take place after this. [20] The secret of the seven stars you saw in My right hand and of the seven gold lampstands is this: the seven stars are the angels of the seven churches, and the seven lampstands are the seven churches.

"I John, your brother and partner in the tribulation, kingdom and endurance that are in Jesus..." This is a key sentence to the understanding of the book of Revelation: John uses the word tribulation (singular) and expresses that the tribulation, kingdom and endurance are <u>in Jesus</u>—in our church age.

The word tribulation here reflects the struggle that believers in Jesus are put through within the fallen world that surrounds them as they live their lives faithfully to Him and offer their living witness of Him. It is what Jesus promised His followers: temporary persecution.

This, however is completely different from the word tribulations or great tribulations that we commonly use as an expression for the period that follows the rapture of the believers, when Satan, through his proxy, the *antichrist* is given free rein over the world. This latter period will be referred to as the *hour of testing* by Jesus as He dictates to John for us (3:10). (Using the Greek thlipsis or qlipsis, which reflects the pressing for a purpose—as the pressing of the grapes to extract the juice or, the pressing of the olives to extract the oil.)

The other important detail in this verse is that John puts the "tribulation" in Jesus. This clearly lets us know that he refers to our time—the space of time between Pentecost and the rapture—when the believers are in Jesus here on earth (as John certainly was when he wrote this). After the rapture, those lifted in Jesus will not experience tribulation, nor will they need endurance: they will be with Him away from this earth. (The few who will reject the mark of the beast and will in extremis turn to Jesus during that fateful time of testing will not have to face tribulation or endurance: they will be immediately and mercilessly beheaded.)

> <u>Note</u>: The pre-tribulation timing of the rapture of the saints will be developed in the text of this book at the proper time and context.

Verses 17 and 18 make clear that the one who came to John is Jesus. The wording Jesus uses leaves no doubt about this.

In verse 8, John gives us God as: *I am the Alpha and the Omega,* later, in verse 17b, Jesus (*the One like the Son of Man,* the One who *was dead but look—I am alive forever and ever*) says: *I am the First and the Last.* Here we see Jesus in God and God in Jesus as Jesus explained in John chapters 14, 15. God the Father does not precede Jesus nor does He extend beyond Jesus. And He does not create Jesus. The First and the Last or the Alpha and the Omega tells us that there is nothing preceding Jesus—or for that matter God. And there is nothing that extends beyond Jesus—or God.

This is important because some religions play loose with this part. Islam and later Mormonism clearly have God the Father preceding Jesus. It allows them to isolate Jesus and make it whatever suits their theology. In Islam, Jesus is just a prophet and in Mormonism, he is created and is actually a blood brother to Satan.

At the opposite end of the time frame, the word tells us that there is nothing extending past Jesus/God. But the same religions above must ignore this reality to fit in their heaven theologies. The Moslems can hope that if they are really, really good, they will get their fiefdom where they will enjoy the sexual favors of 72 virgins for eternity. Thus as gods, they can hope for their own eternity, their own personal Omega where no god has any reach at all; they are free-agent gods, then. The same is true for the faithful Mormon males, they can hope to qualify for their very own planet to populate through the services of as many beautiful women they can dream of having, forever. The Alpha/First and the Omega/Last qualifiers are very important and are non-negotiable.

Finally in verse 20, the "seven" *stars, churches, lampstands* were specific to that time, yet, they are endemic to our time, as they have been relevant to and representative of the world's community of believers in every age. The "seven" represent the total community of believers at any one time and at all times.

Observations

The first line tells us that Revelation is dictated to the apostle John by Jesus. In essence, this part called the *"things that are"* is Jesus' epistle to all believers. Before Jesus went up to heaven He could not give a letter of guidance and corrections to His church because it did not function yet. The church came into existence at Pentecost when the believers received His Spirit.

Jesus waited until it made sense to provide steering instructions: steering a motionless vehicle has no effect. These steering letters had to wait until the church was underway. By the time the apostle John was near the end of his long life, the church had begun to develop and exhibit both the good traits that would honor her and the bad traits that would plague her all the way to the rapture. The time was right for Jesus' epistle.

There was another factor that may have controlled the timing of this epistle. The first believers—especially the Jewish believers—had hoped or even assumed that Jesus would come back for the first Jubilee after His death. Which would have been sometime around 65 to 75 A.D. (Peter had to address this false expectation in his second epistle.) The people had to be clear of that hurdle in order to be receptive to the long term teaching presented by Jesus. They had to have experientially known that the age of grace extended beyond their original thinking to be embrace for this teaching.

This is the only epistle actively and directly dictated by God Himself: *It is the word of God; it is the message from Jesus Christ* (1:2a NCV). The believer should give it ascendance and authority over all the other epistles—that were inspired; but not dictated. The texts of the epistles should be gauged and validated upon the authority of the text of Revelation; not the other way around. Revelation is not an obscure appendage at the end of the Bible, an after-thought, so to speak. Revelation is where the Christian lives; it instructs and it reveals.

The apostle John was the perfect conduit: he had (and still has) credibility with believers. He had been with Jesus during His entire earthly ministry and had witnessed Jesus' transfiguration, death and resurrection. It is appropriate that God should choose him to relay this teaching.

As mentioned above, the term *tribulation* in 1:9 applies to our current era, not to the events of the end times, because John lived and died in our era. That is the era he shares with us. Obviously,

He will not be subjected to the terrible trials that will be visited on the world population following the rapture of the Christians; so we cannot twist what he says here. Being a true Christian sets us apart from the society in which we live, and our lives are fraught with difficulties, even persecutions (Jesus had foretold it). Tribulation, mild or severe, has befallen the true follower of Jesus all through the Church era, and John was no stranger to it.

Thoughts to ponder

The word *angel* of each church here—as in every case in the Bible—means messenger, ambassador, representative or agent. The word angel is not a translation into English; it is a poor transliteration. Messenger is the correct term, whether the word angel refers to a man or to a heavenly being. The various churches or groups of believers often sent messengers to the apostles to get clarifications on topics, concepts and conduct. We read in Acts that they sent such people to Jerusalem while Peter, James and others were still there. It makes perfect sense: emails and telephones did not exist yet.

Thus, decades later when Jesus dictates Revelation, John is probably the only apostle still living and his reputation is well established. Isolated groups of believers would have routinely sent messengers to him to inquire on various subjects and to get guidance. He would have represented the direct connection with the source of Christianity. John would provide answers and explanations and these messengers would report back to their groups. In Revelation, the teachings to be sent were of capital importance so it is Jesus who dictated them and instructed John to write them out. Jesus knew that believers through the ages would need them unadulterated; so they are in writing.

The system of messengers was much more efficient than if the aging apostle John had walked to the various believers' groups in person. When we consider just the seven groups of believers here, they were scattered in what is today Turkey. John would have wasted most of his time walking from one group to the next and would have certainly expended more energy that he could spare at his advanced age. By being stationary, John is more effective. Also, this epistle of Jesus through John, taking place at one time and in one location, provided a better means to collate the data and to keep the information together through time. Plus, John is told to give the entire text to each of the messengers; not just the message specific to his church. No wonder God immobilized him on Patmos.

Another advantage is that there were probably messengers from several groups at any given time meeting with John. In this manner they all heard teachings on several subjects and thus they were able to disseminate more information back to their home group. At this particular time, there were at least these seven messengers at John's side.

These messengers on the way to John would probably stop and layover at Christian homes in various cities. There they would discuss the matters being brought to John and possibly these local churches along the way added some of their own questions. On the return trip, stopping again, the traveling messengers would share with the local church what they had learned at John's side. The impact of John's teaching would be greatly amplified.

Having John stationary was a blessing for the church universal—God was not surprised. God used actual messengers from several groups in Asia to transmit this appropriate teaching to these groups and by extension to every believer who has read them since, wherever they may be and at whatever period of history.

It is no surprise that the seven messengers present at that time happen to be the right ones to provide us with this extensive teaching. In 1:16, we see that Jesus has the *seven stars*—the chosen seven messengers—in His right hand. These specific messengers from these seven specific assemblies of believers were there to hear from John because Jesus brought them. Furthermore, there is no chance that their messages would not be taken back and given to their intended audiences because these messengers were safely in Jesus' right hand (1:20). Finally, the revelation specifically brought by Jesus was too far-reaching and precise to be orally imparted therefore Jesus insisted that John provide it in writing to the messengers.

As explained above, the term "angel" in 2:1, 2:8, 2:12, 2.18, 3:1, 3:7 and 3:14 refers to these human messengers. Interpreting "angel" to mean some heavenly being instead of a human being is just not possible: it would mean that God used John to pass on messages to His own celestial angels. In all the scriptures, God has never used an earthbound human—not even John—as messenger to carry a message to His heavenly angels who are in His presence in heaven. God always used His heavenly *angels* to bring messages to humans; never vice versa.

Some interpret *the angel* of each of these churches as referring to the pastor of that church. This is faulty thinking for the simple reason that the modern office of "pastor" did not exist in the early churches. The believers' groups had elders and deacons as specified in 1 Timothy 3. It is very possible that the assemblies would send one of their elders as messenger to the Apostle John; but that does not make him the equivalent of a modern-day pastor.

There are letters to seven churches: seven represents totality. The implication is that these letters are for all the churches of all times. The teachings in these letters cover the spectrum of Jesus' guidance to the church universal. If He had needed to broaden His teaching further; He could easily have done so—therefore the teaching is complete as is. And it is foundational.

<u>Note</u>: the seven churches represent seven types of believers. In any church today several types may share the same pews: Ephesus types, Sardis types, Pergamum types... So as you read, ask yourself: Am I being addressed personally here? Today, there is not a Philadelphia type church or a Laodicea type church; there are many churches where Philadelphia types of believers can be found, as well as the other types, etc.

Also, as individual believers, we may have to be challenged in our "Ephesus" conduct and frame of mind at one point, yet at other times we may be rebuked for our "Pergamum" or "Thyatira" deviances. So the teaching is both congressional and personal at the same time. At the end, though, the battle is always inside the individual believer.

The seven churches Jesus chose to address in His epistle to all believers of all times were specific and local congregations but they were not monolithic in their doctrines or deeds as modern congregations tend to be. Modern congregations, members of a denomination or not, are held together by a narrow set of tenets and particular organizational practices. In John's time, believers met with all the local believers in their town or area, today, believers assemble by their denomination and preferences but not necessarily locally. They will drive by several churches on the way to their favored flavor of service or beliefs. Denominational fences have been erected, the Nicolaitan principle rules and followers have been corralled by color and flavor. These disobediences have enabled entire denominations—representing millions—to leave the truth and embrace gross evil.

<u>(Return to Table of Contents)</u>

Ephesus

2:1 – 7

¹ Write to the angel of the church in Ephesus: "The One who holds the seven stars in His right hand and who walks among the seven gold lampstands says: ² I know your works, your labor, and your endurance, and that you cannot tolerate evil. You have tested those who call themselves apostles and are not, and you have found them to be liars. ³ You also possess endurance and have tolerated many things because of My name and have not grown weary. ⁴ But I have this against you: You have abandoned the love you had at first. ⁵ Remember then how far you have fallen; repent, and do the works you did at first. Otherwise, I will come to you and remove your lampstand from its place—unless you repent. ⁶ Yet you do have this: You hate the practices of the Nicolaitans, which I also hate. ⁷ Anyone who has an ear should listen to what the Spirit says to the churches. I will give the victor the right to eat from the tree of life, which is in God's paradise."

Jesus begins His addresses by lavishing praises where praises are due. He begins his messages with the group in Ephesus; it is one of the two groups that get the most praises.

What's happening

Today, the community of believers in Ephesus would be considered a model church. Imagine that you have just moved to a new city and you are looking for a community of believers with whom you could worship, grow, learn... And you happen on a church, a community of Christians that is very active, very faithful week after week, year after year. A church that makes no room for the false teachings of evil people, they emphatically reject the evil centered teachings of LGBGTQ+ agenda. They vehemently oppose the killing of the innocent in the womb. They reject the false apostles and their claims and the teachings the New Apostolic Reformation and other "reformation" variants that abound today.

In the Christian faith, apostle means "one being sent [by God]". Throughout the church history there have always been people who claim to be sent by God to us as a group or to you as a person. We must exercise discernment; there are a lot of self-serving quacks out there. Following Jesus involves a lot of judging—that is clear-eyed discernment followed by drastic actions. We must cut out the false messengers, pure and simple, no emotion should enter the process. These Ephesians expose the "apostles" lies.

This congregation has also withstood all sorts of campaigns against them. They have not submitted to illegal threats wielded against them by the authorities, and day after day they have maintained their unerring bearing. What a church! To you, a believer, it would seem to be an ideal group to join.

But, to the unbelievers, to the ones who do not know the Savior... this community would just be another well structured, do-good, group-think. Indeed, what does such a community bring to the unbelievers here and now? And what makes it different from other associations one can join for a time and leave at will without loss?

In Jesus, God makes us His children, love is central to any healthy familial relationship. God does not make us members, He adopts us as His children. Our relationship to God is borne of love (For God so loved the world...) and it functions in love (John 15, John 17...) If we shed the love core of our relationship to our Father; are we still embracing our filial position? Are we still honoring our redeemed heredity?

God wants, requires our love for Him, not just obedience or submission, but full personal love. The good news begins with His love: ...*For God so loved the world...* Our part must also exist on our love of Him and for Him. Indeed, Jesus demonstrates this clearly with Peter, when Peter was about to begin his Christian life: *...Peter, do you love Me?* It is those who love Him that Jesus asks to follow Him. It is after having demanded Peter's love that Jesus said: *Follow Me.*

The main thread of the John's gospel is that we do not go to Jesus on our own. God-the-Father's unflinching and dogged love pursues everyone through life. Through many uncanny, personal prompts He intends to bring us to Jesus where we would become aware of His love and enter in this love. Those who systematically shun these divine prompts will end up separated from their Maker. Those who embrace them will eventually embrace Jesus, in their lifetime if someone presents Jesus to them or after as explained by Peter in 1 Peter 3:19 – 21 and 1 Peter 4:6.

The Ephesians had forgotten what started them!

That is: Someone who loved someone in Ephesus, could not hold the Good News back and came to make disciples of these loved ones, to baptize them and to teach them to obey Jesus commands. The Good News is about life in the here and now. This is why it is called the Good News. Eternity in heaven is the natural continuation of the good life here.

Consider: Islam is not good news even though it touts the possibility of a paradise. It is not good news because it offers no divine help for living life today, down here. It gives an extensive list of "dos and don'ts" that will be used to tally the score for or against the converts as he negotiates the burdens of life. And finally, it leaves the adept alone for his future face to face reckoning with a capricious god. There is no: Allah so loved the world...

On the other hand, the God of heaven loves humans and He invests Himself intimately in their lives... today and every day. He comes to live in them, to guide them through the maze of life, to comfort them, correct them... They are never alone. Anyone who had done life solo for a while can appreciate what a wonderful life saver the Gospel is: the All-knowing, All-powerful Master of the universe proposes to come aboard and pilot him through the shoals to the safely to his permanent mooring. Why did God do this? Because God so loved the world...

Let's develop the contrast between a religion without God's living love and Christianity. When asked if He was really the Messiah, Jesus answered: the blind see, the lame walk, the dead are brought back to life... Translation: God's love is manifested in this life.

Why is it that Muslims are so fond of martyrdom? Why Muslim mothers trudging through life wish martyrdom for their own children? It is because it gives them an escape, a by-pass, from this lonely arduous and uncertain life. Doom weighs on the faithful in all things and all times, he is a stranger negotiating the obstacle course laid before him by an exacting god. Martyrdom opens directly into paradise. One can see that a loving mother could yearn for an assured release, even at the price of her deep mourning. Jesus, however, demonstrated the opposite: He brought back dead people to THIS life. Was this a mean trick? No, it was just the opposite: a glorious adoption into life to the fullest in the care and sponsorship of the all knowing, loving God.

Also, God never answered a display of faith with the following: "You have shown great faith, you have pleased God, so go now directly into paradise." No, He absolutely did not, because Jesus came that we may have life, and life more abundantly—in the here and now. And because He loves us, He does life with us.

Ask any Muslim if Muhammad was really the last and foremost prophet of their god and his answer will not be: "Because through him, wherever he rode wielding his sword, people's lives were transformed; the lame walked, the blind saw, the mute praised, and the dead were brought back to life."

You see, the biblical argument is not about Hell or not Hell, about Hell or heaven. The argument is about life and life more abundantly from a God who loves you. And this is what you want to bring to those you love. This is the fire that sets fires.

The Ephesians had become self-centered, cozily insular. They became God's group and they did church. They had become active members. Jesus is telling them: Following Me is not how you do church on Wednesdays and Sundays. It is not about "being in church" either. If you don't have the love to go out and spread My love to all those who do not yet have it; I will let this community disappear. And He did.

Interestingly, several decades earlier Paul seems to have already sensed this propensity in the Ephesians because he specifically prayed for them about it: *I pray that Christ will live in your hearts by faith and that your life will be strong in love and be built on love. And I pray that you and all God's holy people will have the power to understand the greatness of Christ's love—how wide and how long and how high and how deep that love is. Christ's love is greater than anyone can ever know, but I pray that you will be able to know that love. Then you can be filled by the fullness of God* (Ephesians 3:17 – 19 NCV).

The principle at the core of Jesus' message to these Ephesians is that the Christian walk is all about Jesus, not about the believer. When a believer strays from this understanding, it is bad for him because he loses the peace Jesus specifically provides (John 14:27) and it is bad for others because he loses his triumphant witness.

YHWH's love through Jesus

YHWH's direct love through Jesus provides two fundamental applications in the believer's life that set Christianity apart from every religion. The first application is that Jesus grants eternal life to each believer the moment he converts and chooses Jesus: paradise is attached to the saving conversion.

The second application is that Jesus extends His love through His Spirit into the very life of the believer. Jesus comes to live in and with the believer so He experiences intimately every hurt, sorrow, joy or victory in the believer's life—from the inside. Jesus also advises, guides and protects. He personally insures the process that transforms life. He accomplishes in us that which He asks of us. This makes our faith unique and our relationship with our God exceptional.

Not to belabor the point, but let us look at two world religions to illustrate this point. Consider Islam: when a person is persuaded to choose Allah as his god (or is forced to accept Allah as his god), Allah does not grant that person entrance into paradise at that moment. And neither does Allah offer a relationship with his convert. Instead, the new faith imposes blind subjection to an unknowable god. The new convert does not receive Allah's approval and never Allah's personal love. Instead, the new convert receives a book (Quran) that few people at all can read and fewer can understand, plus a compilation of commentaries to live by (Hadiths). It also imposes a ruling hierarchy of Mullahs, or Imams.

The convert is taught that if he practices the precepts in these "scriptures" faithfully, pray the required rote daily prayers without fail and if he hates the people he is told to hate and makes new Muslim converts through high reproduction rates, indoctrination or coercion; then, maybe, Allah will be merciful and will accept that person into Muslim paradise after death...but there are no guarantees. (The only qualifying by-pass into paradise is to commit suicide while killing non-Muslims; which they call martyrdom.)

In Islam, the onus rests solely on the convert: Allah does not walk with him, does not come to live in him. On a day-to-day basis, Allah is of no use at all to the Muslim.

In contrast to this, a dying man can give his life to Jesus "in extremis" yet he can be sure that he is heaven-bound. He can receive peace instantly (viz. the man on the cross next to Jesus). However, a dying man who opts for Islam at the threshold of death will be judged on his past—that is on the merits of his non-Muslim life—thus guaranteeing Hell as his destination. What good is that? Where is the hope? Where is the peace? What is absent from his god? Love, is what is absent from his god.

The new Islamist convert cannot be heaven-bound because heaven has to be earned. There is nothing there to embrace spontaneously...ergo, the human religion of Islam could only expand at the point of the sword—abject fear had to be the motivator, and fearful submission has been the keeper. It is a religion of enforcement; not of jubilant transformation.

Allah does not pay for the life of each Muslim convert; the convert alone assumes the cost of believing and the burden of living life according to his religion. Allah does not restore the convert piece by piece with patience, understanding as Jesus does, (*a bruised reed He will not break, and a smoldering wick snuff out*, Isaiah 42:3 and Matthew 12:20); which prompts the valid question: since Allah does nothing, then is Allah even real or is he a figment of man's imagination maintained by violence, coercion and slavery of the spirit?

Let's consider Buddhism: a new convert has no relationship and no communication with Buddha (or for that matter with Yamantaka, the conqueror of death or any other deity). Buddha does not intervene in the convert's life—ever! However the convert receives a copious compilation of Buddha's thoughts (as well as the thoughts of other disciples of Buddha) but he has the sole responsibility to navigate the path of life toward a nebulous and never fully defined enlightenment.

The destination of his life's travails remains dishearteningly improbable; he is going to die and be re-born untold number of times at the mercy of a capricious, totally out-of-his-control karma. This karma controls all his hopes: will he develop further or be ruined by whatever persona he comes back as next? And through this intractable process, all the Buddhist has to go on is a compilation of thoughts and theories to ponder upon.

Incidentally, the "scriptures" or sacred texts never identify what the original "bad Karma" was. Not knowing how or why these nefarious cycles began makes it impossible for one generational individual to actually tackle the problem and possibly straighten the "wrong" and free himself from his crushing, adversarial fate. It is the most debilitating religious proposition.

That religion provides no supra-human power that can come and share the life of the lowly convert; comforting him, teaching him and leading him. There is no god to hold his hand and feel his pain. A dying man who decides that Buddhism might be the answer to life receives nothing. All he knows is that whatever karma he has already accumulated will cause him to be re-born somewhere, sometime...but with no assurance that the new persona will continue the quest. What a despairing situation this would be.

In contrast with the above religions, the believer in Jesus has Jesus/YHWH who from the beginning of time has walked with those who chose Him. Enoch walked with Him, so did Abraham, David, Jesus, John, Peter, the Ten Boom family, Joni Eareckson-Tada...so can you.

The trap Ephesians fell for

You have abandoned the love you had at first. [5]*Remember then how far you have fallen.*

In Jesus, the believer is not only a son of the Father, thus co-heir with Christ; he is also Jesus' bride—chosen by Jesus and loved by

Him because of His unabating desire to love His bride. This is why in Jesus we have everything we need: a bride has everything her groom has. Therefore, this situational reality creates in the believer a giddy, groom-centered desire to celebrate, to sing, and to broadcast this marvelous condition.

However, and here I will paraphrase Hannah Whitall-Smith: "As soon as husband and wife perform their expected service out of a sense of duty, the sweetness of the union is lost. And the marriage becomes a bondage and the things that were a joy before become crosses [to bear]. And before long these things become what we ought to do—but dislike doing. And a sort of meritorious penance takes the place of overwhelming joy that was there... and should still be there." And this is what happened in Ephesus.

How far you have fallen or whence you have fallen. The believer's position, his status was that of a beloved bride. The Ephesians had vacated the position of bride of Christ. So this raises the pivotal questions: If the believer is not Jesus' bride, if he does not function as His bride; then what is he? And how is Jesus supposed to feel about it? What will Jesus do about it?

The believer began as the beloved bride goo-goo eyed for her Groom. But eventually, she resigned her position and status to become just a servant, a paid laborer. She wanted to be worth her wages, she wanted to have value outside the value inferred by her Groom. The believers may be doers of good deeds but without their defining bridal identity they do not point to the Savior anymore. They forgot that each of them had been brought into the knowledge of Jesus because someone loved him; just like Andrew did with brother, Peter. This is why I shared Jesus with my own brother.

This is very important because Christianity is not set on the same footing as any other religion. It does not operate like any religion.

The great commission compels us to bring out the good news about Jesus. The Christian faith is the only faith that centers on a person—and a person-minded God. It does not hang on a messenger, nor on a set of scriptures or on a list of rules. It is not based on a philosophy to be applied.

It is unique in the world and in history. The key to Christianity is to come to the person of Jesus and to reside in His presence as His bride. He comes down to us; we do not climb up to Him. He comes to each one of us and says: *Follow me...* enter my company and I'll take you the whole way.

A person is saved the moment he or she comes to Jesus and embraces Him completely as Lord and Savior; regardless of the amount of scripture that person knows at that time. So, the matter of heaven or Hell being settled, what is left is the wonderfully loving provision for the day to day life, down here. The convict hanging on the cross next to Jesus entered paradise on this precept alone. He never learned appropriate scriptures about salvation nor did he receive the Spirit of God and he never shared his faith with anyone. His salvation was God-given. He had to accept it, and he did.

God extends a love bond to us through Jesus. As we respond to Him, we bond with Jesus and we become infused by His love and thus we can begin to love Him and eventually to love others. That is the "mere" Christianity, the nexus for us all; and it must remain so. Man's soul yearns for this love; man is wired for it.

As we love Jesus in return for being loved, we embrace His preferences, His tastes and His choices for us and for our life. We realize that His infinite love for us desires only the best for us moment by moment as well as in the aggregate of life. Loving Him is to trust in His very love for us.

When we have brought the love of Jesus to all the people we already loved; we must continue and love new people, and others, and others to bring the love of Jesus to them too.

That is why the Ephesians had become ineffective witnesses: without that love spark, the great Christian commission is just a compilation of "do rights" and "don't do wrongs". Christ becomes the object of a religion. When the church cares more for people and its various corporate activities than it does the person of Jesus; then it has left the path—and this is Jesus' message to the church of Ephesus.

Sincere members of all human religions labor hard to work and to merit their way up the mythical spiritual ladder of their particular faith. Their curiosity and interest will not be aroused by some other fellow toiling along the mythical ladder of his own religion. And if approached by this type of Christian, the deep reaction will be: What do I gain? What do I gain by leaving my family, my culture and giving up whatever chips I have already accumulated in my own faith?

How do we lose the love?

We Christians fall easily into the prideful and conceited mindset that our works are helping God; we are convinced that God benefits from our efforts. From that position it is but a short leap to believe that it is our works that keep us in God's good graces. At this point, we enter the hamster wheel. The result is that our own performance becomes our focus and since we are well aware that we are not perfect, fears and pressures will dictate our reactions and cloud up our true relationship with our Lord. Legalism follows, overshadowing grace. By trying to placate YHWH for the good things we want and against the loss of the blessings we enjoy, we make Christianity into a religion just like all the religions of the world: we treat YHWH like a man-made god.

There is a second aspect to this loss of love process: we begin to invent, choose and practice our own causes, activities and ministries—social justice for example. These are our own expressions of our Christianity but they become our orthodoxy. And when this happens, we have exited Jesus' orthodoxy.

God's love transforms the life of those who apprehend it. Paul understood this and he concluded his prayer for these same Ephesians: *With God's power working in us, God can do much, much more than anything we can ask or imagine* (Ephesians 3:20 NCV).

I saw myself in Revelation 2: 2 – 5. I have done the Ephesians bit: worked hard and not given up—pugnaciously so—I reject false prophets and false teachings and I have endured... But, I had missed God's love and Jesus' love because I had gauged divine commitment upon my own "unlovable-ness". I dwelled in my depravity and my propensity to fail in my walk with Jesus; so I have felt unlovable and thus I tried harder. I was wrong! God does not base his love on my merits. He associates me with His merit.

Following Jesus has a legal dimension: The Father adopts the believer as his child (co-heir with Jesus). At some point in the future, the believer will inherit his God-given share. Following Jesus has a practical and spiritual dimension: The believer becomes Jesus' bride; as such he comes into instant possession of everything Jesus-the-Groom has. A bride never has to justify her position, her status and her rights.

God decided to love me. Nothing can stop Him from loving me. He expressed His love for me vicariously at Jesus' baptism: *you are my son, whom I love, and I am very pleased with you* (Luke 2:22 NCV). And God expressed the same fact effectively at my own baptism: you are my son, whom I love and I am very pleased to have you. Jesus did not wait until I had cleaned up my act (even partially) to bless me: His care and generosity were evident right away, and they have never faltered since. I am "in", period. I am in

His love, period. My life has been very blessed since then because of the position <u>He</u> has taken toward me: He is very happy to love me and to have me. I am what He paid for.

When Jesus paid for me, He was not buying a good person: He was purchasing a reprobate. He knew full well who and what he was getting into—yet, He was pleased to have me, "as is" so to speak, and to pay for me.

Through Jesus, God purchases useless, broken tools and then He patiently invests Himself to redeem them to the usefulness and to the glory that He had put in each of them before the world was made. It is not about me, it is not about you: it is all about Jesus who is all about God. It is His project—we are only the objects of His projects.

So Jesus dictates to John for the Ephesians: *remember the love you had at first*. Remember the love I lavished on you at your baptism when you came to Me, scoundrels and reprobates, all of you. Remember that free love: My love. It is still the same love that restores you piece by piece, carefully tending to you.

Remember that you came up out of the baptismal water with empty hands; you brought nothing to Me or to the process! ... And you have provided nothing to Me since. I am doing the restoring and the work I will do through you is My work.

This has always been the case with God and way back in time Job had to learn this paramount attribute of God. His experience helps us understand the message here.

As a very wealthy man, Job applied himself to do good because he lived in fear that God would take away all that was dear to him. So he offered sacrifices every time his children held a party; just in case they had sinned. We know of Job's great fear because he tells us: "*the thing I feared has overtaken me, and what I dreaded has happened to me*" (Job 3:25). Job had the wrong perspective on God; he failed to see the immovable reality of God's love for him as expressed when God spoke with Satan: *"My servant Job… no one else on earth is like him"* (Job 1:8 and 2:3). "My servant Job" says it all: there is a satisfied proprietary inference here. Job was securely held in the inner circle of God's love but he did not let this be the basis of his life. God considered him peerless; but Job felt he had to keep earning God's approval by his actions in order to protect the things he loved most.

Do you feel you have to live up to God's expectations to deserve His continued grace, His abiding love? You did not come to Him under that premise, initially. Yet, has this sin of pride invaded your practices?

Having listened to the discourse between Job and his three friends, Elihu warns Job not to question God's actions based on his own perceived self-righteousness—not to think that he had earned God's indebtedness. *"You ask, 'What's the use? I don't gain anything by not sinning'. I will answer you and your friends who are with you. 'Look up at the sky and see the clouds so high above you. If you sin, it does nothing to God; even if your sins are many, they do nothing to Him. If you are good, you give nothing to God; He receives nothing from your hand. Your evil ways only hurt a man like yourself, and the good you do only helps other human beings' "* (Job 35:3 – 8 NCV).

One of the purposes for the process Job went through was to bring him to see God's perspective and to realize that God loves us on a divine scale: His love cannot be bought or placated. It does not depend on man's performance. We see that Job was transformed by this revelation because in the subsequent and longest part of his life there is no mention of Job sacrificing in fear. Job had become secure in the knowledge of God's love for him. His life was transformed. Job expressed it this way: *I had only heard about You before, but now I have seen You with my own eyes* (Job 42:5 NLT). Job could finally enjoy his blessings with joyful thanksgiving, in peace and free from all fears. Note that Job's earthly life was made more abundant; there was no notion of the thereafter. God showed Job His Good News.

The believers in Ephesus had moved away from the declaration of love that God utters at every convert's baptism: "This is my child, I love him/her and I am pleased with him/her". Jesus who was God and Messiah, did not need to be baptized—John the baptizer expressed as much and Jesus acknowledged the point (Matthew 3:13 – 15)—but Jesus needed to exemplify the reality of God's commitment of love for us. So, Jesus demonstrated baptism for our benefit: to show us that we must make the public commitment that our faith requires and more importantly to reveal to us the statement of love and the pledge God makes at that moment to each baptized believer "*this is my beloved son. I take delight in Him*" (Matthew 3:17 HCSB). When a person comes to Christ and makes the public confession of faith through baptism, shedding the old life, he or she becomes the brother or sister of Jesus: co-heir with Him of God's parenthood and love. And he becomes Jesus' beloved and precious bride.

At first, these Ephesians had reveled in the safety and glory of the love God lavished on them: *the love you had in the beginning*. But over time they moved away from that; they drew self-approval from their works which in turn can lead to conceit. Their works may have taken the nature of a bargaining platform in their relationship with God instead of being simply the reflection, the spontaneous reaction to God's love for them. This is what Jesus aims to correct in all of us through His message to the believers in Ephesus.

We feel that over the years of our "Christianity" we ought to be able to build a personal momentum of righteousness that we could personally use to do "good works" or to "live right". That's our pride talking. Consider the light bulb: it may have lit up a room for a thousand hours, yet when you switch it off; it is instantly useless. The light bulb is the perfect modern analogy for Jesus' words: *you can do nothing without Me* (John 15:5 HCSB). Our pride, however, will make us consider our works; it will use our works to give us value. Then our works become our justification to God and the unit of comparison against our peers.

When works are the justification, fear inevitably creeps in: "will this be sufficient to placate God? Am I doing enough?" When this is the case the works acquire a momentum of their own and the divine spark is extinguished. Little distinguishes the good works the Ephesian believers did from the secular social or civic activities carried out by their non-Christian ambient society as it enforced its rules and policed its values.

On the other hand, the works a believer does as a reflection of Jesus' love for him; the works that flow out of irrepressible gratefulness will attract others. Done as the natural response of the beloved, these works have a salutary appeal to the unsaved and bring encouragement to the weaker brothers and sisters. This is essential to the Christian life because God's love through Jesus is the reality that transcends the human condition and transforms all human relations.

Without this divine dimension, the followers of Christ practice a mere human religion, hardly distinguishable from all other human religions that concentrate on applying specific rules and enforcing theologies.

This is the first correction Jesus brings to the church at large. As such it is very important because it addresses the situational core of our relationship with Him: *we love because He first loved us* (1 John 4:19 HCSB). Jesus wants the believers in Ephesus to fill their consciousness anew with the reality of God's love for them in Him as they did in the beginning and return that love wholeheartedly so that their works may have a divine effect on those around them. God gave them His love <u>before</u> they began to do any of the works listed in the text; their works in the beginning were the grateful response to being loved. They had stopped testifying about that love, they had lost the motivating urge to spread its wild fire.

Being loved by God and loving God has always been the core of the relationship God intended to have with man: YHWH says *whoever loves me, I will save* (Psalm 92:14 NCV). Jesus is very serious about this: *"Otherwise I will come to you and remove your lampstand from its place"*. Jesus will not hesitate to remove this assembly from Ephesus (as history will sadly confirm).

Jesus' teaching here is pertinent today; many assemblies who claim to follow Christ do not heed this teaching. They herd people: they meticulously apply "church" rules and keep a close watch over their denominational doctrines. They busy themselves with a multitude of ministries—the fashionable word for works—but they do not free the believers into the fullness of Jesus' transforming reality. Their witness to the adherents of other religions is ineffectual: what is there to find for a Muslim, Buddhist or Animist that he does not already experience under the constraining yoke of his religion? Why should he consider alienating himself from family and culture by changing to "just another religion", another group-think? The love of Jesus is what humanity needs—always.

The words of Jesus to the Ephesians are pertinent to you and to me: have I left the love I had at the beginning? The irrepressibly attractive love had drawn me to Him because it cut through all my shortcomings.

> Note: blessedly, God's love is evident in His scriptures, independent from man's performance.

We must note the plural in "churches" in 2:7. This should catch our attention because this part of John's letter is written to the church (singular) at Ephesus. This simply means that the teaching is not just for the assembly of believers in Ephesus but to every group of believers anywhere, then and now. It is church-universal in scope and in intent. The other clue is: *Every person who has ears* ... we all do. Barring accidents and birth defects, everyone has a pair of ears; therefore this message is for all believers.

Finally, only the victor, the one who makes the needed changes will eat from the tree of life. The others may call themselves "Christians" but their destination is not the new earth—where the tree of life will be.

Observations

Apostles

The theological discipline of these Ephesians would keep them in good stead today as there is a resurgence of the same fraudulent claims of apostleship. There is a large scattering of people who call themselves "apostles"; their claims are preposterous yet few congregations have the integrity to refute, condemn and stay clear of these modern-day false apostles.

God did give the Church at large its apostles—the 12 Jesus selected (Matthias who fulfilled all the criteria for the original apostles replaced Judas)—and these 12 faithful apostles did serve the Church-of-all-times well. They sacrificially spread the Good News and guided the believers, and some left us enough writings to sustain and guide the believers until the return of Jesus.

Apostle is a transliteration, not a translation; it simply means "one who is sent [by God].

That particular gift of apostleship to the assemblies of believers was full and complete when the twelfth apostle died. We know this to be true because the apostles, who had replaced Judas with Matthias <u>before</u> their work began, did not try to maintain their number later when they began to die. For example: when James was killed, they did not appoint anyone to replace him. This is our clue that this "apostleship" is finished; it has accomplished its mission. Furthermore, only these twelve men (the eleven who originally walked with Jesus plus Matthias) will be acknowledged eternally as apostles: their specific names will be inscribed on the foundations of the new Jerusalem—the foundations of the complete and eternal assembly of those who followed Jesus (Jews and Gentiles).

In Acts, Luke uses the word apostle in the literal sense of its translation: one who is sent. He thus uses the word apostle for Barnabas and Paul: they were sent by the church (at God's bidding). Paul also calls himself an apostle of Christ Jesus, meaning one sent by Jesus (Ephesians 1:1 NCV). Paul and Barnabas were certainly "sent"; but they are not apostles of the same order as the twelve core disciples of Jesus.

Having said this, I realize that many Christians see Paul as the replacement for Judas: I did too for a long time. Whether Paul is or is not Judas' replacement does not take away any of his importance to us all. Through Paul, God demonstrates to us that Jesus is able to call us personally, to send us precisely and, through His spirit, to *lead us to all truth* (John 16: 13 NCV). Paul is vital to us today because we are "late comers". Through Jesus' direct dealings with Paul we see that we do not miss anything for not having been there physically when Jesus walked this earth. Jesus will deal directly with every one of His believers.

However, those today who claim to be apostles can only apply the literal translation of the Greek term: one who is sent (if indeed they are sent). They cannot claim special authority or knowledge. They cannot liken themselves to the original twelve...and they have amply proven to be no prophets at all.

The Nicolaitans

Yet the believers of Ephesus did something that was good: they hated the practices of the Nicolaitans. Jesus takes an irrevocable position against organized church, denominations, clergies, rites and liturgies. This is not a minor point: it is important enough for Jesus to mention it again later in His dictation. There is a very stern "do this or else" warning here that churches stubbornly ignore.

The Ephesians did something right: they hated the practices of those who took the truth of Jesus and made it a religion with a hierarchy and an ordained clergy to officiate rites. This is what Nicolaitans is. The word is a transliteration of a Greek word-grouping defining this concept. Preserved written correspondence between various groups in the early centuries show that the Church fell into the trap of hierarchies very early on. Twenty centuries of traditions have only reinforced the tendency.

When I researched Nicolaitans on the web (Google Nicolaitans and you can spend hours sifting through all the sites that discuss it) I found two main positions on the subject. The first one explains that Nicolaitans is a translatable aggregate word. It is built on NIKOS which translates into subjugation or subjugator, dominion or dominator, LAOS: the common people, the common folks or the masses and TON: a generative plural of "the". Accordingly, since Jesus addresses the churches, the term applies to them: so it is a church organization that gains an ascendency over the laity, over the common folks, the common believers. This laity is held in obedience and servility to the ecclesiastical elite (bishops, prelates or other denominational hierarchies).

I believe this interpretation of the word *Nicolaitans* to be the only correct one and will explain later the reasons that shore my belief. Most of today's churches and denominations do not heed Jesus' teaching here and are defined by this "Nicolaitans" qualitative. Please note that we are not talking about the authority of experience that an elder has over new believers to teach them and to bring them up to their full maturity; we are talking about a permanent type of hierarchy.

This is not a new teaching: Jesus had covered the matter in Matthew 20:25 – 28 HCSB *...you know that the rulers of the Gentiles dominate them, and the men of high position exercise power over them. It must not be like that among you...* But the lure of power for the ambitious and the proud, the craving of the insecure for structure proved irresistible and mere decades later; the church is already headed that way; even though Peter had admonished: *not lording it ... but being examples* (1 Peter 5:3).

Paul had been very specific in his first letter to the Corinthians (3:21 – 23): *So you should not brag about human leaders. All things belong to you: Paul, Apollos and Peter; the world, life, death, the present and the future—all these belong to you. And you belong to Christ, and Christ belongs to God* (NCV). Paul kills the idea of a permanent hierarchy managing God's affairs and interests for the believers. He also teaches that no person should be "ordained" to perform exclusive rites or duties that the normal believer would not be allowed to do. *All these belong to you...* Paul had warned about what the *Nicolaitans* do and want to do.

When we consider our human hierarchies, we see institutions where a moneyed or privileged elite makes all the rules. The privileged class is insulated from the needs of the masses and is served by lower classes. The serving class is considered to be the needy class and under this system, it can only have its needs met by obediently serving its "betters". The absence of dire needs confer a higher status to the "betters". When a lower class progresses in its social environment, it too will seek the services of a lower class yet. The system adds layers until everyone is accounted for and fits into his own caste.

All human hierarchies aim to preserve themselves and their privileges so they seek to enforce or demand that their intentions and preferences be catered to—rigidly. When we institute hierarchies in the assemblies of those who follow Jesus, we introduce the same operating principles.

Jesus has this to say about the hierarchies of the world: *the kings of the world rule over their people, and those who have authority over others want to be called "the great providers for the people"* (Luke 22:25 – 27, ERV). Ironically, while the elite see themselves as "the great providers for the people", they insist on being served by the people: so who really needs whom?

This is not how Jesus' Church should operate; Jesus continues: *but you must not be like that. The one with the most authority among you should act as if he is the least important. The one who leads should be like one who serves. Who is more important: the one serving or the one sitting at the table being served? Everyone thinks it's the one being served, right?* (If you look at things from the world's perspective; that's what you'll think.) *But I have been with you as the one who serves*: so draw the correct conclusion. In God's order, the one receiving the serving is the one <u>with the need</u>; the one serving is the one <u>who has what is needed</u>, ergo: he is the more important of the two.

The Father had given Jesus authority over His disciples, He had given Jesus the wisdom they needed, the understanding they needed, the knowledge they needed, and the power they needed... and Jesus spent himself serving them in order to impart these to them. God's system functions on opposite precepts than those of the world system.

Jesus teaches that in His Church there are no hierarchies, no promotions and no social advancements. The one who has must put that into the service of those who need. Ergo, the elders known to have more understanding, more experience, more wisdom or knowledge should put themselves and their assets into the service of those who need those things—new believers, weak brothers... The Church's inner organization is thus streamlined: everything flows through directly from Jesus to all; the elders being conduits (propagators), not lords (receivers).

The thing that God hates about the Nicolaitans is that in creating a pyramidal, hierarchical structure, man organizes Christianity on the model of Satan's organizations which surround it. It assimilates the church to its ambient society; it does not separate it as it should. That will not do for God. Indeed, by not being omnipresent nor omnipotent Satan must organize his realm on a vertical and horizontal structure in order to project his control to the distal parts that escape his constant attention. Satan's model for everything is pyramidal; therefore, every human organization since the fall of Adam is built on this model.

As humans we are comfortable with this mind-set because everything we have known and participated in functions on this model—it is the evil we know. It is difficult for us to conceive a different pattern, so when a group of individuals who believe in Jesus forms and meets; some folks naturally try to give it organization and structure. They go to the only model they have known; instead of going to God for guidance. The world's organizational charts do not work for Christianity and it cuts God out of His main intercourse with His church, which is the direct, hands-on, leading of His individual believers.

God gave us a natural example in the core human organization—the family. It is meant to function on a single level, with a temporary hierarchy (parents) that works toward its own redundancy. Its goal is to bring the young to independence and to responsible maturity. Let's consider this for a moment: the biblical elder's role and function is similar to that of a parent. He is to rear a new believer to maturity in Christ so that every believer may be fully usable by God—just as a parent rears a child to become an independently responsible adult, reaching his full potential.

The family hierarchy stops when the child reaches maturity thus independence. In a dysfunctional family, the hierarchy continues beyond the coming into adulthood. The parent continues to control the adult child, and a tyranny ensues. This dysfunction prevents the offspring from maturing and breeds mediocrity. In this situation, no one reaches his God-given potential and usefulness—adult development is stunted. The same is true spiritually.

In most churches and denominations today, the hierarchical organization is self-perpetuating. When a bishop, a pastor or an elder retires; the structure fills its own "void" regardless of what God thinks about it. Inevitably, in these conditions, the church pews are filled with permanently immature Christians who are useless to God and ineffectual in society. The divine reality however, is that God wants direct access to every believer and He wants the ability to move each one as He pleases.

God is omnipresent, He is omniscient and omnipotent. Unlike Satan, God can keep track of and perfectly lead every single believer from the inside. That's why He gives us His spirit which is His motivation—or the projection of Himself in us. God does not need a pyramidal, hierarchical organization that hinders Him and gets in His way. God jealously reserves the right to move each and every one of His believers as He sees fit, when He wants to, where He wants and without interference. He also reserves the right to team up the individuals He chooses for His actions regardless of which groups they belong to or whether or not a human board approves.

When believers organize in a pyramidal, *Nicolaitans* style, they become limited in their scope by the human arrangement and disposition under which they operate. When an individual is nested in a hierarchical organization, God is muzzled in the life of that individual. We can see why God hates this type of organization.

The *Nicolaitans* principle has a second detrimental effect that reflects its godless societal roots: the hierarchy will seek to insulate itself from the basic accountability of the "common folks" it claims to shepherd. It seems that every additional layer of hierarchy distances the "people at the top" from the probing of the faithful; eventually they can become immune to accountability. This was never meant to be the case in the assemblies of those who belong to Christ. Once we assign a title and a correct form of address to a clergyman, such as "Pastor Jim", "Bishop John" or "Father Andrew", we create an aura of artificial godliness with an invisible hedge which places that person outside our basic scrutiny. Of course, while freeing itself from scrutiny, the hierarchy will demand transparency in the lives of the faithful flock—hypocrisy and double standards are the norm. Nothing good ever comes from this *Nicolaitans* principle.

If we take the time to analyze what happens to "Christian" denominations over time; from the good intentions of their founders down through the years we can see the results clearly. For example I attended a United Methodist Church when I first came to Christ. Historically, the Methodist Church began with good intentions, but the huge multilayered organization it became felt ineffective at the personal level. While some adherents are certainly true followers of Christ, God has difficulty using others because the organization does not foster the unmoored availability of the believer who is attentive to God's Spirit. It has largely replaced God's direct action with Church dogma and tradition, rites and liturgy and its own branded social programs. They have replaced "In the beginning God..." with "the Methodist life". This is what Jesus wants us to avoid.

What the term "Nicolaitans" does not mean

The other mainline interpretation of the term *Nicolaitans* says that the Nicolaitans were members of a cult begun in Jerusalem by a heretical elder named Nicolas. This conception lacks credibility and does not respect the context nor satisfy the integrity of translation. This interpretation is based on the writings of people like Hippolytus of Rome, Iranaeus, Epiphanius, Theodoret and churchmen of what became later the Catholic Church like Thomas Aquinas. There are three logical arguments against this widely held interpretation: the credibility of the writings of these men is questionable, their interpretation compromises the textual integrity of Jesus' message as He gave it and the inherent nature of scriptures weighs against it.

Regarding the credibility of the writings of the men above, there are three aspects to reflect upon. First, all the men above who championed the concept lived much later than John's writing and therefore none had personal contact with such a sect in John's time. The earliest is Hippolytus who lived between 170 and 235 and the latest is Thomas Aquinas who lived from 1225 to 1274—they had no connection with the events. Their opinions are mere speculations.

Second, their criticisms of this "heretical sect" do not harmonize; the writers are not consistent and do not agree on what that man Nicolas taught. From the sum of their writings we cannot get a clear picture of the problem—they cannot even agree where Nicolas led this heretical activity: some of them say Jerusalem others say Antioch.

Third, they were all bishops (prelates) lording it over the masses of the regular believers: they had vested personal interest in steering the understanding away from the straight translation of the term *Nicolaitans*. They were *Nicolaitans* themselves!

Regarding the textual integrity of Jesus' message we must reckon with the fact that when Jesus warns us about a peril in

Revelation, He also defines its errors and gives necessary details for our understanding. Jesus is consistent, He makes sure that any one of us who reads His instructions at any point in history can be taught and thus edified because we understand. Jesus either spells out the reproof; for example: you have lost your first love or you have a reputation for being alive but you are dead. Or He provides information from the scriptures so that at anytime, anyone can go to the Bible and study the relevant passages (as with the references of Balaam and Jezebel). The reader can then understand what is happening and personally appropriate the lesson.

If *Nicolaitans* is not a translatable word aggregate as shown above—but instead refers to an ill-defined sect that existed only briefly—then a believer who reads Revelation has no way of knowing what Jesus warns him about. Jesus' warning is lost. This can never be! This part of Revelation is Jesus' epistle to the Church at large <u>for all times</u>, yet, His message here would only have a transitory benefit at best and its relevance would have been local, not universal—i.e. if *Nicolaitans* were a local sect that existed briefly. Therefore, the inclusion of this warning in the message of Revelation would be at odd with the rest of the text. This first part of Revelation is Jesus' communication to the Church—all the churches, all of the times.

Finally, the inherent nature of scriptures weighs against it: *all scripture is given by God and is useful for teaching, for showing people what is wrong in their lives, for correcting faults, and for teaching how to live right* (2 Timothy 3:16 NCV). Revelation is eminently scriptural—Jesus Himself dictated it—and therefore it must meet these criteria. Try to stand in front of a congregation, ask people to open their Bibles to Revelation 2:6 and ask: "How did Jesus' hatred of the practices of the Nicolaitans help you in your personal Christian walk and what did it change in how you live your faith?" I venture to say that you will be met with expectant blank stares, even though most of those present will have read Revelation. Because *Nicolaitans* was transliterated and not properly translated; Jesus' teaching has been unusable by the common believer for more than 18 centuries. Thus, Revelation 2:6 was prevented from becoming *useful for teaching, for showing people what is wrong in their lives, for correcting faults and for teaching to live right.* *Nicolaitans* of the past made sure of this and *Nicolaitans* of the present do their best to preserve their usurped privileges.

However when *Nicolaitans* is properly translated as: the creation of a spiritual elite that lords it over the common believers; the scripture instantly becomes useful and applicable by all—as Jesus meant it to be.

(Return to Table of Contents)

****

Chapter 2 - Smyrna, Pergamum, Thyatira

Revelation 2:8 – 29

Smyrna

2:8 – 11

8 "Write to the angel of the church in Smyrna: 'The First and the Last, the One who was dead and came to life, says: 9 I know your affliction and poverty, yet you are rich. I know the slander of those who say they are Jews and are not, but are a synagogue of Satan. 10Don't be afraid of what you are about to suffer. Look, the Devil is about to throw some of you into prison to test you, and you will have affliction for 10 days. Be faithful until death, and I will give you the crown of life'. 11 Anyone who has an ear should listen to what the Spirit says to the churches. The victor will never be harmed by the second death."

What's happening

The believers in Smyrna get encouragements from the Good Shepherd; it is what they need. This group represents the Christians who suffer religious persecution. At the time of Jesus' dictation, the assembly of believers in Smyrna was mainly Jewish. The general Jewish population, having rejected Jesus as Messiah, held onto their pre-messianic/Talmudic religion. Their religion became the entity that worked against Christ and against the broadcast of His Good News—the book of Acts amply documents this fact. It worked against the truth thus it became *a synagogue of Satan.*

Here is a biological parallel to express this reality: the true Jewish religion (as opposed to the Talmudic sect it became) was the transitory "placenta" which sustained and fed life until Messiah's birth. After Jesus, its function was over—in popular term, the placenta becomes the afterbirth (a matter unconnected with the continuance of life outside the womb) and it must be discarded. A new-born dies if he is immersed again in that matter; he came out and must stay out. The same is true with the pre-Jesus Jewish religion.Christian Jews had come out of this religion and were now persecuted by its adherents.

Note: There was also a crucial factor at play in that context. Within a couple centuries prior to Jesus' coming, Satan highjacked and suborned the Jewish religion. He created the Pharisaic sect, who became dominant and who were absolutely against Jesus as Messiah. Rejecting Jesus was their entire purpose. They invented an "oral Torah", an oral tradition of rules and structures and laws and theology to which they gave equal—or even higher—authority than the written law of Moses. By the time Jesus came, they were dominant and murderously aggressive and Jewish people feared them. The Gospels abundantly document this fear. The Pharisees created the Rabbinical order and "wrote" this "oral Torah" which is now called the Talmud. They were successful in detouring God's ancient people from the very Messiah they had waited for. Only a few came to Jesus. Judaism since Jesus has been this Rabbinical/Pharisaic/Talmudic religion which is and has been a false religion through and through. However, the written Torah still exists for these people, and as always, some will read the passages of Isaiah, Daniel and others that they are not supposed to read; and as a result do come to Jesus the Messiah.

Since Christ, the believers are threatened by whatever religion they came out of to join Jesus (viz. the persecutions and systematic killings of those who left the Catholic Church to follow Jesus, or the death sentence that is passed by Muslims and Hindus on any one of their numbers who converts to Jesus). Jesus' message of encouragement to the believers in Smyrna is as valid today as it was then.

As it happened often to followers of Jesus, the believers in Smyrna who were about to suffer were accused of blasphemy by the religious Jews. Jesus comforts the Christians: "I know that the blasphemers are the religious Jews and not yourselves". By rejecting Me their Jewish religion has squarely become a synagogue of Satan (which it remains to our days).

Christian believers will be persecuted for their beliefs by those of all other religious creeds. Jesus is aware of this and he specifically gives encouragement to His followers in advance so that they may not be surprised or overwhelmed but will confidently hold on to their faith.

There is a hope-sustaining aspect in Jesus' note: the persecution is not forever. It comes in cycles and will pass—this particular spell would last ten days. For the Christian, persecution is a universal underlying reality, although there are times and places where God shields him temporarily. We should not let this lull us into a state of complacency. Jesus instructs His beloved believers in Smyrna to continue holding onto their faith through whatever cycles of persecution and harassment befall them until they leave this earthly life and receive the rewards He has for them. Jesus will not overlook nor forget any of their fortitude: He will give them the *crown of life*.

In Smyrna, Jesus expresses that when one has the truth as his core, his foundation is unshakable: he only needs the resolve and courage to hold on to what he believes. His life may be threatened on the outside; but his foundation is not. His identity is secure. This is Jesus' message to the believers in Smyrna.

They say they are Jews but are not; that is to say: based upon their religion; these slanderers call themselves people of God. But they are not. Jesus identifies the religious Jews in this verse but the phenomenon is universal and applies to all religions and all religious beliefs. The Muslims see themselves as the people of their god, so do the Hindus to their various deities; it is part of the dynamics of religion.

The religious Jew's opposition to the Christians in Smyrna was not motivated by love. They were not trying to steer aright a dear brother who was diverging. Their motivation was hatred and selfishness: they felt threatened enough in their hegemony of the faith to persecute—even to death—those leaving the fold of their religion to become followers of Christ.

We find this same evil motivation by fear through the ages: how many followers of Luther or Calvin were officially persecuted by the Catholic Church? They were hunted out of their dwellings, deprived of their basic rights, and enslaved on rowing ships, their children forcibly taken away. Others were gruesomely killed—even burned at the stake. The entire province of Franche-Comté, for example, was left practically uninhabited by the murderous religious purges ordered by Cardinal Richelieu. While, it is said, a jubilant Pope Gregory XIII officially celebrated each massacre and urged for more. He even commissioned the painter Vasari to paint the scenes for the Vatican apartments and had special commemorative coins made.

In His message to the church of Smyrna (and later of Philadelphia), Jesus singles out the persecution of Christians by the religious Jews because that is where the persecution came from in those days. Most people who converted to Christ at that time had converted from Judaism; so the reaction against them came from the adepts of Judaism. The Judaism group was far bigger than the smattering of Christians and found itself in the position to exert persecution. But as the Christian group developed and became more numerous than the Judaists; the open persecution stopped from that quarter.

There is an inherent bully effect to every religious persecution; it is always the larger local group that preys on a minority group. The persecution of the Christians by the adepts of Judaism ceased when their relative numbers flipped many centuries ago. The religious persecution of the true Christians since then comes from other quarters: they are persecuted by whatever religion rules the societies where they live: may it be the Catholic Church, Islam, Hinduism, etc. That is to say: the religions from which local new Christians escape into Jesus' arms—it is a reaction of fear or at least of unease at losing members to Jesus—because the defections suggest that the main group may not have the truth after all. Thus Jesus' admonition to the group in Smyrna applies to the believers today in relationship to their respective, locally dominant religions.

Jesus is aware of the suffering that lay ahead for some believers; He is not taken by surprise. He urges us to keep our confidence in Him and to hold on to our beliefs.

Observations

There are only two kinds of wars from the aggressor's standpoint.

1. Secular war: its source is selfish desire and bitter envy driven by selfish ambitions (James 3 and 4). These motives encourage every corrupt human instinct and attract devious individuals like white pants attract dirt.

No matter how sanctimoniously the aggressor justifies a secular war; it is born of these motives. Most foot soldiers have no personal or emotional stake when they begin to fight—as a group they are often referred to as "cannon fodder".

2. Religious persecution is different: religious murders which can reach the scale of war are driven by fear; the untamable fear that results from the destabilization of one's foundation when one's core belief is challenged. Every participant is personally engaged and driven by his own emotions.

Religious persecution is always meted out by a religion, sect or religious faction onto another. (The atheistic state apparatus of a totalitarian regime like North Korea's or China's is also a religion and thus it persecutes its own Christian citizens for the same reason as any other religion does.) In the case of persecution aimed at the Christian believer, truth is always the trigger; or more precisely the lack of truth in the persecutor. Truth exists—it is not a negotiable concept. Truth is an absolute; it always probes the very foundation of the individual.

When an individual whose foundation is the truth is engaged in the wrong direction, truth will create a reaction of self-cleansing and personal realignment. It brings correction to this individual as happened to King David when Nathan confronted him (2 Samuel 12). However, in the individual whose foundation is false or who is determined to reject the implication of truth; truth will always produce anger—uncontrollable, explosive anger. To have one's lack of foundation revealed is unsettling to the core; the primal reaction is to destroy the threat.

The situation we have in Smyrna is universal: truth will bring a reaction of persecution and murder against Christians from those not in Christ; those who reject the truth.

God has created in man the ability to know the truth because truth is an inherent part of being made in God's image. Jesus says *I am the truth* (John 14:6), and it is God's will that man should know God (John 17:3); therefore truth is elemental to man's life. Alas through Adam, man sold out to Satan, the father of lies. Because man can now lie to himself convincingly; he is able to live with a lie as well as to live a lie. He is able to fashion his conscience to serve his beliefs and preferences. Yet, in the deepest recesses of his person there is the inerrant warning that tells him that he has stepped off the solid foundation upon which his species was originally created and is now treading on an illusion.

Our conscience cannot define truth, but truth should define our conscience. Conscience is usually the product of the ambient society—it is highly moldable. The widely divergent acts that are done with a good conscience around the world are proof of this. A Hindu who will not kill a cow will feel fully justified in killing a Muslim or a Christian. Some mothers in certain tribes used to kill one of a set of twin girls at birth because the culture demanded it; they experienced no pangs of conscience about it. Either example would be anathema in other cultures. When a person comes to Him, Jesus will begin to construct a new conscience in that person. Based on permanent truth, this conscience is now immutable—the only universally useful conscience.

Few people—from any religion—will embrace the truth of Jesus when they come in contact with it (*only a few find that road* Matthew 7:14 NCV). But if they do, it is with the relief of a drowning man grasping the life ring thrown to him. The individual who embraces the truth will now regain the steadfast footing his species had lost through Adam's rebellion.

This need for God's foundation in man is so strong and so deep that it cannot be consciously expelled by the individual. It cannot be brainwashed out by theology or by tradition: it is always there. Yet it can be tolerated by the individual who chooses to believe what pleases him and to surround himself with likeminded people.

Thus, since Adam's fall, man has learned to live with this instability and to accommodate himself to the situation. The individual in pursuit of his own selfish desires will opt for the lie and live with its instability <u>until</u> he is faced with the truth. His artificially maintained equilibrium cannot withstand an exposure to the truth; he will either embrace the truth with joyful relief or he will strike against its messenger with uncontrolled rage.

Now let's consider the persecutor: when exposed to the truth, he will attempt to curb or counteract the untamable fear that grips him by striking out—very often murderously. The clergy of such a group (sect or religion) feels the threat on two fronts: on the individual foundational level like his coreligionists plus on the social level: his favored standing in his society is imperiled. Thus the clergy—whether prelates, mullahs or others—will invariably fuel the fears, invent threats and bless the violent outcome; stridently whipping the masses to commit repulsive acts of barbarism. Fear pushes them. Remember how the *teachers of the law* (Jewish clergy) incited the mob into demanding Jesus' death from Pilate (Matthew 27:15 – 23, Mark 15:10 – 11, Luke 23:20 – 23 and John 18:38 – 19:16).

This covers the situation where the victim is a Christian; but what explains the religious anger, murders and wars between sects that have no connections with Jesus as Messiah (for example the Hindu/Muslim endemic violence in Asia)? The process is simply an application of the same principle. When one does not have the truth, he does not have the sure footing for his life that his species requires and somewhere deep down below the surface his spiritual toes are striking around anxiously for a foothold. Among his coreligionists, he has a false sense of security; however, when this individual is confronted by a belief at odds with his own, that contact intensifies the deep reality of his lack of footing. Therefore he will strike out with verbal violence if alone, and with physical violence and murder if in a mob. God created man in His image; when we deny this, there is no end to the misery we attract and dispense.

Thoughts to ponder

Blasphemy

It is interesting to notice that it is always the members of non-Christian religions who shout "blasphemy" at the Christians. It seems that their gods need human protection to pamper their thin skin. In the past, how many true Christians were harassed to death by the Catholic brutal repressions under the accusation of blasphemy? And by Muslims today? Those who live in Jesus and by Jesus never seem to invoke "blasphemy" in regard to people of other creeds; they do not need to: the God of the followers of Jesus is the Big God, the Only God—He does not need human defenses.

Truth

Because of its inescapable effect, truth is inconvenient to some. This explains why philosophers and social engineers try to make truth irrelevant by pretending that it is a flexible notion entirely modifiable by each person to serve his self-gratification.

This is futility. Picture this as an example: uneasy with heights, I may choose to redefine gravity in a way that will allay my fear and I may pontificate about my theory convincingly; but the day I step off a cliff, gravity will express its unchanging reality—regardless of my preferences. Truth does the same.

<u>Note</u>: In Revelation 22:11, Jesus gives a useful order to prevent the Christian from becoming a religious persecutor: *let the unrighteous go on in unrighteousness; let the filthy go on being made filthy; let the righteous go on in righteousness; and let the holy go on being made holy.* The true Christian should emulate John: he should present the Good News, display it with deeds and reject aberrant behaviors but never should he coerce. Tragically, people who have called themselves Christians have persecuted the adherents of other faiths. These people, contrary to their boasts, were not Christians at all.

(Return to Table of Contents)

Pergamum

2:12 – 17

12 "Write to the angel of the church in Pergamum: 'The One who has the sharp, double-edged sword says: 13 I know where you live—where Satan's throne is! And you are holding on to My name and did not deny your faith in Me, even in the days of Antipas, My faithful witness who was killed among you, where Satan lives. 14 But I have a few things against you. You have some there who hold to the teaching of Balaam, who taught Balak to place a stumbling block in front of the Israelites: to eat meat sacrificed to idols and to commit sexual immorality. 15 In the same way, you also have those who hold to the teaching of the Nicolaitans. 16 Therefore repent! Otherwise, I will come to you quickly and fight against them with the sword of My mouth'. 17 Anyone who has an ear should listen to what the Spirit says to the churches. I will give the victor some of the hidden manna. I will also give him a white stone, and on the stone a new name is inscribed that no one knows except the one who receives it".

What's happening

We see Jesus' compliments and encouragements; they show again that Jesus is perfectly aware of our living conditions. The believer finds himself embedded inside Satan's sphere of influence. Satan affects all life around us. We must understand and not be surprised by this; God knows about it. Our righteous struggles do not go unnoticed. These believers had shown courage.

Today, we live in a society that practices evil more and more openly and flaunts it. Do we resist? Do you resist? Or do you accommodate? Personally, and as a group, do you preach and stand firm on the sanctity of life, the sanctity of the biblical marriage even against the ungodly, secular, regulatory mandates? Have you gone silent in voice and deeds? Have I? No wonder teenagers leave our churches: the heroes are gone. They do not leave because the music is boring or the services not hip enough; they see no stars to look up to.

However, courageous as they are, the believers in Pergamum compromise with the ambient society. They want to assimilate into their lives the values, tenets and practices of the ambient society in order to receive the benefits that society bestows on its "good" members. They want to mitigate the threat, to ease the pressure points.

Every society imposes a burden of conformity to its people; it bears down into the details of every life. The bullying pressure to align with these expectations is very real. Unlike the Jews in the desert at Acacia, the believer in Jesus chooses the rule (Kingdom or kingship) of God and must therefore resist the desire to conform to the ambient rule of Satan—instead, he must be set apart unto Jesus in every way. Some believers in Pergamum did not want to be excluded from the sinful society amidst which they lived, nor did they want to be excluded from their family members who reveled in that society's morass. They wanted ease the frictions, to fit with man.

Jesus praises the faithful believers in Pergamum who did not bow to political or philosophical correctness. They did not cave in to social pressure even when it meant a loss to them—even the loss of their lives. Would many believers in Europe and in North America be praised today for the same staunchness? ... We live in an age when even our mainline denominations have completely caved in to political and social correctness. We live in a time when Christian principles are not the authoritative norm anymore, so just as in Pergamum, we are relentlessly bullied to accept—even promote—deviant behaviors and thoughts. We are strongly encouraged to participate in repulsive activities and lifestyles... We kill our babies, we shack up, and we submit our young to sinful and destructive influences... We do not correct or discipline our children, young or adults. Aggressors are painted as victims while we malevolently bully the real victims as we seek to "belong".

The righteous reality is: there is no room for promiscuity with the world that surrounds the believer (the Balaam effect). And the second point that Jesus makes is: there is no place for the encroachment of the world's hierarchical system on the believer's relationship with God (Nicolaitan).

> <u>Note</u>: Interesting enough, our most Nicolaitan-esque denominations (United Methodist, Episcopalian Church, and others) who have rigid hierarchies are the worst accommodators. Nothing has changed in nineteen centuries.

The Christian is not called to fight the believers of non Jesus centered faiths; but he is commanded to set himself apart from them and from their practices. A Christian's desire to blend in with the ambient society and to be accepted—even loved—by its members is not benign: he provokes God's anger and incurs His mighty retribution. The follower of Jesus must respect YHWH and Jesus as being superior and immensely different from all other gods. There is no blending possible. When you add dirty water to a pail of clean water, you always end up with a pail of dirty water—it does not qualify as clean water anymore.

Now to the text: *But some hold the teaching of Balaam.* When we look at Balaam's actions in the Bible, we see two separate transgressions in the Balaam/Balak incident: One does not affect God's people negatively and one does.

1. We have Balaam's personal transgression when by greed he persisted against God's original answer (Numbers 22 – 24 further explained in 2 Peter 2:16) ... *by abandoning the straight path, they have gone astray and have followed the path of Balaam, the son of Bosor (Beor), who loved the wages of unrighteousness.* This is not the transgression Jesus is concerned with here in Pergamum. Even though Balaam went against God's first answer and persisted in his own greed; his action resulted in him pronouncing blessings upon Israel instead of curses.

2. But we also have the transgression of the Israelites who, by intermingling with the Moabite women, followed them into idolatry: this evil was also the consequence of Balaam's action. In an effort to undermine Israel, Balaam urged Balak to encourage the Moabite women to lure the Israelites into worshipping their false gods. *While Israel was staying in Acacia Grove, the people began to have sexual relations with the women of Moab. The women invited them to the sacrifices to their gods, and the people*

[of God] *ate and bowed in worship of their gods. So Israel aligned itself with Baal of Peor, and the LORD's anger burned against Israel* (Numbers 25:1 – 3). We can read further in Numbers 31:15 – 16 *Have you let every female live? He asked them. Yet they are the ones who, at Balaam's advice, incited the Israelites to unfaithfulness against the LORD in the Peor incident*. Balaam's suggestion is clearly inferred in this passage. This is the matter that concerns the believers in Pergamum.

God had specifically said in Deuteronomy 7:3 – 4 *do not intermarry with them* [other cultures, other religions of the inhabitants of the land]. *Do not give your daughters to their sons, or take their daughters for your sons, because they will turn your sons away from Me to worship other gods*. God understands man's nature and its inherent weaknesses; even Solomon—in spite of his wisdom—fell into this trap and incurred God's anger (1 Kings 11:1 – 13). Israel was still purging itself from this Balaam-suggested trespass during Nehemiah and Ezra's lives (Nehemiah 13:1 – 3 and Ezra 9 – 10). This idolatrous deviation of the people of Israel was serious and it is this particular deed that got Balaam executed when Reuben's tribe took over the territory God assigned to them (Joshua 13:22). Balaam was not executed for his greed or for blessing Israel in front of Balak, but for advising Balak as to the manner with which he could weaken Israel by turning its men away from YHWH.

Just as the Israelites of old had lived among the enemies of God (*The surrounding people have filled it* [*the land*] *from end to end with their uncleanness by their impurity and detestable practices*, Ezra 9:11); the Christian believers live among the non-believers. Christians live in a world manipulated by Satan (*I know where you live—where Satan's throne is!* [Revelation 2:13]). Adverse social surroundings do not excuse the believer; Jesus expects him to fully differentiate himself.

There are a couple of practical implications here: the first is that when a believer in Christ dates or marries a believer of another faith (or simply someone whose faith is not in Jesus); the latter will influence him with—and in the direction of—his convictions. For every aspect of life, the true believer must get his instruction from the word of God and should be led by the Spirit of God to cast his fears upon Jesus and to actively trust in Jesus' provision.

The unbeliever, or the believer of another faith, on the other hand has no way to live above his ordinary human fears; so his fear induced coping mechanisms are always idolatrous—whether he does it by the subterfuge of superstitions or through various man-made deities, or simply by surrendering the leadership of his life to others and their man-made coping mechanisms. Invariably, this leads the Christian spouse to compromise in the direction of the non-believer. A family unit cannot function according to active trust in Jesus and according to a human/idolatrous coping mechanism at the same time. The non-Christian spouse cannot live under the Godly trust of the other's: the fear is too great. One can only live by trust when God's Spirit (motivation, equipping) abides in him.

Let's look at a practical example of this: *There was no one like Ahab who had chosen so often to do what the LORD said was wrong, because his wife Jezebel influenced him to do evil. Ahab sinned terribly by worshiping idols, just as the Amorites people did* (1 Kings 21:25 – 26 NCV). In a union between a believer and an unbeliever; it is the believer who compromises himself and his beliefs. The unbeliever acts consistently with his worldly ways and does not violate any of his principles. As a consequence, the union does not weaken the unbeliever, but the believer. Having forsaken the strength of his foundation the Christian will invariably fail to remain firm on God's principles.

The matrimonial union of a believer with a non-believer is proscribed as follows: *Do not be mismatched with unbelievers. For what partnership is there between righteousness and lawlessness? Or what fellowship does light have with darkness? What agreement does Christ have with Belial? Or what does a believer have in common with an unbeliever?* (2 Corinthians 6:14 – 15) This is not a condemnation of the unbeliever as much as it is a protective hedge for the believer.

The implication of Jesus' message here goes beyond matrimony: when a believer desires what the non-believers aspires to or when the believer wants to be included in the camaraderie of the non-believer's society; he will be influenced in that direction and will compromise. He will adopt the standards, priorities and social deviances of the world around him; and these are never God's. James teaches this clearly: *You people are not faithful to God! You should know that loving what the world has is the same as hating God. So anyone who wants to be friends with this evil world becomes God's enemy. Do you think the Scriptures mean nothing? The Scriptures say, "The Spirit God made to live in us wants us only for himself"* (James 4: 4 – 5 ERV). When the believer allows himself to be seduced by what the unbelievers pursue avidly; he will end up acting just like them. James 5:8b admonishes further: *you who are trying to follow God and the world at the same time, make your thinking pure* (NCV).

A Christian must forsake the means unbelievers use—as well as reject their fears—otherwise he will end up being just like them. Some of the believers in Pergamum were both "of Jesus" and "of the world"; this ambivalence is eternally fatal.

Holy means "set apart for a specific reason". In the biblical context, the terms saint, sanctify, consecrate, set apart, distinguish, hallow and holy are used to translate the same Hebrew word Kadash. God always requires that His people distinguish themselves from the world around them to become identified with Him who is not of this world. God is separate (Kadash) and this is what He demands: *be holy because I, YHWH your God, am holy* (Leviticus 19:2) and *consecrate yourselves and be holy, for I am YHWH your God... I am YHWH who sets you apart* (Leviticus 20:7 – 8). The apostle Peter confirms this for the Christian believers: *as obedient children, do not be conformed to the desires of your former ignorance but, as the One who called you is holy, you also are to be holy in all your conduct; for it is written, Be holy, because I am holy* (1 Peter 1:14 – 16).

The warning message through Pergamum to us believers today is that we should not identify with the world system around us. The true believer should not aim to establish his success and security through the world's social and professional networks around him. He should not strive to reach an exalted position within that system. God's Spirit in the believer is jealously possessive—for the good of the believer—and will oppose all human avenues built upon pride.

The true believer is a new creature thus he cannot prosper in his old ways because God Himself will oppose proud people and their means. However, God will be gracious to the believer who humbly chooses to go by God's ways and means; and thence will come his successes. (This is what James 4:4 – 6 teaches.) This also means that we should not be vanquished by the fears that control the people around us.

Even while in the midst of Satan's sphere of activities, we Christian believers must live with our Almighty Spouse and be true to Him. We must follow Him and identify with Him, impervious to the ambient, prevalent evil and the godlessness around us. Most of the believers in Pergamum did this toward Jesus, drawing His praise.

Jesus' command to His believers is drastic and exclusive: *I tell you, don't worry about the food or drink you need to live, or about the clothes you need for your body... Don't worry and say, "What will we eat?" or "What will we drink?" or "What will we wear?" The people who don't know God keep trying to get these things, and your Father in heaven knows you need them. The thing you should want most is God's kingdom* (choose His sovereignty) *and doing what God wants. Then all these other things you need will be given to you. So don't worry about tomorrow...* (Matthew 6:25 – 34) Today, in the countries where Christians are not persecuted; very few Christians—pastors included—obey this. Instead, most Christians live under, and struggle with, the same fears that grip the ambient society. They want the security of a good job, the protection of the government for the free pursuit of their faith and the promise of a golden old age—all the attributes that society praises in people and for which shallow, ungrounded Christians strive. Jesus gave the believers His peace so that they would not live under the fears that rule mankind.

When a believer fears things like lacking money or the insecurity of old age he may become a slave to his job or a slave to having a job, he may fixate on getting a retirement, on securing medical coverage, etc. When this happens, he lets go of the trust that should have remained rooted in Jesus and allows the uncertainties of his own "what ifs" to dictate his choices and actions. His faith is dead, useless; so he grabs and holds onto things (like money, human services, government programs, etc.). When we do this we are just like the people around us so we do not shine with the light of the gracious hope that we have in Jesus. We become worthless in our witness. We are not salt nor are we light.

This is what this Balaam/Balak reference is. God will strike these people of Pergamum. God will strike the same people today.

This also covers all the aspects of superstition which is the fear of false gods. Some outward signs of this are: good-luck charms, St. Christopher medals, crosses, flapping prayer flags, statues of saints or of the Virgin. For some it is the adoption of oriental philosophies or the blending of ancestral beliefs into the Gospel.

Nicolaitans

We also find the *Nicolaitans* in Pergamum: some people in the church seek security and status in permanency thus they find comfort in establishing rules and hierarchies. This attracts people who fear exposure and want the false comfort of a socially dominant group.

Some who begin churches set them under a government mandated status for security against harassment. Most occidental churches are organized that way in order to be civically sanctioned as legal non-profit entities, conforming thus to the ambient humanistic culture and disobeying God's order to be set apart.

Some seek rituals or church services with specific liturgies. Others seek status and power through clergy positions. They want to impose a hierarchy and a form of ritualistic worship. Believers should not be absorbed by the worldly, established "Christian" religion that insulates them from the simple Gospel message.

The sobering reality is that Jesus will come and fight against both these groups of people (2:15). True believers should not associate themselves with either of them; if they do; they will get hurt. Jesus will fight anything that dulls our witness. Giving credence to popular occult fears really undermines God's credibility as the cornerstone of our faith with those around us—so He will act. He leaves us here on earth after giving us His Spirit in order that we may showcase His grace. If we don't; why should we be left in place?

Again, the plural in "churches" in the closing statement means that the letter is universal and applies to us today as well. Nineteen centuries of church tradition should not dull the reality of Jesus' teaching for us today: do we accept tradition or do we obey this teaching?

In 2:17, there is an exclusively personal attention given to each believer from Jesus. Jesus' relationship with the believers is not a group phenomenon, not a herd principle; instead it is personal. Not only the relationship to Jesus from the believer's standpoint is personal; it is personal and exclusive from Jesus' standpoint as well. Jesus loves each and every believer with the unshared intimacy of true love: the exclusive intimacy of a groom to his beloved bride.

Observations

The throne of Satan

The actual great throne of Satan referred here did actually exist in Pergamum. Early in the twentieth century, it was moved to Berlin, Germany and exhibited there. It served as a Nazi inspiration to some of the Satanists among the elite.

At the end of World War II, the Communist Russians moved the whole structure to the USSR. It was not exhibited in a museum but it is said to have been be used as a Satanic ritual center for the elite. Communism is Satanic at its core, its propagandists and originators (Hess, Engle, Marx, and others were Satanists above all other considerations). Communism is just one of Satan's front organizations (read Wurmbrandt's *Satan and Marx*). Just like in Pergamum, invariably, Communism outlaws Christianity, actively persecutes and kills believers. Think of the Chinese Communist Party and of North Korea!

The great throne of Satan was real and unfortunately is still real today. Believers should be aware.

To eat meat sacrificed to idols...

In our days, we are browbeaten to become more generously inclusive. Do you feel that way? Would you attend a multi-faith symposium aimed to build harmonious co-existence and integration? Would you participate—actively or passively—in ecumenical prayers from other faiths, prayers to Krishna, Manitou, Allah, Mary or the saints? When you joined them, do you think Jesus went with you? Do you really think that in your befuddled or maligned mindset of "being inclusive" you brought these other people into the fold of the Living God? You certainly did not. But, <u>you</u>, on the other hand, left the fold of the Almighty, and, solo, you went and joined yourself to Jesus' enemies. You have included yourself in them; and you have severed your eternal connection.

May be you feel limited, old fashioned or hemmed in by being faithful to only what Jesus says (after all this is the twenty-first century)? So, you feel that you should enlarge your horizon, get a "balanced" perspective; and you attend a Wicca meeting. Do you think for one moment that Jesus went with you? The reality is that you fell for the same trick as Eve did. You did not witnessed to them; you simply slipped into their fold (as the Jews did in the text's reference to Balaam). You walked away from the goodness that was yours in Jesus. By going from a filial relationship with the all-knowing God to the company of those who worship limited creatures, you have not expanded your horizon; you have clipped it to the quick.

To commit sexual immorality...

Your unbridled feelings and emotions toward a homosexual son, nephew, grand-daughter or neighbor lead you to misguidedly try to include the homosexual agenda into the tenets of Jesus' kingdom. You erroneously think that you are bringing the practitioners of this sin to your Lord. But, Jesus never followed you there. When you try, by this approach, to bring people to Jesus; He is not there, because you left Him to go there. You left Jesus to travel down a path that has, or will, cost you everything. We cannot bend God to our sinful wishes and emotions. He does not have to. The only hope for these people is to walk out of the kingdom they have chosen and come <u>to</u> Jesus where He is and as He is. He will welcome them because He is wholly capable of ridding them of their sin—and change them, and He will. They have the same opportunity as everyone else (and will receive the same welcome); but in Jesus' terms. There are indeed a lot of Pergamum's problems in today's Western church. What is so shameful is that we have the witness of the scriptures and of history, so we ought to know better.

The white stone

Every inner-spousal relationship is unique. It has certain markers, traits and intimate references that are known and shared only inside that relationship. Marriages are not standardized. The believer in Jesus is the bride of Christ; therefore there is an exclusivity of form and content in every believer's relationship with Jesus: no two are alike. To anyone who has fallen in love and married, the *white stone* with *a new name inscribed on it that no one knows except the one who receives it* makes sense. For example, when my wife and I were married, we chose to have wedding rings made in a unique shape and thickness to symbolize that our relationship was unique and special to the both of us—it was and is unlike all others. And we still cherish the concept. The *stone* here expresses the same idea.

A stone is a building block, it can be foundational piece upon which Jesus will build our Christian life. And each foundational building block is customized to each believer.

Common place instances of Pergamum compromises

There are nuances of this Pergamum deviation that seem innocuous because they are so commonplace, or because they make us feel good—they connect us to our society. For example, the benign superstitions people succumb to when they change their chosen habits or adapt their behavior to ward off the same fears non-believers live by. Do you touch wood, or cross your fingers when you want a certain process to go well? Why?

How about religious ecumenism where all other beliefs are viewed sympathetically and even given equal honor? This is what tripped the Jews at Acacia Grove: it is the antechamber of the idolatrous trap, the invitation to a promiscuous bastardization of Jesus' Good News.

There is also religious and political correctness that give priority to man's preferences and emasculates God's exclusive and divinely mandated message. When people submit to religious or political correctness *they lie to one another; they speak with flattering lips and deceptive hearts* (Psalm 12:2).

(Return to Table of Contents)

Thyatira

2:18 – 29

18 "Write to the angel of the church in Thyatira: 'The Son of God, the One whose eyes are like a fiery flame and whose feet are like fine bronze, says: 19 I know your works—your love, faithfulness, service, and endurance. Your last works are greater than the first. 20But I have this against you: You tolerate the woman Jezebel, who calls herself a prophetess and teaches and deceives My slaves to commit sexual immorality and to eat meat sacrificed to idols. 21 I gave her time to repent, but she does not want to repent of her sexual immorality. 22Look! I will throw her into a sickbed and those who commit adultery with her into great tribulation, unless they repent of her practices. [23] I will kill her children with the plague. Then all the churches will know that I am the One who examines minds and hearts, and I will give to each of you according to your works. [24] I say to the rest of you in Thyatira, who do not hold this teaching, who haven't known the deep things of Satan—as they say—I do not put any other burden on you. [25] But hold on to what you have until I come. [26] The one who is victorious and keeps My works to the end: I will give him authority over the nations—[27] and he will shepherd, them with an iron scepter; he will shatter them like pottery,—just as I have received this from My Father. [28] I will also give him the morning star. [29] "Anyone who has an ear should listen to what the Spirit says to the churches.

What's happening

Jesus finds the congregation in Thyatira worthy of high praises. He particularly notes their love, their faith, their service and their patience... And all these works are increasing. Every believer today is challenged by this address. I know I am: love (ouch), service (ouch), patience (ouch).

It would seem that all is well with these followers. Yet, something rotten threatens the integrity of the group.

I am the One who examines minds and hearts—or *God is the one who searches out the thoughts and intentions of every person* (NLT)—this key sentence helps us understand the message here: we are not talking about physical sex or about open participation in satanic religious services. *Sexual immorality* and *eat meat sacrificed to idols* are physical images of a spiritual reality.

Regarding *sexual immorality,* the straying is likened to sexual sins because the erring folks in Thyatira don't limit their contentment to what God offers—to what their rightful spouse,

Jesus provides—they seek more elsewhere. They seek *deeper truths* (NLT): new revelations, new prophecies, and new extra-ordinary acts on command.

They revel in the fantastic: they seek the showy testimonies of men and give these the same weight as scriptures—or they twist the scriptures to validate their experiences. They use man-flattering means born of ego-stroking sensual emotions.

Regarding *meat sacrificed to idols*, they don't feed exclusively *on every word that comes from the mouth of God* (Matthew 4:4) as Jesus did in the desert. They go outside the black and white reality of scriptures to other "food sources" to satisfy their cravings. They put their own spin on things. Jesus is not the only master of their spiritual lives anymore. And, having entered into this sensual ego-stroking mode, they don't want to give up its practices. But God will act and punish because He indeed is *the one who searches out the thoughts and intentions* (motives) *of every person* (NLT).

Paul warns us, Peter warns us, John and Jude warn us ... and now Jesus warns us: do not tolerate false teachings and false teachers. If you do; you are guilty. Here again, we see that Jesus is completely aware of our actions and situations.

How is *Jezebel* of Thyatira different from *Balaam* of Pergamum's?

In Pergamum, some of the believers allow themselves to be tempted by what the world offers, what the world seeks and pursues. The erring people in Pergamum are both "of Jesus" and "of the world against Jesus" at the same time: eventually, their compromise estranges them from Jesus. Jesus wants His believers to Himself.

In Thyatira the situation is different: some Christians change the truth. They do not have a foot in each kingdom as those in Pergamum have; but they embark on false teachings, on a false faith.

They unilaterally change the relationship with Jesus. They silence the truth, or more accurately they out-shout the truth with the proclamations of their false and deadly teachings.

They create and cater to their own prophets—like *Jezebel* did—and they choose those charlatans' word over the truth. For our own good, the parameters and qualities of our spousal relationship with Messiah are set by Him because He is perfect. Jesus will not accept our emotional druthers on the subject because this would rob us of what is perfect.

A true prophet of God is chosen by Him and will only say what God says. But the "prophets" of these people spout off their own teachings, their new revelations and their followers give preference to these over God's. Both anomalies (Pergamum's and Thyatira's) wreck the sanctity of the believer's relationship with Jesus.

The believers in Thyatira who resist and who resolutely reject and condemn the deviant adepts and their theories will reign with Jesus, in Jerusalem, during the 1,000 year reign—as His bride. They will be un-dissociable from Him. But those who tolerate this deviant faith will suffer along with its agents.

Who was and what is this Jezebel?

We have information about this Jezebel in the Old Testament; she was the wicked wife of wicked Ahab. She led him and the masses to worship idols.

The Jezebel in the Church of Thyatira claims to be a prophetess, but by her teachings she leads people to follow their emotions and carnal instincts instead of what YHWH commands. She condones and promotes immorality—and she does not want to change.

When we read about the original Jezebel in the Old Testament, we surmise that she lived and rationalized all things according to her emotions and capricious desires (1 Kings 21). She was the epitome of selfishness on the spiritual level. Everything must accommodate her whims.

We note that she knew about YHWH—her husband was Israeli and there were powerful prophets of God like Elijah proclaiming the truth. But she wanted her own way. So she had YHWH's prophets killed (1 Kings 18:4) to silence the truth she did not want to hear. Then, in an effort to dictate her "truth" she imported into the midst of God's people 450 prophets of Baal and 400 prophets of Asherah and she paid them (1 Kings 18:19). They promoted her agenda and influenced people. Each of these prophets claimed to be the anointed of his respective deity, they claimed to be able to channel the power of that deity (See 1 Kings 18:18 – 40). And of course their claims were false.

In our church age, in order to be successful, an individual who aims to impose non-scriptural beliefs on others must place himself above the written word. He must appear to be the holder of a greater revelation that permits him to surpass that of the scriptures (or at least to have received a newer revelation that would "complete" older scriptures).

He must present himself as a prophet and broadcast his preferences as prophecies, as new truths. We find this approach in the religions that use the Bible to infer legitimacy as for example in Islam where Mohammed defined himself as the true prophet, depositor of a greater truth than the holy book of the Jews and the holy book of the Christians. His followers become the only true people of Allah. We find this also in Mormonism where Joseph Smith, Jr. claimed to have discovered the missing key scriptures that completed the content of the traditional Bible and provided superseding teaching for life and eternity. Of course Joseph Smith, Jr. proclaimed that his followers were the only true believers.

Sadly, these two examples are not exclusive; we find the same process at work in movements that claim to be mainline

Christianity. In our modern times, the newest iteration of this shameful deviation is the Pentecostal/Charismatic Movement and its various sub-movements like the Third Wave of the Holy Spirit Movement and the New Apostolic Reformation, to name only two.

Consider the following quote as a representative sample of what is being preached: "And the Lord says 'I'm giving you new grace to begin to operate and function apostolically and prophetically like you've never known before... For I break off the limitations that have tried to hold you back and have tried to hold back your gift and have tried to hold back your church, I begin to break the limitations through apostolic and prophetic release' so the Lord said 'get ready, I'm shifting you, I'm moving you into a new grace. For all over the earth there is a new breed being raised up. There was a new leadership coming into place and many men and women are taking their place in leadership and the apostles are rising and the prophets are rising and even the elders of the local churches are rising into a new dimension of grace to begin to release that which is not being released in generations...' The Lord said 'that which you walked in, in the past is not sufficient for today or for the future'. But the Lord said, 'I'm calling you into another realm of faith, into another realm of grace, into another realm of my anointing...' So the Lord says, 'do not draw back but press into this dimension, for it is a new dimension for my leaders,' and the Lord said, 'and each city and each region a new breed of prophetic and apostolic leaders shall be raised up and you shall begin to do what you could not do before and you shall begin to release my grace and my anointing upon the people.' (John Eckhardt, National School of The Prophets-Mobilizing The Prophetic Office, Friday, 5/2/00, 7:00 p.m. Session 12; quoted from www.deceptioninthechurch.com/narfaseprophecies.html.)   This exemplifies precisely the evil *deeper truths* (verse 24 NLT) Jesus speaks against here.

Here we have it in a few lines and the variations on the theme are endless. These people claim that Jesus did not give us all we needed; that He allegedly held back. But fear not: this "new breed" of self-professed apostles and prophets will now usher a new faith, a new grace and a new spiritual reality. These imposters have to make such extravagant claims because the faith, the grace and the spiritual life Jesus gave us do not provide for their ambitions.

In spite of the evident spuriousness of these boasts, a multitude of immature and carnal Christians flock to these deceivers and proceed to emulate them in their own churches. I have attended church services at Pentecostal churches on three continents. Inevitably, a percentage of each congregation considered themselves to be prophets and prophetesses. However, what spewed out of their mouths as prophecies was verifiably false and their self-serving predictions never realized. Yet the circus continues week after week.

For these congregations, emotional catharsis in whatever outrageous form serves as proof of orthodoxy. Feelings validate everything, showmanship trumps integrity and boasting is the norm. Jude had forewarned about this when he wrote: *In the end of time there will be scoffers walking according to their own ungodly desires* (Jude 18).

These Pentecostal/Charismatic groups also study the devil's moves and thoughts as 2:24 states: "having *known the deep things of Satan*". They find numerous ways to be scared of him and to attribute their personal and collective failures to his interference. With formulas and rituals they claim to bind Satan and to cast out imaginary demons in great public shows. They conduct ritualistic inner-healings and spiritual deliverance events. Every ailment from hot flashes to Alzheimer's is proof of demonic possession or at least demonic activity in that person. If these afflictions were simply demonic possessions, then a sufferer who comes to Jesus should systematically be released from them. Yet, it does not happen this way, doe it? So the premise is wrong. The followers of this movement are misled further and further away from the joy of Jesus—they have a huge Satan and a very small Jesus.

> <u>Note</u>: every disease and every imperfection is a consequence of man's rebellion through Adam—but not necessarily the expression of a specific demonic possession.

Jesus taught the biblical reality of demonic possession in Matthew 12:29: *If anyone wants to enter a strong person's house and steal his things, he must first tie up the strong person* (NCV). God's very own Spirit inhabits the believer in Christ; no fallen celestial creature can overpower Him in order to possess the believer.

> <u>Note</u>: In areas of the world where people do not have access to the Word of God because of endemic illiteracy or by the unavailability of the physical script, God, <u>at times</u>, still validates the work and words of His evangelists by wonderful, miraculous healings and other signs as He had done to validate the apostles status and message in the early church. But that is not at all what happens here with the charismatic movement and its high profile shysters.

Here is an example of such a Charismatic muddle: John Wimber (1934 – 1997) of the Vineyard and Third Wave of the Holy Spirit movements—whom some in England called Mr. Miracle—had prayed extensively and publicly for David Watson's recovery from cancer. Watson (1933 – 1984) was a prominent

Anglican Charismatic leader who invited Wimber to the UK in 1980. Yet Watson died of that cancer. When questioned about it afterward Wimber answered: "The devil won that battle but we're gonna make him pay!"

What poppycock! God owns the time of our death and allows the manner thereof; He does not lose a stand-off with the devil. If a person belongs to God, yet Satan "wins sometime"; then that person has the weaker god: why trust such a god?

Satan never wins a battle against God. Even during the three and one-half half years when God allows him to rampage the earth, Satan will only be able to do what God allows him to do. And finally, men do not make Satan "pay"; Jude tells us that even powerful *Michael the archangel, when he was disputing with the Devil in a debate about Moses body, did not dare bring an abusive condemnation against him but said "The Lord rebuke you!"* (Jude 9). Mr. Wimber's Charismatic assertion is humanistic hubris; it is wishful thinking made into policy and doctrine, and it is delusion. Jesus will have none of it.

The Pentecostal movement in all its forms and offshoots seems to encourage such empty boasting; but no one checks back to demand an account on its realization. There is no one who insists on "how specifically did you make Satan pay, Mr. Wimber?" Jude 16 says: *their mouths utter arrogant words*; they truly do.

There are good people doing a lot of good works in the Charismatic churches; sincere souls can be found in many of the mission fields assiduously and selflessly "working for the Lord". Their *love, faithfulness, service and endurance* are commendable and Jesus acknowledges these points specifically.

But these folks have a tendency to accept the testimonies and teachings of leaders and molders-of-beliefs who are the Jezebels that Jesus warns about. Relentlessly, the poison erodes orthodoxy and many good-intentioned people are sliding off the biblical track. The Gospel they teach is alloyed and the teachings of the Jezebels are passed onto unaware new converts. The good works become tainted, compromised—the good works that Jesus will weigh (verse 23). Emotions play a leading role in these people's walk, fueling high human expectations; and therein lays the weakness: the pathos of human considerations often trumps doctrine. And this is what will be developed in the next section.

We have looked at the false prophets and apostles phenomenon; let's now look at the other phenomenon of the Pentecostal/Charismatic movement: the authoritative importance given to human testimonies and experiences over the facts of God's word.

Experiential testimonies seem to rule their theology. Awed by the testimonies of purported supermen of the faith, multitudes flock to showmen for healing and deliverance of evils—real or imagined. These Christian gurus, showy charlatans, often claim the irresistible gift of healing; of course: who does not desire to be healed? Credulous folks are attracted by the superlative testimonies of these showmen and their ever rising fame, and lured by the promises they adopt their faulty theologies.

A friend gave me a clue as to what had drawn her into this nonsense: "But they have such fantastic testimonies! It is such an inspiration for us; we are awed." And this is the key: these fooled folks seek the testimonies of men.

The legends of these showy "superheroes of the faith" grow in the retelling and through their self-promoting campaigns in churches, through books, radio and TV. Paul understood this dangerous tendency in people and he vowed to teach *Christ only, and Him crucified*. Paul realized that the only testimony anyone needs is Jesus': His acts, His words and His cross (the judgment of sin and the justification of the believer). Seeking the testimonies of men and of other Christians is a trap; it leads to the unbridled pursuit of the sensational. *Many will follow their unrestrained ways, and because of them the way of truth will be blasphemed. In their greed they will exploit you with deceptive words* (2 Peter 2:2 – 3). This last sentence has proven to be accurate: most of these leaders have become scandalously rich from the milking of their followers' emotions.

Whether their fame is local, national or international, these men are cunning deceivers; they are the *springs without water* and the *waterless clouds* that Peter and Jude warn us about. These charlatans arrogantly confront Satan and demons publicly and order them about, but their boasts are empty, they are dangerous delusions. *Bold, arrogant people! They do not tremble when they blaspheme* (curse) *the glorious ones* (fallen angels)*; however, angels* (God's angels)*, who are greater in might and power, do not bring a slanderous charge against them before the Lord. But these people, like irrational animals—creatures of instinct born to be caught and destroyed—speak blasphemies* (curses) *about things they don't understand, and in their destruction they too will be destroyed, suffering harm as the payment for unrighteousness... They are blots and blemishes, delighting in their deceptions as they feast with you, having eyes full of adultery, and always looking for sin, seducing unstable people, and with hearts trained in greed. Accursed children! By abandoning the straight path, they have gone astray and have followed the path of Balaam, the son of Bosor, who loved the wages of unrighteousness... These people are springs without water, mists driven by a whirlwind. The gloom of darkness has been reserved for them* (2 Peter 2:10 – 17). Jude speaking of these charlatans of the faith says this: *These are the ones who are like dangerous reefs at your love feasts. They feast with you, nurturing only themselves without fear. They are waterless clouds carried along by winds... wild waves of the sea, foaming up their shameful deeds; wandering stars for whom is reserved the blackness of darkness forever!*

The perceived appeal of these showmen is often directly proportional to their confessed former depravity: an early life of drugs or alcohol addictions, gang membership or even Satanism boosts their credentials. A testimony that originates in the lowest, seediest strata of society has more power, more "wow effect", thus the audience gives it more value, and puts more faith in its message.

The gullible people who follow these showmen pursue relief for their personal problems or success for their ambitions on their own terms; and that is where the heart of the matter is. In their impatience or rebellion they seek a shortcut to the solution; and the "Christian guru" seems to offer just that. The perception is that if the "guru" who began at such a low station in life made it to the public forefront of the faith, then his approach must bring a fail-proof quick-fix for them...if he intervenes, if he applies his so-called "anointing" for them—if he gives them the trick, the formula.

Thousands pathetically submit themselves to ignominious practices like the hypnotic "slaying in the Spirit" in order to share in the "anointing". They debase their humanity and offend their Creator to acquire the "superman's" favor in the quest for their goals. The followers who flock to these "Christian gurus" focus on the claims of mere men, instead of focusing on the only good, the only perfect testimony: that of Jesus.

This slavish infatuation of the naive spurs the unprincipled "gurus" to greater and greater claims. These quacks boast of healings, of demon cleansings, each new claim more spectacular than the last—none of which are ever submitted to factual scrutiny. There are no medical verifications of symptoms, no recorded medical history and there are never confirmations of results by the same tools that diagnosed the malady in the first place. If you suggest a third-party verification process; your faith is questioned. These charlatans are skilled crowd manipulators and they exploit the mob effect to create a blinding frenzy in their—all too willing—audience.

These Christian quacks must continually expand their bombastic claims because they love the adulation of the crowds and the financial sponsorship it brings, plus they'll do anything to keep their exalted status. So the claims grow and the multitudes are led deeper and deeper into the lie. The guru's legend grows, fueled by the retelling through his cronies who have a stake in his fame. Peter was clear: *the gloom of darkness has been reserved for them. For uttering bombastic, empty words, they seduce, by fleshy desires and debauchery, people who have barely escaped from those who live in error* (2 Peter 2:18 – 19).

When unable to heal someone from a <u>real</u> affliction, these showmen typically blame the failure on that person's lack of the "right faith". Interestingly, these showmen seem incapable of healing themselves: for example Wigglesworth who is exalted as a super healer never healed himself: he suffered of gallstones and chronic sciatica. He never healed his deaf daughter either. Mary Boddy lived the last 16 years of her life as an invalid... and the list goes on. So it is fair to ask: "Mr. Wigglesworth what wrong kind of faith do you have that prevents you from healing yourself or your own daughter for that matter?" Of course he would explain away the issue with some pious poppycock, some martyr-syndrome excuse.

Smith Wigglesworth was a fraud, a teacher of false theology, yet many still buy his biased biography *Smith Wigglesworth: Apostle of faith* today and drink its sugary lies. Sadly, large numbers of gullible souls, today still exchange a scripture-based faith for this *waterless cloud*. I have used him as the example here, but you can see these showmen on TV, YouTube and in many churches and convention venues. They are numerous and ubiquitous, they poison Christianity on every continents with their self-serving theology and empty promises.

Unlike Jesus, and in spite of their boasts, they never accept to take on the clinically proven invalids and the terminally ill patients that competent and unbiased doctors (with medical data on hand) would bring to them for healing. My wife and I sat in Mombasa with Mary, a seriously handicapped lady who had invited us to attend church with her. She faithfully attended the Sunday services led by a "Christian guru" of local fame. Predictably, she remained in her infirmities while we watched people forwarding handkerchiefs to be "anointed" by the holy man as he boasted that these would carry his anointed healing powers into the villages.

Mary was never invited forward to be considered for a healing prayer and touch by the quack. Why? Because her problems were real and visible; therefore so would his failure be. Jesus never shied away from the obvious cases because His healing was real. Jesus is the only testimony the Christian needs to seek and to study.

These Pentecostal/Charismatic people "à la Jezebel" bring divisiveness in the community of believers because they consider themselves to be the ones who have been anointed and have the qualifying gift(s) and all the non-Pentecostal/non-Charismatic believers are the lesser Christians who do not have the gifts but should strive to get them. It does not matter that the gifts are fake or imaginary. Jude tells us: *these people create divisions and are merely natural, not having the Spirit* (Jude 19). In spite of their claims of having the "baptism of the Holy Spirit", these people still have the spirit of this world, the spirit of Jezebel. Jesus does not live in them.

The blame does not lay exclusively with the "Charismatic gurus" because, while they are skillful predators, their efforts would be in vain if the average believer at large refused to be deceived. Indeed the crowds who flock to these "Christian gurus" are not coerced to do so: they willingly seek them, they travel from afar to attend their seminars and revivals, and they even pay them—liberally! They deprive themselves in order give the gurus their financial sponsorship! These charismatic showmen (and women) would be powerless and exposed if believers at large looked to Jesus' testimony and to no other.

When believers apply the discipline of scriptures they are neither swayed nor duped. The predators could not become obscenely rich and powerful if the masses shunned them. The sad reality is that the deceived are the willing enablers; the sponsors of their own doom.

The Pentecostal/Charismatic leaders will receive what the text of Revelation promises: *great tribulation*. Some have already been exposed and publicly disgraced, however, the scandals that have exposed them have tarnished Christianity by association. Greed is not their only shortcoming: they exhibit a propensity to sin like the unregenerate. From what I read, this was evident from the start of the movement: quite a few of the Azuza Street original and early leaders were caught in sexual scandals (some even in sodomy). They were truly *fruitless* (they had no good actions), *twice dead* (Jude 12).

The Christians at large should have reacted and not tolerated this movement; the believers in Thyatira were rebuked for having tolerated such a deviation. Today, God is still giving the folks in the Pentecostal/Charismatic movement time to repent (to change their way) but soon He will strike. Then they will pay, eternally, alongside the doomed deceiving "gurus" they have chosen to follow.

From the anonymity of the pews to the spotlight of the podium, all the Pentecostal adherents must change their practices. However, that infers being willing to humble themselves first. They are very proud of their unbridled practices and they want to hold on to their claims of having special faith positions and privileges (prophets, apostles, gift of tongues...) even though these are delusional claims. For these believers, changing their ways means that they will lose face; a hard thing to do because their theories and practices are ego flattering.

I have often laid solid, basic scriptural evidences before individuals who were drawn into the Pentecostal movement. But, in every case they brushed aside the scriptures that were meant precisely to rebuke them. Jesus is right in Revelation 2:21: these people demonstrate a dogged determination to continue in their errors because this fits their own religious ambitions. Jesus is correct here when He dictates: *but she does not want to repent.*

There is nothing benign about the Pentecostal/Charismatic movement: in the end, the deceivers will be punished eternally... but so will the deceived! The deceived did not care enough to love the truth and they did not respect the Savior enough to make Him the exclusive authority, the last word in their lives. They did not reject the false Christianity of the Charismatic "gurus".

When Jesus strikes Jezebel and her followers, true believers will face the practical and inescapable reality of Jesus: righteousness and justice. And for the believers who do not dip in any of those things, God does not add any additional burden; indeed, He came to give us rest for our lives (Matthew 11:28 – 30).

We also notice Jesus' fairness: God deals with each believer independently; He can differentiate between every one of us. This capability of God and the fairness it reveals also implies our personal responsibility. No one who adheres to the Charismatic/ Pentecostal movement will be able to claim a "mob effect" in his defense: each will be responsible for his choices and his walk.

Verses 26 and 27 are a reference to the 1,000 year reign. During that time, the non-Jews will be subjected to Jesus' rule; not as friends nor as bride but as vanquished enemies—mere serfs.

Again, church is plural in the closing statement: the message is not just for Thyatira; it is meant for all assemblies anywhere, anytime.

The "gifts" Jesus bestowed upon His original apostles

Early in His earthly ministry, Jesus revealed who He is to His own people in Nazareth: *The Spirit of the Lord is on Me, because He has anointed Me to preach good news to the poor. He has sent Me to proclaim freedom to the captives and recovery of sight to the blind, to set free the oppressed, to proclaim the year of the Lord's favor* (Luke 4:18). These feats were Jesus' Messianic finger-prints, a copy of which was deposited, in advance, in the archives of the prophets so by matching them the Jews could identify Messiah.

Jesus made sure that the Jews would recognize Messiah by the Messianic prophecies He fulfilled. When John the Baptizer sent his disciples to Jesus to ask: *Are you the One who is to come, or should we expect someone else* (Matthew 11:3)? Jesus answered: ... *Go and report to John what you hear and see: the blind see, the lame walk, those with skin diseases are healed, the deaf hear, the dead are raised, and the poor are told the good news* (Matthew 11:4 – 5).

Prior to the above exchange, Jesus had empowered His twelve apostles to go ahead of Him: *heal the sick, raise the dead, clean those with skin diseases, drive out demons* (Matthew 10:8). He specifically limited their mission to the Jews; the healings heralded the good news for the Jews. These "gifts" had the purpose of qualifying the claims the disciples were making: "Messiah has come, we have met Him, rejoice!"

Jesus and His original team carried out these signs so that the Jews could validate Jesus as Messiah by examining the Messianic prophecies. Many lunatics or scammers had pretended to be Messiah and many since have done so: but only Jesus can be recognized by the fulfillment of prophecies. These signs and wonders were for the Jews' benefit. They were the validation of Messiah's credentials for God's people. Isaiah 55:5 – 6 said: *Then the eyes of the blind will be opened, and the ears of the deaf unstopped.*

Then the lame will leap like a deer, and the tongue of the mute will sing for joy... Isaiah 42:7 said: *...In order to open blind eyes, to bring out prisoners from the dungeon, and those sitting in darkness from the prison house* (drive out demons). And finally, Isaiah 61:1: *The Spirit of the Lord God is on Me because the Lord has anointed Me to bring the good news to the poor...*

Jesus never cancelled these original gifts; His eleven disciples (plus Paul to some extent) went on exhibiting these gifts after Pentecost when they began to reach out. These wonderful signs demonstrated to the Jews of that time that Messiah had indeed come and that the good news was real. For a few decades, and throughout Paul's outreach, the disciples presented the good news first to the Jews, they taught first in the synagogues. The fulfillment of these Jewish prophecies was needed and useful, even required, because a Jew was supposed to verify any Messianic claim. That purpose was accomplished and is amply recorded for us all...and the need for it is no more. It has done its work. The British and the Prussians do not have to re-enact the battle of Waterloo for every generation: the battle and its outcome are recorded, and that's enough for any historian. The same apply here: the fulfillment of prophecies is amply recorded and that is enough for the remainder of time.

As for the gift of tongues, Jesus who truly was in the Spirit at all times and communicated intimately with God never went into a fit of gibberish. His disciples could understand any prayer He uttered. The gift of tongues God provided to the disciples and to a few other people (there never were entire communities gifted with it) was a specific manifestation to impress <u>upon the Jews</u> the reality of the apostles' preaching and message. It was the fulfillment of a prophecy given by Isaiah (28:11): *I will speak to these people by people of other languages and by the lips of foreigners, and even then they will not listen to me.* "these people" refers to the <u>Jews—and</u>

<u>only to the Jews</u>. This phenomenon validated the fact that the new believers in Jesus at Pentecost, and for a short while after, presented the promised Messiah.

That validation was made first to the Jews in Jerusalem. Then it was extended to the Samaritans so that the Jews would understand that salvation was offered to these "almost Jews" as well. And finally it was extended to Gentiles so that the Jews may understand that salvation is universal. We know that this gift continued for a while as the first missionary journeys reached new territories because Paul wrote specifically to curb its abuse in Corinth. Again, it was useful because Paul and the others followed the protocol of preaching to the Jews first in any city they reached. The Jews needed to be convinced by this prophetic actualization. Paul even confirms the Isaiah 28 prophecy when addressing the Corinthians.

There is no need to duplicate this phenomenon today. In the same way that Jesus having fulfilled the Law of the Old Testament did not continue (and does not continue today) to do the things He did while walking on this earth. He does not continue to die every day, for example. Fulfilled prophecies do not need to be duplicated "ad nauseam" into the present.

Tongues were real languages; they were not the Pentecostal, Charismatic gibberish called glossalalia which has its root in pagan religious incantations and practices. What struck the Jews of different local languages was that they could hear their own local dialect clearly spoken by people who had no reasons or way of having learned it. The fulfillment of this prophecy stunned them; it made them comment about it and ponder. It made a huge impression on them because these were their own regional dialects. It fulfilled its intended purpose. If these words had been senseless incantations; the hearers would not have been impressed at all. I have listened to Pentecostal/Charismatic "tongues" on two continents many times and I can assure you that I have never been impressed, stunned or awed.

The "gifts" Pentecostals claim today

Pentecostal's/Charismatic's argument that God is the same today as He was two thousand years ago, ergo: these gifts continue today. But they miss the point entirely: the purpose of those ancient gifts was accomplished long ago. If we carry the Pentecostal reasoning through its logical development, we could argue that Jesus who died and was resurrected should do it again and again in our present age... why should we be deprived of this greatest feat of all? We should be demanding that John the Baptizer continue his pre-conversion work nowadays. The reality is that Jesus fulfilled the Law and the Prophets, once...and it is done. The "gifts" the original apostles demonstrated were ethnic-specific: they were for the Jews who had the prophecies.

Healings in the infancy of the Church age did not simply hide symptoms of ill defined afflictions and vague pains. Jesus and His direct apostles brought dead people back to life. They cured advanced leprosy, deafness, muteness and blindness: these were real ills; ills everyone knew about. They healed the cause, they regenerated bodies.

God heals today as He always had; no one questions this. He heals believers and non-believers alike. Therefore, miraculous healing does happen—a lot: God answers the sick who pray to Him and He also answers the prayers of their loved ones who pray. But that is not the "gift of healing" as proclaimed—and fraudulently showcased—by the Pentecostals/Charismatics. God does send believers to pray for someone or to pray at a distance for someone and He heals that person. Even in cases too far gone for human medicine or cases impossible by human means. We should bring all our need to Jesus in prayer; including healing—ours and other's. But this is not the process the charlatans of the Charismatic movement claim.

The apostles healed conditions that medicine at that time could not heal. The same criteria should apply today: let the charlatans of the Pentecostal movement cure acute generalized lymphoma, AIDS, Ebola epidemics or Alzheimer.

Since the Charismatics claim the same gifts as the apostles; let them stop the funeral procession and go to the casket and order the dead to rise! Let them walk into any hospital and clear all the wards of the sick or injured, no matter the sickness or the trauma. Let them empty the surgical wards. If hospitals had existed in Jesus' time; that is probably what He and His disciples would have done. (In those days, the sick were not grouped into hospitals—hospitals did not exist—but their families and friends brought them by the hundreds to Jesus and He healed them all...)

Observations

While Jesus condemns the folks who follow that Jezebel; He also chastises the remainder of the Thyatira congregation: *you tolerate* (2:20). They were not being true to their faith; they did not keep their Savior's interests in mind: they preferred to be nice to the erring folks. The choice of word *tolerate* is still appropriate today because there has not been a vigorous scriptural rejection of the Pentecostal/Charismatic movement by the Church at large. The world assemblies of those who follow Jesus have *tolerated* this movement.

The Pentecostal/Charismatic movement came on the heel of a century of extreme erosion of the authority of the scriptures by liberal theologians (especially in Europe). The practical and binding value of the words was discounted and the concrete foundation of the apostles' faith became a metaphysical miasma. Christians and especially pastors lost their spiritual footing. Thus, when the Pentecostal/Charismatic movement came on the scene, they tolerated it: it is hard to push back when your own feet are on slippery ground.

<u>Aside but in context</u>: a fraction of the modern Church strives to expand its "tolerance". Can Jesus' warning be applicable to the Churches in Western countries today who promote the "gospel of tolerance"? In some congregations and from some pulpits, to tolerate everyone's druthers and being considered tolerant by the non-Christian society abroad trumps all considerations of orthodoxy, morality and righteousness. As long as the Christian is tolerant and acts as a doormat for all the deviant behaviors, theologies and philosophies of men; then he is a "good" Christian—a "good" Christian then is one who kowtows to man, not to God. God, not society, must define the Christian; so I believe that this passage is also a personal wake-up call for today's spineless social Christians.

The Bible version I am using for this study translates Jesus words in 2:20 as *My slaves*. It is a good choice of words because there is a proprietary aspect to this statement: Jesus purchased us at the ultimate high price one can pay. We are His and He expects us to comply with His preferences. A human master would not tolerate a slave's diversion from his purposes. When believers allow this Jezebel to divert their minds and actions, the beloved servants of Jesus become useless to Him—and His supremely costly investment is lost.

By its actions, the Pentecostal/Charismatic movement of today denies the sufficiency of scriptures. They infer that God supplements His "inadequate" original communication to man by new revelations through modern day apostles and prophets (all self promoted). Yet Jesus was finished with His doctrinal communication as He said through John: *If anyone adds to them* [the prophetic words of this book], *God will add to him the plagues that are written in this book* (22:18). And we shall see that the plagues will only hit the ones who do not belong to God, the message is clear: those who add new doctrinal revelations do not belong to Christ and will suffer the same consequences as those who oppose God. Jesus taught: *Beware of false prophets ... Not everyone who says to Me, "Lord, Lord!" will enter the kingdom of heaven, but only the one who does the will of my father in heaven. On that day many will say to Me, "Lord, Lord, didn't we prophesy in Your name, drive out demons in Your name, and do many miracles in Your name?" Then I will announce to them, "I never knew you! Depart from Me, you lawbreakers!"* (Matthew 7:15 – 23).

Two rigidly organized religions are built upon claims that new revelations were necessary to fill in beyond the inadequate biblical text—Islam and Mormonism. The Charismatic/Pentecostal movement is different from these religions because it is not monolithic. New prophets and apostles sprout continually all over these churches with "new revelations" whereas Islam and Mormonism have a trunk of fixed theories. (Although, in Mormonism revelations seem to continue from a designated number of official "apostles" as the need arises in order to modify the original doctrine—as with the recent revelation to include non-white people into their complicated system of heavens.) The Charismatic/Pentecostal movement does not have a designated number of accredited apostles: anyone can claim to be one and to prophesy. It is a free-for-all where personal ambitions rule.

Finally there are two more points on the subject. First, the theologies of the Pentecostal movement have had a downgrading lateral effect on the faith of Christianity as a whole. I have observed a lack of rigorous scriptural authority in the lives of those who do not personally share into the practices of the Pentecostal/ Charismatic movement but who are in close proximity with its theologies (perhaps attending a Charismatic church). They exhibit a tainted theology where their wishes and feelings outweigh scriptures. They approach decision-making from the premise that they will not deny their pursuits, but will find a way to validate them. If they can find a verse or a portion of a verse that they can use to their own end, they will give it the authority of "this is the will of God". If they cannot find a useful verse; they will then search for signs in their circumstances and will use such subjective artifices to validate their decision and action. The guiding principle seems to be: if it grants my wishes or if it feels good; then it must be from God. When we do this, we become our own god—we become our own final authority.

And second: I have noted a yearning for ecumenism toward the Catholic Church in many adherents of the Pentecostal/Charismatic movement. In this they are motivated by sentiments, not by obedience to any scriptural mandate.

The New Apostolic Reformation movement's emphasis on unity, on spiritual "togetherness" at the expense of obedience and respect of what God expressed in His Word, coupled with its "dominion" aims shows us that the trend toward the fateful one-world-religion and one-world-government of the Anti Christ is already apparent.

The huge popular rallies organized by various leaders of the movement feed on sentiments and create a mob feeling of belonging. The various threads of diverse religions are drawing together: New Apostolic Reformation, Roman Catholic Church and Islam. The common, universal yoke begins to emerge as we see the head of the Roman Church extending a welcome hand to the others—not as a move of Rome toward the others; but as a solicitation for them to join in (more about this later in the text). Jesus told us that we do not know the day; but that we should recognize the season...so, let the discerning reader beware.

Jesus, who knows all things, tells us that *only a few people* will find the narrow gate and walk the exclusive, demanding path of the redeemed and that one should *beware of false prophets who come to you in sheep's clothing* (Matthew 7:13 – 15). Yes, these false prophets look good, sound good and their message feels so good...they seem so benign, so gentle...unthreatening. We must sober up and realize that among the more than one hundred million Americans who call themselves Christian, only a sprinkling actually are ... the majority have settled for a Christian-flavored organized religion or have attached themselves to these mass movements—both harbingers of the evil to come.

Lulled by modern affluence and comfort, most people who call themselves Christians do not fear YHWH/Jesus. They have lost—or never had—the overwhelming respect for the person of the Almighty demonstrated by John at the beginning of Revelation. When John, the beloved apostle of Jesus, came in contact with Jesus, he *fell at His feet like a dead man*. John's relationship with Jesus, his Lord and Savior, was far from the casual—buddy type—relationship these false prophets entertain with the "Holy Spirit" and with "Jesus". They speak of their buddy-buddy visitations by Jesus, very casual affairs... The psalmist tells us: *obey YHWH with great fear. Be happy but tremble* (Psalm 2:11 NCV). There is no fear of the Lord, therefore no knowledge (read Proverbs 1) in these predators, and yet huge crowds follow them.

Thought to ponder

The Pentecostal/Charismatic movement often focuses on the danger and power of Satan. True, the devil exists; but need we fear him? Peter tells us in 1 Peter 5:8 – 9. *Be serious! Be alert! Your adversary the Devil is prowling around like a roaring lion, looking for anyone he can devour. Resist him and be firm in the faith, knowing that the same sufferings are being experienced by your fellow believers throughout the world.*

How is this warning "*be serious!*" compatible with the peace and rest a believer should find in God's love as Jesus intimated to the Church of Ephesus in Chapter 2? And does Peter really tell us to fear the devil and to fight him, to bind him where we find him? He does not.

Let's consider an example to bring Peter's teaching to a personal level. I love flying airplanes. When I am not actually flying; I am daydreaming about it. Yet, I am totally serious about my flying and as alert as I can be. I insist on thorough maintenance on my plane, I do not let any "squawk" go unfixed. I preflight thoroughly and shut down methodically. I don't fly when I am tired or sick. I plan my flights and I take voluntary recurrent training.

This is what Peter is writing about. He is not advocating that we should fear the devil or that we should see him in everything and keep a wary eye on him. Peters tells us to concentrate on the right procedures for the successful life in Christ: to be serious and alert about doing the right thing, saying the right thing and thinking the right thing. That way we won't fall victim to the prowling devil.

Gravity works 24/7—it never lets up and never fails—and under propitious circumstances it will always crash an airplane. My relationship with flying would not be viable if I considered it from the point of view of its foe—gravity—and the certainty thereof. Yet flying is perfectly workable when I seriously concentrate on applying the principles of flight that manage insulate the effect of gravity. As soon as my wheels leave the ground, gravity does its work relentlessly. Gravity rules our world; we can say that it is prowling the skies looking for any airplane it can devour. But I am committed to adhere to the principles that neutralize gravity so I am not imperiled nor stressed about it. Every airplane that you see in the sky is in the same circumstances. The reality is that almost all crashes are due to pilot errors—errors in handling the plane, planning contingencies, in making decisions about weather, in inadequate maintenance or in lackadaisical pre-flight inspection—no crash is due to the "devil" of gravity alone. Yet gravity is overwhelmingly present.

Peter is saying that Satan does not have to rule our lives. In the same way that it is impossible for a pilot to consider flight successfully if his main consideration is gravity and its negative intents; the believer cannot attempt the life in the kingdom if his preoccupation is with the devil. The believer must resist him by keeping firm in the faith and acting accordingly (in doing what Jesus asks him to do). All believers share the same circumstances and conditions; no one is singled out—just as all the airplanes in the sky are subject to the same gravity. Peter does not in any way strengthen the theories of the Pentecostal/Charismatic movement on spiritual warfare; he disproves them.

(Return to Table of Contents)

****

Chapter 3 - Sardis, Philadelphia, Laodicea

Revelation 3:1 – 22

Sardis

3:1 – 6

¹ "Write to the angel of the church in Sardis: "The One who has the seven spirits of God and the seven stars says: I know your works; you have a reputation for being alive, but you are dead. ²Be alert and strengthen what remains, which is about to die, for I have not found your works complete before My God. ³Remember, therefore, what you have received and heard; keep it, and repent. But if you are not alert, I will come like a thief, and you have no idea at what hour I will come against you. ⁴But you have a few people in Sardis who have not defiled their clothes, and they will walk with Me in white, because they are worthy. ⁵In the same way, the victor will be dressed in white clothes, and I will never erase his name from the book of life but will acknowledge his name before My Father and before His angels.

⁶ "Anyone who has an ear should listen to what the Spirit says to the churches.

What's happening

The followers of Jesus are known in Sardis, and they are well thought of by society. Their programs and outreaches are noted. They are not indifferent to Jesus but they are reverting to the world principles of life. They slide back to being motivated and guided by the spirit that moves man's society—not by God's Spirit. Their divine faith is fast becoming a mere religion; they are disconnecting their deeds from divine inspiration. Jesus issues an alert: what little you have left is about to die.

With the perspective of 2,000 years of Church history behind us we can see the effects of Jesus' judgment here: the world scenery is littered with the skeletons of dead assemblies. Their human organizations and buildings have endured for centuries. Generations after generations of their members have gone through the routine and carried on their elaborate, yet empty, rites. But Jesus has divorced them a long time ago: they are devoid of divine light and life. They are considered a cultural heritage by mankind; but God has nothing to do with them. They began, but somewhere down the line, they were distracted then diverted.

This is the first group that receives no kudos in Jesus' initial address. Faith is not philosophy, faith is not mental knowledge; faith is the unrestrained, unopposed and practical <u>application</u> of our knowledge and beliefs. Faith is the seal of authenticity of our convictions. Conviction not translated into action is hypocrisy—our opinions on God's prescription for life have no value: only our actions speak.

The Good News is so thoroughly good that it will necessarily have a transforming effect on our earthly lives. In Acts 5 the angel tells the freed apostles to *tell everything about this new life* and in Acts 11 the Jewish believers praised God for allowing even the Gentiles to *change their hearts so that they can have the life He gives.*

However, actions not anchored in conviction will quickly lead back to human hubris and apostasy. At this point there would be no difference between our actions and the "good" actions of an atheist or a Hindu or a Muslim: nice gestures...but devoid of God's eternal promise.

The symptom of discarding the Good News is a drying out of the effects it had in our life. If left unattended, our convictions will dry out. The conviction of the Good News is our core; when it withers, it will deaden the whole and eventually whatever little of it we put in effect will die too. Our only provision for salvation is our faith in the Son of God which translates into the permanent action of following Him day by day, moment by moment. The absence of the effects of faith condemns us. And the penalty is absolute: eternal damnation—notwithstanding our claims of "knowing" Jesus.

Ours is a love relationship with God and because it is true love; God will always grant us our liberty. Without this liberty, we would not love Him: we would only submit to Him as a master. This liberty implies a responsibility on our part. The plus side of our relationship with God is awesome; the downside of our casualness is fateful. With Sardis, Jesus addresses complacency: He wants a pure love with His followers. The price He paid prohibits any indifference and complacency on our part.

Jesus is not distant; He knows their works and the state of their souls. He is very much in attendance and is perfectly aware of all that goes on.

Sardis is the congregation that falls into a routine. The people may have loved Jesus at one point; but Jesus calls them *"dead"*. They do not particularly sin in a gross way. They started in Jesus but eventually they let the human concerns around them reassert themselves in their lives—suppressing what new life there was. This is the seed that fell among the thorns in the parable of the seeds (Matthew 13:3 – 9 and 18 – 23). The Good News was swamped out and their belief has regressed into a mere intellectual exercise devoid of conviction.

The believers of Sardis have let go of the Good News; Jesus tells them: *Remember therefore what you have received and heard* [the Good News]; *keep it and repent* (3:3). They are not animated nor moved by God's spirit anymore; instead they function like the community around them. God's inner prompts do not control their actions anymore; personal preferences, circumstances and society do. They have disconnected their walk from what had been their embraced conviction.

A true Christian must appear completely at odds with his human surroundings; but here, in Sardis, the believers fit perfectly in their local society. The spiritual reality of the Christian is that he must set himself apart and be readily identified as belonging to Christ: he is bought and paid for; he is not his own. Being the bride of Christ is not a marriage of convenience.

But again, Jesus will be fair: He will pick out the individuals who remain attached to, and identified with Him. They have kept Jesus' pardon and His grace as the living principle of their existence. Belonging to Jesus is a personal commitment and the responsibility remains with the individual.

Jesus does not abandon us; but some of us abandon Jesus. This was the reality in Sardis and it is a reality today. Here is a practical example to illustrate the principle: take an apple tree with a bumper crop on it. God gives the crop freely, yet it only benefits someone if he picks the apples; if he appropriates this bounty. That's the principle of the universal redemption offered through Jesus but embraced by so few. Now consider the person who did pick a basket of apples but on his way to his cellar lays the basket along the path and walks away. He abandons the free bounty. When he gets home, will he be able to benefit from that wonderful crop of apples that God provided? No, he will not. Yet, the apples were given and at one time were in his possession but he discarded them. This is what happens here in Sardis, and it happens today for a lot of people who call themselves Christians. They continue to see themselves as Christians; but it is now an illusion. Let's guard against this; Jesus has forewarned us.

<u>Note</u>: Let's make this personal: Embracing Jesus the Savior, steadfastly putting your faith, your trust in Him assures your eternal destination. Your past works—good or bad—have no bearing on this matter... and neither will your future works—good or bad. Your works will affect the quality of your earthly life, not your post-life destination. Good works have blessed consequences, bad works have negative consequences. The people of the old testament understood this perfectly. They knew that their faith made them the people of God. By faith Abraham was made righteous. They also knew that obeying the Law made their daily life much nicer but disobeying it brought hardships—in this life. As the psalmist wrote: *All good things come from you Lord.* Disobeying the Law did not revoke their status; faith controlled that.

When you put your faith in Jesus, He puts His cuing breath in you for the successful practice of life. Thus it is expected that your works down here will improve, will get transformed as the logical expression of His blessed leadership of your life (James 2).

Your decision to trust Him is voluntary; it is of your free will that you embrace Him, that you opt to trust Him. It will always remain a matter of free will to continue and deepen this faith, this trust. At any point, you can withdraw your trust, your faith, and reject His Lordship. Should you do so, this fateful decision will be irreversible and permanent. The writer of Hebrews makes this point absolutely clear in chapter 6 and Jesus lays it clearly for the seed in the shallow ground and the seed in the thorny briars.

Paul says: *Now, brothers and sisters, I want you to remember the Good News I brought to you. You received this Good News and continued strong in it. And you are being saved by it if you continue believing what I told you. If you do not* [continue believing what I told you] *then you believed for nothing* (1 Corinthians 15:1 – 2 NCV). And how did Paul define this Good News? *I passed on to you what I received, of which this was most important:* 1) that Christ died for our sins, 2) that He was buried, and 3) that he was raised to life on the third day after His death and 4) that He was seen by a slew of witnesses. In Sardis, many had discarded *what they had received and heard.*

This is extremely sobering: their names once written in the book of life will be regretfully erased by God. Not because God deserted them; but because they detached themselves from God. The author of Hebrews lays the point out clearly: *Some people cannot be brought back again to a changed life. They were once in God's light, and enjoyed heaven's gift, and shared in the Holy Spirit. They found out how good God's word is, and they received the powers of this new world. But they fell away from Christ* (Hebrews 6:4 – 6 NCV). Or as the ERV says: *they left it all behind*—just like the basket of apples in the example above.

Again the closing statement refers to churches in plural making it universal and timeless.

Observations

Jesus is clear: *I have not found your works complete before my God* (3:2). *What can we do to perform the works of God? They asked. Jesus replied, "this is the work of God: that you believe in the One He has sent"* (John 6:29). It is our committed conviction of the Good News that maintains the ground necessary for our transformed earthly life.

When this is the case, believing is doing what we know to be true. Believing is not an intellectual concept it is the concrete application, the working-out of what we claim to know. Jesus says *the only people who will enter the kingdom of heaven are those who <u>do</u> what my Father in heaven wants* (Matthew 7:21 NCV).

Every believer must critically inspect his life and see whether he merely nods his approval to Jesus' words or whether he drastically changes how he lives to put into practice Jesus' dictate.

For example, in Matthew 6:33 – 34, Jesus says: *What you should want most is...doing what he* (God) *wants you to do. Then he will give you all these other things you need.So don't worry about tomorrow* (ERV). Do you do what God instructs you personally to do day by day, moment by moment? Do you trust that He knows what He will want to do about your children's college education (He may have other plans) or about your career plans and retirement? Or do you pursue assiduously these socially acceptable goals by any human means at your disposal, hoping that God will not disturb your plan by placing a conflicting demand on you or by giving you different marching orders? In other words: are you today employed at your current task because God specifically gave you that task? If you can answer "yes", then you are indeed a follower of Jesus. On the other hand, if you are tied to your occupation because you seek to provide stability, respectability and comfort for yourself and your family or simply because you are pursuing a personal goal of your own; then you are not a follower of Jesus: you are balking at the threshold of His kingdom.

Have you effectively stopped your personal pursuits and do you actively trust God to provide? Only you can answer the question, but answer you must (and no: God does not need "tent makers"). You might not find encouragements from your congregation on this because your walk may expose the shallowness of their own beliefs. So you will hear excuses like "that was fine in Jesus' time;

but it does not apply now" or "you have to be reasonable about this"—or worst of all: "we have to be good stewards". What these statements would really express is that Jesus' teaching is just too hard, too inconvenient to be heeded as told and should Jesus live in our modern times, He would surely modify his discourse to accommodate our modern life's druthers.

Do you have the backbone to practice your faith? To follow where God leads you? Or do you ignore His voice; quenching the effects of His Spirit (inspiration) in you?

This teaching of Jesus is not new; God's relationship with His people has not changed: *I have carried you since you were born; I have taken care of you from your birth. Even when you are old, I will be the same. Even when your hair has turned gray, I will take care of you. I made you and I will take care of you. I will carry you and save you* (Isaiah 46:3 NCV). If we think that it was not God who took care of our every need when we were newborns, we are foolish. And if we think that we must provide for ourselves when we are mature adults: we are not saved at all.

In Sardis, Jesus warns: *I will come against you* and in Matthew 7:21 He had unequivocally declared that only those who do what God wants are in His kingdom. Jesus says that it is people who don't know God who keep trying to provide these things for themselves (Matthew 6:32). Do you know God? This principle of exclusive practical alignment with God must apply to all areas of our lives, without exclusions.

Thoughts to ponder

Sardis is where the blade of God's word cuts through our preconceived notions; are you shying away from the blade? If so: you are not in Him. You may be in church every Sunday or lead the study every Wednesday, you may be known in your community as a pillar of your congregation—you may even be its pastor—but if you have not sheared off the strings of your own security; you have not completely believed. You have the reputation among men for being alive; but you are dead.

There may be some secondary areas of your life in which you exercise a true faith; but have you surrendered the core aspects of human life? Wake up and act or even what little faith you now exhibit will die off.

Change the source for all the needs and processes of your life; change the way your life flows. If you don't, Jesus will not come for you; He will come against you. Your name will be erased from His book of life because you insisted in keeping your life according to man's books (20:12).

<u>(Return to Table of Contents)</u>

Philadelphia

3:7 – 13

7 "Write to the angel of the church in Philadelphia: 'The Holy One, the True One, the One who has the key of David, who opens and no one will close, and closes and no one opens says: 8I know your works. Because you have limited strength, have kept My word, and have not denied My name, look, I have placed before you an open door that no one is able to close. 9Take note! I will make those from the synagogue of Satan, who claim to be Jews and are not, but are lying — note this — I will make them come and bow down at your feet, and they will know that I have loved you. 10Because you have kept My command to endure, I will also keep you from the hour of testing that is going to come over the whole world to test those who live on the earth. 11I ' coming quickly. Hold on to what you have, so that no one takes your crown. 12The victor: I will make him a pillar in the sanctuary of My God, and he will never go out again. I will write on him the name of

My God and the name of the city of My God — the new Jerusalem, which comes down out of heaven from My God — and My new name. [13] *Anyone who has an ear should listen to what the Spirit says to the churches".*

What's happening

What a contrast between this assembly in Philadelphia and the one in Sardis! Jesus defines the believers in Philadelphia as being limited in strength yet acting on Jesus' impulses. They unblinkingly do what their convictions show and demand. They choose to deny their fears, to deny their pride, to deny their social integration in order to avail themselves totally, unequivocally to their Lord Jesus.

> <u>Note</u>: The open door Jesus placed before the Philadelphians was not an absence of opposition—God had not cleared a smooth path before them. In fact the text suggests the opposite: *because you have kept my command to endure* tells us that going down the divine path was strenuously opposed by the religious people there. But these faithful Philadelphian believers knew what God expected of them and they faithfully and doggedly pursued it.

> Facing a decision, we often ask God to guide us by "opening or shutting" the correct door; by this we mean: God, please remove all obstacles that are in the way; thus, make my choice a no-brainer. But the Christian walk does not work that way. We must seek God's will and intention and receive His quiet, intimate assurance and then, regardless of how the landscape appear, we must walk the path of our blessed conviction.

When we read the life stories of heroes of the faith, we often see that they acted on this deep, intensely private, divine conviction and walked against persistent and nasty opposition. From a human point of view, there was no clean swept path for them to walk on.

The Philadelphians are not appraised on the meager results of their works but on the condition of their hearts. It is crucial for us to know that we "follow" Jesus; we do not "produce" for Him. The ungodly Egyptians demanded production quotas from their Hebrew slaves; that's the world's mentality. God is the opposite. In the end, our eternal rewards will be based on: "did you walk with Me?" "Did you let me accomplish My work through you?"

Their opportunity to serve Jesus is due in no small part to the fact that they keep no reserves; they commit their all to living the new life. They keep nothing of their former life to go back to and they banish all regrets about it. They endure. Jesus has their all. Jesus urges them to continue living that way till the end. No corrections are needed. Their reward is assured.

Jesus never asks His followers to do anything more than what He specifically asks of them. The true followers of Jesus will be honored amongst all forever. Understandably, we all want to consider ourselves "Philadelphians". But the reality is different. We must frankly assess our lives, actions, comfort zones and motives. If we don't, Jesus will have no compunction being ruthless with the reality of our lives. In our Western societies, where Christians are not actively persecuted, very few people who call themselves Christians hail from Philadelphia.

These Philadelphians are the beautiful, true Christians. Sadly, they are few in number.

Because you have kept My command to endure: "endure" is a key concept of this passage. Committed endurance defines the

Philadelphian believer. To endure, at God's prompting, implies the willful and sustained denial of our fears and the committed eschewing of the "world reality" that surrounds us and aims at defeating us. This is the first principle Jesus demonstrated for us after His baptism. The first temptation: Jesus has submitted to the Spirit's leading and walked deep into the wilderness. He had not heard any command to the contrary since. He could have given up after a few days, or a few weeks and walked back. He knew the way: He had walked in. But He waited on God's lead. He voiced His intent to persevere in His endurance this way: I may need bread badly; but I will live by God's word... (not by your words). I will wait for God's instructions.

The believers in Philadelphia had endured faithfully. Jesus could open the door for their *good works* (Eph. 2:10), for the life He has for them: they were His ready tools.

> Note: the believer does not choose his own life in Christ. The believer cannot substitute his own preferred works or his own socially integrated ministry. God did not accept Moses arguments and He will not accept yours. The door He opens for the true believer is the door to the very life Jesus has chosen for that believer.

About endurance: let's say you had the best job you ever had, just received a significant pay raise and were recently put on a fast track for promotions, when God's gentle, yet unmistakable voice urges you to "leave now". Did you obey and told your bosses the actual reason for your leaving and did you respond frankly to your family and friends' inquiries. Then, did you endure in this uncomfortable limbo, while God was teaching you that He is utterly reliable and that He provides for His believers? Did you endure when the time dragged on, when weeks turned into months and months into years? Did you endure when your reserves dwindled to nothing? Then, did you endure through the pointed criticisms of your friends, of your brothers and sisters in Christ? Did you endure through your crushing doubts and bewilderment? Did you endure when your pastor threw you out of the church because your obedience threatened his comfortable faith (even though you never asked for any aid from anyone)?

Or instead, did you begin on the path God showed you, but at some point decided that enough was enough; did you go back on the job market, rekindled old connections and became a "good steward" again? In other words, did you endure until God Himself brought the teaching to its divine conclusion? Or did you "walk out" at some point?

... Hold on to what you have so that no one will take your crown (verse 11). God will do what He has planned to get done; nothin will deter Him. God will do through a faithful follower what He has planned to carry through a human agency. Esther 4:13 – 14 makes this principle clear. If you turn down the purpose God would accomplish through you, He will do so through someone else But you will miss the divine reward that would have been allocated to you. It will go to the follower who accepted the mantle.

Every follower of Jesus will appear before the *"bema"*, the reward/judgment seat. This is the divine podium where the performance awards are meted out. Some will receive many crowns, some will be left naked, without any reward at all. This is what Jesus speaks about here to the Philadelphians: continue to make yourselves available to God's purpose—to what God intends to do through you—so you will receive the corresponding rewards (eternal crowns)... Someone will get those specific crowns; make sure it is you.

Jesus provided us with the example to follow. Jesus endured in the desert; He had obeyed willingly, had placed Himself trustingly in a situation of human hardships at God's prompting. And then

He endured beyond any reasonable parameters. He froze through the long desert nights and baked under the relentless sun during the day while He was tormented by hunger. As a man, He only had three years to accomplish His mission, yet God led Him to a long, idle isolation; it must not have made sense to the man in Jesus. At any point He could have walked out; He knew the way (He had walked in). Only His determination to endure, His unwavering decision to trust kept Him there. And when his resistance was worn down, He still turned down the easy, ungodly "outs" that His weakening flesh could have welcomed. Please note that at this point, He did not know how much longer his situation would last; yet He chose to endure and turned down Satan's offers. This is our example. It is God who brought on the end of Jesus' endurance training; Jesus did not choose when to quit.

Then, having rested in the care of God's angels and been restored through their ministering, Jesus *returned to Galilee in [with] the power of the Spirit, and news about Him spread throughout the entire vicinity. He was teaching in their synagogues, being acclaimed by everyone* (Luke 4:14 – 15). God had placed an open door before Jesus so when He came out of the desert, no one was able to close that door. Jesus completed His mission, all opposition being powerless to stop Him.

Job is another of our early biblical examples here: after his friends exhausted the human argument of cause and effect, and after God questioned him; Job chose to endure. God revealed Himself through His questions: I personally attend to and am aware of everything that happens in creation; do you think that I am oblivious of your situation? And: I have power over all things; do you think that I could not set you free in an instant if I so chose? At that, Job embraced God personal attributes and His sovereignty. Basically Job submitted totally and surrendered wholly to God's chosen fate for him—<u>without</u> knowing that God would end his misery soon: for all Job knew, his misery would last through his last breath. God never hinted at the outcome but Job chose to endure. The Philadelphians had endured. And they were urged to continue doing so.

So Jesus tells the Philadelphians: *I have placed before you an open door that no one is able to close*; it is the door to accomplish the *good works God planned long ago for them to live their lives doing* (Ephesians 2:10, adapted). The picture for us is that once we reach the benchmark maturity of endurance, we are readily usable by God. That is our model for the necessary principle of obedient endurance that Jesus praises in the Philadelphians.

The circumstances of your endurance will be tailor-made for you; but make no mistake: God will require endurance from every one of His believers. If your life has been middle of the road and ruled by the same imperatives as those of the society around you; you do not hail from Philadelphia...yet.

Building the endurance that your faith requires will always be a personal process, never a group endeavor. Jesus whose ministry was completely public demonstrated the endurance of His faith in isolation, privately. This will be true for you as well. If you are married, your spouse will be implicated by association; but the process will isolate you: it is your personal faith that will be exercised, never a collective faith.

Every Philadelphian type of believers must pass through the threshold of endurance; if God has not brought the teaching to you yet: He will. If He has already and you balked; will you submit to it again—with the commitment to endure—when He offers it to you again? ... For He certainly will.

When the trial comes, it is always offered gently, yet firmly by God and it is always "out of the blue", unexpected. It is never in line with your existing plans, your emotions, nor does it match someone else's suggestion for your life. It never lines up with your lifelong dream either. But it will define your life; as James says it would: *Consider it great joy, my brothers, whenever you experience various trials, knowing that the testing of your faith produces endurance. But <u>endurance must do its complete work, so that you may be mature and complete, lacking nothing</u>* (James 1:2 – 4). The Philadelphians were mature and complete and lacked nothing: they were ready for an eternity with Jesus and, while on earth they were the honed tools in His hand.

> <u>Note</u>: If you are suffering, if you are in dire straits because of disobedience or rebellion (promiscuity, greed, fear, lying, selfishness or other sin) do not for one moment imagine that you are "suffering righteously"—you are simply reaping the consequences of your willful sin. The maturing process of your faith expressed here does not begin as a consequence of your unrighteous, negative actions and it does not use your bad actions or your regretful choices as the trigger either. God always offers His call to the believer at a time of quiet obedience and of intimate walk with Him—He is not punishing; He is building his very dear child. Remember Job.

There may be several areas in your life where faithful endurance is needed, and accordingly, each will come with its tailor-made training. So, having already endured in one area, God may shift to another.

For example: when God, later in your life, told you to leave your country and go where He showed you, did you go? Did you go without "raising support" and without seeking the sponsorship of a board? And once there, did you stay? Did you endure as your "productive years" slowly drifted by, unused? Did you stay, doing the small things God asked you to do day by day, feeling inconsequential, getting weaker in body and mind? Did you stay until God Himself brought you home, older, much older? Your human prospects for expected outcomes like a profession or a retirement plan now foregone, yet having been whittled to fit His hand and ground smooth like a favored tool, you are now ready for His work ... not by your own strength or power, but by God's Spirit (Zechariah 4:6). God is not afraid of long projects; I know: it took several long processes for me.

Jesus says that the believers in Philadelphia have limited strength. These people are not the elite among the men of their community or country, they are not important members within the organized church setting, but God is with them. Jesus has made a way for them; their path is secure, and their place is defended by the Almighty.

In the end these Philadelphian believers will be with Jesus for eternity. When the "Christians-in-name-only" lumped with the rest of the unbelievers come to pay homage to Jesus they will automatically pay homage to these Philadelphia believers (v. 9) who will be securely at Jesus' side.

In 3:10 Jesus promises that the Philadelphian believers will not go through the terrible *time of testing* of the end, because they have kept the faith. They will be raptured before it begins. This *time of testing* is exactly what the words say: to obtain everyone's spiritual position. Jesus will put to the test (apply pressure in order to extract the essence) all the inhabitants of the earth so that none who would have come to Him may be lost. The process will also demonstrate that everyone He will condemn at the last judgment was indeed unconvertible. These Philadelphians had truly come to Jesus and allowed Him to change their lives now; there is no need to test them, to squeeze them about it.

The Philadelphians are the ones who will never leave God's presence; they will be incorporated into His very surroundings in the *new Jerusalem*. They will be tagged as God's very own property and pride. Jesus will indelibly write God's name on them (brand them as God's) and will give them an intimate name for Himself.

Again, the closing statement refers to churches plural: the message is universal and timeless.

Of the five other groups already addressed, only those in Smyrna were ready to go through the necessary maturing of endurance, and Jesus tells them that the process is coming and encourages them to endure through it. The other four groups were sidetracked by issues that needed clearing up before they could walk the road toward completion and maturity of their faith.

If you are a believer in Jesus, are you sidetracked by some of the same issues? If you are: He has addressed you clearly and you are accountable for your active response. If God is beginning the process of maturation through endurance in you; be encouraged to persevere and to hold tight. If you are like the believers of Philadelphia; you already know where you are, and you already understand the process.

(Return to Table of Contents)

Laodicea

3:14 – 22

14 "Write to the angel of the church in Laodicea: 'The Amen, the faithful and true Witness, the Originator, of God's creation says: 15I know your works, that you are neither cold nor hot. I wish that you were cold or hot. 16So, because you are lukewarm, and neither hot nor cold, I am going to vomit you out of My mouth. 17Because you say, 'I'm rich; I have become wealthy and need nothing,' and you don't know that you are wretched, pitiful, poor, blind, and naked, 18 I advise you to buy from Me gold refined in the fire so that you may be rich, white clothes so that you may be dressed and your shameful nakedness not be exposed, and ointment to spread on your eyes so that you may see. ¹⁹ *As many as I love, I rebuke and discipline. So be committed and repent.* ²⁰*Listen! I stand at the door and knock. If anyone hears My voice and opens the door, I will come in to him and have dinner with him, and he with Me.* ²¹*The victor: I will give him the right to sit with Me on My throne, just as I also won the victory and sat down with My Father on His throne.'* ²² *"Anyone who has an ear should listen to what the Spirit says to the churches."*

What's happening

This is the first group in which Jesus finds no acceptable deeds. The Laodiceans are the only group who does not yet have a part of Jesus even though they call themselves Christians. They have kept Jesus from the core of their lives, yet He gives them a personal invitation to let Him in. This letter is the ultimate appeal to all of us who may be like these Laodiceans.

This letter to the Laodiceans addresses the crux of Christian life. It harkens almost word for word to Jesus commands: *You cannot serve two masters... You cannot serve God and worldly riches* (Matthew 6).

This letter is the spear into the heart of the North-American church.

Jesus practical teaching is clear and straightforward: God <u>must</u> be your provider. You <u>must</u> choose your provider. You <u>must</u> choose to be supplied by God for all things, to depend on Him only—practically, not theoretically. Only then will you escape the lordship of money, the lordships of the world. If you do not resolutely walk that way in your <u>practical</u> life, you are no Christian at all. Jesus is still knocking at your door—precisely because He is not in yet!

This message to the Laodiceans echoes directly Jesus' commands in Matthew 6: *So, don't worry about the food and drink you need, the covering you need...* These are commands, not suggestions. Jesus said to go into all the world and make followers, baptize them <u>and</u> teach them all the commands He gave us. These are the types of commands He means.

The assembly of Laodicea could afford what the world had to sell so they felt pretty good about it. They could afford all the necessities, they could maintain a decent social status, and if sickness threatened them, they could afford whatever medicine offered at that time. Humanly speaking, life was good.

But they were not Christians at all. What Jesus teaches in Matthew 6 is not optional, and now just a couple generations later this assembly exhibited the traits of the fallen humanity of the non-believers.

They based their peace of mind on the earthly treasures they had. Whereas Jesus demands that His followers choose to get supplied by Him (He is never short and His reserves are never plundered or at risk).

So because in their minds, in their hearts and in their actions they lined up with the world's system, they were not hot about Jesus. Mind you, they were not against the idea of Jesus being the Messiah; but they could live with or without Him in their everyday routine... And so it is for most "Christians" around me, in North-America.

Jesus' pastoral letter hits where they err: They are missing the whole life, life to the fullest that Jesus brought.

> • *Buy <u>from Me</u> gold made pure in fire* (NCV). God will supply even actual financial needs that you will face. But He will do so without the enslaving tentacles of the human money systems. This is not theory; this is

absolutely practical. In Jesus you will have what you need to procure food, beverage, housing, transportation...

• *Buy <u>from Me</u> white clothes, so you can be clothed and you can cover your shameful nakedness* (NCV). As Jesus commanded in Matthew 6: *And why worry about clothes? Look how the lilies of the field grow.* They don't rely on the human system at all, yet *Solomon with his riches was not dressed as beautifully as one of these flowers.* Protection, covering and status: You <u>must</u> get those from Jesus and from Him only.

• *Buy <u>from Me</u> medicine to put on your eyes so you can truly see* (NCV). This principle extends to all areas of life: get your health solutions from the author of life, from the One who heals. Do not depend on human health. Of course, the solution Jesus may choose could involve human solutions, but as a means; not as a policy.

The Laodiceans thought they had it made. They could placate God at the weekend by sitting in the pew, singing along with the choir because they had it all covered. They could be smug or feel safe because they had the means to pay for groceries, housing, transportation, vacation, education, retirement... They had the means to maintain social status and to purchase whatever health solution the world offered at that time. Except they were not born of the Spirit. They were headed for the awful eternity. Jesus is graphically clear: He is going to puke them out. That means, God was repulsed by their lives. Yet, Jesus was reaching out from outside their lives: *I am outside your door, knocking; will you let me in?* If you don't, with all your money, your status and the human connections you can afford, you are headed for Hell.

This message to the Laodiceans is not theoretical and it is not optional; it is practical and mandatory.

It is amazing that within mere decades of Jesus' glorious resurrection and supernatural departure, believers had already reached the "blahs" in their association with God. How many of the professed believers since that time—and today—belong to this category?

We think that things are all right because Jesus does not come back; we are philosophically lackadaisical. We have an "Oh, well..." mentality. There was no "Oh, well..." in Jesus' torture on the cross for us, there was no "Oh, well..." about his glorious resurrection. His reality must be relevant moment by moment. Being a Christian is all about God, not about us.

These folks are nauseating enough to Jesus that He can't stomach them as they are (He can't take them fully in); He can only vomit them out; there is a gag reflex here. He finds nothing that tastes like Him in them. Vomiting them out is a gross choice of words but Jesus expresses it this way and it represents accurately His feelings on the matter. Those whom God will vomit out will be permanently out; He will not take them back in again: only dogs go back to their vomit.

This group is doing well world-wise. Today, the Church of Laodicea would be a successful, reputable denomination or even a mega-church. The members smell good, look good and can afford lunch at the club. On the world scene they compare well with the secular important and influential crowd.

Unfortunately, because they never let Jesus transform them from the core; they are just like the world around them. They are not against God or against the idea of God but they keep Him "in his place" and grant Him limited access to the fringes of their lives. They never entered into the life of Jesus' kingdom where the believer deliberately comes to Jesus and does what God tells him to do moment by moment (righteousness), trusting God to supply all his physical and spiritual needs (Matthew 6:34).

Because their lives fit perfectly within the social setting around them, their faith does not generate human conflict or even social uneasiness, neither for them nor for those around them. Today, in western society, a significant section of those wearing the label of Christianity are in this group. Society considers them "good Christians"... meaning they are tame, they are not upsetting to the non Christians' way of life and system of values.

Laodiceans see themselves as movers and shakers; but really they are *wretched* because they are not moved by the Spirit of God who gives life to the fullest.

They are *pitiful* because they deceive themselves. A person living in self-deception or delusion is always a pitiful sight from an observer's point of view.

They are *poor* because although Jesus promises abundant life, the Laodiceans are really living at the restricted level of their human surroundings and understandings. They may think that they have many worldly possessions, but when it comes down to it; they only enjoy a few of these while the bulk of their other possessions simply weigh their lives down. What they have do not necessarily compliment their core personalities.

They are *blind*: their scriptures present the light but they have not incorporated this light into their hearts, refusing to let it illuminate and guide their lives. The available light has been useless to them.

They are *naked*: they eschewed God's protection. Considering that God even clothes the lilies of the fields (Matthew 6:30); how sad that these people ignore God's proffered cover for their protection. Without Him we are naked, vulnerable to all threats.

This covering goes beyond protection. Our clothes also reflect and project our social status, our relative position in the group. The blue suits of IBM, Proctor and Gamble and other status conscious firms are an application of this principle. Routinely, when someone is invited to an event or to a home, he or she will automatically consider: "what should I wear?" Clothes express status for the wearer and honor for the host. The traditional caste-based sartorial etiquette of Egypt is designated to expose everyone's social status at first glance—clothing there is foundational. In his time, Solomon was without peers socially and his sumptuous attires made the point (inferred from Matthew 6:29).

Here, the Laodiceans saw themselves as relevant socially because they could afford fancy clothing, but Jesus says: *you are naked*. You have no eternal standing at all: you would be turned out at my popular kingly wedding banquet because you do not have the right clothes. You do not have <u>My</u> covering. Those who will be in Heaven with Jesus will receive from Him a robe of white linen: it expresses the status that the wearer enjoys with God and it honors God. The white clothes refer to the true Christian who has washed his clothes in the blood of the Lamb. Jesus will adorn His bride in linen as white as snow.

In 3:18 Jesus tells these people to switch supply centers; God must become their selected, exclusive provider. They must come to God for everything because there is no safety for them in gauging themselves on a comparative scale with their worldly neighbors. There is no stability either; no matter how they delude themselves into thinking they are rich and doing well. Their lives must flow in another direction in order to please Jesus. They must decide to choose God and His ways.

God loves these people and will apply discipline before spitting them out if no changes take place. They had never come face to face with the reality of Jesus, so He causes this personal encounter: He knocks at their doors so that they will have to either take Him in fully or reject Him there. The Laodiceans know <u>about</u> Jesus but they have not embraced Him for who he is. Jesus is on the outskirts of their lives. They are "for" the idea of God but they have never allowed themselves to be challenged by the sovereignty of Jesus; they have never submitted to its transformation.

Jesus is willing to make the first step (He knocks); He is making the offer. Their future hangs on their response to His knock. They have the responsibility to let Him in and to assume His nature. Jesus had defined the eternal position of the faithful believer: the Philadelphian is by the side of Jesus who is on the throne—only a bride could be granted this closeness. These folks in Laodicea are one life-changing response away from that glorious intimacy. Conversely, they are one compromise away from falling off eternally.

Again the closing statement changes to the plural form in churches indicating a timeless and universal message.

Thoughts to ponder

Today's Laodiceans may be individuals whose parents and grandparents were church goers. They have "grown up in the church" and have participated in various church activities all their lives. But they have never surrendered themselves to Jesus. They have not tasted the heavenly gifts, they did not become companions with the Holy Spirit nor did they taste the goodness of the word of God and the powers of the coming age described in Hebrews 6:4 – 5. They are social Christians in their community and intellectual Christians personally. There is a significant ratio of Laodicea types in most established denominations.

If you are one of these Christians, watch out, because you have been lulled by the appearance of Christianity. Jesus addresses you specifically. From the <u>outside</u>, He knocks at your door. He says clearly: *be committed and repent* (relinquish your will and change the flow of your life) 3:19.

Then and now

This "epistle" of Jesus to the seven churches sums up every type of Christian believers who ever were and together in one form or another they populate our church pews today.

We should note that Jesus does not compare any one group to another. He never says: "Why don't you be more like the Ephesians... why don't you perform like the Thyatirans..." We must follow Him and live our Christian life in step with Him, and Him only. Often, we want to emulate this "successful" church or this "growing" church—those are human artifices and pursuits.

When we compare ourselves with other Christians or congregations, we lose the essence of our relationship with Jesus: *Come to me...and you will find rest for your life...my burden is light and my task is easy...* The reality is: our pride urges us to live up to others' performance—we want to be able to humanly justify ourselves.

When we analyze the corrections Jesus provides, we notice that none are burdensome. For the Ephesians, Jesus relieves the burden of performance and commands them to rest in His love. To the Smyrnans, Jesus adds no burden. The corrections for the people of Pergamum or Thyatira add no burden. Sardis' believers are being redirected, not burdened. The Laodiceans are called out and invited to begin what they have been missing.

What is the practical relevance of Jesus' epistles to us? To understand the implications, let's look at the applied consequences of Jesus' words: if the rapture had happened in John's time, based on Jesus' omniscient words in these letters to the churches: who would have been raptured?

Out of Ephesus, Jesus is clear: before the letter, no one would make the cut—although they were sincere "Christians". After Jesus' letter only *those who change their hearts and do what they did at first...those who win the victory* would be spared—the implication is:

a few. As a witness to this reality, we have the testimony of history: the assembly in Ephesus ceased to exist a long time ago just as Jesus had warned.

Out of Smyrna, it is logical to expect that most of them would have been raptured before the letter. And after the letter, those who continued to be faithful would also have been raptured.

Some in Pergamum would have been raptured; but two groups in that assembly would not. After receiving John's letter, of these two groups, only those *who change their hearts and minds, who win the victory,* would have been raptured. How many would have made it? How many did change? How many in your assembly will change?

Out of Thyatira, Jesus would have lifted those who *had not followed the false teachings* and had continued steadfastly loyal to Jesus' orthodoxy. From the text it appears that the prevalent spirit in the remaining majority would have resisted the change. Is your assembly guilty of the same deviations as Thyatira? Then don't expect a massive and glorious rapture from your group, in spite of what your pretended prophets and false apostles promise you.

Out of Sardis, we know that only *a few had kept their clothes unstained* and Jesus will gladly lift them up. But how many others in Sardis will choose to change their *hearts and lives* after reading Jesus' letter? In your group, how many of the people who exhibit Sardis' symptoms will make the radical turn around? Will you?

The entire assembly of Philadelphia would have been lifted and *kept from the time of trouble that will come to the whole world to test those who live on earth.*

Out of Laodicea, no one would have been lifted outright, before they received the letter. Yet, upon reading the letter, how many completely changed their worldview and their life? How many felt the urgency to do so when life seemed to go on just as before?

The sobering reality is that, already in John's time, only one group out of seven who called themselves "Christians" would have been raptured and one other was on the cusp. Out of all the other assemblies who considered themselves to be legitimate "churches", only a few souls would have met Jesus' criteria. The witness of history shows us that assemblies through the centuries have not migrated into the Smyrna or Philadelphia molds.

Today's pre Gog and Magog time, existing churches still fall within the parameters of these seven permanent examples therefore rapture would only lift a smattering of believers from among the "Christians". God leaves the choices of obedience to each individual who claims to believe, the choices that lead to rapture are not entrusted to the congregations or to the denominations.

Above all, we must keep in mind that Jesus is speaking to everyone, individually, in these letters. Your congregation may be described in several of Jesus' letters and some of its members may have their personal lives defined in more than one of the letters. You may see yourself also in several of the letters, and that is the very purpose of Jesus' epistles: that we all may be exercised personally so that we may change accordingly.

Final note: the word "victor" is repeated for almost every group. No one is a victor who does not stay in the fight until it is over. The redundant fact is to never, never quit, never let go of Jesus' hand.

From today's perspective: after God's universal revealing at *Gog and Magog*, how many Christians-in-name-only will choose YHWH/Jesus during the great harvest? (Refer to: *The Rock Breaks the Globalists' Empire*.) How many then will decide against the God they now cannot discount anymore?

I am often asked whether I think many "left behind" people will turn to Jesus after the rapture of the saints. Let's be sober about this: how many who chose to stand against YHWH/Jesus after *Gog and Magog* will have the courage to make the frightful choice for Jesus when the knife is pressed against their throats? Today, every "Christian" must ponder the reality check Jesus provides in His universal epistle. Now is when the choice is still easy and voluntary.

From now on, you who read these lines should ponder the reality of Elihu's question: *Should God repay you on your terms when you have rejected His?* (Job 34:33).

Conclusion on Jesus' pastoral letters

These letters to the churches are our God-dictated epistles. It is my opinion today that when we study Paul or the other apostles' writings, we should balance them out and weigh them against these letters of Jesus. We should never extrapolate any meaning in the apostles' epistles that would differ from what Jesus has dictated here.

Jesus meant these letters as scriptures; that's why He dictated them and they are completely trustworthy. Just as Jesus was very succinct when He explained the Good News in the Gospels, He remains succinct in His "how-to" pastoral letters. Jesus could have given many more pages of corrections and exhortation—John was not running out of writing material—but He chose not to because He had said all that would be needed. Jesus' epistles are complete. He has addressed those who have come to Jesus and He extends His invitation to those who think they are Christians.

Peter tells us that Paul's writings are sometimes hard to understand; but there is nothing hard to understand in what Jesus tells us here. The only reason that the apostles did not reference these letters of Jesus in their epistles is simply because Revelation was not available at the time they wrote.

Personally, when a person inquires about the hope that is in me I lead him first through what Jesus did and said by sharing the gospels. From now on, if they accept Jesus; I will lead them to study what Jesus teaches here in this first part of Revelation.

These first three chapters of Revelation are the most relevant chapters for Christians; they are the "how to" book for life in the kingdom and a stern "wake up" call. They are the timeless reality of those who follow Jesus.

The remainder text of Revelation will be most important for those who will be a part of the tragic times of the end, those who had not accepted Jesus as their saving Messiah before the rapture. But as for us, who study them this side of the rapture, the next chapters are useful in urging us not to be a part of these events. The last chapters of humanity are pre-published; no one will affect any aspect of them. Because everyone can read what will happen later; no one will have an excuse. And that too is an aspect of God's fairness.

(Return to Table of Contents)

****

Chapter 4 - Timeline of the Events, Gog and Magog

4:1

After this I looked, and there in heaven was an open door. The first voice that I had heard speaking to me like a trumpet said, "Come up here, and I will show you what must take place after this."

Timeline of future events

We now enter the long text of Revelation that deals with the events of the end, the text calls it: *What will happen later, after this* [after the Church age]. In 4:1, the *open door* in front of John expresses that there is a threshold that separates the now from what he will see next. Things revealed on the other side are not visible from this side. We are done with the practical pastoral letters and now we enter the prophetic message of Revelation. Basically, God says: "come to My side and see what's next".

Perspectives

Note: I will use the terms Jew or Jewish when the text refers to the two tribes of Benjamin and Judah. I will use the terms Hebrew, Hebraic when the text refers to the twelve tribes, the entire family line of Jacob. The ten tribes of the Northern Kingdom were dispersed and "lost" into the world prior to the Babylonian exile of the two tribes of the Southern Kingdom. We do not know how many people comprise these "lost" tribes today.

As my study of Revelation proceeded, I became aware of a peculiarity: Revelation is a stand-alone document as regards to its specific content. Earlier prophecies provided through the Hebraic prophets of the Old Testament focused mostly on what will affect

123

Israel; that is to say the end-time events from a Jewish/Hebraic perspective (Daniel chapter 2 is one of the rare exceptions). These Jewish/Hebraic revelations are, for the most part, complete; we can see God's plan for the descendants of Jacob all the way to the end of the thousand year reign of Jesus.

In Revelation, Jesus broadens the picture by revealing the things of the end as they relate to mankind—universally. The bulk of the details in Revelation pertain to the Gentiles. Revelation documents the *time of testing* which is the last phase of the hope prophesied in Isaiah 42:1 – 4 and confirmed in Matthew 12:21: *in him* [Jesus] *will the non-Jewish people find hope* (NCV). This *time of testing* is not the joyful harvest that we have known since Pentecost; it will be the last gleanings after the harvest is taken in.

Since Pentecost, a person chooses life in Jesus, and life more abundantly: life here and now. During the *time of testing*, everyone living will have to choose their death; not their life. The text will show this.

Revelation is a complete, detailed and relevant disclosure for the Gentiles. It also provides the reasons for the events of the end. It offers greater information for the three and one-half years of Satan's rampage and for the short period of God's calamities that follow it; more specific information than what the Old Testament prophets had provided. The reason is simple: God does not test the Hebrews through these periods *of testing*; He tests the Gentiles. Revelation 3:10 is specific: *Because you have kept my command to endure, I will also keep you from the hour of testing that is going to come over the whole world to test those who live on the earth*. This is not Israel specific at all; it is Gentile. By the time Jesus gave His revelation to John, the Christian congregations, especially in Turkey, were not Jewish anymore; they had become decidedly Gentile.

As we will soon see in the text the ethnic descendants of Jacob will have a separate dispensation during the *time of testing*. In the same way, Revelation does not give a lot of details about Jesus' 1,000 year reign since that phase is for the benefit of the Hebrews; therefore, other specific Hebraic prophecies have already covered this.

The text of Jesus' Revelation is clear and straightforward. However, it is not linear. Jesus breaks down His narrative into individual tableaux that allow us to picture events within their specific context and the text fits them in their respective places in history. Revelation is not a mystery—actually by definition it is the opposite: it reveals; it makes clear. Jesus dictated it for the understanding of the masses, He entrusted it to a former fisherman, not to a religious scholar. Jesus chose John, not Paul who was an "expert" of the Law.

Over the centuries, Bible theoreticians have tended to use Revelation as the apocalyptic catch-all into which they try to fit the Old Testament prophecies they failed to grasp. When commenting on Revelation, they attempt to make all these arcane bits fit; they make the error of adapting the understanding of Revelation to allow for all the unresolved mysteries (the prophesied events of Revelation being the ultimate deadline when, time-wise, all loose ends must tidy up).

These attempts cloud the simple meaning of Revelation and spawn awkward theories and scenarios that never satisfactorily explain everything. For example, some say that the temple in Jerusalem must be rebuilt and be in use for the end times to begin—it will not. Some say that the city of Babylon must be rebuilt to reclaim its dominant splendor and influence—it will not.

The clear text of Revelation allows us to discount these theories. We can say with authority: "yes, this Old Testament prophecy fits in the end-times." Or "no, this does not fit in the time between the rapture of the believers and the *great white throne* judgment; therefore another understanding must be gained to place it correctly in time and context." We should not attempt to validate Jesus' message to John through the filter of our own inadequacy at solving Old Testament mysteries.

Jesus gave Revelation in its entirety to John for the believing laymen of all times (*I, Jesus, have sent my angel to tell you these things for the churches* [*you* being plural in Greek] 22:16 NCV) and its message should be taken as valid by itself (*blessed is the one who keeps the prophetic words of this book* 22:7). We should not add to it nor subtract from it in order to coordinate our preferences or our limited understanding of Old Testament prophecies: *if anyone adds to them* [*the prophetic words of this book*], *God will add to him the plagues that are written in this book. And if anyone takes away from the words of this prophetic book, God will take away his share of the tree of life and the holy city, written in this book* (22:18 – 19).

For this study, we will concentrate on what Jesus revealed to His apostle John; Jesus meant it as a complete message.

Introduction

The goodness of God and His faithfulness are demonstrated during our time as well as the times of the end: *He* [*YHWH*] *sits on his throne to judge, and He will judge the world in fairness; He will decide what is right for the nations. ... Those who know the LORD trust Him, because He will not leave those who come to Him... He remembers who the murderers are; He will not forget the cries of those who suffer... The nations have fallen into the pit they dug. Their feet are caught in the nets they have laid. The LORD has made Himself known by His fair decisions; the wicked get trapped by what they do. Wicked people will go to the grave, and so will all those who forget God... The wicked people are too proud. They do not look for God; there is no room for God in their thoughts... The LORD is in His holy temple; the LORD sits on his throne in heaven. He sees what people do; He keeps his eye on them...* (These verses are taken from Psalms

9 through 11 NCV). The remaining chapters of Revelation will demonstrate the truth of these words.

Chapters 4 through 22 foretell the events of the end: events that will happen after the Church's age of grace—the age of the harvest—in which we now live. For some 2,000 years we have been wooed by a gracious and generous God through His Messiah. Choosing Jesus has meant life in His kingdom and life more abundantly—albeit with various degrees of persecution or discrimination. As we enter the fourth chapter of Revelation, this benevolent era is closed.

We will see that the first thing God reveals to John about these events is that Jesus is now going out *as a victor to conquer.* This is the first seal and it sets the tone for everything that follows: Jesus personally directs from here on. He will orchestrate every event; He will extract the very last people who would choose Him—by rejecting the mark of Satan (the gleanings after the harvest)— and He will punish the rest. He will complete the gathering of the eternally redeemed from the earth by picking up the post-rapture gleanings and He will rid creation of Satan and his minions. Finally He will create the new heaven and earth as was His plan from the beginning of time.

To steer us through the study, I include here a chronological timeline of the events as they will proceed from the rapture of the Christians at the end of our benevolent era of grace.

The chronological stages

First: Jesus brings our era to an end and harvest His Church (Jews and Gentiles). He is not pressured into it by a presumed evil ascendency; He is delighted to do so because the last person who will choose Him has voluntarily done so—a victory for Jesus.

Next: Satan is given three and one-half years to rampage the earth.

Next: Jesus brings on terrible calamities.

Next: Jesus reigns over the world and creation from Jerusalem for one thousand years.

Next: Jesus judges and sentences the doomed people of all times and makes this creation disappear.

Finally: Jesus creates the new heaven and the new earth for eternity.

The main events of each stage

Jesus closes our grace era, what we often call the church age:

1. From Israel, Jesus lifts 144,000 Jews who have been faithful to God. They had come to Jesus prior to the events I call God's march of Glory: That is the destruction of the fourth empire, the culling of the Hebrews followed by Exodus 2.0 for those who accept Jesus' alliance, the Gog and Magog war; they will never leave Jesus' side. *They were redeemed from the human race as the first-fruits for God and the Lamb* (Revelation 14:4).

2. Jesus will also transform and pick up (rapture) the Gentile true followers of Christ alive at that time, they receive their eternal body. He will also provide resurrected bodies to the believers in Christ who were already dead—Jews and Gentiles. These resurrected believers will be in His presence forever. The *time of testing* does not concern those who had come to Jesus.

3. God separates the remaining ethnic descendants of Jacob from the Gentiles who live among them in Israel; He removes all these Hebrews to a safe haven where He will care for them throughout the entire *time of testing.* The *time of testing* does not concern Jacob's people. They are His already.

4. Satan and his fallen angels are thrown out of heaven and Satan is allowed to rampage the earth for three and one-half years.

5. God will preach the Good News supernaturally through His heavenly messenger to all people living. This will fulfill Jesus' prophecy: *this good news of the kingdom will be proclaimed in all the world as a testimony to all nations. And then the end will come* (Matthew 24:14).

6. God will suddenly stop the world system we have lived in since Adam yielded his authority to Satan. God will impose very strict allotments—whether by penuries or by calamities. God ordains that things will be bleak and restricted for all. Gone is God's generous provision that had prevailed as witnessed in scripture: *He causes the sun to rise on good people and on evil people, and He sends rains to those who do right and to those who do wrong* (Matthew 5:45 NCV).

7. God will supernaturally warn all living persons against following Satan and accepting his mark. His heavenly messenger (angel) who proclaims this message will be seen and heard by all living people. He will spell out clearly the consequences of everyone's choice.

8. Through His two human witnesses in Jerusalem, God will provide a very visible and constant counterpoint to Satan and the *antichrist's* pressure. These two witnesses will be able to continue their support and exhortations through the life of the very last person who will choose death in Jesus over the mark of the beast. Satan will hate these two witnesses because they will constantly undermine his message. The whole world will hear these witnesses words and see their miraculous deeds.

Satan runs amok for three and one-half years from the moment he is thrown out of heaven. Here is his agenda:

1. After failing to inflict harm to the sheltered nation of Israel, Satan will turn his anger on the non-Hebraic population (Gentiles).

2. Satan is not omnipresent nor is he omnipotent; so he will build an organization around his *antichrist* to project his control. The *antichrist* and the *false prophet,* two distinct but thoroughly evil entities, will set up a politico-religious empire (a revived Roman Empire) with 10 vassals afield to control the population of the world.

3. Satan will mark his people indelibly; all of them Gentiles.

4. He will systematically kill (behead) those who choose to attach their fate to Jesus during these three and one-half years by refusing the mark of the beast (all of them Gentiles).

5. During that time, he will rage powerlessly against the two witnesses in Jerusalem who encourage the world population to resist the *antichrist* and Satan.

6. After the last person who will choose to entrust their fate to Jesus during this period of testing has done so and died for it, God allows the *false prophet* to have the two godly witnesses in Jerusalem killed—their work is done.

7. At the end of those three and one-half years, the *antichrist* and the *false prophet* will gather a huge army to come against Jesus and His heavenly army of angels for a battle that has no specific name in the text of Revelation. Jesus will destroy them with His word and birds will feed on the carcasses.

8. As Jesus destroys this army, He will throw the *antichrist* and the *false prophet* into the *lake of fire* (Hell).

9. The three and one-half years are over. As Jesus destroys Satan's army, he orders him bound and sequestrated until Jesus' 1,000 year reign is over.

Following these three and one-half years, Jesus brings His divine pressure to bear on the remainder of the non-Hebraic world population.

1. Jesus will prove that He has been completely just and fair. He will bring terrible pressures to bear on the Gentiles still living in order to demonstrate that none will accept Him. There will be stinging locusts that will relentlessly sting everyone for five months, boils and sores will affect all the mark bearers, a third of the oceans and fresh water will become toxic, a third of the earth will be scorched, a third of the day will be without light and God's heavenly army, 200 hundred million strong will wreak death everywhere.
2. Nothing in the text of Revelation gives a time limit for this specific phase of Divine calamities—except for one five month event (9:1 – 12). It might be quite short; we simply do not know. All we do know is that everyone will suffer horribly. Those will be divine calamities; no one can escape.
3. The reduced population of Gentiles who survive these calamities will live through the coming 1,000 year reign of Jesus.

Jesus reigns for 1,000 years.

1. This is the reign the Jews have been waiting for. Jesus will reign with an iron hand; His rule will be universal and absolute.

2. Jesus will reign on this old earth. He will reign over normal flesh-and-blood people, that is to say: Satan's marked Gentiles who survived the previous calamities plus the Hebrews God had protected.

3. The post-rapture saints will be resurrected to rule over their former tormentors as Jesus' administrators at large. This class of people are resurrected therefore they are of a different nature.

4. Every Gentile on earth will come to Jerusalem and pay the mandatory homage to Jesus and to the Jews in Israel.

5. At the end of the 1,000 years, Satan will be released. He will muster the non-Hebraic people to come against Israel. Jesus will incinerate their army and crush the rest of the Gentile population like grapes in a winepress, somewhere in a central location. The blood from this ultimate killing field will run as high as a horse's bridle over a considerable surface. Jesus throws Satan into Hell.

6. The earth and the sea give up all the dead people who chose to oppose God since the beginning of time, they now receive their resurrected bodies. Having released its dead, the earth will not be needed anymore.

7. God will make the current earth and sky disappear. Man will not destroy the earth. God made the current creation appear out of nothingness and He will make it disappear into nothingness.

8. Jesus judges all the now resurrected enemies of God who are not found in God's *book of life* from the beginning of time. Jesus throws them, eternally alive, into the *lake of fire*.

Finally Jesus creates the new heaven and earth.

1. Every Hebrew who had lived through the preceding

phases receive their eternal bodies. They join up with the murdered Gentiles who chose to die in Jesus during the three and one-half years of testing and all the believers of all times. The wedding of the Lamb can now take place in Heaven.

2. God foreknew that He would produce this new creation.
3. The true believers—His bride—are called to the *new Jerusalem*.
4. Glorious eternity follows.

Observations

After God lifts up the true believers of the Christian era to heaven and gathers the Hebrews into a safe haven in the desert, He will begin the *hour of testing*. This will be the time for hard choices, life will be miserable at best. Every Gentile alive will have to choose his death. Every non-Hebraic person living then will have to decide without delay between two options:

1. Choose Christ and be killed immediately at the hands of Satan's minions, but receive a blessed, redeemed eternity with God, or
2. Surrender to the *antichrist* and accept his mark, getting a limited life now and unabated misery for eternity.

This process of testing will last three and one-half years; until the last person on earth who would choose Jesus has done so and has been killed for it. These three and one-half years will be the time of Satan's attempt to establish himself as god on earth and his opportunity to inflict as much suffering as he can. My opinion about why it will take this amount of time is that Satan is not omnipresent therefore the implementation of his plan to the most remote population groups will take a while.

After these three and one-half years, God will apply great calamities with a divine ferocity on all the gentile population that remains on earth (the ethnic descendants of Jacob are spared). The Hebrews were promised dominion over all the other nations; therefore a certain number of Gentiles will survive these ordeals in order to be the "other nations". By this final "wringing" God will prove that no matter how hard conditions become, how intense the pressure exerted, not a single person will turn to God anymore. Every person remaining has validated his eternal punishment.

<u>(Return to Table of Contents)</u>

God's March of Glory

Let's cover the last few years before the rapture. The rapture is the apotheosis of the good news, of the age of grace. Jesus' own rapture was the glorious lifting of the victor; He had accomplished flawlessly what he had to accomplished during His time on earth. Similarly, the rapture of the believers will be the glorious exit of the winners. It will be preceded and ushered by some very intense, world-changing, divine events, long predicted throughout the old testament.

This specific set of promised events will lead to the rapture. I call these events God's March of Glory because God's purpose is for the whole world to see Him. Nothing and nobody will foil His plan. This leitmotif is like no others: God/Jesus will be seen!

Another aspect will be unique: the audience will be universal. Wherever man lives, We will all watch in real time on our personal screens (Telephone, tablets, computers, TV...) as each event unfolds. When these divine events were predicted, and for many centuries thereafter, this explicit exposure seemed impossible: How could the whole world see an event? Humans could only witness what happened within their horizon. But God knew that in our time, readily available technologies would bring the far corners of the world into everyone's sight. These technological breakthroughs that we all use every day now serve as harbingers placing the timing of the divine events in out time.

Chronologically:

1. The first event is the divine destruction of the fourth empire, the most powerful and destructive human empire ever; everyone alive will see Jesus do this. Read about this empire in Daniel 2. We live in this powerful and destructive empire: The Globalists' One-World-Government/New-World-Order.   This empire's power is global, its control is invasive and coercive and it is absolutely opposed to Jesus and His commands. It is led by the evil master it worships and serves. It opposes free worship and aims to curb and crush allegiance to Jesus. The Globalists' One-World-Government/New-World-Order is the fourth empire God showed Nebuchadnezzar in a dream and explained through Daniel in Daniel 2.   Through this divine destruction process, the entire humanity will learn that there is a God and that man—even at the peak of his power—is no match for this God. (See Daniel 2 or read *The Rock Breaks the Globalists' Empire*.)

2. The second event is the global and final exodus of Jacob's descendants to Israel. This process will begin with the identification of the descendants of Jacob. Today, no one can vouch for being or not being a descendant of a Hebraic line. The archives and documentation of the ten northern Hebraic tribes disappeared at their exile a few centuries before Jesus. They have been lost to history

since then. The archives and documentation of the two remaining Jewish tribes were destroyed with the temple. So, am I a descendant of Jacob? Are you? Are those who claim to be Jewish, actually Jewish? Many who joined the Pharisaic/Talmudic/Rabbinical false religion centuries ago have eventually claimed to be Jews; but without any verifiable data. But God knows every living descendant of Jacob and He will bring them out to the light.   Therefore, as Ezekiel prophesied (the valley of the dry bones, Ezekiel 37), God will first identity every descendant of Jacob in every county of the world, including Israel. Having identified them within the ambient national communities, God will separate them from the local Gentile populations and will judge each one of them on the basis of His covenant. The only covenant is: Jesus is Messiah. (The very truth that the Pharisaic/Talmudic/Rabbinical religion has systematically refused and fought against.) Those who will refuse Jesus as Messiah will be destroyed right there and then by Jesus, in view of the whole world. Jesus will usher all the others out of all the countries of the world at the same time, with Him covering from the front and from behind, He will move them to Israel. None will be left in another country.   Because everyone in the world will follow the entire process in real time on their screen, everyone will know that the God who is doing these amazing things is the God of Jacob. He is the same God who had just vaporized the greatest human power.

3. The third event is the divine destruction of the Muslim armies of the god that billions of humans consider as the most powerful god. The scripture refers to this battle/war

as the war of Gog and Magog. This process will show everyone that there are no other divine powers in all of creation. By demonstrating that Allah is no god at all, the God of Jacob vanquishes all man-made gods. (A reference could be *The Great Harvest of the Post-Allah World*.)

4. The fourth process is the great harvest of God's fields. Everyone on earth will have seen God through His actions. Everyone will want to know this God, who He is. So, there will be two humanities: the Hebrews in Israel who have all embraced Jesus will get to know Him through the teaching of their peers who had come to Jesus in our time. These Christians are now the knowledgeable ones who will bring out the good of the old and the good of the new to their brethren. God will rejoice for at least seven years as the Hebrews, all in Israel, get to know Jesus.   God will also rejoice with the Gentile population of the rest of the world: it will be the great harvest of souls. Indeed, every Gentile will know that God exists, that man is no match, that God is the God of Jacob, Isaak and Abraham and that no other gods exist. Therefore, everyone will want to know the God they have seen. Some will embrace the true Jesus, other, seeking their own way will opt for the false Jesus of the false Christian religion. This is the parable of the wheat and the tares. These years (7+) are an absolutely joyful time for God. Nobody will cheat Him out of this. It is God who sets up this munificent harvest.   The Gentiles who embraced the real Jesus will follow their Savior up to Heaven at the rapture. Those who decided against the true Jesus will harden their hatred of Him and will remain on the earth. The antichrist will come to this thoroughly anti-Jesus-Christ

population. He will come and appeal to his own. It is not a victory for him: he just inherits the losers.   God's actions in His March of Glory sets the field for the antichrist. God's March of Glory saves the Hebrews, saves the Gentiles and dooms the Gentiles who shun the true Messiah and instead choose a "Jesus" after their own hearts. Satan never wins; even here, he can only rule when God has finished His projects... And even when ruling, Satan remains on God's leash: He can only do what God allows him to do, for the length of time He allots.

The impetus will build all the way through these events and will culminate with the joyful, celebratory lifting of the faithful: the rapture.

When will this March of Glory begin? It could begin soon. Many supporting aspects are now present for each of these steps. The terribly destructive supra-national empire exists and is becoming more and more overt as each day passes. Gog and Magog is not hard to predict now, the coalition of Muslim states exists (even traditional enemies like Turkey and Iran have joined up in a synergetic coalition and odd countries have joined, like Libya and Sudan. A northern "dome" of islamic countries is in place as the "Stan" republics are closely related to the Turks.) Technologies have enabled people everywhere to connect globally and to witness events in real time. The conditions seem to exist.

Note: A significant number of "Christians" have embraced a faulty theology. They propose that as evil increases in our era, it will become more and more difficult for Christians to exist and prosper. Eventually, the evil hordes will back the "Christians" into an impossible corner and Jesus, out of options, will just have to take us out of here. This view is wrong, dead wrong. These "Christians" do not have Jesus as God—Jesus, the Conqueror who sits at the right hand of God. They do not know God. The reality is that Satan does not win victories against God's church. He does not dictate our fate; Jesus does. They fail to see that the followers of Jesus have never, ever been as many as they are today. The Good News is conquering today! In China alone, there are more than one hundred million true believers. There had never been so many Chinese harvesters ready for the great harvest. In Indonesia the Islamic government estimates that 15% of its population has now converted to Jesus. Each believer only has to reach six people around him for the harvest. In Iran, it is estimated that more than one million people have come out of Islam and follow Jesus—risking their lives in the process. There had never been that many missionaries in Iran, ever. In spite of the intense Islamic persecution wrought everywhere in Africa, conversions to Jesus are reaching flood proportions... And so on.

In the parable of the wheat and the tares, the Master does not say: "We better get what we can of the good wheat because it is taken over by the tare". No, the Master's eyes are on the good harvest. He enjoys the full harvest, then He disposes of the opposition.

Most Christians I know fail to see that between the increase of evil and the departure of the saints, there will be a time of great divine victories, what I call here God/Jesus' march of glory.

<u>Note</u>: The increase of the intensity and level of evil predicted for the times of the end is a logical phenomenon. Satan and his fallen angels, while smarter than man, are not all-knowing, nor are they all-powerful and they certainly do not know the end from the beginning (a God-only attribute). Therefore, they relentlessly practice their evil and have learned as they go: they get better and better at it. Many of Satan's schemes have failed over the years; but he and his cohorts have ceaselessly worked at it for some 6,000 years, all along learning, so it is natural and understandable that they are getting more and more proficient as the years go by. And this is a plausible explanation as to why evil will increase in the times of the end.

The great testing time will be selective

God's *great testing time* (what people call the Great Tribulation) has the purpose of sifting out the very last people who will turn to God through Jesus—meaning: the last people who will turn away from the proposition of evil...and, through death, will join the Savior they had spurned in life. This is why the twelve tribes and the true Gentile Christians will not be touched by the testing—they have already come to Him, they do not need to be tested.

God's calamities during the tribulations do not affect any of His people

Revelation 6:9 – 11 clearly indicates that the post-rapture saints of the three and one-half years will be killed by men. They will be the object of Satan's wrath (beheading); but not of God's. Therefore, none will be killed by the sweeping means of death God will send: the 200 million strong mounted army or the sea of blood and the toxic springs of water, etc. The fact that the post-rapture saints are killed by men points to one conclusion: the God-ordained massacres and calamities will take place <u>after</u> the three and one-half years, after the last post-rapture saint is by Jesus' side and has joined the saints who were raptured.

Perspective for our troubled times

The national and international political brouhaha that batters us incessantly can be daunting. Can we step away from the craziness to recalibrate our perspective? Can we take encouragements from the pattern of history? And can we take comfort and reassurances from the prototypes of things prophesied that have already happened just so? If we can, then we will understand that in our very near future Gog and Magog prophetically dooms the geopolitical enemies of Israel and by extension their inspiration: Islam. Let's look into this.

Today's frantic political furor and terrorism by Islamists worldwide could possibly reflect the desperate—yet ultimately futile—latest charge by their master to derail YHWH's plan. Historically, though, that evil master has failed at every juncture. Please consider:

Through his proxy, Pharaoh, Satan tried to kill all Hebrew newborn boys in Egypt to foil God's plan for the miraculous and very public liberation of His people through Moses. Satan failed.

Later, through his proxy Herod, he tried to kill all the Jewish boys around Bethlehem in an effort to interdict Messiah's ministry—he failed.

Later, through his proxy Hitler and all who joined into his rabid anti-Semitism, Satan tried to deny the return of the Jews to Israel through the horrible genocide of the 1930s and 40s which was meant to kill every last Jew once and for all time. You see: if there were no Jews left, there would be no need for a country for the Jews—a country where Gog and Magog could take place someday.

So right now, through new proxies—the Islamists in general and the so-called Palestinians in particular—the evil master is trying to deny the promised mass redemption of God's chosen people (Jacob's descendants) in Israel. The reasoning goes: if today's Hebrews are pushed into the sea so that Israel does not exist anymore, then, the complete salvation of the descendants of Jacob and the great universal harvest of the Gentiles are thwarted. But the witness of history asks: what are the chances that Satan's plan will succeed this time?

The evil master is busy stoking worldwide anti-Semitism, he is weakening and poisoning the perception of God's ancient people by massive Muslim immigration and he is preparing a huge international military conflagration to push the Hebrews into the sea, killing them all—he will fail again. What is so tragic is that every time he is at it, innocents suffer by the thousands and by the millions.

Because Gog and Magog will happen during our unique time in history when the dissemination of information is instantaneous and universal, its impact will be global. Minute by minute, Muslims everywhere in the world avidly follow the feverish build up toward the longstanding Islamic goal of killing all the Jews. The eradication of Israel and of the Jews represents the ultimate validation of their religion; the condition for the return of the Mahdi.

For fourteen centuries, with much anger and great efforts, through sustained and terrible bloodshed of innocents, mere men have propped up a god who existed only in their minds. Thus, at Gog and Magog, when YHWH unilaterally and with His own hand crushes this huge Islamic coalition; He will have killed more than the belligerents: He will have decimated their god.

Today is not a time for Christians to cower and to accommodate; we should know and understand the immutable truth upon which we stand and we should trust the God who stands for us. We should not make allowance for what the Enemy is doing in our country or internationally. Jesus is marching on to His victory step by step.

We should not let ourselves be moved to comply with, nor should we tolerate a doomed world view. We should wholeheartedly and confidently resist it. We should strive to be one of the *lands who trust in Me [God]* (Isaiah 60:9). So far, Satan's proxies have lost every engagement that he has devised to evade his own doom at the end of the 1,000 year reign of Jesus. He will lose this one also.

No one knows the day or hour

Jesus tells us in Matthew 24 that the period nearing the rapture of the saints and the rapture itself will be like what happened in Noah's time: the people did not know; they were unaware of the impending doom. But this cluelessness affected only the people who were not listening to God.

While the godless people did not know, Noah (and his family) knew. Noah's family did not know the exact moment to the minute or even the exact day, but as the work on the ark was completed they knew the time was short. When the animals showed up; they realized time was shorter yet. When the animals proceeded up the ramp; they knew time was really short. And when God told them to get in; they knew that God's action was at hand...

So Noah and his family knew, they could read the signs perfectly; it was only the other people who did not know. And it is the same for believers today regarding God's march of glory: like Noah before us, we know the time is short because we recognized the markers God has given us as we passed them or as we see them taking shape today and looming upon us. But the people who reject God do not know because they do not want to know. Facing judgment is the most inconvenient truth there is, and those who are not in Jesus find it easier to ignore the facts than to face the reality these imply. But if you are a believer, you should recognize the times in which you live.

Allow me to expand on this point. The ELV says in Matthew 24:32: *the fig tree teaches us a lesson: when its branches become green and soft and new leaves begin to grow then you know that summer is very near. In the same way, when you see all these things happening you will know that the time is very near, already present.* Today this very phenomenon is taking place before us as we observe that, for the first time since the early church, more and more Jews are coming out of their Talmudic prison and to Messiah using their Old Testament scriptures and these are on fire for Jesus. So we observe that the fig tree which is God's people—the Hebrews—is beginning to turn green. New leaves are coming out, here and there and more and more. Not the whole tree yet; but *new leaves begin to grow*: *the time is very near, already present.* Believers attuned to Jesus can see this unmistakable budding process. This strong resurgence of Jewish conversions, so long after the early church's, is one of our surest markers.

<u>(Return to Table of Contents)</u>

****

Chapter 5 - Glimpse of Heaven, Introduction of the Scroll

Revelation 4:1 – 5:11

4:1 – 11

¹ After this I looked, and there in heaven was an open door. The first voice that I had heard speaking to me like a trumpet said, "Come up here, and I will show you what must take place after this."

²Immediately I was in the Spirit, and a throne was set there in heaven. One was seated on the throne, ³ and the One seated looked like jasper and carnelian stone. A rainbow that looked like an emerald surrounded the throne. ⁴ Around that throne were 24 thrones, and on the thrones sat 24 elders dressed in white clothes, with gold crowns on their heads. ⁵Flashes of lightning and rumblings of thunder came from the throne. Seven fiery torches were burning before the throne, which are the seven spirits of God. ⁶ Something like a sea of glass, similar to crystal, was also before the throne. Four living creatures covered with eyes in front and in back were in the middle and around the throne. ⁷The first living creature was like a lion; the second living creature was like a calf; the third living creature had a face like a man; and the fourth living creature was like a flying eagle. ⁸Each of the four living creatures had six wings; they were covered with eyes around and inside. Day and night they never stop, saying: Holy, holy, holy, Lord God, the Almighty, who was, who is, and who is coming.

⁹Whenever the living creatures give glory, honor, and thanks to the One seated on the throne, the One who lives forever and ever, ¹⁰the 24 elders fall down before the One seated on the throne, worship the One who lives forever and ever, cast their crowns before the throne, and say:

¹¹Our Lord and God, You are worthy to receive glory and honor and power, because You have created all things, and because of Your will they exist and were created.

What's happening

In 4:1, we have the same voice as in 1:10: the one that sounded like a trumpet; so it is Jesus himself who tells John: *Come up here, and I will show you what must happen after this* (NCV).

This is the first time a human prophet is brought up into Heaven to see what is there for the specific purpose of recording what he is shown for us. To all the great prophets of the Old Testament, God brought the visions down to them on earth. It makes sense that John should be invited up: only someone who is in Jesus can access Heaven. Note that in 2 Corinthians 12:2, Paul claims to know one who went to heaven (whether himself or someone else; we do not know), but we at large do not benefit from that event. Here, however, John is invited up to God's court in order that we may all benefit from God's revelation to him.

Jesus chose to say "must" happen; not "will" happen because these coming events are necessary in order that every person living then may declare himself for or against Jesus. The divine deadline has arrived; it is the *time of testing* that Jesus spoke about in His message to the congregation of Philadelphia (3:10).

Right at the beginning (4:3), John attempts to describe YHWH but YHWH surpasses human explanation and understanding. He is too big, too complete and beautiful to be fully comprehended by one of His creations. This is one of the reasons God chose to become a man; so that, in Jesus, we would have a representation of Himself that we could relate to.

The *sea of glass* (as it will be defined in Chapter 15) represents the raptured believers and the believers of times past who embraced Jesus' salvation when they lived and have been in His presence since then. In short, the saints are joyfully in God's heaven already.

The seven spirits of God means the complete spirit of God. Today, His spirit is present throughout the world inside and around every true believer. However we are told in 4:5 that the complete spirit of God is with God. This reflects two facts: first, at this point in Revelation, the church (i.e., the assembly of those who have set themselves apart onto Jesus) is not on earth anymore. So the Spirit living in each of them is not on earth anymore. And second, the Spirit of God who was also mitigating all things on earth has left that post. This universal mitigating presence and effect of the Spirit of God in the world will be absent for the duration.

It is not paramount for our basic study here to know who the four creatures are or to identify specifically the 24 elders; the text does not provide their identity nor specify their nature. The important fact is that they worship God wholly.

> Note: The four creatures are interesting (4:6 – 9). They obviously exist. And they are living creatures. They were obviously created by God for His purposes only (here it seems that the purpose is for endless praise as well as introducing each horse and rider that the seals reveal). In Ezekiel 1, we also have creatures of a different nature and aspect. So we do not know all the various living creature God has made. However, one thing we know for sure: the creatures we find in the bible are not aliens. They are not independently functioning beings with a life of their own who may live on some far away celestial body. And these creatures do not have the privilege of deciding their actions. So, the aliens of science fiction will remain just that: fiction.

However, there is a telling detail in the wording of their praises to the throne of God, as they address YHWH: *Lord God, the Almighty, who was, who is, and who is coming.* Jesus is the one who is coming—not the Father—the following chapters are very specific about this. With their wording, the four creatures express the biblical reality that no dividing line exists between the Father and Jesus. The attributes serve seamlessly the Father and Jesus. The Father and Jesus do not form two distinct persons with their own volition or motivation as we naturally picture persons from a human point of view. Jesus is the expression of God to us humans (Logo is the Greek word used for Jesus as the "Word of God"; it means the expression, the easily identifiable symbol). Jesus is an intrinsic part of God.

Observations

We western believers have trouble with the concept of the trinity. Yet, the working relationship of the Father, Son and Spirit did not seem to pose a problem for the apostles nor for the early Jewish believers. We know this because the apostles did not feel a need to teach or explain the concept in their epistles. And Jesus in the first three chapters of Revelation did not expand on it either. The implication is clear: the triune God was not a mystery for the early church.

However, as time went by, the occidental mindset of non-Jewish converts had difficulty with the Father, Son and Spirit relationships. YHWH, in substance, does not square off with the Greek style of logic that became prevalent through the Church in later centuries. The people demanded a definition or an adaptation of YHWH to fit into their thought patterns and parameters. Actually, it is the emperor who demanded a definitive consensus on the matter because he wanted one single empire-defining religion.

He needed a uniform faith that could define and shore up his power.

While our God is triune, the concept of "trinity" fails to capture His essence and identity. The word "trinity" is never found in the Bible because it is a Gentile's attempt at explaining God logically. It was not until the third century that Tertullian used the term Trinity in reference to the Father, Son and Spirit of God. Later in the fourth century, under great pressure from the Emperor, the churches' representatives at the councils of Nicaea and later of Constantinople expressed the canonical belief in the Father, Son and Holy Spirit to prevent heretical theories and to satisfy the emperor's insistence of a unified doctrine. That basic belief, which in itself did not explain the triune God, developed its own momentum and in time sealed the term "Trinity" for posterity. It became a pillar creed of "Christianity", yet it misses the reality of God. These fourth century men made a mystery out of a concept that was never obscure in the first place. Unfortunately, Trinity, with its murky definitions, remains an official doctrine to this day, a doctrine that prelates and bishops qualify as "mystery".

What is a mystery? Let us look at an item that was actually labeled as "mystery" in the Old Testament: the good news. It <u>began</u> as a mystery...until it became a reality and after this, the mystery was no more (Colossians 1:25 – 27 and Revelation 10:7). But the trinity is different: the three persons of God <u>did not begin</u> as a mystery at all. The apostles had difficulty accepting that Jesus, the man speaking to them, was God, one with YHWH. But the triune God was not an issue with the early Christians. And it is never labeled as a mystery in the scriptures. I am not being iconoclastic here; I am simply pointing out the incongruity between two notions deemed to be mysteries. It is high time that we believers move past conventions and dare to believe as the original believers did! And let's stop branding as heretics those who have the courage to consider scriptures, history and reality.

These here thoughts about the person(s) of God take absolutely nothing away from God's glory, from God's function or from God's mode of relationship with us. Let's face it: bad faith in using the trinity definition of Nicea has been the basis of many false religions that have battered humanity ever since—like Islam, Mormonism, Catholicism, et al.

The sad part is that the Jews of Jesus' time and of the apostles' time had no problems with the "triune" reality of God as He presented Himself. However, since the regrettable interpretation of the Nicene Creed, the Jews have been alienated from the Christian beliefs because for them this Nicene position made God a three persons God: it made 3 gods. Since then the Jews have always countered: "YHWH is one; your gods are not our God!" And with that perceived inappropriateness they discard the Gospel. The Godhead is not a quorum of three having a morning meeting to synchronize their schedules and activities then split up for the day to get it done. We cannot go to one or the other with our petitions as the mood or our superstition strikes us.

Let's go back to the identity of Jesus: He is the Word, Logo, the easily understandable representation of YHWH. The logo of a company is the easily recognizable expression, the popular symbol of that company. It allows the public to perceive and identify the company without having to know every line on its accounting ledgers, the state of its current orders or the various technical skills of every one of its employees. The logo does not exist apart from the company; it has no identity outside its representation of the company. The logo is an integral part of the entity of a company; but the logo is not an entity in itself.

It is the same with God. YHWH is far too complex and awesome for us to grasp comprehensively; even John in Revelation

4, looking at Him on the throne cannot adequately put into words what he sees. Through Jesus' humanity, God the Father made Himself discoverable by mankind. He chose to reveal the part of Himself that created all the things that we see, hear, feel and taste so that He may relate to us and be eminently attractive to us. Jesus is God's logo to man. He is a sample of God...but only from our end; from God's end, Jesus is fully God. But Jesus is in no way a separate person from the Father. This is why the four creatures can say: *Lord God* (the Father) ... *who is coming* (the Son).

There is no division of persons between the Father and Jesus as we humans define personhood. God said in Isaiah 9:6 that Jesus will be *Father who lives forever* (NCV), *Eternal Father*. Jesus says: *whoever believes in me is really believing in the One who sent me. Whoever sees me sees the One who sent me* (not a separate person) (John 12:44 – 45 NCV). Revelation 7:17 makes the point clear: *the Lamb who is at the center of the throne.* There is only one throne in heaven—not three. From 7:10 (*Salvation belongs to our God, who is seated on the throne, and to the Lamb*) we know that God is on the throne. These verses tell us that Jesus is the core of God; the core that we humans can apprehend.

God gave us a human model of this to help us grasp the concept of God the Father, of Jesus and of the Spirit of God: He gave us fatherhood. Indeed, God who created all things did not need to create fathers to establish a species; but He wanted to give us a pattern that would help us understand Him. At the personal level when I think of fatherhood, I can only see a few aspects of it: the ones my own father modeled for me. But the concept of fatherhood as a whole escapes me: it is greater in totality than what my intelligence plus my experience can know.

However, I have a representation of fatherhood, a logo of it in my earthly father. Having been blessed with a good father, I am able to have a good representation of what fatherhood stands for. My father exhibited care, protection, provision and education plus an unfailing commitment to my becoming the man I ought to be or could be. So when I think of fatherhood, I see my earthly father: he is what fatherhood did for me, what fatherhood looked like for me and what fatherhood represents for me in a useable way. When I need help from what fatherhood can provide; it is to my dad that I go. In the same way, in regard to God: I go to Jesus; He is what God did for me, what Godhood looks like and represents for me. And Jesus attests to this: He instructs us to come to Him and to pray to Him (John 16).

Then, as I entered adulthood and left home, I no longer lived in my earthly father's presence. That's when I noticed that my dad had imparted to me a significant part of himself; his impulses and his values. His teachings live in me; they motivate me, they urge me in the way he wanted me to go and they give me the ability to recognize situations he had lived through or taught about. A part of him truly lives in me. I can say that the person of my father is present in me, the spirit of my father. This spirit also gives me the ability to continue learning how to live life.

My father's spirit replaces his physical presence thus it gives me the ability to function responsibly wherever my life takes me. When I speak of my father's spirit, I say "he"; because it is truly a part of my father—there is nothing in my father's spirit that is distinct from my father. My father's spirit is a real thing; it is part of the effect of my father's person, he is not a separate person.

Basically, this is the example God gives us to understand the deity: YHWH (God the Father) is the essence of God, the complete entity of God. YHWH-Saves (Jesus), while being the complete entity of God (Colossians 2:9), is the aspect of God that we can relate to, the part of God that did and does things (created all things, walked with us, died for us and will come back for us). And the Spirit of God—the Holy Spirit—is what Jesus left us; what

He puts in us. And because Jesus is eternal and omnipresent, there are no limits to the capabilities of His Spirit in us. The Spirit of God is the motivation <u>of</u> God, the motivation <u>for</u> God and the motivation <u>toward</u> God. It is the likeness of thoughts that moves us His way; it moves us to act according to God's will and continues to teach us. The Spirit of God is not a person of God: it is a part of God—it is the divine inspiration, the divine impulse in us, God's direct projection into us. It is in this triune understanding that we can know our God. He had to break His reality down for us so that we could apprehend Him and know Him.

We can understand why Jesus said *it is for your benefit that I go away, because if I don't go away the Counselor will not come to you* (John 16:7). As long as Jesus was contained in the shell of a mere man; His Spirit and the effect of His Spirit were limited to His immediate vicinity. Jesus resumed His heavenly position within the Deity, so that His Spirit would escape the confines of the Man and could by God's omnipresence indwell every believer.

It is absurd to address the Holy Spirit or to pray to the Spirit. We pray to Jesus directly and He, through His Spirit (His motivating breath), guides us and works in us and for us. This is why Jesus tells us that the Holy Spirit does not act as a separate person but only brings to us what YHWH has for us (John 16:13 – 14). Putting it another way, using the earthly example God provides for us: when I am in a quandary on a matter that I know my dad understands or a field where he has experience; I do not ask the little voice inside myself what I should do. No, not at all: I call my dad to talk to him personally. This is the same with Jesus in regard to His Spirit. Jesus always said: *come to me* (Matthew 11:28).

The author of Hebrews had defined the matter with this beautifully simple presentation: *The Son is the radiance of God's glory and the exact expression of His nature, sustaining all things by His power* (1:3 HCSB). The radiance emanates from God and that radiance, which is the exact expression of God, or "the expressed image of God" is Jesus. That is what Jesus is and who Jesus is—period. The radiance is in no way separate from God. It is not a distinct person; it is God in action (John 1:1 – 5). The early believers were not confused on the subject; it was not a mystery to them.

A light bulb radiates light. You cannot take the light separately from the light bulb; the light is the very function of the bulb, the expression of the bulb that is usable to us. A light bulb without its radiance is just a glass object; it is not a light bulb. No one ever buys a bulb to have a bulb. We all buy light bulbs for their expression: for the light that emanates from them. And the light does not exist outside the bulb.

YHWH without Jesus is not the God of the Bible. How could He be and still meet Paul's succinct description: *All of God lives in Christ fully (even when Christ was on earth)* (Colossians 2:9 NCV). God has always been the same, John tells us that it is through God's expression that all things were created (John 1: 1 – 3). No one can go to the Father except through His expression. God leads to Jesus all those who seek the light for their lives.

In the same way: the Spirit of God is an intrinsic part of Jesus, like a function of Jesus. John says: *He* (Jesus) *had seven horns and seven eyes, which are the seven Spirits of God sent into all the earth* (Revelation 5:6).

The ill-conceived and ill-defined concept of the trinity did not come from God or Jesus' teaching; men elaborated the concept much later in Nicaea. Church councils, no matter how well intended, were men's efforts to manage institutionalized Christianity (and to satisfy the political power of the emperor). We must remember that the Good News <u>began</u> right, Jesus gave it correctly—eternally correctly—men corrupted it later. In every instance, for every quandary we can find the answer by going back to the original, to the source—truth is not served by expounding new concepts or variations of understanding to fit the questions of the time; which is what the men in Nicaea did. By the time Jesus gave His revelation to John the church (those who believed) had already lived through at least two generations. Obviously, the harmonious identity of the Father, the Son and the Holy Spirit was no issue. If it had not been so, Jesus would have addressed it here, in His final epistle to us.

The unerring availability a Christian has to go back to the source does not exist in other theologies. Muslims are taught that later verses have greater authority than earlier ones do. This makes sense: as the early Muslims went about making up their theology and dogma, they regularly had to amend earlier premises that did not fit anymore. Mormonism does the same thing: a research of the earlier utterances and writings by Joseph Smith, Jr. and the early leaders shows that the original theories are at odd on various key points with today's doctrines. Why? Because the early Mormon men were making up their theology as they went—as served their interests at the time. Eventually, progress in sciences and the basic questions from new converts of different walks of life led to serious rewritings or the whole edifice would have collapsed under the weight of its absurdities. Christianity is the opposite: it cannot be propped up by doctrinal facelifts. It can however be marvelously cleansed and revitalized by returning to its sources—which were perfect.

So, it is high time that we go back to the scriptural reality of Jesus and shed our superstitious adherence to the mysterious concept of Trinity that we do not grasp nor can explain clearly. Let's go back to the reality as Jesus presented it and as the original apostles passed it on to us.

<u>Note</u>: the concept of three distinct yet unified persons (Trinity) is not benign: it has opened the door to the falsification of Jesus. Indeed because it seems to present Jesus as a distinct person; people who set out to create their own religion will simply remove Him to the periphery of the Father. They marginalize Jesus in order to serve their purposes.

Major world religions that name Jesus in one capacity or another have done this very thing. This is what happened in Islam: Jesus is portrayed as a prophet (a creature, not The Creator); accordingly, He is not considered God Almighty. For the Jehovah's Witnesses, Jesus is Michael the Archangel. In Mormonism, Jesus is defined as one of God's sons (there are even Mormon writings that present Jesus and Satan as blood brothers).

Having defined Him thus, anything becomes permissible when it comes to interpreting what He can and cannot do. (Mormonism and Islam often come up together as examples in this book because they are similar in so many ways as to be almost two copies of the same thing.) Those who by ignorance or by design claim that Christianity and Islam share the same God or that Christians and Mormons have the same Jesus are wrong—dead wrong.

In Catholicism—a world religion that proceeded from council to council to continue defining itself through the ages—there exists an irrational attachment to Baby Jesus. Why? Because a baby's place is in the care of his mother: she is his upholder—not vice versa. Having "neutralized" Jesus' awesome "Almightiness", they can, in their minds, place Him permanently under Mary's tutelage and she can be made the queen of Heaven. Thus she can be petitioned instead of Him by those who pray to her. We are told that she can affect—and even dictate—Jesus' decisions regarding our own wants and preferences.

When we change Jesus, we do not follow the Savior anymore. What was expedient for the emperor at the council of Nicaea was not good for the believers thereafter.

The relevance of the sea of glass to the concept of the rapture

John is taken up to see what was to come next. He is brought there before the beginning of the time of testing so that he could record the whole process. The verses above set the tableau of the situation at the beginning or just before the bad times of testing begin. I am often confronted with the following comments: "Christians will go through the great tribulations". And: "Revelation does not mention the rapture at all. So maybe there is not a "rapture" or maybe the rapture is pre or mid or post-tribulation". This is all bunk.

First, Jesus has given us the prototype of the Jewish wedding process to help us get our perspective. The groom, bringing the dowry, goes to where the maiden lives and he proposes. The maiden can accept his offer and commit herself to this groom. If she does, from that point on, she wears his name. He leaves her there and goes back to his place to builds a home for her with him. His father inspect the works and tells him when he can go and fetch the bride. Note: There is no testing of the intended bride; she does not have to pass any type of purifying gauntlet. <u>He</u> brings the bride to the place he has made. And there, the wedding feast takes place. And they live together in intimacy for ever after. How he brings the bride to his place is immaterial: if he is wealthy, he may carry her on a richly adorned camel, if not; she may ride a donkey. But, <u>he</u> takes her there.

Jesus came to us, and made his offer and paid our dowry. Those of us who respond and embrace Him live a different life from this point on, because wear His name. Someday, He will come for us and <u>He</u> will take us with him to the place He has made for us. The Groom will not put us—His intended bride—through a time of testing to assert whether we will choose Him, (we have already done that), or through a gauntlet of proof. No: He comes with joy, picks us up and take us Home. There, we will be the subject of the wedding of the Groom when we become the bride. And forever live in intimacy with Him.

In this chapter we have the verse: *Something like a sea of glass, similar to crystal, <u>was</u> also before the throne* (4:6). Later, (15:2) we will have: *I also saw something like a sea of glass mixed with fire, and those who had won the victory over the beast, his image, and the number of his name, were standing on the sea of glass with harps from God* .

A sea of pure humanity, clear as glass, is the right picture. And the tense (*was*) tells us that it had already happened: this sea of blameless humanity has already arrived in God's heavenly presence.

A diamond is valued by its clarity; that is to say the absence of debris that would lessen its absolute transparency—like pure glass or crystal here. We, who follow Jesus have been made clean as snow. In God's eyes, we are free of all impurity. John sees us already in the heavenly because at that time: we have been brought there—before the time of testing begins.

And before the wedding of the Lamb, the souls who have refused the mark of the beast and chosen to die in Jesus through the process of testing, will be joined to the saved of all times (15:2).

How does this relate to the "rapture"?

Imagine that you went to a family reunion in an other state. There you saw members of your extended family. As you write about the event to a distant cousin, you tell him that you saw uncle Joe there, as well aunt Silvia and cousin Jack, and the twin cousins Melanie and Julie... And in a return correspondence, your cousin writes: "Yeah, but did they travel there before the reunion, or in the middle of the three day reunion or did they travel after the reunion? I am wondering because your letter did not say". Of course, you would roll your eyes and shake your head, and leave his inane comment unanswered. The fact that these people were there means only one thing: they traveled before the reunion. Whether they flew, drove or rode trains: they got there before the reunion.

The term rapture is not important, if you get hung up on it; then call it the "lifting", the "picking up", the "transfer", or the translating into God's presence by the loving Groom. But advancing the argument that the rapture is not explicitly mentioned in Revelation makes absolutely no sense. However Jesus chooses to execute the transfer, <u>the saved are found already there</u>—period.

<u>(Return to Table of Contents)</u>

5:1 – 14

1 Then I saw in the right hand of the One seated on the throne a scroll with writing on the inside and on the back, sealed with seven seals. 2I also saw a mighty angel proclaiming in a loud voice, "Who is worthy to open the scroll and break its seals?" 3But no one in heaven or on earth or under the earth was able to open the scroll or even to look in it. 4And I cried and cried because no one was found worthy to open the scroll or even to look in it. 5Then one of the elders said to me, "Stop crying. Look! The Lion from the tribe of Judah, the Root of David, has been victorious so that He may open the scroll and its seven seals." 6Then I saw One like a slaughtered lamb standing between the throne and the four living creatures and among the elders. He had seven horns and seven eyes, which are the seven spirits of God sent into all the earth. [7] He came and took the scroll out of the right hand of the One seated on the throne. [8]When He took the scroll, the four living creatures and the 24 elders fell down before the Lamb. Each one had a harp and gold bowls filled with incense, which are the prayers of the saints. [9]And they sang a new song: You are worthy to take the scroll and to open its seals, because You were slaughtered, and You redeemed people for God by Your blood from every tribe and language and people and nation. [10]You made them a kingdom and priests to our God, and they will reign on the earth. [11]Then I looked and heard the voice of many angels around the throne, and also of the living creatures and of the elders. Their number was countless thousands, plus thousands of thousands. [12]They said with a loud voice: The Lamb who was slaughtered is worthy to receive power and riches and wisdom and strength and honor and glory and blessing! [13]I heard every creature in heaven, on earth, under the earth, on the sea, and everything in them say: Blessing and honor and glory and dominion to the One seated on the throne, and to the Lamb, forever and ever! [14]The four living creatures said, "Amen," and the elders fell down and worshiped.

What's happening

The scroll has writing on both sides (front and back): it is complete. This fact also tells us that what is coming has all been decided, planned and settled; it will now be carried out: God is not reacting. At the end of Revelation we will see that Jesus promises a curse to anyone who adds to the prophecies of this book.

John could not satisfactorily describe God on the heavenly throne. But now, while God is still on the throne, John recognizes and describes Jesus who is at the center of the throne. The explanation is perfect: Jesus is the core of God that man can readily recognize and comprehend. This is why God became man. Thus, on the throne and within God, John perceives and easily identifies Jesus, the *Lion from the tribe of Judah*, the one who is worthy not only to reveal the things of the end to John, but also to bring them about.

To understand the vision of the "Seals", we must remember that a document is information; it is not the execution of that information. We seal documents so that their contents are hidden until the one authorized to access them does so. The breaking the seals only reveals; breaking the seal does not carry out the unveiled actions. No created being is qualified to open the seals: only God can reveal what is in the document. It is fitting that it should be Jesus who reveals the contents of the scroll to man.

The Lamb that had been killed is Jesus. I think that his resurrected body keeps the marks of his wounds so that we can recognize Him. It certainly allowed John to recognize Him.

Jesus has the seven spirits of God. The text defines further that these seven spirits had been sent into the entire world (from Pentecost on). The past tense indicates a finished action therefore the complete Spirit of Jesus is now back in heaven in Him. The apostle Paul alluded to this in 2 Thessalonians 2:7 – 8 *for the mystery of lawlessness is already at work, but the one now restraining will do so until he is out of the way, and then the lawless one* [antichrist] *will be revealed.*

Observations

At that point in time (beyond our current grace era), the Spirit of Jesus is not needed in man anymore on earth because, from this time forward, the person who chooses Christ over the *antichrist* is killed right away. This "new convert" does not have to live by God's

Spirit like today's believer does. The new life we can experience today is good because the Spirit of God in us becomes our effective teacher and guide. After the rapture, the person who chooses to die in Jesus will not be left on earth to illustrate grace for others and share his hope; instead, he is martyred promptly.

Indeed, at that time, none of the functions of the Spirit that Jesus described when He promised His Spirit in John 16 will be needed anymore. There will be no need to *convict the world about sin, righteousness and judgment to come* because our age of grace is past and the angels will have broadcast the eternal gospel to all as well as the consequences of choosing the beast (chapter 14). There will be no need to *teach and to guide* (the new believer) *into all truth* because the soul who opts now for Christ will be swiftly murdered. It is the same situation as happened on the cross; the felon who turned to Jesus never received Jesus' Spirit (Jesus' Spirit was sent to dwell in man at Pentecost, 53 days after that felon's death). The felon believed in Jesus being the Messiah, died and was presently with Jesus in paradise. That felon chose to die in Jesus.

Furthermore, Jesus does not act through His Spirit during the events of the end; He intervenes in person as conqueror. This is what the first seal reveals with its rider. Jesus has left the throne and rides His horse of destiny. This is Jesus with His resurrected body—He is also omnipresent, omnipotent and omniscient.

<u>(Return to Table of Contents)</u>

****

Chapter 6 - First Six Seals

Revelation 6:1 – 17

Now John writes about seals. As mentioned, they are not the actual events; instead the seals are snapshots that simply give an overall picture of some of the things that will take place. They reveal God's plan—what He will roll out presently. The seals are not sequentially chronological; they are thematic in nature. They do not cover all the events that will take place. They just hit some of the high points to give the tone. Details will be filled in and additional events will be brought out later in the revelation to John.

The seals, the trumpets and the bowls

Let's bring some light on these matters. We seal things to hide a content and we unseal to reveal. The content—God's action plan—was already prepared, approved and ready to go. God is not reacting, He is simply enacting the plan He has worked out from the depth of time. The first four seals—commonly referred to as the horses and riders of the Apocalypse—reveal divine actors who will concretely accomplish certain missions. The last three seals reveal aspects or direct divine actions.

The seals are not presented chronologically; they are brought out by categories. God uses the seals to set the stage for the rest of time and eternity—and within these new parameters, He will let the process follow its course.

From the concomitant rapture of the saints and trouncing of the rebellious angels out of heaven time is divided into sections. There is the redemptive span of three and one-half years of the time of testing, followed by a punitive retribution of roughly 6 months, followed by Jesus' reign on earth, followed by the last judgement and by settled eternity.

However, the conditions of life on earth have been drastically altered and new conditions are imposed—all by God. So, the seals set the stage. During the three and one-half year redemptive span, God does not intervene on the behalf of the living Gentiles as He would do on earth now. The Gentiles living during that period had all rejected a relationship with Jesus. They wanted no part of God; so He respects their will. It is without God's presence or succor that they will navigate their final—and for some: fatal—choice.

The first seal covers Jesus' actions that begin with His rapture of the saints and the booting of the Satan and his cohort out of heaven: Jesus, the eternal victor will actualize His victories in every way and all times. This first seal continues throughout time and eternity.

As for the other seals, some are sequential but some run concomitantly. The second, third, fourth and fifth all begin at the rapture and set the conditions and attributes of life that will apply to all the Gentiles until Jesus comes to reign for a 1,000 years. They last three and one-half year plus around six months of divine calamities.

The sixth seal reveals the end of this world at the conclusion of the 1,000 year reign. The seventh seal is in a category of its own thus is listed separately, but chronologically, it will precede the sixth.

As we will see in details later in the text, the post-rapture/pre-millennium span of roughly four years is divided in two different sections: the last redemptive allowance of three and one-half years when those who rejected Jesus in our time will have to decide how they will test for their eternity. Do I die with Jesus and live a blessed eternity? Or do I submit to be marked for a miserable life now and an abysmal eternity? (In our era, we have the choice to <u>live</u> with Jesus, down here then to transition into to eternity with Him, but at that time, the Gentiles will only have the choice of <u>dying</u> with Jesus in order to live with Him on the other side.)

The trajectory of human history is like the parabolic arc of a rocket. Redemption shot up fast at Pentecost and has kept going up and up. After the rapture it will be close to the end of it upward arc, it will eventually slow to a standstill as the last person dies in Jesus. There, for a short moment (the text mentions half an hour), it will hang still before precipitously hurtling down. The angel with the little scroll will announce that divine salvation is now closed, finished. The redemptive phase ends at that standstill and at that point, the divine wrath begins its earthly, punitive, and implacable retribution.

It is in this wrath that we find most of the trumpets and the bowls. Some of the trumpets represent the same events from slightly different perspectives: trumpets #1, 2, and 3 and bowls # 2 and 3. (The fourth trumpet and the fourth bowl are similar because they strike the solar system, but their effects are not identical; they are supplemental. And they apply all through the redemptive era; not just after the "standstill".) The first bowl is poured at the onset of the redemptive phase, right after the rapture of the saints.

Trumpets 1, 2, 3, 5 and 6 and bowls 2, 3, all happen in the short six months period that follows directly the three and one-half years of testing (redemptive phase). These calamities will severely reduce the world Gentile population.

The trumpets are announced by seven angels, the bowls poured by seven angels, however, we cannot assume a total of seven woes. There will be total of eight calamities. We will list them chronologically later in the text when we study the bowls.

Bowl # 6 is different from all the others. It takes place after the 1,000 year reign. It has an evil spiritual element, at the onset humans are the actors not the victims, and finally it has its own divine retribution.

While discussing the message of Revelation, there always seem to be confusion as to what is what and when what takes place; hence the above aside. Now, let's follow the text.

6:1 – 2

¹ Then I saw the Lamb open one of the seven seals, and I heard one of the four living creatures say with a voice like thunder, "Come!"² I looked, and there was a white horse. The horseman on it had a bow; a crown was given to him, and he went out as a victor to conquer.

What's happening

One of the four creatures ushers in the first horse and its rider. This is an overall vista of everything that follows: Jesus conquers. Even while Satan is on the rampage, Jesus sets his limits. In this first seal we see Jesus with His attributes: He has the authority of heaven (crown), and He goes forth *as a victor* to conquer. There is no doubt as to the outcome. Step by step, He will manage and control the events. Jesus goes out as conqueror because He already has the victory, so now He will go and claim it. As we will see throughout His Revelation: everything now follows Jesus' dictate.

Other translations identity this rider more clearly: ... *He rode out to defeat the enemy and win the victory* (ERV). God is never referred to as the *enemy*. And the One who defeats the *enemy* is none other than Jesus. Men may resist the enemy; but man does not defeat him. *Win the victory* is a second clue: Satan—and his representative the *antichrist*—never wins a *victory*; let alone *THE victory*. They may be allowed to win some battles; but victory is never theirs.

When Jesus leaves the throne and takes direct actions, some events will happen concurrently, immediately at the end of the grace era in which we are living today:

1. Jesus marks and raptures up the faithful 144,000

Hebrews.
2.	Jesus raptures the true Christian believers and all believers in prior history.
3.	He airlifts the nation Israel to safety.
4.	Satan is thrown out of heaven and immediately tries to strike at the Hebrew people.

As we will see later in the text, this is a very quick sequence; the first three events could be instantaneous and simultaneous. When the world abroad is apprised of these events; they will already have happened.

6:3 – 4

3 When He opened the second seal, I heard the second living creature say, "Come!" 4 Then another horse went out, a fiery red one, and its horseman was empowered to take peace from the earth, so that people would slaughter one another. And a large sword was given to him.

What's happening

The second creature ushers in the second horse and its rider. The second and third seals take effect in the same time period: right at the beginning of the three and one-half years of Satan's rampage that will begin just after the believers are raptured. These seals remain pertinent until Jesus begins His 1,000 year reign. The breaking of these seals reveals what happens to the Gentiles who are against God.

God removes peace on earth. The benevolent decency that the Spirit of God had maintained on earth to buffer the murderous inclinations of men is now removed. There will be no empathy, no pity nor mercy left in people. Killing will come naturally. The old inhibitions being absent, no human bonds or relationships will be able to buffer or prevent this absolute violence. Fear will dominate.

Read *Justin's Tomorrows* as a reference for what life will feel like for the individual.

Chapter 18 of Revelation will delve into how the action of this horseman will play out in details and what the universal and instantaneous consequences will be. This seal simply gives us a "heads-up".

Observation

Jesus had given His peace as His ongoing legacy to His believers (*Peace I leave with you. My peace I give you*, John 14:27). Now that all the grace era believers have been gathered to Him in heaven, Jesus retrieves His peace. The effect on the population will be instantaneous and devastating.

God will rapture His own when the last person who chooses Jesus freely has done so. Logic dictates then that 100% of the left-behind population had rejected Jesus—they had all opted for evil at a time when they could have weighed good versus evil and chosen the Savior. So when Jesus removes His peace from earth, the dam that had constrained evil will burst everywhere and within all. There will be no delay in the implementation of evil, because the population was already pressing for it: evil will cascade forth unhindered.

> Note: The few souls who will eventually refuse the mark of the beast will be souls who, at the last moment will reconsider the implication of that mark. As we will cover in subsequent chapters, everyone on earth will see and hear the two angels who will preach clearly the Good News (embrace Jesus; it is the only way) and will urge to resist the Devil and the *antichrist* during the short time between choosing to die in Jesus and getting beheaded (Hell is real and is irrevocable) plus they will

hear the incessant urging of the two godly prophets from Jerusalem. Therefore, at the moment of being marked, a few will shy away and desist...and will be beheaded for it.

These few souls who wise up at the threshold of their doomed destiny had not been "almost Christians" in our era who had not made the decision in time to make the rapture. No, they were those who did not want to embrace Jesus and had gleefully welcomed the *antichrist*. We can be sure of this because Paul teaches that God will wait for the full number of those who will choose Jesus' redemption before closing our era.

Also, the people who refuse the mark will not be souls who "sat on the fence" trying to conceptually decide between Jesus and the *antichrist* when the marking became mandatory. No, they were, and had been, full-bodied, evil-minded sinners who did not want to embrace Jesus; yet who, realizing the import of the messages of the angels and of the two witnesses, will at the last moment reconsider the eternal implications of getting Satan's mark. God is indeed fair and generous: He will embrace even these "Johnnies-come-lately". Jesus does not redeem us because we are almost good; but because we are helplessly bad.

6:5 – 6

5 When He opened the third seal, I heard the third living creature say, "Come!", And I looked, and there was a black horse. The horseman on it had a set of scales in his hand. 6 Then I heard something like a voice among the four living creatures say, "A quart of wheat for a denarius, and three quarts of barley for a denarius — but do not harm the olive oil and the wine."

What's happening

The third of the four living creatures ushers in the third horse and its rider. We must keep in mind that these creatures are Godly heavenly being; they work for God and take their orders from God. They are not evil and are not commanded by the evil one.

Everything is measured, weighed and accounted for ... and all necessities are limited. Gone is God's unending bounty, His generous watering of the fields of the wicked as well as those of the righteous that we have taken for granted throughout history. Isaiah spoke of this principle: *when your judgments are [in] the land, the inhabitants of the world will learn righteousness. [But if] the wicked is shown favor, he does not learn righteousness. In a righteous land he acts unjustly and does not see the majesty of the LORD* (Isaiah 26:9b – 10).

From times immemorial until the end of our era of grace, YHWH has showered undeserving man with His favor and man has refused to credit YHWH for it. Paul tells the people of Lystra: *in the past God let all the nations do what they wanted. But God was always there doing the good things that prove He is real. He gives you rain from heaven and good harvests at the right times. He gives you plenty of food and fills your hearts with joy* (Acts 14:16 – 17 ERV). One of the first judgments of the end will be the abrupt cessation of this generous favor; it will make evident what was always true: everything we have, everything we enjoy, comes from God and points us to Him.

No new crop will grow anymore and the crop already growing will not mature or will be lost. The earth will not produce anymore. All there will be is the surplus God generously gave during the seven years of the great harvest. Ezekiel tells us that a jubilant God will give Israel bumper crops, the same jubilant God will most like likely have celebrated the great harvest by giving the rest of the world bumper crops too. That surplus will be miserly administered by the enemy of mankind—you talk about a grim prospect!

> <u>Note</u>: How will the abrupt cessation of all crop and fruit happen? A possibility is given with the fourth trumpet and the fourth bowl which are applied right away after the rapture. These greatly and instantly affect the climate. The nights will be a third longer, which means that even along the equator, nights are now sixteen hours long, three hours longer than they are in Fairbanks, Alaska in December and January. The effect if bitter cold, within a day or two, all normal crops—fruits, grains and vegetables—are killed. And that's only the first half: the sun, during the shorter days burn much hotter. Besides making life miserable for the humans and animals, the sun will grill everything to a crips, so, within a day or two, frost-resistant crops are burnt out of existence. It is a devastating one-two divine punch.

I am told that a denarius was the wage for a day's work: it represented what a person was worth, one day at a time. Here, each day a person will only have access to a quart of wheat or three quarts of barley—that is all a person will warrant, all he or she will be worth—and no disposition made for improvements. Necessity will tether people to their local food distribution center: you cannot undertake to travel far when all you get is a one day's meager ration. Food, the availability of it, is a universal control tool.

<u>Note</u>: at the time of the third seal, the conditions of earth have drastically changed. With His saints being safe in Heaven with Him, and all the Hebrews tucked away in their safe haven, God does not protect anyone anymore. *If you are to be killed with the sword, then you will be killed with the sword,* (Revelation 13:10 NCV). This is worth repeating: God does not intervene in favor of the living anymore. At that time, God is handing over the handling of humanity to Satan and the *antichrist*. And God allocates and restricts precisely the supplies that Satan and the antichrist will have access to. They cannot create new supplies. This is the time <u>God</u> has set for the testing of the rest of the people—the people who, so far, had refused Jesus. But as always and in everything, Satan and his people are dependent on God's permission and God's providence: the third seal.

The One-World-Government elite already controls all the money and the supply of it. But money is a fragile control: it depends on the masses' tacit acceptance of this medium of exchange. Should the masses or a rich country decide to opt out of the globalist money framework; the whole construct could collapse and the One-World-Government would be imperiled (read *None Dare Call It Conspiracy* to understand the globalists' panic when Lincoln proposed to do just that). This money control is only maintained because enough people in key places of power in the various countries of the world are profiting greatly from the Globalists' agenda and the pay-offs they receive from it, and they keep the masses in fearful ignorance. These nabobs naively think that their kind will somehow bypass the obvious reckoning when the overall plan comes to fruition.

The Globalist elite understands the precariousness of money as control and has recognized that the ultimate control weapon is food: he who controls the food supplies owns the population. Experiments in developing countries have proven the point. However, in our era, God's restraining Spirit does not yet allow the global implementation of these plans. Satan's power and knowledge is always insufficient to dominate a world where God's restrainer is calling the shots. Therefore it is God—on the day of His choosing—who hands over the total control of the remaining humanity to the evil actors of the end. When the God-sustained earth suddenly stop producing food (and possibly food already growing will not reach maturity or will die out promptly), he who controls the harvested reserves controls the population. And when he begins his rule over the uniformly evil population, the *antichrist* will be able to bypass money and to control all the food supply...eventually, food will be meted out only to those who accept his mark.

Without God's universal action on the food production of the earth, the time of testing would take many decades to reach everywhere and everyone. Without God's new curses on nature, people in remote places could continue their subsistence farming for a long time. However, as it is prophesied, hunger will be the driving force. The single, exclusive source of existing foodstuffs will quickly create a massive exodus of the hungry, peripheral masses toward the centrally located food reserves; making the logistics of implementing the mark of the beast and the beheading of the "resisters" far easier and much quicker. Food is the most powerful control, we have a recorded example of this in the time of Joseph in Egypt. During the famine, people came from everywhere for food. They progressively gave up everything for that food and eventually even gave themselves up.

God's action makes it impossible for an individual to survive "off the grid". Come to think about it: "off the grid" means off man's supply route and onto God's supply route—which is precisely what God will have shut off. So, forget all the touted theories and schemes of survival during the "Great Tribulation" that are based on man's ability to supply his own needs because that possibility is obliterated at the onset by this divine reality: the horseman with the scales.

Observations

These restrictions will affect the post-rapture saints less than the rest of the population because these resisters/believers are killed as soon as they are identified. Someone trying to purchase anything without the mark will be prompted to get the mark of the *antichrist* on the spot ... or to be killed. Those who refuse the mark of the beast become de-facto post-rapture saints; they have chosen to die in Christ.

We will see later that the grinding mills will be idle during the *time of testing*; this information indicates that the earth has indeed stopped producing crops. There will be no new grain to grind. The rations announced by the horseman on the black horse represent the metering out of the crops harvested <u>prior</u> to the announcement. The mark of the beast will give a person access to meagerly metered supplies; it will never satisfy.

Do not harm the olive oil and the wine. God does not leave these two valuable goods for the enjoyment of the people wearing the mark of the beast because we will see in later chapters that the olive oil and the wine will not be available to the population during the *time of testing.* "*The merchants of the earth will also weep and mourn over her [Babylon, the world system], because no one buys their merchandise any longer—merchandise of ...wine and olive oil ... they will never find them again* (18:11 – 14)."

The olive trees and vines are deep rooted species that have long fruit bearing lives, so possibly by ordering these untouched by His wrath God will bless His people (the descendants of Jacob) with the goodness of olive oil (comfort) and wine (celebration) early when Jesus begins His good reign.

The third seal does not say that people will die of hunger—they won't. What it says is that they will never have enough; the necessities will always be in insufficient supply. Nothing will satisfy. The dwindling supplies will reflect what man can provide, or manage, by himself: Nothing. Life will go on but shortages will be the norm and no one will ever be satiated (until Jesus' 1,000 year reign).

Thoughts to ponder

God's stroke imposes extremely strict restrictions and there will be no human opportunities to better one's situation in life. Throughout history, God had generously made available resources far in excess of the basic needs of the people. Even in countries known for food shortages, famines today are artificially controlled by man: there usually is a hideously rich dictator or cliques of warlords who have stripped the country of its wealth and bounty, and have waylaid the humanitarian relief. Not then anymore: The restrictions of the third seal will take effect suddenly when the world system that we know is shattered by God in one blow (*in one hour*). No one will be satiated. This side of Jesus' reign, these restrictions, as shown later, are permanent and universal; there is no escape. Only Jesus' reign will ease these restrictions.

There is a terrible reality in a "day's pay": there is no possibility of getting ahead by entrepreneurship or speculation. Also, it leaves the people with no margin of error or of disobedience: they cannot work harder for a few day in order to save food for a day's rest.

There is no rest. The control exerted on the population is direct and relentless.

People will not have the ability to spontaneously help one another; the second seal saw to that: everyone will have murderous intent toward everyone else. People will have not enough, and no succor.

We will see later that the natural restrictions revealed above will be magnified by the instantaneous disappearance of the world system, within which entrepreneurship had flourished. The individual will have no rights and no recourse. Satan will have no reason to accommodate anyone.

Getting the mark of the beast on one's hand or brow will not increase the quantity of goods available to each person. It will only give access to "not enough". The limitations are ordained by God. Satan is powerless to satisfy.

6:7 – 8

⁷ When He opened the fourth seal, I heard the voice of the fourth living creature say, "Come!" ⁸And I looked, and there was a pale green horse. The horseman on it was named Death, and Hades was following after him. Authority was given to them, over a fourth of the earth, to kill by the sword, by famine, by plague, and by the wild animals of the earth.

What's happening

The fourth living creature ushers in this last horse and its rider. This heavenly host is empowered to roam over a fourth of the earth's habitable surface to kill systematically using every means conceivable: *sword, famine, plague and by wild animals of the earth.* Existence on earth will be devoid of "quality of life". Conditions will be bad all around. People far from the food reserve centers may not be able to get there and will die of hunger. During the three and one-half years of testing everything will pressure, will test the people left on earth. This does not take place during the great divine calamities that follow the three and one-half years of testing. If one chooses not to embrace Jesus in our era of grace; he will face dismal life as never seen before. Even the animals will enter into the action of killing humans.

We are also told specifically that this rider named "Death", is followed by Hades. Most people killed by the sword, famine, plague and wild animals is scraped into the Hell-bound basket (Hades). The few people who will heed the warning of the angels in chapter 14 are the only ones who will not transition to Hell.

The four horses and their riders were all ushered in by God's creatures. They represent actions that will truly take place; these actions are quick, unwavering and unstoppable.

The next three seals are of a different nature.

6:9 – 11

9 When He opened the fifth seal, I saw under the altar the people slaughtered because of God's word and the testimony they had. 10 They cried out with a loud voice: "Lord, the One who is holy and true, how long until You judge and avenge our blood from those who live on the earth?" 11 So a white robe was given to each of them, and they were told to rest a little while longer until the number would be completed of their fellow slaves and their brothers, who were going to be killed just as they had been.

What's happening

John now has another vista where he sees the post-rapture saints. These are the latecomers who were beheaded by the antichrist forces. These are the Gentiles who before the rapture had rejected Jesus and were bent on evil like everyone else then, but who chose to listen to and accept the post-rapture heavenly preaching of the

Good News by God's angel. As we will see later, these people had drawn encouragement from these messages and from the two godly witnesses in Jerusalem and they turned down the mark of the beast. These new believers remained steadfast in their choice for Jesus during the very short interval of time between their decision to reject the mark of the beast and their murder. They are beheaded immediately when Satan's minions identify them and God receives them into His eternal care. The *antichrist* provides no trial and offer no reprieve.

These martyred saints petition God to punish the men of the earth who continue to kill the new saints of God. Jesus hears their plea but He gives them an understanding: this will continue until the last person who would choose Jesus has done so and has been martyred for it. These are the hardscrabble gleanings of the harvest; God will not abandon even one soul to his horrible eternal fate. We will see this from a completed point of view in 15:2 – 3 and 16:6. But there will be no reprieve coming from heaven—*those meant to die will die.*

> <u>Note</u>: These martyred saints are not the martyrs of the pre-rapture era, because Paul tells us that all the dead saints—martyred or not—will receive their eternal bodies before the living are transformed in the blink of an eye, to join in the common rapture. The raptured saints are the sea of glass, they are not under the altar.

> We can see clearly that the post-rapture "Christians" are all murdered by men, famine, plague or wild animals; they are not decimated by the divine cataclysmic events of the trumpets and bowls. This fact is useful to assist us in placing the cataclysms <u>after</u> the last post-rapture believer is in heaven; that is to say <u>after</u> the three and one-half years of Satan's rampage.

This fifth seal thus documents the plight of those saved during the three and one-half years of Satan's rampage. Those who will choose to die in Jesus and refuse life-then-death with Satan. They are the kernels gleaned after the harvest.

Observation

God applies the same principle today as Jesus' salvation is offered freely to all who desire to choose Him. Paul tells us that God will wait until the last person who will freely believe in Jesus has done so before bringing our current grace era to an end. When He does, He will lift His believers to Him—the dead and the living. That's why we cannot calculate when the rapture will happen; only God knows the hearts of men.

Thought to ponder

During the three and one-half years, will there really be people who will choose immediate and gruesome death in Jesus rather than submitting to the beast? The text tells us that some will (6:9 – 11). We can foresee this because today, people do convert to Jesus in Muslim countries where such conversion often carries the death sentence; yet some do choose Christ.

It seems that the ultimate penalty (death) is not as powerful a deterrent to doing right as we would consider it to be. The penalty seems to reveal the weakness of the enemy, not his strength. Once he has killed a man, what more can Satan do to him? Nothing; killing the believer is the admission of Satan's ultimate helplessness. The butchered soul gets eternal, blessed life. So who loses? Satan loses.

6:12 – 17

12 Then I saw Him open the sixth seal. A violent earthquake occurred; the sun turned black like sackcloth made of goat hair; the entire moon became like blood; [13] *the stars of heaven fell to the earth as a fig tree drops its unripe figs when shaken by a high wind;* [14] *the sky separated like a scroll being rolled up; and every mountain and island was moved from its place.* [15] *Then the kings of the earth, the nobles, the military commanders, the rich, the powerful, and every slave and free person hid in the caves and among the rocks of the mountains.* [16] *And they said to the mountains and to the rocks, "Fall on us and hide us from the face of the One seated on the throne and from the wrath of the Lamb,* [17] *because the great day of Their wrath has come! And who is able to stand?"*

What's happening

This seal reveals God's mighty deeds. This image foretells the actual end of the world, when the last living Gentiles will be pounded to death and to oblivion. This will be followed, as we will read later, by the earth giving up the dead of all time before finally disappearing altogether.

Verse 15 – 17 tells us that there will be no changes of hearts or minds in that crowd. No one surrenders to Jesus. All remaining harden their Hell-bound stand.

These people who hid in caves, under rocks are the immense remainder of the doomed humanity that will be crushed after the battle of *Armageddon*. They know without a doubt that this is the end for them. They seek an escape through oblivion; but there will be no reprieve. They will be rounded up and physically crushed to death, then eternally doomed to perpetual suffering at the White Throne of sentencing—upon which Jesus will sit.

We will see similar images twice more, both times in reference to the same point in time and the same events: the aftermath of *Armageddon* prior to the setting of the White Throne of judgment.

The sixth seal also gives the human perspective from the victims' side, how it will feel to the people on earth. Their human conclusion is *who is able to stand?*

(Return to Table of Contents)

****

Chapter 7 - 144,000 Sealed, Raptured Believers

Revelation 7:1 – 17

After the sixth seal, God sets aside the linear description of the *things yet to come* in order to cover some very important items. We go back to the threshold at the end of the age of grace. Before Satan is allowed to begin his three and one-half year rampage and force the choice of *antichrist* or death on every Gentile, God will remove those who have already declared their allegiance to Him.

7:1 – 8

1 After this I saw four angels standing at the four corners of the earth, restraining the four winds of the earth so that no wind could blow on the earth or on the sea or on any tree. 2 Then I saw another angel, who had the seal of the living God rise up from the east. He cried out in a loud voice to the four angels who were empowered to harm the earth and the sea: 3 "Don't harm the earth or the sea or the trees until we seal the slaves of our God on their foreheads." 4 And I heard the number of those who were sealed: 144,000 sealed from every tribe of the Israelites: 5 12,000 sealed from the tribe of Judah, 12,000 from the tribe of Reuben, 12,000 from the tribe of Gad, 6 12,000 from the tribe of Asher, 12,000 from the tribe of Naphtali, 12,000 from the tribe of Manasseh, 7 12,000 from the tribe of Simeon, 12,000 from the tribe of Levi, 12,000 from the tribe of Issachar, 8 12,000 from the tribe of Zebulon, 12,000 from the tribe of Joseph, 12,000 sealed from the tribe of Benjamin.

What's happening

In the first 3 verses, the *land*, the *sea* and the *trees* will be the targets of the cataclysms heralded by the first three trumpets. These coming calamities are still in the future.

The heavenly messengers are told to hold off beginning the end-times events until the 144,000 descendants of Jacob *who serve our God* (NCV) are marked with God's very own seal and are given their special status at God's side. Great details are given to show that the 144,000 are all ethnic Hebrews. They must be lifted from the earth because we see later that they will be in the constant presence of Jesus. The other Hebrews will be protected by God also, but they will remain on earth in their earthly body.

Later we will see that these 144,000 Hebrews were the ones who *had been redeemed from the earth* (14:3). The only redemptive transaction ever performed for any man was the one effected by Jesus and paid in full at the cross. Therefore, these Hebrews had made Jesus their savior and had been faithful to God all their lives whereas the great majority of them had only come to God and His Messiah when they saw Him, through the triage and transfer processes of the second exodus. These later converts will have believed because they will have seen what God did (Ezekiel 20"34 – 38, Ezekiel 38 and 39 respectively).

The 144,000 are rewarded early with permanent intimacy and presence of their Messiah. They gain 1,000 + years worth of intimacy with God over the other Hebrews. It seems to me that the 144,000 are the Hebrew people who came to Messiah Jesus by trusting the words of God without requiring God's supernatural demonstrations listed in Ezekiel (chapter 20:34 – 38 and chapters 38 and 39). This is the meaning of Jesus' teaching: *Because you have seen Me, you have believed. Those who believe without seeing are blessed* (John 20:29).

Soon in our days, at the coming Exodus 2.0, the entire Hebrew people who will be brought out of all the countries of the world toward Israel and who will surrender to God's covenant at that time will do so because they will have <u>seen</u> God gloriously destroy the rebellious then take the others out and lead them out. They will personally see God [Jesus] going before them and going behind them with great power. I believe that because they did not believe until after they saw the divine demonstrations; they will now be treated differently than the Messianic Jews who had also returned to Israel in their midst. In the same way, their brethren who already lived in Israel and who had not come to Jesus prior to personally seeing God [Jesus] destroy the fourth kingdom amongst them and bring their brethren back will too stay on earth. Whereas the messianic Jews in today's Israel will be raptured for having believed without seeing. It is my opinion from the text that the Messianic Jews, everywhere who are alive at that time, those who had believed prior to either event, will be blessed...with a thousand years of intimacy with their Savior and Creator. John 20:29 is a Jewish/Hebraic clause. It is well within God's foresight to know in John's time that the number of the messianic Jews at the time of Exodus 2.0 would be 144,000.

Observations

Nowhere does the text of Revelation give any credence to a post-Jesus Jewish religion based on the Law. All actions and dispensations are in regard to the Hebrew race—never the Jewish religion. The Jewish religion was fulfilled by Jesus, the Messiah. Obeying and following the Old Testament rules and rituals today while ignoring Jesus as Messiah is an anachronism; it has essentially been idolatry since Jesus announced His Good News (Matthew 11:12 – 15). This erroneous attachment to a religion has held back ethnic Jews from coming to their long promised Messiah.

While their scriptures unerringly point back to Jesus the Messiah, the religious Jews pursue their religion for religion's sake, heedless of their scriptures. They feel their religion validates them. Through the process of Exodus 2.0, the Hebrews God spares will have personally come to the Messiah. However, it will not be as a validation of his religion; but through his belated acceptance of the eternal, unchanging Messiah.

The record of the Old Testament Jewish/Hebraic faith is useful to us all, to teach us about God (YHWH) and to give us the background of salvation. It brings us prophecies, fulfilled and yet to be fulfilled. Paul tells us: *All Scripture is inspired by God and is profitable for teaching, for rebuking, for correcting, for training in righteousness* (2 Timothy 3:16) and by scripture, Paul meant the scriptures that existed at his writing: the Old Testament. We are grateful for and cherish the Old Testament. In it we can observe God; through it we can know God, His character and His heart. It pointed to salvation, but it is not the vehicle for salvation by itself: one must pass through Messiah Jesus.

Also, Judaism is not a bypass of God's wrath for the times of the end; so it would serve no purpose for a Gentile to convert to Judaism. The Hebrews who will be led back to Israel by God are ethnic descendants of Jacob; something no one else can become—either one is born into the twelve tribes to Hebrew parents or he is not a Hebrew.

(Return to Table of Contents)

7:9 – 17

⁹After this I looked, and there was a vast multitude from every nation, tribe, people, and language, which no one could number, standing before the throne and before the Lamb. They were robed in white with palm branches in their hands. ¹⁰And they cried out in a loud voice: Salvation belongs to our God, who is seated on the throne, and to the Lamb! ^{11}*All the angels stood around the throne, the elders, and the four living creatures, and they fell facedown before the throne and worshiped God,* ^{12}*saying: Amen! Blessing and glory and wisdom and thanksgiving and honor and power and strength be to our God forever and ever. Amen.* ^{13}*Then one of the elders asked me, "Who are these people robed in white, and where did they come from?"* ^{14}*I said to him, "Sir, you know." Then he told me: These are the ones coming out of the great tribulation. They washed their robes and made them white in the blood of the Lamb.* ^{15}*For this reason they are before the throne of God, and they serve Him day and night in His sanctuary. The One seated on the throne will shelter them:* ^{16}*They will no longer hunger; they will no longer thirst; the sun will no longer strike them, nor will any heat.* ^{17}*For the Lamb who is at the center of the throne will shepherd them; He will guide them to springs of living waters, and God will wipe away every tear from their eyes.*

What's happening

This vision is timeless: it pictures the eternal reality for those who embraced Jesus as the good news. It begins at the rapture and will never end.

In 7:9, the vision reveals a multitude of people so great that we could not count them. These are Hebrews and Gentiles; they are from every nation and tribe, from everywhere on earth. Jesus had commanded His disciples to go and make disciples of every nation, tribe and country on earth; and they have. These are:

- The true Christians who died between Pentecost and the rapture—Hebrews and Gentiles.

- Those who lived before Jesus came to whom *the gospel was also preached to those who are now dead, so that, although they might be judged in the flesh (dead), they might live by God in the in the spirit* (1 Peter 4:6).

- Plus the living Gentiles (and of course the 144,000 Hebrews) who were raptured while living.

The believers of our age (between Pentecost and the Rapture) will have come out of about 2,000 years of opposition, discrimination and persecution as anticipated by Jesus in Matthew 5:11 – 12.

There is another aspect to this "coming *out of the great distress*": Since Adam's sin, we have lived on a stressful earth which ground was cursed by God. In Jesus, we get relief right away from this situation (even though we will have trials, difficulties and physical duress and death). Jesus tells us: *Come to Me all of you who are tired and have heavy loads, and I will give you rest. Accept My teachings and learn from Me, because I am gentle and humble in spirit, and you will find rest for your lives* (Matthew 11:28 – 29 NCV). Jesus will take away the earthly adversarial reality for those who come to Him: *Do not worry about the food or drink you need to live... Seek God's kingdom* [in Jesus]...(Matthew 6:25 – 34 NCV). Everyone there had come out of that distress and now they have the full benefit of it.

These realities are what the *great tribulation* (or *great distress*) refers to in verse in 7:14. These believers had lived in the midst of Satan's kingdom as foreign sojourners and have been subjected to his ire. The apostle John who belongs to our era says: *I, John, your brother and partner in the <u>tribulation</u>, kingdom and perseverance in Jesus* (Revelation 1:9). Also the letters to the churches in the first 3 chapters of Revelation document the hardships and persecutions of the Christians. The expression *great tribulation* in 7:14 does not refer to the period of testing and of God's calamities in the events of the end; it defines the condition of life of the true Christian between Pentecost and the rapture.

In 7:16 Jesus tells us that those with Christ will never be thirsty again and that the sun will never hurt them or the heat burn them as will happen to the people still living during the bowls of God's wrath in Chapter 16. We will see from God's planned calamities (trumpets and bowls) that the people remaining on earth (except the descendants of Jacob) will suffer from thirst as a large part of the drinking water will become toxic. They will also burn as the sun will be made hotter to inflict burns to the living. Clearly, from the text, those who have trusted Jesus will be spared all of this. The argument for a post-tribulation rapture has no basis.

These people can gratefully sing *Salvation belongs to our God, who is seated on the throne and to the Lamb* because they have experienced the joyful result of salvation. The believers in Christ are held securely by God, next to His throne where Jesus sits. They worship Him day and night. They are free from all distress. By showing this vision to John, Jesus reassures the true believers of our era; He wants to make sure that we understand how good and secure our hope in Him is.

The raptures

As we have just seen, chapter 7 of Revelation is the chapter of the raptures; the rapture of the 144,000 descendants of Jacob from Israel and the rapture of the believers of all times (the living Gentile and the dead Hebrews and Gentiles of all times). Before the unpleasant events of the end-times begin, God lovingly gathers to Himself all those who, during this age of grace have spontaneously chosen Jesus as savior and Messiah. God had fully adopted them and now He protectively spares His children, co-heirs of Christ, from the discipline He will mete out to the rest of humanity.

<u>(Return to Table of Contents)</u>

****

****

Chapter 8 - Last Seal, First Six Trumpets

Revelation 8:1 – 9:21

The silence, the worship

8:1 – 4

¹When He opened the seventh seal, there was silence in heaven for about half an hour. ²Then I saw the seven angels who stand in the presence of God; seven trumpets were given to them. ³Another angel, with a gold incense burner, came and stood at the altar. He was given a large amount of incense to offer with the prayers of all the saints on the gold altar in front of the throne. ⁴The smoke of the incense, with the prayers of the saints, went up in the presence of God from the angel's hand.

What's happening

This seventh seal is a multilevel tableau. There is solemn worship in God's presence as the era of redemption has now closed. This acknowledges the momentous and irreversible change of paradigm that is being effected.

The paradigm of redemption began way back at the beginning when God promised Eve the redeemer seed from her. Actually, it began even before the world began, as God committed Jesus to become the redeemer.

There is a pause to mark the end of a process millennia old, a pause before the wrath of God's retribution is poured out on the Gentiles of the earth.

The pan full of fire thrown to the earth

8:5

⁵The angel took the incense burner, filled it with fire from the altar, and hurled it to the earth; there were rumblings of thunder, flashes of lightning, and an earthquake. ⁶And the seven angels who had the seven trumpets prepared to blow them.

What's happening

The action of the angel causes flashes of lightning, thunder, loud noises and an earthquake. From subsequent chapters we will be able to locate these events precisely in God's sequence when He brings His calamity on the doomed Gentiles—all wearing the mark of the beast. The seals have given us a panoramic preview of the events Jesus will orchestrate.

Reviewing the seals

After the rapture of the true Christians, God will allow Satan to wreak havoc on earth for three and one-half years. Satan along with his fallen angels and men who are dedicated to him takes complete control of humanity. They can do so because God has planned for them to do this and He has removed all His barriers: His Spirit and the Spirit filled believers.

God withdraws His generous providence of all goods and necessities. Killing is the order of the day, every person turns against everyone else, there will be no more thought of marrying and giving one's children in marriage (18:22 – 23). Every available supply will be metered and controlled because no new crop will grow ... *the sound of a* [grinding] *mill will never be heard... again* (18:22 – 23). Over a fourth of earth will be submitted to death *by the sword, by famine, by plague, and by the wild animals of the earth* (6:8).

What an unusual and instantly recognizable time of global struggle and strife. We can conclude with certainty that the believers of the grace era will have been raptured prior to these three and one-half years because Jesus had specifically told us that normal human activities will continue right up to the instant of the rapture (Matthew 24:36 – 44). He includes the example of *two women will be grinding at the mill: one will be taken and one left*—when these events in Chapter 8 begin there will be no more grinding at the mill.

During the three and one-half years that follow the rapture, Satan will try to establish himself as god. He will have every person killed who chooses not to worship him. The people who belatedly give their devotion to Jesus are exposed publicly and are ushered through martyrdom into heavenly eternity. They had rejected Jesus totally before the rapture; but now, facing the reality of their eternity according to God's terms some will demure and refuse the mark of the beast.

After the three and one-half years allotted to Satan, it is God's turn to act and He will bring incredible pressures to bear on every Gentile alive then. Later (sixth seal), after God's programmed anger and after Jesus' 1,000 year reign, our creation will disappear. The sun will become black, the moon will turn like blood, the stars will fall and darkness will be deep. Every mountain and island will be moved from its place. The terrified Gentiles on earth will hide underground. They will wish to die as they realize that they face YHWH's anger without any buffer... and they will indeed be pounded to death. Here we have the heavenly perspective of what the sixth seal had shown us.

(Return to Table of Contents)

The trumpets

While the seals had set the stage, the trumpets set events in motion. The trumpets of Revelation do not necessarily reflect a chronology because, for example, more than one of the first 4 trumpeted events may run concurrently.

The first, second, third and fifth trumpets announce God's direct actions <u>after</u> the three and one-half years of Satan's rampage and before the 1,000 year reign. The first 4 trumpets describe the same type of calamities. The last three trumpets will be of a different nature and their impact will set them apart, this is why they are specifically highlighted by the eagle. The latter three will also ramp-up in severity from physical torments (non-fatal) to wholesale physical killing and finally to the eternal living death of damnation. The last three do reflect a chronological progression that begins right after the three and one-half years of Satan's rampage and finishes at the end of time.

> <u>Note</u>: There are two aspects to keep in mind when reading about the trumpets: they do not present the totality of the calamities that will be visited at that time on mankind and on earth—two more calamities will be mentioned later (the burning sun and the boils). Second, the calamities are revealed by class not by chronological order. The first four trumpets announce God's actions on nature, on the ecosystems; man suffers because he lives in the affected ecosystems. The last three trumpets announce God's direct actions on humanity while the ecosystems are untouched.

8:7

⁷ The first angel blew his trumpet, and hail and fire, mixed with blood, were hurled to the earth. So a third of the earth was burned up, a third of the trees were burned up, and all the green grass was burned up.

What's happening

This first trumpet heralds God's strike. *Hail and fire, mixed with blood* rain upon a third of the earth's surface, no grass nor trees remain. The regions affected cannot sustain life. Imagine: the sum of the areas affected will represent a third of earth's habitable surface. No natural disaster has ever produced so great a desolation since the flood in Noah's time.

The first trumpet's calamity creates desperation and death for those hit by it; but it does not touch every living Gentile. People living in unaffected areas will not suffer directly from it. Also, death will come rather swiftly because no human or animal can survive any length of time on bare mud and rocks. We are not told the duration of this calamity. We are not told how many people will die from it.

8:8 – 9

[8] *The second angel blew his trumpet, and something like a great mountain ablaze with fire was hurled into the sea. So a third of the sea became blood,* [9] *a third of the living creatures in the sea died, and a third of the ships were destroyed.*

What's happening

A large block like a mountain is thrown into the sea causing a third of the sea to turn into blood. A third of the creatures of the sea die and a third of the ships of the world are destroyed.

Consider the stink, the desolation, and the world-wide loss in transport ability. Imagine the Northern and Southern Atlantic Ocean plus the Mediterranean Sea, the English Channel, the

North and the Baltic Seas; all turned to blood. Can you picture the mass of humanity that lives along those shorelines?

This second trumpet creates desolation to every area it touches but it is not universal so some people are unaffected. Those in the affected area die rather quickly: the blood quagmire is toxic and the ships can't stay afloat. We do not know how long the effects of this calamity will last or how many will die as the result of it.

8:10 – 11

10The third angel blew his trumpet, and a great star, blazing like a torch, fell from heaven. It fell on a third of the rivers and springs of water. 11The name of the star is Wormwood, and a third of the waters became wormwood. So, many of the people died from the waters, because they had been made bitter.

What's happening

A large burning star poisons a third of all the fresh water supply of the world. We do not know if it will affect one great contiguous area or will poison separate pockets but the scope of this calamity is gigantic. Imagine a combined area as large as Russia plus Asia without any drinking water. Millions of people maddened by thirst die from drinking this toxic water.

Again, this third trumpet brings desperation. Death in the affected area will be swift. People do not live long without water so they will either die of thirst or die poisoned by the water. However, the people in the areas unaffected by the trumpet are not really touched by it. We do not know how long the effects of this calamity will last but we are told may people will die because of it.

Observation

With the additional information of Chapter 16 we see that the first three trumpets all have a *blood* element. It is interesting because we are told that blood is the substance of life, and Jesus' blood is the substance of our eternal life. Here, however we have the reverse aspect: blood spilled brings death.

The three preceding trumpets will affect the Gentiles who have chosen the *mark of the antichrist*. These cataclysms will kill millions, possibly billions; and *the other people who were not killed by these terrible disasters still did not change their hearts and turn away from what they had made with their own hands* (9:20 NCV). The people are unsalvageable: they have the mark of Hell on them.

This process excludes the post-rapture saints because they were not killed by disasters but by men in the service of the *antichrist*. It also excludes those victims of the fourth seal who had accepted Jesus and would have refused the mark. This aspect helps us position these disasters after the three and one-half years; that is: when all the post-rapture saints are safely in heaven. (*...until the number would be completed of their fellow slaves and their brothers, who were going to be killed just like they had been* [by men in the service of the *antichrist*] Revelation 6:11.)

8:12

21 The fourth angel blew his trumpet, and a third of the sun was struck, a third of the moon, and a third of the stars, so that a third of them were darkened. A third of the day was without light, and the night as well.

What's happening

This trumpet takes effect at the onset of the time of testing, right on the heel of the rapture of the saints.

A third of the sun, a third of the moon and a third of the stars are darkened. Daytime, even on the longest day of the year, will be drastically shortened and nights will be really dark. Night time temperatures will drop significantly. This calamity affects the whole earth. Even today in a "functioning" world, our systems could not cope with this change. They could not cope with the consequences; our infrastructures could not possibly adapt to the instantaneous extra demands for light and heat. But actual conditions will be far worse for these people than they would be if this calamity had hit today. Socially, because of the second seal, everyone will face these calamities alone and without any recognizable social framework, no support and no respite.

People will not be able to insulate themselves from this cold. They will not be able to band together to protect themselves from the dangers lurking in the scary night because all human relationships are murderous (see second seal). Abject fear will rule the night.

Nothing is normal anymore! Something larger than what mankind can fathom or control is at work here; the whole planetary system is haywire. The resulting fear and panic will be worldwide yet it will be suffered at the personal level.

Thought to ponder

Consider the events heralded by the above trumpets: what does this do to the prevalent dismissive consideration of God as a "benevolent old guy who cannot help himself from indulging our whims and transgressions"? Do you see Him as a soft granddaddy type, an out-of-touch god whom you can con into doing your wishes? Is He the "man upstairs", as some people casually refer to Him in conversations? Or is He reduced to being just "Providence"? Sobering, isn't it?

8:13

13I looked again and heard an eagle flying high overhead, crying out in a loud voice, "Woe! Woe! Woe to those who live on the earth, because of the remaining trumpet blasts that the three angels are about to sound!"

What's happening

As if the above curse and calamities were not severe enough, a strange messenger (an eagle flying high) gets John's attention; basically, it says: watch the next three announcements. The eagle shouts "trouble" three times because there are three sets of troubles yet to be introduced to John by the last three trumpets. These calamities are of a different nature and scope: they target people, not the ecosystem. The coming fifth trumpet will herald a stand-alone event that God ordains.

9:1 – 12

[1] The fifth angel blew his trumpet, and I saw a star that had fallen from heaven to earth. The key to the shaft of the abyss was given to him. [2] He opened the shaft of the abyss, and smoke came up out of the shaft like smoke from a great furnace so that the sun and the air were darkened by the smoke from the shaft. [3] Then locusts came out of the smoke on to the earth, and power was given to them like the power that scorpions have on the earth. [4] They were told not to harm the grass of the earth, or any green plant, or any tree, but only people who do not have God's seal on their foreheads. [5] They were not permitted to kill them but were to torment them for five months; their torment is like the torment caused by a scorpion when it strikes a man. [6] In those days people will seek death and will not find it; they will long to die, but death will flee from them. [7] The appearance of the locusts was like horses equipped for battle. Something like gold crowns was on their heads; their faces were like men's faces; [8] they had hair like women's hair; their teeth were like lions' teeth; [9] they had chests like iron breastplates; the sound of their wings was like the sound of chariots with many horses rushing into battle; [10] and they had tails with stingers like scorpions, so that with their tails they had the power

to harm people for five months. [11] They had as their king the angel of the abyss; his name in Hebrew is Abaddon, and in Greek he has the name Apollyon. [12] The first woe has passed. There are still two more woes to come after this.

What's happening

This is a timed event—precisely five months. Its duration sets it apart from the previous four calamities. It also happens at a different time than the calamities that bring death because no one will die during this five month period, so logic tells us that this event precedes the other calamities. It brings pure torment. However, it does happen after the gleaning of the time of testing is completed. It affects only the damned.

One of God's messengers—a powerful angel—receives the key to the abyss. We'll see later that his name is Apollyon or Abaddon—his name means Destroyer; but there is nothing that indicates that he is Satan's angel: he is God's righteous angel of punishment.

Apollion will direct pain onto all the people who have resisted God. This particular messenger may be the one who will appear again in Chapter 20 with his key to lock Satan in the bottomless abyss. This agent of God unleashes pure agony on Satan's marked people.

> Note: We will see later that the *false prophet* is made up of the fallen angels, the demons. Before the locust event of the fifth trumpet begins all the demons are already in Hell. There are none available to *open the shaft of the abyss and neither are they available to create pain*; therefore Abaddon/Apollyon is an angel <u>of God</u> who at His command orchestrates this divine punishment. It cannot be any other kind of angel. Neither Satan (he

is bound up in the abyss) nor his angels (demons) take any part in this (they are in Hell). The Abyss or the depth of the earth is not a demon controlled area; it is the temporary place of suffering for the demons—and Satan—until they are exiled permanently into Hell. God rules the Abyss. This is why the demons begged Jesus not to send them into the Abyss: because the Abyss is an unpleasant place for them—a place of suffering.

This calamity does not occur during the three and one-half years because Jesus does not unleash His punitive wrath until all who will choose Him have done so. This fifth-trumpet event takes place right after the three and one-half years and before Jesus begins His 1,000 year reign. It will not touch the Hebrews who are being cared for by God in their desert haven. On earth, at that time these Hebrews are the people who have God's seal—they are His elects. They have God's seal on their heads.

> Note: in these particular verses, God is not referring to the 144,000 Hebrews of Chapter 7 who have been sealed (marked) on the forehead by God; because we see in Chapter 14 that the 144,000 Hebrews are already in heaven and never leave the presence of Jesus: "*The 144,000 who had been bought from the earth... They follow the Lamb everywhere He goes. These 144,000 were bought from among the people of the earth to be offered to God and the Lamb*" (14:3 – 4 NCV). John is provided *a measuring reed like a rod ... to go and measure God's sanctuary and the altar and count those worshipping there.* The only people allowed to do this were the Hebrews. This is the reference to God doing a census of the remaining Hebrews, those He would hereby airlift to His desert haven where He will keep them safe and cared

for through Satan's rampage and the following calamities.

The means to apply this unbearable 5 month torture is described as locusts of a very different sort. Whatever the nature these monsters may be is not critical to our understanding today: suffice to know that the people will suffer enough to go out of their minds.

The physical suffering has now become personal and universal; everyone with Satan's mark is in exquisite pain. The calamities of the first three trumpets will not affect everyone, some people living in unaffected areas do not suffer directly from them, however these locusts will affect every single Gentile still living—universally.

With this calamity God introduces terror. These horrifying monsters are inescapable and relentless, the pain they inflict is excruciating. People will yearn for death but death will evade them during this entire phase. The tormentors will not be allowed to kill anyone, and people will not be allowed to find a way to die. There is no reprieve. There are no shelters to hide from these monsters. Their merciless stinging persists night and day for 5 long months.

The sixth trumpet will be another one of God's mighty strikes.

9:13 – 21

13The sixth angel blew his trumpet. From the four horns of the gold altar that is before God, I heard a voice 14say to the sixth angel who had the trumpet, "Release the four angels bound at the great river Euphrates." 15So the four angels who were prepared for the hour, day, month, and year were released to kill a third of the human race. 16The number of mounted troops was 200 million; I heard their number. 17This is how I saw the horses in my vision: The horsemen had breastplates that were fiery red, hyacinth blue, and sulfur yellow. The heads of the horses were like lions' heads, and from their mouths came fire, smoke, and sulfur. [18]A third of the human race was killed by these three plagues — by the fire, the smoke, and the sulfur that came from their mouths. [19]For the power of the horses is in their mouths and in their tails, for their tails, which resemble snakes, have heads, and they inflict injury with them. [20]The rest of the people, who were not killed by these plagues, did not repent of the works of their hands to stop worshiping demons and idols of gold, silver, bronze, stone, and wood, which are not able to see, hear, or walk. [21]And they did not repent of their murders, their sorceries, their sexual immorality, or their thefts.

What's happening

The sixth trumpet adds a greater horror to the cataclysms described by the previous five trumpets. It will happen through the same period as the other trumpets, that is to say: during the short time God puts maximum pressure on the remaining population right after the three and one-half years of Satan's rampage and before the beginning of the 1,000 year reign.

A map of the region will show that geographically, the four messengers of God are on the section of the Euphrates that goes by Al-Thawrah, Ar-Raqqah and Dayr Al-Zawr in today's Syria. This tells us that the four messengers of God are on Israel's northern border and that they will go out in all four directions to do their terrible killing. We must remember that no Jew will be living in the land of Israel during this period so the killing wave of the Gentiles will also go through the Holy Land.

These four messengers of God who had been specially equipped for and assigned to this task from long ago are now given the order to proceed. This is an army from heaven, 200 million soldiers strong, larger than any human army ever seen on earth. Its troops are not human soldiers thus are untouchable by human defenses. (At any rate, there will be no organized human resistance in the form of an army. The lastest human army up to this point was thrashed by Jesus at the end of the three and one-half years—just before this time of calamities begins.)

These 200,000,000 heavenly soldiers kill by various yet specific means: fire, smoke and sulfur. Jesus had said to Pilate: *my kingdom does not belong to this world. If it belonged to this world, my servants would fight so that I would not be given over to the Jews* (John 18:36 NCV). Jesus is now using His own army; and it is not of this world.

In my opinion, the fact that there are four messengers means that they will lead their portion of soldiers into the 4 directions of the compass, that is to say everywhere. Zechariah 2:6 uses the same image to mean everywhere (*I have scattered you* [the Hebrews] *like the four winds of heaven*—NCV). It is safe to deduce that this army of 200 million will spread out in all directions to leave no pocket of population untouched.

These are not earthly horses and the riders are not humans. The understanding of their precise description is of no consequence for the believer today: he will not see them. These death agents are gruesome and pitiless: they are implacable and efficient. No area of the globe is spared. These swarming soldiers add visual terror to the death they generate.

These soldiers accomplish exactly what God had prepared them for: they kill a third of all the Gentiles still on the earth. If we use today's world population as reference, this could mean billions of people.

The Gentiles remaining, all wearing the mark of the *antichrist*, will not change their hearts. God again is proven right. He knew that these people were against Him to the core. They proved it by adopting the mark of the beast. God proves that no matter what, they will not turn to Him (similar to Pharaoh's hardened heart). God had waited three and one-half years, until the very last person who eschewed the mark of the beast and chose Him was martyred and safely at His side in heaven before sending this army. At this point, grace and pardon would be useless: there are no takers left. Indeed, the entire Gentile population that is left lives in the chaos of their un-regenerated nature. There is no structure, no wisdom, no societal cohesion—only selfish individuals bent on murder, sorcery, sexual immorality and theft—it is universal, morbid depravation.

By mentioning here that the people remaining would not turn to YHWH but would resolutely give their worship to demons and to assorted idols, we have the proof that there is no one left interested in pardon and reconciliation with YHWH. God has demonstrated that He has provided salvation to absolutely everyone who would accept it. When the last post-rapture saint is beheaded at the end of the three and one-half years, Jesus' redeeming work will indeed be complete. God has been totally fair and just. As we will see later, an angel in heaven will proclaim that the Good News is indeed over.

Observations

The trumpets show us what God does; He displays His power and relentlessness. He accomplishes all that He had planned and with the events of the trumpets He concludes what we commonly refer to as the Great Tribulation.

The three and one-half years that preceded most of the events announced by the trumpets were the apogee of Satan's romp and power on the earth. Satan marked his followers and killed those who rejected his dominion, finally, at the end of the three and one-half years, he organized and motivated a great army against Jesus and His heavenly army in a battle to which Revelation gives no name. Jesus smashes Satan's army, and birds feed on its rotting flesh. At that juncture the *antichrist* and the *false prophet* were thrown alive into the *lake of fire*. His allocated three and one-half years having run out, Satan was bound and will remain sequestrated until the end of the 1,000 year reign.

Following this battle for which Revelation gives no name, God will hit the remaining Gentile population with His selected expressions of anger. Calamities are instantly applied to start out the process while the others will follow in sequence.

This is a good place to recap the redemptive curses as well as the punishing calamities of the post-rapture time in their chronological order. The first redemptive curse destroys the human relationships at the horizontal level. Indeed: The second seal removes peace from the earth, so that people will slaughter one another... all the time, everywhere. This is the background reality throughout all that follows. The calamities previewed with the seals, exposed by the trumpets and the bowls do not happen all at the same time; they actually span a little more than a thousand years:

1. Some calamities/curses are meted out right at the onset of the time of testing—right after the rapture of the believers. The murdering urge that will inhabit all Gentiles when God remove His peace right after the rapture. The purpose of this one is redemptive: do you want this world or God?

2. At that time also, the darkness imposed by the fourth trumpet (8:12) will make the days eerily short while the longer nights are brutally cold—as winter nights in the far north. The fifth bowl (16:10 – 11) tells us that this will be the conditions of life during the rule of the beast (the three and one-half years of testing). Again, the purpose is redemptive: Do you want this or God? In this punishing nature, [The beast's] *subjects ground their teeth*

in anguish (NLT). The only time the Gentiles are subjects to the beast are during the three and one-years of testing. After that the beast is in Hell.

3. Also, right at the onset of the time of testing, the sun burns the people harshly during the day (chapter 16). Verse 7:16 tells us that the raptured people will never be scorched by the heat of the sun. This shielding of the saints does not refer to their eternal situation because the sun will not be recreated then. It refers to the bowl of 16:8 –9. We can deduce that the burning sun will be a feature of the three and one-half years of testing. Both these climatic calamities will continue through the short span of the greater, devastating calamities that will quickly follow the ending of the three and one-half year. All these hardships and calamities will end when Jesus comes to reign.   <u>Note</u>: The third seal and several other passages let us know that from the onset of these three and one-half years, no new crop will grow—and existing crops in the field will perish, un-harvested. Only plants with deep roots will be able to survive those three years: Olive trees and grape vines. There will be no new grain to grind. The acute ecological conditions (extreme cold and extreme heat) of the first two divine curses above will instantly kill any crop in the field and preclude any new crop from growing. Today, our gardens do not survive one night of unseasonal freeze at the wrong time of the year. Imagine: the worse heat of the worst summer anywhere in the day followed by the harshest, deep freeze of the arctic the following night. Food will indeed become instantly scarce as given by the third seal. Indeed, extremely long nights will bring glacial temperatures akin to—or worse than—those of

Fairbanks in December/January, freezing any normal crop and fruit tree. At the same time, day time temperatures will soar and the action of the sun will burn beyond what is experienced anywhere on earth today; thus searing and killing any crop that may be cold-resistant.

4. At the same time, also from the onset of the time of testing, terrible boils that afflict every Gentile who accepts the mark of the beast (chapter 16); this affliction lasts all the way till Jesus begins His 1,000 year reign, because we are not told that it would abate. An argument can be made that this curse strikes is meted from the beginning of the time of testing from the text of 16:11: *And they cursed the God of heaven for their pains and /.* It is hard to tell what services will be available during the rule of the *antichrist*, but we know that after his defeat, nothing will function: no pharmacy, no salve, drug or other palliative… and no healing—no organized leadership; bad as it was.

5. After the time of testing, when Satan is tied up in the Abyss and the beast and the false prophet are in Hell, things get worse yet: Otherworldly creatures will mercilessly torment every Gentile for 5 months—night and day with no reprieve, no escape. On top of their awful boils, of their intense freezing at night and their heat exposure every day, every Gentile is tormented by these creatures.

6. After these initial five months, there will be an army of 200 million heavenly fighters unleashed on mankind. They will kill a third of the remaining Gentile population. Billions will die. This will not take long at all: based on today's world population, 200 million fighters

will make short work of it.

7. Following these killers, a third of the earth will be pounded, scorched and bathed in blood, millions more will die. This calamity cannot extend for long otherwise all the people touched by it would die.

8. A third of the sea will be turned to blood and the ships on it destroyed, millions more will die. This calamity cannot extend for long otherwise all the people touched by it would die.

9. A third of the fresh water on earth will be poisoned; entire populations, crazed by thirst will die. This calamity cannot extend for long otherwise all the people touched by it would die.

These last three events could happen simultaneously. They will not last long otherwise no one would survive (how long can one live without drinking water?).

Note: this chronological progression of the trumpeted events can be logically argued. For example, the stinging locusts happen before the scorching of the earth, the sea of blood and the poisoned springs because no one dies during the 5 months the locusts are active. Also for example, if the event of the first trumpet happened before the fifth's, people caught in the vast areas reduced to mud and bare rocks by the *hail and fire, mixed with blood* would have nothing to survive on and would all die of hunger long before the five months of torments of the fifth trumpet would run out. And so forth... the calendar chronology of the calamities can thus be logically deduced.

The seventh trumpet and the sixth and seventh bowls are not calamities.

There are two important points to be made with the last verses of the above passage: *The rest of the people, who were not killed by these plagues, did not repent of the works of their hands to stop worshiping demons and idols of gold, silver, bronze, stone, and wood, which are not able to see, hear, or walk. And they did not repent of their murders, their sorceries, their sexual immorality, or their thefts.*

The first point is that grace is now over, eternal reprieve can be withdrawn because these people—all Gentiles—will never, ever change. Thus, we will see in 10:6 – 7 that: *There will be no more waiting! In the days when the seventh angel is ready to blow his trumpet. God's secret will be finished. The secret is the Good News God told to His servants the prophets* (NCV).

The second point is that while Jesus reigns for a thousand years with a rod of iron, these Gentiles will not be able to carry out any of their evil deeds. As Jesus rules, there will be no unpunished sinning on this earth. These people will hold their behaviors in check because the price will be too high. They will amass a huge weight of pent up frustration and bitterness for a millennium which explains why they will embrace Satan's return so readily and follow him to their final physical destruction. He will release the flood of their iniquity.

Thoughts to ponder

When Adam and Eve chose their course of action in defiance to God, Eve blamed the deceiving serpent and Adam blamed Eve. Satan's part in inciting them to sin did not constitute a valid excuse; Adam and Eve personally paid the consequences of their choice. The same will be true when God deals with humanity at that time: the people will personally pay the dire consequences of their choices independently from their Deceiver's fate. Each one of us is responsible for our choices; no excuse will ever release us from the penalty of our rebellion.

Those who dismissed God and His warnings during the three and one-half years now pay dearly. They chose to side with Satan; but he is powerless to help them now. The people who had put their trust in him are in absolute despair: they realize that there will be no help forthcoming from the liar whom they have believed and worshipped, yet they will continue their rebellion against God. What a revelation this is: they demonstrate their personal choice...and by doing so, they demonstrate their personal responsibility.

The terrible disasters God metes out after the three and one-half years of Satan's rampage may not last very long, the text of Revelation gives no indication as to the overall duration of this phase. We only know that one event will last 5 months. The events of the first three trumpets that bring this campaign to a close may last only a very short time otherwise no Gentile would survive to enter the 1,000 year reign of Jesus. This is why I take the liberty to time this period as "around six months".

> <u>Note</u>: the number of deaths God will mete out through these trumpets is mind boggling. My imagination cannot grasp the scope or the implications. Yet, there exists today an insidious and well organized worldwide group of people who actively contemplate the elimination of large portions of the current world population. Indeed, the Globalists have calculated "scientifically" that the maximum population the earth can sustain long-term is 500 millions.
>
> In 2013, I watched an interview where a high ranking United Nations executive in Geneva posited the above calculation. The interviewer asked what the

organization would do with the excess 7 billion people already on earth. His response was amazing. Without any qualms he averred that indeed this was the rub. Yet, according to him, they must find ways to kill these excess people. His group has not yet finalized how they will do this; but they are committed to eliminating the excess population. They must! He spoke matter-of-factly and with confidence because he simply mouthed the precepts under which he is employed and the end toward which he works. And since 2013, we have seen some of their plans take effect.

However, through the six trumpets, the reader of Revelation gets a diametrically different and insightful understanding: there will indeed be massive population elimination campaigns, but the evil—satanic—planners above will not be the implementers; they will be the targets, the victims. Many verses of the Old Testament tell us that evil people will be snared by the very trap they set for others; and this certainly is one application.

The God-inflicted cataclysms we have just read about in the text of Revelation will be visited upon the very godless humanity that threatens us today! We can only muse: "Yeah, who knows? May be only 500 million Gentiles wearing the *antichrist*'s mark will be left to live out the 1,000 year reign of Jesus."

In our time, because of its immense political clout and financial power the liberal progressive elite who hatches such plans feels unassailable. But these people can plan all they want; they are dead wrong as to the actual implementation.

Let us develop the thought-flow from these premises. I have noticed that Globalists in their preparation for world control insist on two evil precepts: unrestricted abortions and homosexual unions. It is all about population control.

How effective is abortion for controlling population numbers? Very; here is an example: when six generations of the descendants of only one set of my great-grand-parents met a few years back, those still alive numbered more than 800. Had just these two progenitors been murdered in the womb, more than one thousand people would not have lived...as of today—and the "hole" into future generations widens from there. It is not difficult to picture the gigantic effect on world population that the ongoing killing of millions of unborn human beings creates.

The present humanistic elitists see themselves as the cream of humanity and as such they consider their own offspring to be a valuable addition to humanity...the seed of a better race, as it were... Therefore they do not necessarily favor abortion when it comes to their own children or grand-children; but they heartlessly sponsor it for the hoi polloi. For them, abortion is an effective means to reduce the latter's numbers. Stupidly, the masses who kill their own think they have been given a liberating favor.

The second issue is also obvious: homosexual unions are sterile unions; there is no population growth to be feared from them; so the more of them the better!

In the same way, the elite do not necessarily favor homosexuality for their own lives; they simply see it as a population containment option for the masses. Homosexual marriage is the legal expedient that makes these unions permanent and more difficult to walk away from; that is why this political elite pushed for it. A settled homosexual lifestyle ensures no new population growth from that segment of the population. Homosexual marriage is simply a make-believe way to give permanency to these sinful relationships. In the past, when some individuals practicing homosexuality felt social qualms about their choice and they would opt out. Quite a few redeemed their lives, married and even had children. By legalizing their wrongful choice the elite removed some of the natural and social pressure that have mitigated the vice.

Also, it is harder to leave a legalized relationship than a casual one: there is paperwork involved and a legally contestable division of assets... Plus, now a person leaving such a relationship for a healthy heterosexual lifestyle must endure the opprobrium of the media as traitors to his/her "homosexual genes".

Finally, the political elite neutralized the deep-seated yearning for parenting that had urged many to leave the homosexual lifestyle in the past: homosexual couples can now adopt children and thus remain sterile till the end. This carries an embedded Trojan horse: the children raised in that mindset are not expected to question homosexual lifestyles and could be more prone to choose a homosexual lifestyle as well...and thus, the adopted generation has been neutered too.

This global humanistic leadership thinks that it will be on this earth for ever; so they think long term. Thus, a baby aborted today or two progenitors neutered through homosexuality effectively eliminates thousands of potential humans within just a few generations—which equates to less people to be killed by other means. The victims are their own willing executers.

Another example is revealing its fruit today. China's one child policy in force for decades did two things. It created a mass genocide of the unborn extra children. The parents felt they could choose what sex they wanted to keep for their one child; so culturally, this favored male children being spared. So now, they have a negative population outlook made worse by a systematic deficit of child bearing females. So, all the threads of this satanic policy are coming to roost: the Chinese population is in precipitous decline with no hope of ethnic survival for the Chinese race.

Sadly, the Godly people who oppose this global elite never publish, never expose the actual motives: population elimination. The Godly people endlessly argue the issues, but they never expose the global agenda or the true motive. They never demand that the elite justify their deep agenda. This is where the battle should be waged. The humanistic elite are very skilled at keeping all discussions on the issues while shutting out any discussion on the morality of the motives.

At the issues' level, the masses feel that they are being given something they want: that is the right to do whatever they want with their body—even though deep down most of them know that killing an innocent baby is wrong. In reality, the weak and the scared are duped and they are cheated of something better that was truly theirs ... and the whole human race is impoverished and destabilized. Exposure of its true agenda is the greatest threat to this evil movement. Exposure is always the greatest threat to a lie.

Knowingly in some cases or misguidedly in most others, the Globalists assiduously prepare the way for the one-world-government-with-one-world-religion of the *antichrist*; thus their spiritual master will never let them abandon these two premises that are central to his grand strategy. The coming absolute control apparatus based on evil must be ready to roll at the rapture, so they think; therefore their preparations are underway today, and that's why we face these phenomena. In this too they are misguided: Read *The Rock Breaks the Globalists' Empire*.

However, as long as the true Christians are still on earth and God's Spirit is at large among them, the enemy cannot place the capstone on his edifice: he can only prepare. So it behooves the Christians to push back. We can neither be complacent about—nor complicit to—this massive murderous movement and its social degradation. Let us stop being politically correct pansies and let us stand on what we believe is true and eternal...and let God provide for the world population—all 7 + billion of us.

Christians will not add a single day to the pre-rapture era; but until then they should unblinkingly live their lives as their faith dictates. Christians should throw out of their lives anything that is blatantly against God and accept whatever this may cost them today. The apparatus of the *antichrist* seems to be rolled out in our days; but to us, it is a paper tiger.

True Christians please stand up! It is OK for us to say: No...and to stand resolutely against the pressures of evil.

Among the so-called Christians, there is a nonsensical theological school of thoughts. We are wrong when we believe that Satan and his cohort will build up their resistance to the Godly and will eventually make life almost impossible to live for the Christians thus at that point, Jesus will have no choice but to rapture His followers. This approach is absolute bunk. Satan does not win. He may temporarily gain an edge in a battle here and there; but he never wins a campaign. He is never attributed the victory.

The time preceding the rapture of the saints (beginning with the coming exodus of the Hebrews out of every country, followed by the battle of Gog and Magog, followed by the greatest harvest of souls ever, and culminating with the glorious rapture) is God's blessed time. It is God's march of glory. Satan does not derail it, and he does not impede it, Satan does not detour it; in fact the time remaining between today and the rapture is Satan's worst nightmare.

It is also wrong to think that Satan and the *antichrist* will conquer the population of the world in order to rule it. They will not. Jesus will remove the winning team, and those who were opposed to Him will be left on the field—they are the losing team. Every single one of them is against Jesus. Every single one of them is ready to fall for the liar who will sing their tune. It is God who makes it possible for Satan and the *antichrist* to rule! And the irony is that the two nefarious entities begin with a one hundred percent following, yet they will continue to lose people all through the three and one-half year of their rule. Indeed, every Gentile who demure at the last moment and refuse the mark of the beast and is decapitated for it will be picked up by Jesus! None of these will be lost by Jesus, yet every one of them will be lost by Satan!

<u>(Return to Table of Contents)</u>

****

Chapter 9 - Small Scroll, Daniel 9, Two Witnesses, Seventh Trumpet

Revelation 10:1 – 11:19

The text leaves the trumpets to cover two vignettes: one in heaven, the other in Jerusalem.

10:1 – 11

¹Then I saw another mighty angel coming down from heaven, surrounded by a cloud, with a rainbow over his head. His face was like the sun, his legs were like fiery pillars, ²and he had a little scroll opened in his hand. He put his right foot on the sea, his left on the land, ³and he cried out with a loud voice like a roaring lion. When he cried out, the seven thunders spoke with their voices. ⁴And when the seven thunders spoke, I was about to write. Then I heard a voice from heaven, saying, "Seal up what the seven thunders said, and do not write it down!" ⁵Then the angel that I had seen standing on the sea and on the land raised his right hand to heaven. ⁶He swore an oath by the One who lives forever and ever, who created heaven and what is in it, the earth and what is in it, and the sea and what is in it: "There will no longer be an interval of time (there will be no more waiting, NCV, ERV), ⁷but in the days of the sound of the seventh angel, when he will blow his trumpet, then God's hidden plan will be completed, as He announced to His servants the prophets." ⁸Now the voice that I heard from heaven spoke to me again and said, "Go, take the scroll that lies open in the hand of the angel who is standing on the sea and on the land." ⁹So I went to the angel and asked him to give me the little scroll. He said to me, "Take and eat it; it will be bitter in your stomach, but it will be as sweet as honey in your mouth." ¹⁰Then I took the little scroll from the angel's hand and ate it. It was as sweet

as honey in my mouth, but when I ate it, my stomach became bitter.
¹¹And I was told, "You must prophesy again about many peoples,
nations, languages, and kings."

What's happening

With the arrival of this mighty angel, we return to the end of the
three and one-half years of the *testing time*. The offer of salvation
to mankind is now closed because the last person who chose Jesus
during that period is in heaven. This is the official expiration of
God's pardon, His *hidden plan* (the Good News) *is completed*, verse
10:7. God has been more than fair; He paid the price for our
redemption at Calvary and offered it freely and graciously to all.

After His enduring patience through the church age, God had
explicitly defined salvation and the consequences of not choosing
Jesus to all mankind still living at the onset of the three and
one-half years of testing. He then gave one last opportunity to
everyone to declare his eternal allegiance, a process that took up
these three and one-half years. This is fair and just. At this point, it
is time to apply the consequences.

The *little scroll* of these verses may be a reference to Ezekiel
2:10 – 3:3. If this is the case, it portends terrible pain, suffering and
despair for the people remaining. Which is exactly what is coming
to them.

John is exhorted to tell this truth to many people, nations,
languages and kings. And through his writing of Revelation he has
fulfilled his assignment. Apparently whatever God said through
the seven thunders in 10:3 – 4 was meant for John's personal
understanding and is not necessary for us. God gives graphic
descriptions throughout Revelation of how the events will take
place so that by any means possible He may warn and persuade men
to turn to Jesus and receive His blessings instead of His anger and
curse. This ends the first vignette.

(Return to table of content)

Synchronizing Revelation with Daniel 9 prophecy

Some modern teachers assume seven years for the *time of testing* of Revelation 3:10 (the Great Tribulation, they call it). They usually divide this span into two halves, the first one being rather peaceful and benign while the second is brutal and evil. It seems that they use the message Gabriel gave to Daniel (Daniel 9) to elaborate this theory.

Context here is important: Daniel had only queried God about the Jews, their fate and their future; so the heavenly messenger Gabriel only brought answers that related to the Jews—the first half of the seven year week. Now, studying Revelation, we see that it is Jesus who fills in the details about the last three and one-half year of that 70th week.

Let's take a few paragraphs to harmonize this passage of Revelation with the Jewish prophecies of Daniel. Here, in Revelation, between the 6th and 7th trumpets, the angel declares: *there will no longer be an interval of time, but in the days of the sound of the seventh angel, when he will blow his trumpet, then God's hidden plan will be completed, as He announced to His servants the prophets* (i.e. Daniel).

There will no longer be an interval of time means that the seventy weeks of Daniel are now all accounted for. The 69 weeks are finished and the 70th week is closed. And indeed, the 7th trumpet will declare: *the kingdom of the world has become the kingdom of our Lord and His Messiah and He will reign forever and ever!*

And *God's hidden plan*—the good news—is now accomplished and finished. Access to Heaven is now closed. The page has turned.

What are the seventy weeks of Daniel chapter 9?

Gabriel, the messenger for the Jews uses a count of seventy weeks (or seventy groupings of sevens) to summarize the rest of God's history with <u>His people and their City</u>—not universal humanity. In Daniel 9:24, he lists the key points, each of them will be fulfilled by Jesus:

To bring rebellion to an end, the rebellion Adam and Eve began for us all. The very rebellion Jesus redeemed. Put a check on that one.

To put a stop to sin, the process that doomed all of humanity was overcome by Jesus on the cross. Put a check on that one.

To wipe away iniquity, the consequence of sin is now reversed by Jesus. Put a check on that one.

To bring everlasting righteousness is exactly what Jesus did. Put a check on that one.

To seal up vision and prophecy, Jesus fulfilled and put a cap on the relevant prophecies. Put a check on that one.

And to anoint the most high place: in Jesus, we have access to His presence, to God's intimacy. Jesus lives in the believers. Put a check on that one.

Gabriel's revelation is *for your people*; it is relevant to Daniel's people: <u>the Jewish people</u>. Each of the points in the verse above was fulfilled by Jesus for the Jews first. All these points were fulfilled at the time of Jesus. We must not lose track of this fact.

As he continues his presentation to Daniel, Gabriel uses a specific format: a back-and-forth set of images. He gives a snapshot of the divine and follows it with a corresponding snapshot of the evil. Gabriel uses this style for both the 69weeks and the 70th week; there is continuity in how he presents his message. If Gabriel were recorded today, the writer would use bullet points and possibly a two column table; a format we would readily relate to.

Gabriel groups the first sixty-nine weeks together (7 plus 62) and he ties up that part of the message on the divine side as follows: *Messiah will be cut off and have nothing.* Indeed, right on Gabriel's time line, Jesus died a lonely death and his followers abandoned Him. Then on the evil side Gabriel gives two separate predictions: *the people of the coming prince will destroy the city and sanctuary.* And the second: *The end will come with a flood, and until the end there will be war; desolations are decreed.* The first information obviously refers to Jerusalem and the temple. The second, however, refers to the whole world, to humanity in general. Let's look at it in more details:

Messiah's death brings closure to the sixty-ninth week but it does not end it: *until the end...* tells us that the run-off of these sixty-nine weeks will span out till the end of humanity. Therefore, the 70th week will be laid on top of the continuously on-going 69th week. The 70th will not be tacked on at a chronological end of the 69th. This is because even though sin was effectively dealt with by Jesus' death, evil will be allowed to run on *until the end.* Every person born after Jesus' death begins life under the curse of sin; that type of life continues and will continue. The 69 weeks are a type of life, the 70th is another type of life. This temporal juxtaposition of the two types of lives is not surprising because all of humanity will continue to begin life under the same sinful nature that has been the human condition since the original sin. Viz. consider the parable of the wheat and the tares. We all know that evil has continued. Ergo, the 69th week of Daniel does continue until the end.

History has played out exactly as predicted: *After those [7+ 62] weeks the Messiah will be cut off;* and indeed, at precisely the 483 years mark from the edict to rebuild the <u>City</u> of Jerusalem, Jesus entered Jerusalem to die and to be resurrected. On the godly side, the sixty-nine weeks were rounded up and accounted for as predicted. Jesus did not stop the 69 weeks; He breached them. He inserted the overall demise of that system. Even though, evil will continue on until the end, a permanent breach has been created in its system. Actually, it is more like a splice: the 70th week—the new type of life—is spliced on the 69th. It is a way out of the 69th week's doomed continuum.

As predicted, a few decades after Jesus' atonement, the people of the coming prince, the Roman legions, did come and destroyed the city and sanctuary. Almost 2,000 years ago, history fulfilled Gabriel's words: the city was sacked and the temple destroyed, and the on-going universal continuum (war, desolations) has followed its course ever since—just as predicted.

Having covered the subject of the 69 weeks and followed its course out, Gabriel now lays out the seventieth week. It is a different week, chronologically and qualitatively. The reason it is different is because it is the week of the new covenant, the week of the good news. It is an entity of its own. It ties the old to the new and to the beyond. And within that week (that grouping of seven years), the second half is not for the Jews at all; therefore Gabriel leaves it out. Gabriel only covers the first three and one-half years of those seven years.

The 69 weeks are the weeks of the fallen humanity. The 70th week is the week of redemption, the week that marks the time of the redeemed. The good news about the new life began with Jesus' ministry. Since the cross at Calvary, since the middle of the 70th week—the apex of the week—a person can, at anytime, leap out of the 69 week system he was born into and live in the 70th week dispensation. The criminal on the cross next to Jesus who turned to Him passed from the doomed 69th week to the 70th and died within the new covenant of that week.

Another aspect differentiates the nature of this 70th week: it is not exclusively Jewish. It is the week for the Jews <u>and</u> for the Gentiles: the good news is universal—the firm covenant predicted by Gabriel is with the *many* not just the Jews (Daniel 9:27). Jesus confirms this premise precisely in Mark 14:24. So Jesus increased the covenant to include all humans. He also increased the covenant to include all of history: *for this reason the Good News was preached to those who are now dead. Even though they were judged like all people, the Good News was preached to them so they could live in the Spirit as God lives* (1 Peter 4:6 NCV). The new alliance has increased the covenant in every way. This is what Gabriel lays out for Daniel.

The 70th week has a Jewish component of three and one-half Biblical years and it will have a Gentile component of also three and one-half Biblical years. Gabriel is silent about the second—the non-Jewish component. It is Jesus who will reveal it to us and develop it fully in His revelation to John. The 70th week—the week of the good news—begins when John-the-Baptizer began his work and Jesus launched his ministry. The first three and one-half years were the planting of the good seed and its harvest. The last three and one-half years will be gleaning that follows the actual harvest.

Remarkably from Daniel's text we see that the sixty-ninth week and the seventieth week interconnect—cross if you will—at the most important point of history: Jesus' death! Indeed, we read that Messiah is cut-off (69th week) and at the very same moment Messiah ends the sacrifice and offering (middle of the 70th week: three and one-half years into this "different kind of week"). This amazing juxtaposition of timings is the literal crux of history: Jesus dies for our sins and at the same time God accepts His sacrifice wholly—the curtain that separated the holy of holies from the people is rent (Jesus did indeed *anoint the most high place*, Vs.

24). The perfect sacrifice ends all sacrifices. The way into the very presence of God is now open to all. The splice is now operational.

The temple has two functions: its outer parts were where the priest submitted the sacrifices and the innermost part where the high priest presented the offering to the representation of God (Ark of the Covenant). Jesus accomplished the final and total sacrifice for all humans of all time, and at that very moment, God's representation in the inner-sanctum became obsolete. At the moment of Jesus' sacrifice, God tore down the curtain that made the Holy of Holies separate, indicating that from now on, God (Jesus) would live in the believers. Nobody else did this, nobody else ever had or would have the power to do either. Jesus is the center of Gabriel's message to Daniel.

The sacrificial temple and the First Covenant are closed: *It is finished* (John 19:30). Jesus could thus end the sacrifice and offering because with His death He has spliced in a broader, superior and permanent dimension that escapes the definition of the 69 other type of weeks.

It is God through Jesus who puts an end to the sacrifice; not the enemies of God. In the time between Daniel and Jesus, the enemies of God had interrupted the sacrifices (first the Babylonians, then the Greeks); but these human invaders had not ended the sacrifices. Sacrifices were still needed. Only God who instituted them could end them. *It is finished!*

In antiquity, for the other times, when the human situation reversed, the sacrifices began again. With God's blessing, the temple was dedicated again. However, since Jesus ended the sacrifice and offerings, a sacrificial temple will never again be dedicated with God's blessing.

Plus the temple as the receptacle of God's presence among His people was also made obsolete and void as now God in Jesus dwell directly with and in His people. We are His temple. So the second and most sacred function of the temple in Jerusalem also ended with Jesus.

Daniel's text is beautifully clear and God's timing is perfect: Jesus death and the abolition of the sacrifice and offering fall in the middle of the seventieth week (the middle of the batch of seven years that are represented by that "week"). This tells us that three and one-half years have already elapsed in that seven years period: the duration of Jesus' ministry—the planting. The Jewish half of the seven year period is done. At Pentecost, the harvest began, and the harvest will last until the last person who would embrace Jesus voluntarily in our time has done so. The harvest includes both Jews (Hebrews) and Gentiles. The three and one-half years of the time of testing that follow this harvest exclude the Hebrews; it is Gentile specific. The Hebrews bypass this phase as they are in God's direct care in the desert enclave He will provide for them.

Erroneous readings of Daniel 9 in recent centuries have inserted the *antichrist* as the one making a peace deal with the many—especially with the Jews—and he will allow the rebuilding of the Jewish temple, so they say. Then, according to this scenario, three and one-half years later, the *antichrist* will renege and desecrate the rebuilt temple... It is from this theory that scholars developed the premise for a seven year Great Tribulation. It is to be noticed that the text of Revelation <u>never, ever</u> mentions seven years: it mentions three and one-half years. There are no scriptural supports for a seven year tribulation anywhere in the Bible.

The *antichrist* is not for the Jews; he does not figure in Daniel 9 at all; more on this later. The chronology of Revelation places the Jews and the other ten Hebrew tribes out of the grasp of the *antichrist* prior to the *antichrist* being identified by Satan (Revelation 12:13 – 13:2).

The two equal parts of three and one-half years that make the 70th week of Daniel 9 are already separated by about 2,000 years; they bookend the great age of grace, the harvest so to speak. Jesus refers to the Good News—His expanded covenant—as a seed because its purpose is the harvest of humanity into God's fold. The harvest began at Pentecost and will end at the rapture. The three and one-half years of Satan's rampage on earth will be the time when Jesus picks up the last post-harvest gleanings of the good news—none of them Jewish. No one who would ever choose Jesus will be left out.

In the middle of the 70th week, before returning to heaven Jesus' last command opened up the kingdom to all who would follow Him: *Go, therefore, and make disciples of all nations* (Matthew 28:19). From then on, the Spirit-filled, God-commissioned harvesters have worked at the universal harvest—this harvest has been going on ever since. Jesus refers to the good news as a seed because its single purpose is the harvest. We are in the harvest age, the age of grace.

In short: The second half of this famous seventieth week (three and one-half years) is left out by Gabriel—the messenger to the Jews—because Gabriel was sent specifically to Daniel's people [the Jews] and their City [Jerusalem]. The Good News is what makes this 70th week distinct: it is a new way of life. In the early years, Christianity was called "the way". At the rapture, the main harvest is over; but the Good News is not closed yet. It has three and one-half years to go yet; thus begins the gleaning. And just as it was with any farming operation in biblical times, the harvesters do not participate in the gleanings.

The 69 weeks had a metered component (to mark, to time-stamp precisely the timing of Messiah's death). This was crucial because it pinpoints the identity of Messiah to any Jewish person of that time. And verifies Jesus' identity to us all retrospectively. In addition, the 69 weeks have a permanent qualitative component (that determines life for the fallen humanity until the end): the new life. Since Jesus' death this component has also continued for almost 2,000 years.

In a similar fashion, the 70th week has its own metered component of seven years that are divided into two halves: one Jewish (fulfilled by Jesus) and one Gentile, yet to be fulfilled. And between the two parts of the 70th week we find the qualitative hiatus has run almost 2,000 years.

Nobody foresaw this long interval between the two halves of the 70th week. Actually, by all accounts, it seems that the Jews dismissed the reality of the second half. When Jesus was resurrected, His disciples assumed that now He would begin His 1,000 year reign. But the reality was far more marvelous: the intention of the resurrection was universal—not myopically Hebraic—as the covenant would now be universal. Over-imposed above the on-going 69th, the 70th week will be allowed to "run off the clock".

There are both symmetry and continuity between the two types of weeks. They cross at one precise point in history (the cross) and they finish at the very same time: three and one-half years after the rapture when the angels raises his right hand to heaven swears by the One who lives forever: *There will no longer be an interval of time* (Revelation 10:6). And the heavens mark this ending with a half-hour silence. There will be no more delay!

At the rapture, the godly harvesters had gone home with the Master. However, the covenant of the good news still remained, that is to say: come to Jesus, the Messiah, and receive eternal life. But following the rapture, the covenant's modality is different; this is why this phase begins with three heavenly pronouncements (14:6 – 12). These announcements proclaim how things will be run from then on—for the last three and one-half years of the covenant of redemption.

These heavenly announcers—that everyone on earth will hear and understand—will stipulate how things will be and what is at stake. The first (14:6 – 7) will confirm the good news: choose Jesus for eternity (there is no other way). The second (14:8) will announce the end of God's benevolent generosity that has sustained mankind so far (no new food production plus the world system collapses instantly). The third (14:9 – 12) exposes clearly what choosing the *antichrist* and his mark will mean (eternity in permanent misery).

With these announcements, the second half of the 70th week will begin. The course has been set; Satan is allowed to rampage for the next three and one-half years. The tares on the harvest field are now left to be baled up for burning by the evil workers: they are marking up the weeds to be burned. And Jacob's descendants have no part in this process.

For that time of testing, there are no God-commissioned, harvesters left, no missionaries because the good news has been given to everyone on earth by the first angel so every living being can make his/her informed choice. Grim reapers will demand the immediate answer. They identify those who will get the mark of the *antichrist* and they indelibly stamp them for Hell. In the process they trample (behead) the few kernels of the good seed that are identified on the field.

These are the few who, after the rapture, will demure from getting the mark and embrace Jesus when the knife is on their throat. Through this process the gleaning of the Good News is accomplished and these decapitated souls are welcomed in heaven by Jesus; they will be with Him forever. In our age of grace, we can choose to <u>live</u> this life in Jesus, during the time of testing, the gleanings will choose to <u>die</u> in Jesus.

Here, in Revelation 10:7 we have reached the end of the second three and one-half year period: we have reached the end of the seventieth week of Daniel (the portion Gabriel left out). The covenant, the good news is now closed, finished. And this is what the heavenly announcer broadcasts now (10:6 – 7).

So, what is left at this point? After a short time of divine reprisals against the bearers of the mark of the beast, the thousand-year righteous reign of Jesus will begin. From the moment this reign begins, no one will be allowed to carry out any sin.

Gabriel had finished his prophecy to Daniel with: *the abomination of desolation has been on a wing of the temple…and will continue to be until the decreed destruction is poured out on the desolator*. In *The Great Harvest of the Post-Allah World* I logically develop the argument that the Colosseum in Rome fulfills this prophecy precisely. I will not, therefore, develop the theme here because the text of Revelation at this point concerns only the end of the Good News.

> <u>Note</u>: There is tragic component to Gabriel's message to Daniel. Indeed, with it God pinpointed Messiah's death to the day. The Jewish leaders, the Pharisees, priests and teachers of the law knew Gabriel's message to Daniel. They intended to murder the man in front of them who said he was Messiah and had exhibited all the divine and messianic attributes predicted by the prophets <u>on the very date Gabriel predicted the death of Messiah</u>! Their hatred for God and for the truth was so strong that they persisted in carrying out His death. You would think that one of them would have suggested that they'd wait a week or a month... Just to see. Gabriel's message pre-condemned them, their actions confirmed their disposition.

Thoughts to ponder

At His resurrection, Jesus became the *firstfruits* (1 Cor. 15:23), the first of the great harvest of the humanity who would choose Him. (Our time is the time of the harvest; we call it the age of grace or the Church Age: but it is God's harvest.) This phase of the harvest will climax with the *en masse* turning of Jacob's people to Jesus and through Him to YHWH around the second exodus and the war of *Gog and Magog*. Then, a few years later, the rapture will follow. The last interim years will also be the years of the greatest harvest of the good news among the Gentile population.

As I write this and as you read these lines we are very close to *Gog and Magog*. Here is a harbinger: a curious phenomenon began very recently that should get our attention: for the first time in over 19 centuries, a significantly large number of Jewish Rabbis, studying their scriptures, are finding Jesus as Messiah and they embrace Him as such. They leave their Pharisaic/Talmudic rejection of Jesus and embrace Him. As far as I can tell: such an awakening of Jewish Rabbis was never in evidence in any previous period of history. I believe this to be intrinsic to the approach of the times of the end: God is preparing His team of 144,000 preachers (12,000 per tribe) who, for seven years after their divine return to Israel and Gog and Magog, will teach their Hebrew brothers and sisters in Israel all about Jesus, the Messiah they have accepted for their return to the land of Israel, but don't yet know. They will teach the descendants of Jacob to obey everything Jesus commanded (Matthew 28). They are the knowledgeable teachers who will bring out the good of the old and the good of the new.

(Return to Table of Contents)

11:1 – 13

¹ Then I was given a measuring reed like a rod, with these words: "Go and measure God's sanctuary and the altar, and count those who worship there. [2]But exclude the courtyard outside the sanctuary. Don't measure it, because it is given to the nations, and they will trample the holy city for 42 months. [3]I will empower my two witnesses, and they will prophesy for 1,260 days, dressed in sackcloth." [4]These are the two olive trees and the two lampstands that stand before the Lord of the earth. [5]If anyone wants to harm them, fire comes from their mouths and consumes their enemies; if anyone wants to harm them, he must be killed in this way. [6]These men have the power to close up the sky so that it does not rain during the days of their prophecy. They also have power over the waters to turn them into blood and to strike the earth with every plague whenever they want. [7]When they finish their testimony, the beast, that comes up out of the abyss will make war with them, conquer them, and kill them. [8]Their dead bodies, will lie in the public square of the great city, which prophetically is called Sodom and Egypt, where also their Lord was crucified. [9]And representatives from the peoples, tribes, languages, and nations will view their bodies for three and a half days and not permit their bodies to be put into a tomb. [10]Those who live on the earth will gloat over them and celebrate and send gifts to one another because these two prophets brought judgment to those who live on the earth. [11]But after 3 1/2 days, the breath of life from God entered them, and they stood on their feet. So great fear fell on those who saw them. [12]Then they heard a loud voice from heaven saying to them, "Come up here." They went up to heaven in a cloud, while their enemies watched them. [13]At that moment a violent earthquake took place, a tenth of the city fell, and 7,000 people were killed in the earthquake. The survivors were terrified and gave glory to the God of heaven.

What's happening

With this snapshot, we go back right to the time of the rapture of the saints and before Satan begins his rampage, <u>before</u> he identifies the *antichrist*. God does a complete census of the Hebrew people in order to set them safely aside and protect them during the time of testing and the divine calamities because their destiny is live as normal human beings for Jesus' thousand-year reign.

The temple is figurative:

- As he received this order, John is very aware that the temple did not exist anymore. It had already been completely torn down by the Romans more than twenty years prior, never to be rebuilt.

- John is very aware that Jesus is the temple: John 2:21.

- John is very aware that the followers of Jesus will worship in spirit, not at the temple (John 4:23).

John understands that the vision is about the descendants of Jacob who follow Jesus as Messiah.

The reference to Sodom and to Egypt makes sense (verse 8). Both are historical events when God extracted His people and took care of them while He destroyed or disabled the rest of the population. This will be the same process. The angels took the hands of Lot, his wife and daughters and ushered them out of the area. God went before and after the Hebrews as He led them out of Egypt, leaving no one behind, then He took care of all their needs through the years in the desert. Here, we will see that it is God who lifts His people out of Israel and take them to a safe haven where He will shield them from all the actions of Satan and the antichrist as well as from the divine plagues He will punish the Gentile humanity with. He will take care of all their needs throughout that those times (verse 12:6).

And as it has been the case at anytime in history: some Gentiles continue to live in Jerusalem and Israel.

Through the processes of the second exodus and in the aftermath of *Gog and Magog,* every Hebrew will have come to Jesus the Messiah and from that point on they will have full direct access to God—as every believer since Pentecost has had. They are in harmony with God and in His presence and they truly worship Him. God will maintain this privilege through the years of Satan's rampage. God will lift the Hebrews away from the *hour of testing* and the calamities to come. He will deliver them to a safe haven in the desert.

This makes logical sense: having come to Jesus, why should they be *tested* now for something they have already passed? Why should they be made to choose their death when they have chosen the new life? The events we popularly call the Great Tribulation will only target the Gentiles who did not chose Jesus during the 7+ years after the war of *Gog and Magog.*

Again, the reference to the temple is symbolic: it refers to the legitimate descendants of Jacob. It does not mean that a temple will have been rebuilt and that temple rituals will have restarted. It simply refers to the Hebrews, who were the only people would could enter the specifically listed areas of the temple in antiquity. It is a nice clear way to identify who the angel refers to.

In 11:2 we are told that the Gentiles will *trample on the holy city for 42 months* (three and one-half years). They can do this without effecting duress on the descendants of Jacob because the latter will have been removed to a safe haven. There is a non-Hebraic population already in Israel today and it is conceivable that even after *Gog and Magog* a non-Hebraic population will remain. The

Gentile population will be the only population living in Israel and Jerusalem during the three and one half years of the time of testing.

In 11:7, the *beast that comes from the bottomless pit* is different from the "*star*" (God's angel) who has the key to the bottomless abyss (9:1). The *beast that comes from the abyss*, here, is not the *antichrist* either, because the *antichrist* comes from the sea of humanity (13:1). This second *beast* is the *false prophet* who comes from the earth (13:11); he is the collective body of Satan's fallen angels—the demons. It is under this *false prophet*'s manipulations and urging that people will eventually kill the two witnesses of God in Jerusalem. We will see that the earth had swallowed this army of Satan (demons) when Satan hurled them against Jacob's people in their safe enclave. These demons are now coming out of the earth that had swallowed them.

God will establish His two human righteous witnesses in Jerusalem; they will tell the truth. They will broadcast the doom that awaits anyone who will worship the *antichrist* and accept his mark. Of course, this will infuriate the *antichrist*. He does not want anyone to present the truth about his aims. The two witnesses of God will encourage the people to resist the *antichrist* and to place their trust in Jesus—all the way. They will echo the message of the angels in chapter 14.

The credibility of these two human witnesses will be boosted by the awesome powers that they will display against those who oppose them. These two witnesses will be effective encouragers for those who will consider turning down the mark of the beast and instead opt to believe in Jesus and choose to die in Him. These two witnesses will stand out against the bleak backdrop of life revealed by the seals: no interpersonal peace at all, not enough food, plagues, murdering wild beasts... It is very caring of God to provide these two witnesses—shining lights—to boost the morale and determination of the post-rapture saints and to assist them in the very short time between their decision to refuse the *antichrist's* mark and their beheading.

> <u>Note</u>: Again, these verses must have made no sense in past centuries, but now with our technology, the witnesses' words and pictures can be seen anywhere in the world, in real time. We can see in a practical way that these events in these pages could take place in our present time.

God's two witnesses will prophesy for 1260 days, which is basically 42 Biblical months. They will prophesy through the entire process of identifying every post-rapture saint and provide encouragement to them through their martyrdom. While these two witnesses will have awesome powers, we will see later that the *false prophet* (demons) will also have mind-defying powers. (Which they already have and have amply demonstrated throughout history.) This situation reminds us of when Moses did miracles to impress Pharaoh while Pharaoh's magicians produced similar phenomena.

Then, once their task is completed, the *false prophet* will war against the two witnesses of God and will have them killed. God will allow this to happen because the witnesses are done. But they will be dramatically resurrected and visibly lifted to heaven. The entire world population will watch these events, live, as they happen.

To a man, the entire Gentile population remaining will rejoice when the two witnesses are killed, because among them no one remaining has chosen to die in Jesus; they are all against these two witnesses and against God. The all have the mark of their doom.

The bodies of the two witnesses will be left exposed so that the inhabitants of the earth can gawk, jeer and celebrate their death. People will even exchange gifts to celebrate the occasion of their perceived victory over these pesky enemies. However, the universal celebration will turn to raw fear three and one-half days later when God resurrects the two witnesses (11:11).

The power of God will be acknowledged and for those still on the earth, a terrible, nightmarish era will begin. A great earthquake will leave 7,000 people dead and will destroy one-tenth of Jerusalem. Remember: only Gentiles will live there at that time. Some people give glory to God (some translations only say: *pay homage to YHWH*, which is not worship; only acknowledgment of God's power.) They have indelibly marked themselves as Satan's; their worship at that point cannot be voluntary.

> <u>Note</u>: When the age of salvation began at Jesus' death, the earth shook and dead people came back to life in Jerusalem. When salvation came, it brought new life (Matthew 27:51 – 53). When the age of salvation closes, the earth will also shake and seven thousand people will die in Jerusalem. When salvation leaves, it reveals death!

God is fair and Satan always loses

The antichrist and his ten vassals supported by their armies and by millions and millions of demons will rule viciously, insanely (insanely because they do not have wisdom). They will strive for absolute power over every life and every aspect of every life. It will seem to all that there is no other power on earth, and will never be other powers.

...Yet, this is God's earth! Every living Gentile—including the antichrist—will be painfully reminded that there is an immeasurably greater power. Everyone will see these two witnesses in Jerusalem impose duress at will anywhere at anytime, by-passing and ignoring the powers of Satan and his antichrist. And everyone will feel the effects of these witnesses actions. Everyone will personally suffer great thirst when these two withhold the rain. They will be personally sickened by the stench of rotting blood each time these two turn bodies of water into blood. Everyone will intimately suffer all kinds of distasteful and painful ailments every time these two plague them. And they will see time and time again that the soldiers and agents sent to kill these lowly witnesses are incinerated by the fire that comes out of the witnesses' mouths. Satanic and human powers are no match.

These two witnesses, who don't have an army, are untouchable. They are living proofs that God is far, far greater than the devil and his cohorts.

God is so good and God is so fair; He provides all information needed to make the right decision of dying in Jesus or dying eternally by submitting to the antichrist and his mark. In chapter 14, the first angel tells all that Jesus is the only hope. Then another angel lay out for them what eternity will be like for the damned. And day by day, God provides guidance and discipline through His two witnesses. Yes, every Gentile will face his/her choice personally and alone; but God gives them all the tools to make the right choice. God is fair.

Finally, when the last Gentile who will refuse the mark has done so and is beheaded, and everybody else is marked, the witnesses' job is done. God will allow them to be killed. People will rejoice, but their victory is pyrrhic. The death of the two godly men is no victory at all for Satan and his system. Satan never wins. God will revive and gloriously scoop up his two faithful servants. And with that, the Gentile humanity who momentarily rejoiced and their masters will enter the worst period of all history. Shortly after, the demons and the antichrist will be sent to Hell and Satan will be tied up and thrown into the Abyss. Then, on the human side, the Gentiles will face the punishing divine calamities such as the world has never known. Satan and his followers always lose.

11:14

14 The second woe has passed. Take note: The third woe is coming quickly!

With this verse we go back to the trumpets. In Chapter 10, we had left the narrative of the trumpets after the second woe: God's heavenly army of 200 million mounted troops.

(Return to Table of Contents)

The seventh trumpet will be the terrible and irrevocable judgment of God, the third woe.

11:15 – 19

15 The seventh angel blew his trumpet, and there were loud voices in heaven saying: The kingdom of the world has become the kingdom of our Lord and of His Messiah, and He will reign forever and ever! 16 The 24 elders, who were seated before God on their thrones, fell facedown and worshiped God, 17 saying: We thank You, Lord God, the Almighty, who is and who was, because You have taken Your great power and have begun to reign. 18 The nations were angry, but Your wrath has come. The time has come for the dead to be judged and to give the reward to Your servants the prophets, to the saints, and to those who fear Your name, both small and great, and the time has come to destroy those who destroy the earth. 19 God's sanctuary in heaven was opened, and the ark of His covenant appeared in His sanctuary. There were flashes of lightning, rumblings of thunder, an earthquake, and severe hail.

What's happening

This seventh trumpet gives a digest of this section of events from God's point of view—a heavenly perspective. From the beginning of the events heralded by the trumpets, Satan, his *antichrist* and his *false prophet* are immaterial to what is happening on earth: they had been shunted (two were in Hell and one was in the abyss). The final battle of all times: *Armageddon*, has played out, Satan is now in Hell. The nations will never be angry again, ever. Instead, the rebellious dead will be judged and sentenced. *The time has come to destroy those who destroy the earth*!

Now that the remainder of the Hebrew people have been harvested and given their eternal bodies, the people who chose evil all the way will receive their fateful reward.

The opening is an overview: *The kingdom of the world has become the kingdom of our Lord and of His Messiah, and He will reign forever and ever*. There is no more rebellion, whether angelic or human: *The nations were angry, but Your wrath has come*. It is done!

You have taken Your great power and have begun to reign.

Now, at the end of the 1,000 year reign, the last of the righteous Hebrews have received their eternal bodies and have been welcome in heaven, so *The time has come for the* [righteous] *dead to be judged and to give the reward to Your servants the prophets, to the saints and to those who fear Your name, both small and great*. This is the "bema" seat, the podium where crowns will be awarded to the faithful of all times. This is the medal ceremony of all times. It is not the meting out of divine punishment.

What a contrast with what is going to happen to the rebellious of all times: *and the time has come to destroy the one who destroy the earth*. The doomed humanity will also receive their perfect eternal bodies in order to be sentenced to Hell at the White Throne of judgment. What a stark difference is expressed here in just one sentence.

Note: *destroy those who destroy the earth*. Pollution is a by-product of corruption; it is the fruit of Satan's activity on earth as Isaiah 24:5 tells us: *The earth is polluted by its inhabitants, for they have transgressed teachings, overstepped decrees, and broken the everlasting covenant.* Pollution is the direct result of man's rebellion. Therefore, man cannot fix pollution without first fixing his rebellion. All the progressives' agendas to end pollution and save the planet are utopias.

Everyone in heaven celebrates the fact that now God/Jesus rules. All unpleasantness has disappeared forever for those who are with God.

<u>(Return to Table of Contents)</u>

****

Chapter 10 - Messianic History of the Hebrews, Dragon

Revelation 12:1 – 17

A parenthesis to describe God's care of the Hebrews

12:1 – 17

¹A great sign appeared in heaven: a woman clothed with the sun, with the moon under her feet and a crown of 12 stars on her head. ²She was pregnant and cried out in labor and agony as she was about to give birth. ³Then another sign appeared in heaven: There was a great fiery red dragon having seven heads and 10 horns, and on his heads were seven diadems. ⁴His tail swept away a third of the stars in heaven and hurled them to the earth. And the dragon stood in front of the woman who was about to give birth, so that when she did give birth he might devour her child. ⁵But she gave birth to a Son—a male who is going to shepherd all nations with an iron scepter—and her child was caught up to God and to His throne. ⁶The woman fled into the wilderness, where she had a place prepared by God, to be fed there for 1,260 days. ⁷Then war broke out in heaven: Michael and his angels fought against the dragon. The dragon and his angels also fought, ⁸but he could not prevail, and there was no place for them in heaven any longer. ⁹So the great dragon was thrown out—the ancient serpent, who is called the Devil and Satan, the one who deceives the whole world. He was thrown to earth, and his angels with him. ¹⁰Then I heard a loud voice in heaven say: The salvation and the power and the kingdom of our God and the authority of His Messiah have now come, because the accuser of our brothers has been

thrown out: the one who accuses them before our God day and night.
[11]They conquered him by the blood of the Lamb and by the word of their testimony, for they did not love their lives in the face of death.
[12]Therefore rejoice, you heavens, and you who dwell in them! Woe to the earth and the sea, for the Devil has come down to you with great fury, because he knows he has a short time. [13]When the dragon saw that he had been thrown to earth, he persecuted the woman who gave birth to the male child. [14]The woman was given two wings of a great eagle, so that she could fly from the serpent's presence to her place in the wilderness, where she was fed for a time, times, and half a time. [15]From his mouth the serpent spewed water like a river flowing after the woman, to sweep her away in a torrent. [16]But the earth helped the woman. The earth opened its mouth and swallowed up the river that the dragon had spewed from his mouth. [17]So the dragon was furious with the woman and left to wage war against the rest of her offspring—those who keep God's commands and have the testimony about Jesus.

What's happening

We now go back to the Old Testament, to the very beginning, and we see a fast recap of what has happened. When man surrendered to Satan and rebelled, God told the woman (Eve) that she would give birth to the One who will crush Satan. When man passed on his authority to Satan, the latter pulled all the rebellious angels (demons) down with him to plague the earth and earthlings. We also find God electing Israel as His people. We find the traditional Israel (the woman) and its twelve patriarchs (the heads of the 12 tribes) expressed in these verses.

Satan's cohorts of demons have been active on earth ever since the fall of man. They gained Adam's authority through his original sin. God had given Adam great authorities on earth (see Genesis 1:28 and Psalm 8:4 – 8) and situated him just a little lower than the angels. When Adam, by his sin of willfully attempt to attain the knowledge by which he would dethrone God, placed himself under the controlling influence of Satan; his God-given authority went with him and Satan and his angels have abused it ever since.

> <u>Note</u>: In contrast to the demons, God has used His faithful angels (messengers/agents) punctually throughout history—I find no reference that indicates that God's faithful angels roam the earth on their own volition as the fallen angels do. The righteous angels had not been swept down to earth by Satan's tail (12:4); they remain God specific emissaries to humans.

The text figuratively explains the arrival of Jesus the Messiah, Israel was pregnant with the savior of the world for a long time. Indeed, God had foretold to Abraham that the Messiah would come from his lineage.

<u>(Return to Table of Contents)</u>

Satan, the *great dragon*, hovers around to try to kill the newborn Messiah. He killed all the young boys in the vicinity of Bethlehem to try to eliminate Jesus; but of course this was futile: he could not thwart God's plan. The woman (Israel) gave birth to the Messiah who accomplished His work and will rule the world with a rod of iron. The latter aspect will be fulfilled during the 1,000 year reign. And the woman's child (Jesus) was taken to YHWH and to His throne in heaven: Jesus ascended to heaven forty days after His resurrection.

God's messengers led by Michael (the specific messenger appointed for the Hebrews) successfully fight Satan and his cohort and throw them down to earth. This takes place around the same time Jesus raptures His Gentile believers and the 144,000 Hebrews.

As the true believers rise and leave the earth; the now outcast devil and his cohorts are hurled down to it.

<u>Note</u>: How much choice does the devil have? How much control does he actually have? According to these verses: None! He is unceremoniously beaten out and swept off—with his entire cohort. God does not even get involved in the cleansing of heaven—the good angels clear out of the rebellious angelic host. (While Jesus tends to His own: He personally welcomes the true believers out of the earth.) The devil cannot even enforce how long he will roam the earth to carry out his nefarious damning of the tares: his deadline is imposed on him and he cannot even appeal! God gives him three and one-half years; and that's it. The devil is impotent and that makes him mad. And if God did not remove His own true, Spirit-indwelled believers from the earth; the devil would not be able to carry out his plans at all!

The devil has never been God...and he never will. He is only a make believe actor. He is the original transvestite: he cloaks himself artificially to appear one way or another, a sham entity who appeals to those who reject the true God—those who reject the implications of an Almighty, all-knowing and sovereign creator God.

As a creature, the devil only has the limited powers given to his kind. He never had more and he will never succeed in wrestling more out of God's hand. And in these verses, God has just curtailed the devil and the demons' reach: they are now exclusively earthbound...and God has assigned them a non-negotiable expiration date.

Now, let's look at the scheduled progression of events, because once we understand the schedule, we avoid all the wrong theological presuppositions about Israel in the Great Tribulation. *The woman fled into the wilderness, where she had a place prepared by God, to be fed there for 1,260 days. Then war broke out in heaven* (12:6 – 7)... *The woman was given two wings of a great eagle, so that she could fly from the serpent's presence to her place in the wilderness, where she was fed for a time, times and half a* time (12:14). Now we see the purpose of 11:1, the "measured" (identified) Hebrews are brought out of harm's way <u>before</u> Satan and the demons are thrown down to earth. When the war of angels began in the heavens, the Hebrews are moved out of reach, to their place of safety.

This puts the Hebrews out of harms way when Satan's evil hordes go after the *woman* (Israel). Ergo from the text: the war in heaven and safe transfer of the Hebrews happen before Satan identifies the *antichrist*. Before any of the unpleasantness of the "tribulations" begins, the Hebrews will be lovingly tended to by God in their impenetrable desert haven. The *antichrist* and the great tribulations have nothing to do with the Hebrews.

<u>Note</u>: the event of 12:3 is separate and is distinct from the event of 12:9. The event of 12:3 refers to what happened at the beginning of time in Genesis as a consequence of man's sin: Satan was given access to mankind and creation so he pulled down his cohort of rebellious angels with him to harass the earth alongside him. At that time, he rebellious angels (demons) were not thrown down by the righteous angels. However, as we can read in Job, these rebellious beings still have access to God in heaven while they nefariously roam the earth. This is still our conditions today. But it will end

dramatically at the time of 12:9. The rebellious angels will lose their vertical reach.

Now to 12:9: The timing of the event is totally different: it happens at or around the rapture, before the three and one-half years of testing begin. The righteous angels will at that time throw the demons out of heaven permanently. These rebellious angels (including Satan) are thrown down to earth. They permanently lose their access to God and to the heavenly realm. They cannot accuse the redeemed anymore: their access to the throne is cut off. Their power from now on is earthbound, their activities horizontal. They cannot interfere with God's angels and their given messages like they had done in Daniel's time—and by extension at all times till then. This is why, from that point on, any righteous angel's message will be heard clearly by everyone on earth. Satan and the demons have lost the power to interfere vertically.

> <u>Note</u>: The entire passage here that describes the tossing of Satan and the demons out of heaven as well as the scooping up and safe transfer of the Hebrews to their desert haven, is devoid of human factors and of human actions or solutions. The entire set of actions is divinely—and angelically—carried out and the fight is done by other forces than humans. Therefore, the "two wings" provided to fly the Hebrews away are not manmade airplanes or contraptions.

Then I heard a loud voice in heaven say: The salvation and the power and the kingdom of our God and <u>the authority of His Messiah have now come</u>. The first seal (the white horse and the horseman) reflects this verse.

So the dragon was furious with the woman and left to wage war against the rest of her offspring—those who keep God's commands and have the testimony about Jesus. An argument can be made here that, failing against the woman, the dragon will now turn against the Christians—but will find them raptured thus the dragon's intent become moot. On the other hand a point can be made that those who keep God's commands and have the testimony about Jesus are the people who belatedly heed the teaching of the angels and choose to die in Jesus during the three and one-half years of testing (tribulations). The distinction here is not of vital importance as it does not affect the process nor the outcome.

A recap of the passage's timeline

Before leaving the subject, it is worth laying down the timeline again because this timeline precludes the heretical teaching that the Great Tribulation is meant for the Hebrews:

1. Jesus, the promised child, was caught up to God and to His throne forty days after his resurrection (verse 12:5b). From this image, the narrative skips some 2,000 years.

2. The first event: The woman—Jacob's descendants—*fled into the wilderness where she had a place prepared by God, to be fed there for 1,260 days.* This is the first chronological event of the end-time. From the text, it seems that this divine dispensation either precedes the rapture or happens simultaneously with it.

3. The second event, time-wise: God's faithful angels throw Satan and the demons out of heaven. God's heavenly crew clears up heaven in time for the arrival of the raptured saints of all ages. Satan will never again accuse them. The saved of all times and Satan and the demons will never share the same venue, the same space again.

4. The third event: the newly banished and destitute evil host (Satan and the demons) will attempt to attack

Jacob's descendants in their protected haven.

5. This is a re-statement of the second event as God stresses the point: God anticipated the evil move (12:6 and again 12:14) and thus He had securely moved the Israelis to that safe haven in the desert where He will feed them and provide their needs. The evil attempt against the Hebrews is described in no uncertain terms: Satan unleashes the demons against the descendants of Jacob.

6. The evil party does not succeed! God's earth swallows Satan's cohort. Only Satan remains on the surface at that time. Shortly later (13:11), the demons will emerge back out of the earth that had swallowed them as the *false prophet* to resume what they have always done: Mislead people with falsehoods.

And all these sequences <u>precede</u> the apparition and presence of the *antichrist*. Satan turns to the rest of humanity to locate his evil servant (antichrist) <u>after</u> having tried to strike at the descendants of Jacob.

I find no possible support for the popular theory preached today that proposes that the *antichrist* will appear first, making an alliance of peace with the Israelis and with the world. The theory proposes also that the *antichrist* will facilitate the construction of a sacrificial temple in Jerusalem and will allow it to function. Then three and one-half years later, he will supposedly desecrate the temple, install himself as god and turn against the Jews. There is just no way to construct such a theology from the text of Revelation; yet, unfortunately this ideology has become prevalent. It provides believers with wrong expectations. Parsing the word of God correctly on this subject is crucial in our time as we may presently live our part of these events.

The Old Testament passage that speaks directly of the antichrist is Daniel 8:23 – 25 and there is no hint of a peace deal or a temple. The New Testament passage that describes the antichrist, his character and *modus operandi* is Revelation 13:1 – 11 and 13:18; and there is no indication of a peace deal or of an accommodation to build a temple. By the time the antichrist shows up, there is no need for either artifice. <u>Daniel 9:24 – 27 has nothing to do with end-time events</u>.

<u>Note</u>: Twice God tells us that He will feed His ancient people for the entire $3^{1/2}$ years (verses 6 and 14). This is important in the general context of the period because, during that same time span God withholds the production of food everywhere for all Gentiles (3rd seal)—yet, God will feeds His ancient people. Since the time of creation, food has always been the ultimate control. God never relinquished His control over food. At the onset of time, He made food abundant and deliciously enjoyable for Adam and Eve, then, He made food difficult and laborious to produce for the fallen Adam (and for everyone since). Throughout history, famine struck when and where God withheld His generous provision...and times of plenty blessed the populations when God was pleased. We can take the thought even further: it was food that got us in trouble through Adam (Genesis 3) and it is food that restores us (Mark 14:22). And here, for the three and one-half years of testing we find the same principle: the entire Gentile population will have to make do with the unsatisfactory, limited allotments of what was left of earlier harvests...while the Israelis will be abundantly and deliciously fed by God.

After the three and one-half years, Satan is overwhelmed, bound up and sequestrated in the abyss. His human apparatus—political and religious—will crumble instantly as its diabolical leaders—the *antichrist* and the demons— are thrown into the *lake of fire* (Hell). God's calamities that follow this will also by-pass the Hebrews in their protected enclave without hurting them.

To resume: Concurrently to the rapture of the believers, the fallen angels will lose their access to heaven forever. Satan will have a limited time then to wreak havoc on earth: three and one-half years. Being thrown out of heaven brings a big shift in Satan and his demons' span of activities; they have no more over-worldly reach—they are limited to the earth. For example, when God's angels broadcast the Good News and the warnings from heaven, Satan from the earth is powerless to oppose them or to prevent anyone from hearing the messages (unlike what happened in Daniel 10:12 – 13).

All the people who had believed in Jesus and chosen to follow Him are told to rejoice in Heaven. For them this is the permanent fulfillment of the sum of all their hopes (Revelation 12:11 – 12).

... But it will be terrible for the earth and the sea, because the devil has come down to you! (NCV) Satan has one goal now: to vent his evil on earth. He is filled with anger because he knows he only has three and one-half years of action remaining. The first thing Satan will do is to strike at God's people: he will seek to destroy the Hebrews in their safe enclave. *From his mouth the serpent spewed water like a river flowing after the woman, to sweep her away in a torrent.* The river that comes out of the dragon's mouth is not a natural river of water; it is the rush of evil angels: the huge number of demons. They proceed at the urging of Satan (out of his mouth). So much for the erroneous theory that the *antichrist* will make a peace deal with the Hebrews!

The use of similar floods of water analogies to express a military force that overwhelms people and nations is not new in the Bible. It has been used to describe exactly the same type of processes for example: Isaiah 8:7 *so I the Lord, will bring the king of Assyria and all his power against them, like a powerful flood of water from the Euphrates River. The Assyrians will be like water rising over the banks of the river, flowing over the land. The water will flow into Judah and pass through it to Judah's throat...* (NCV) We know this is an analogy because if the actual Euphrates jumped its banks its waters could not flow to Judah—geographically or topographically. Other examples are Isaiah 28:2 *look, the Lord has someone who is strong and powerful... like sudden flood of water pouring over the country, He will throw Samaria down on the ground* (NCV) or Isaiah 59:18 – 19 *[the LORD] will punish the people in faraway places as they deserve like a fast-flowing river, driven by the breath of the LORD* (NCV). And, Jeremiah 47:2 – 3 *A flood is coming from the north to overflow the land... Hear the clatter of hooves and the rumble of wheels as the chariots rush by* (NLT).

This river in Revelation 12:15 – 16 is the army made up of Satan's fallen angels (At this stage, Satan does not have a human army yet because he does not have his human leader). These fallen angels have just been booted out of Heaven and thrown down to earth. They are just as mad as Satan. Driven by his shouts they rush like a torrent to harm God's elects. The earth swallows them and we will see later that it is indeed from the earth that they will re-emerge to fulfill their mission as the *false prophet* (13:11).

Note: It is God's action that makes His earth swallow Satan's army of demons. Under the earth is not a comfortable place for them. Indeed, in Matthew 8:28 – 34, the demons begged Jesus not to send them down to the abyss and later a chained up Satan will be thrown into the abyss to his total discomfort. God owns and rules the earth including its abyss, the abyss is where the demons suffer; not where they rule.

Also, this is not an army of humans; because there are no indication or support for a huge human army to be swallowed up. The only two human armies dealt by Jesus will be at the battle with no name at the end of the three and one-half years of testing and a thousand years later at Armageddon: both times Jesus Himself spectacularly crushes them. The depths of the earth is not Satan's realm; it belongs to God.

The descendants of Jacob are the only group still on earth who will not be affected by the doings of Satan. They will also remain safe through the divine calamities that follow the three and one-half years. These Hebrews must remain on earth because God promised them an earthly reign with their Messiah (the 1,000 years reign) during which time all the other nations will pay homage to them.

Again: it is interesting that Satan should go against Israel before he enrolls his human helper, the *antichrist*. The *antichrist* is an apparatus for the Gentiles, not for the Hebrews: all the descendants of Jacob have already turned to Jesus and God. Anyone who belongs to Jesus has no contact with and nothing to fear from the *antichrist*.

The antichrist is not Jewish, he is not a descendant of Jacob. Every Hebrew who rejects Jesus at the divine culling that precedes Exodus 2.0 is killed by Jesus. Every Hebrew left alive in the whole world will be taken to Israel by Jesus—none will be left behind. So, every Hebrew alive is a follower of Messiah Jesus! There is no possibility that the antichrist could be of Hebrew descent—none.

There will be no Hebrew left abroad within the Gentile populations of the world.

Completely angered for being thwarted in his attempt against the Hebrews, Satan will now turn his anger to "her other children". These are the non-Jews who will turn down the mark of the beast and abandon their lives in the Messiah's hand—the post-rapture saints. All Gentiles who will decide to believe Jesus and die in Him are the *other children* of Israel; her spiritual legacy.

In 12:17 we find the individuals who will choose to accept Jesus' Good News, those that Satan will order killed. The issue is expanded again in 13:7.

Observation

Is this what Jesus was talking about in Matthew 24:15 – 21? No, for the following reasons: Revelation Chapter 12:7 – 18 refers to the precise moment when Satan and his fallen angels are thrown down from heaven, before the great duress of the *time of testing* begins. The Hebrews will be given *two wings of an eagle so she* (the Hebrew population) *could fly from the serpent's presence to her place in the wilderness* (12:14). This bears no resemblance at all with the episode in Matthew 24:15 – 21 when *those in Judah must flee to the mountains*. This admonition in Matthew applied during the Roman punishing invasion of AD 67 – 135.

In Revelation 12, there is no panic, the descendants of Jacob are gathered and moved without duress. The passage in Matthew tells the Jews to *pray that your escape may not be in winter*; but here in Revelation, it does not matter whether the escape happens in winter or not—the people are not escaping to the mountains and they are not slogging it on foot. They are not escaping a clear and present danger; instead, they are lovingly moved before the threat and the attack manifest themselves. The prophecy in Matthew 24 is not about the end-times, it is not about when Satan is thrown out of heaven after the 144,000 Hebrews and the Gentile Christians are raptured.

What Jesus prophesied in Matthew 24 has already happened long ago when the Roman legions campaigned against the Jews from 70 to 135 AD. These punitive campaigns killed two-thirds of the entire Jewish population. This series of events fulfilled the prophecy God gave through Zechariah: *Sword, hit the shepherd. Attack the man who is my friend, says the LORD All-Powerful. Kill the shepherd, and the sheep will scatter, and I will punish the little ones. The LORD says, "Two-thirds of the people through the land will die. They will be gone, and one-third will be left. The third that is left I will test with fire, purifying them like silver, testing them like gold"* (Zechariah 13:7 – 9 NCV). The Jews rejected Jesus, the shepherd—Jesus—was killed, and within a couple of generations the Jews were scattered. And since then, the innocents have indeed suffered. At that time, the temple of Jerusalem was desecrated, then destroyed to the last stone and the Jews had to flee for their lives. Because the vast majority of the Jews lived in Israel then, the entire Jewish population was directly affected—the effects of these historical events relative to the total Jewish population of that time was far greater than that of the abominable European Shoah during World War II.

As predicted by Jesus in Matthew 24:21, that time of 70 to 135 AD was the *great tribulation* [for the Jews], *the kind that hasn't taken place from the beginning of the world until now and never will again!* And true to Jesus' word it has never happened again in such a manner and it never will. There will not be an end-times tribulation for the Jews; God will keep them out of these coming miseries because by then they will have fully returned to God and Messiah for the second exodus.

Today, there are misguided speculations about the rebuilding of the temple in Jerusalem before or for the end-times in order that *the abomination that causes desolation* of Matthew 24:15 could take place. These speculations are theological distractions. The rumored preparations made for the new temple will not come to fruition. And whatever concept the Pharisaic/Talmudic/Rabbinical false religion floats will have no effects at all.

Today, Israel does not have the clout to rebuild the temple against the political and religious fervor that would oppose it. After *Gog and Magog,* when there will be no foreign opposition, Israel will not rebuild the temple because Jesus' eternal sacrifice has made it obsolete forever. And the Hebrews living there will know this. And the "Holy of Holies" will be within the heart of every Hebrew. The Jews, and the rest of the Hebrews, having come back to YHWH through Jesus will worship in spirit as Jesus commands in John 4:23 – 24. There will not be a third Old Testament style Temple rebuilt in Jerusalem.

The Old Testament ritualistic sacrifices offered to YHWH took place in the outer areas of the temple because the Holy of Holy was the repository of the Ark of the Covenant. The Ark of the Covenant represented God's presence with His people. This second function of the Temple (the housing of the Ark of the Covenant) was permanently closed by Jesus' sacrifice. It will not exist after the turning of the Hebrews to Jesus for their second exodus and it will not exist during the thousand year reign either. God specifically addressed this issue through Jeremiah 3:16 – 17: *at that time people will no longer say, 'I remember the Ark of the Agreement'. They won't think about it anymore or remember it or miss it or make another one. At that time people will call Jerusalem The Throne of YHWH"* (NCV). There will not be another Old Testament-style temple rebuilt in Jerusalem where Mosaic sacrifices would again be carried out and where a recreated ark of the covenant would be deposited. This issue is developed at length in *The Great Harvest of the Post-Allah World.*

(Return to Table of Contents)

****

Chapter 11 - Antichrist, False Prophet

Revelation 12:18 – 13:18

12:18

18 He stood on the sand of the sea. Or *and the dragon stood on the seashore* (NCV).

What's happening

Verse 18 does not belong with the rest of the text of Chapter 12. By its content and sequence it belongs with Chapter 13 (as some Bible versions have it).

Satan now faces the multitude of humanity; he is looking for "his man", his weapon of mass destruction so to speak—the man who will become the *antichrist*. We are right at the beginning of the three and one-half years, just after the rapture of the saints. He is looking for a perfectly evil man, a man who has divested himself of all of God's attributes that made man a creature in God's image.

> Note: the text of Revelation uses the term *beast* interchangeably for the *antichrist* as well as for his political empire. Some versions of the Bible also refer to the *antichrist* as the *first beast*. For simplicity and clarity, I will try to use the term *antichrist* throughout this book to refer to the *first beast* and will specify when the word *beast* refers to this political empire and not to the person of the *antichrist*. In the same manner, the *false prophet* is sometimes referred to as the *second beast* but I will use the term *false prophet* in the text.

Satan's setup for complete control

13:1 – 10

[1]And I saw a beast coming up out of the sea. He had 10 horns and seven heads. On his horns were 10 diadems, and on his heads were blasphemous names. [2]The beast I saw was like a leopard, his feet were like a bear's, and his mouth was like a lion's mouth. The dragon gave him his power, his throne, and great authority. [3]One of his heads appeared to be fatally wounded, but his fatal wound was healed. The whole earth was amazed and followed the beast. [4]They worshiped the dragon because he gave authority to the beast. And they worshiped the beast, saying, "Who is like the beast? Who is able to wage war against him?" [5]A mouth was given to him to speak boasts and blasphemies. He was also given authority to act, for 42 months. [6]He began to speak blasphemies against God: to blaspheme His name and His dwelling—those who dwell in heaven. [7]And he was permitted to wage war against the saints and to conquer them. He was also given authority over every tribe, people, language, and nation. [8]All those who live on the earth will worship him, everyone whose name was not written from the foundation of the world in the book of life of the Lamb who was slaughtered. [9]If anyone has an ear, he should listen: [10]If anyone is destined for captivity, into captivity he goes. If anyone is to be killed with a sword, with a sword he will be killed.

What's happening

Please note that the text describes Satan and the *antichrist* using the same formula: *ten horns and seven heads* (12:3 and 13:1). Throughout his life up to that point, the *antichrist* has developed into Satan's image, so to speak. He has shed all vestiges of decency, honor, goodness...

I considered two applications of 13:1, the first is symbolic of the *antichrist*'s attributes, and the second reflects his objective power base and headquarters. Considering the symbolic aspect, from the ten crowned horns we see that this man will have a lot of power and authority in the world. From the seven heads we can assume that he has all the knowledge and all the intelligence of humanity (he is as smart as a man can be). But this intelligence rejects any notion of YHWH, and, as his name implies, he is against Jesus. And he displaces Jesus for these people. He is well equipped to hunt effectively and to inflict harm. Among men, he is a predator (the text describes him as a leopard, a bear and a lion). He is called *the beast*. Every thought-process of that man is decidedly against God.

Considering the objective aspect, we will see later that the 10 horns represent the 10 regional rulers that the *antichrist* will appoint who will pledge their unconditional allegiance to him. In this context, the seven heads have a geographical relevance: they represent the seven hills of Rome.

> <u>Note</u>: We often philosophy about who these ten rulers are and we try to identify them and their countries today. However, the text of the bible does not say that these rulers will already be established before the rapture and already have an existing, established constituency. It is therefore much more likely that the *antichrist* is the one who will choose these individuals from his intimates, set them up and assign their territories. Cronyism has always been the hallmark of every evil, perverse, authoritarian regime.

Paul tells us that, when Jesus was on earth, all of the Father was contained in the physical Son. Here, verse 2 tells us that all of Satan's attributes are now bestowed upon the man *antichrist*. A copycat triune deity is being constructed. The triune Deity who created man existed so as to appeal to man; man was made to recognize the Godhood. In a devious, evil way, the fake triune deity of the end times proposes to use this God-given affinity or man for YHWY/Jesus to appeal to all who have rejected the real God. It will provide a semblance of divine reality, of "that's how things are".

Being satisfied that there are no godly characteristics at all left in this man; Satan confers to him all his assets, powers and attributes (13:2). The *antichrist* is Satan's ultimate machine; Satan bestows on him all of his power and authority. Again: *The beast is absolutely devoid of godly attributes: love, joy, peace, patience, kindness, goodness, faith, gentleness and self-control* (Galatians 5:22) are not found in him. Humans are made in God's image, when a human has none of God's attributes, he can only be called a beast. Thus biblically, his name—the *beast*—fits.

This *antichrist* will even copy Jesus to the point of falsifying his death by a "mortal" wound. And of course, the "mortal" wound is showily conquered by its subsequent healing; hinting at a resurrection of some sort. Naturally the world is amazed, and having resisted the real Christ (Jesus) they are primed to be deceived by the fake one (the *antichrist*). The *antichrist* will not come to the people as gentle as a lamb as Jesus did; he will be a predator of men, equipped to destroy.

People will worship Satan because of the powers they see he has given to the *antichrist*. They will also worship the *antichrist*. Satan is an imitator, so just as God manifested Himself through Jesus, Satan will aim to copy God, by becoming "incarnate" through an existing man: the *antichrist*. It is ironic that even for his master plan, Satan has to depend on God for his supplies: he cannot create his own incarnation; he must use a creature that God made.

Verse 5 infers that Satan and the *antichrist* can only do what God allows and only for the time God has allotted. Indeed: *And* *he was <u>permitted</u> to wage war against the saints and to conquer them*; this tells us that the reason the *antichrist*'s agents will be able to decapitate those who refuse his mark and choose to die in Jesus is because God <u>permits</u> them to do so! They can rant all they want but they remain firmly on God's leash.

Nothing will stop the *antichrist* from speaking terrible things against YHWH and against Jesus in order to rally the population against the post-rapture saints. The *antichrist* will be in power for 42 months (three and one-half Biblical years). It is God who allows this power and who limits its duration. The *antichrist* will be given the power to fight against the post-rapture believers (those who choose to die in Christ rather than accept the mark of the beast) and to defeat them (kill them). The *antichrist* and the *false prophet* will be able to do so because God specifically allows them to.

In the same way, God will give the *antichrist* power over every Gentile, everywhere. And all these Gentiles will worship the *antichrist*. The world at that time will be basically evil, unified under one mandatory religion: Satan's. In a uniformly evil world the people making the choice to die in Jesus will really stand out; they will be evident targets for immediate murder.

If anyone is destined for captivity, into captivity he goes: there is no freedom in Satan's and the *antichrist*'s realm; there is only abject subjection—a total captivity of bodies, minds and emotions. That's what those who opt for the mark of the *beast* get. All the others, the ones who belatedly chose Jesus, are killed: *If anyone is to be killed with a sword, with a sword he will be killed.* God will not interfere with either of these processes; He will not intervene. There will be no mitigation—just the stark reality of the eternal culling taking place.

<u>Note</u>: God does not interfere, does not intercedes for people during that time, even for those who turn to

Him. That era is done. The fifth seal makes this clear. People who ended in the terrible predicament of the time of testing had chosen evil thus they get the world they wanted...and that world is ugly in every way. They thought God was an impediment to life—the life they wanted—now they experience the reality of their utopia. Everyone finds himself in the very world they had wanted—they did not want God to have any part of their world; so God gives them their wish. Therefore, it is alone and without divine support or solace that those who reject Satan's mark will face their gruesome death. They will be told to remain resolute in their choice until they are beheaded, the onus is on them, personally. Today, when we embrace Jesus, He comes to live in us, to guide us, encourage us, give us life more abundantly and to mitigate outside factors; what a different life it will be then.

Observations

The *first beast* is variously called the *antichrist*, the *beast* or the *first beast*; he is Satan's best attempt at being incarnate. Just as God meant for Christ to be worshipped; Satan intends for the *antichrist* to be worshipped.

Chapter 13 introduces two nefarious entities, the *antichrist* and the *false prophet*. After describing these two terrible entities, the text (13:18) makes sure that we know that the first one is actually going to be a man: *the one who has understanding must calculate the number of the antichrist, because it is the number of a man*. Satan will copy God's provision: Jesus was God-made-man; the *Antichrist* will be Satan's human version of himself. The first verses about the *antichrist* make him a monster; he does not seem human: that's why verse 18 clarifies that he is actually a man. The other beast, the *false prophet* is not human.

We will see a hierarchy develop in the next few chapters.

1. Satan establishes the *antichrist* and the *false prophet* (demons) as his extensions. They are His tools to mirror—in evil—what God had done for the good. We will see that the *antichrist* is a human but the *false prophet* is made up of Satan's fallen angels (the demons)—the text never qualifies the *false prophet* as human—because "he" is not human.

2. In their turn, the *antichrist* with the action of the *false prophet* will set up a temporal universal administration (a revived Roman Empire) which will rise on the foundation of the old Roman Empire that the Roman religion has maintained in place for such a time. The Roman religion will morph into the World Religion and will reach the fullness of its purpose at that time ... and it will also meet its demise (ordered by God but carried out by men in the service of the *antichrist*).

There is a confusing aspect here because both the *antichrist* and the human organization he sets up to serve his purposes (the revived Roman Empire) will be called the *beast*. The word "*beast*" applies to his person or to his institution because the term expresses an entity that is not willed by God, not rooted in Him and not motivated by Him. Because such an entity is not divinely inspired it is "beastly" or "beast-like". Usually the text will provide defining details that will help us understand whether *beast* is the person or the institution in a particular passage. God made man is His own image; Satan seeks out the *antichrist* in his own image to raise the revived Roman Empire in his own evil pattern.

Satan at that time is still the prince of this world; he has lost his position and status in heaven but he still has his powers on earth. From now on his priorities are:

1. To set himself as god of the earth and to impose the worship of his "incarnation" (the *antichrist*) through the coercive enticements of the *false prophet* (demons).
2. To control the world's population and take it down with him to his final destination (Hell). For this end he will set up a totalitarian human empire, a political power (also called the *beast*)—a Roman Empire reborn. He will brand the Gentile population as his.

13:10 when God turns away

Nothing is the same during the three and one-half years that follow the rapture of the saints of our era. *If anyone is destined for captivity, into captivity he goes. If anyone is to be killed with a sword, with a sword he will be killed.* To me, this is one of the most dreadfully ominous verses in the entire bible. Indeed, since the beginning of mankind, anyone can turn to God and God will respond. Any soul who earnestly appeals to Him is heard and God always responds. Anyone can take refuge in Him; He is our fortress...not anymore: this had just ended.

God has turned away from humanity. Anyone who is put into captivity, slavery or any other coercive situation after the rapture does not have the option or the succor of turning to God: God had turned away; He is not available to these people anymore. He does not interfere in, nor does He arbitrate man's affairs. People have to face what happens to them on their own. They wanted no part of God and God honors their chosen preference.

In the same way, killings will be rampant and gratuitous from the rapture on (second horse); without mitigation or protection from God. God is not available anymore. The victims are on their own. This reality also applies to the people who will refuse the mark of the beast. They will have to stand on their own decision, without God's direct help inside them through His spirit or outside them to mitigate their sentence. They will have to face their gruesome death on their own, they will have to keep their own wits. God does provide them with the exhortations of the two witnesses in Jerusalem; but there is no help at the personal level. The help that has sustained the martyrs through the ages is not available. This reality gives the context to 14:12 – 14: the *saints*—those who refuse the mark—must *persevere* and *keep* their choice of *faith*. They will be rewarded though *with rest from their labors for their works follow them*. Things are indeed very different after the rapture.

Also, according to the fourth seal, God's universe, at God's command is now hostile: famine terminally affect a fourth of the earth. Plus plague, for which no defense exists, affect a fourth of the earth. Plus the animal of the earth have lost their God induced reserve toward humans and will kill human wantonly. If Jesus had not specifically revealed all this, it would be impossible for us to imagine such a world.

Thoughts to ponder

Even though Satan and the *antichrist* will claim to be god they will never have the attributes of God, they will remain mere creatures. They will never be omnipresent, omnipotent and certainly never omniscient. It is in order to overcome these limitations that the *antichrist* will set up a coercive political and administrative human government, a totalitarian regime to represent him, to extend his presence and to impose his will throughout the world.

<u>(Return to Table of Contents)</u>

13:11

11 Then I saw another beast coming up out of the earth

What's happening

This second beast does not come from the mass of humanity (the sea), it is not human. It comes out of the earth because the earth had swallowed it (Revelation 12:16).

13:11 – 15

Then I saw another beast coming up out of the earth; he had two horns like a lamb,[l] but he sounded like a dragon. 12 He exercises all the authority of the first beast on his behalf and compels the earth and those who live on it to worship the first beast, whose fatal wound was healed. 13 He also performs great signs, even causing fire to come down from heaven to earth in front of people. 14 He deceives those who live on the earth because of the signs that he is permitted to perform on behalf of the beast, telling those who live on the earth to make an image[m] of the beast who had the sword wound and yet lived. 15 He was permitted to give a spirit[n] to the image of the beast, so that the image of the beast could both speak and cause whoever would not worship the image of the beast to be killed.

Our clues

The *second beast*, also called the *false prophet*, is an altogether different creature; he is an actor of a different order. He does not come from the pool of humanity as the *antichrist* does: so who and what is he?

The clues as to the *false prophet* are found in these few verses and will be confirmed later in the text of revelation. The clues are as follows:

1. The *false prophet* comes out of the earth. Who did God's earth just swallow? Satan's army. At that time, Satan did not have a human army. He will only get a human army once he has a human general in chief: the *antichrist*. Satan's army is the army he took down with him at the

original rebellion when he swept a third of the angels down with him with his tail (in his train).

2. The *false prophet* has all the authority of the first beast. Who's power did the beast just received? Satan's. The reason the *false prophet* has <u>all the authority</u> of the first beast is because he has the same nature and abilities as Satan's. Demons are the same type of creature as Satan. They are the fallen angels just as Satan is—same creatures, same attributes, and same authority. Except now they will obey the *antichrist*—just a realignment of the chain of command.

3. The *false prophet… compels the earth and those who live on it to worship the first beast* or: *By this power it makes everyone living on earth worship the first beast* (NCV). This *false prophet* has the same clever power of persuasion as Satan demonstrated in the garden… and has applied ever since to all of us. This power has been applied by the millions and millions of demons relentlessly all through history. The *false prophet* can compel the whole earth because these innumerable demons can indeed fool the billions of humans. As they have demonstrated through history as well: today, they compel more than eight billion humans. This aspect also shuts down the possibility that the *false prophet* is a human person. No human person can multiply himself to con billions so successfully and in tempo.

4. He has the power to *perform great signs* (*…and the second beast does great miracles* [NCV]). Indeed, demons have the same power to do great signs that Satan has had all along. As a matter of fact, countless signs we assign to Satan are probably miracles done by demons.

So, using logic and elimination, we can deduce that the *false prophet* is made up of Satan's fallen angels—the demons. For this time of testing, they have been booted out of Heaven down to earth and the earth had swallowed them when they went against Jacob's descendants. Now the demons are coming out of their earthly prison to serve their master.

While the *antichrist* was specifically referred to as a man; the *false prophet* is never referred to as a man. This is a critical point. The text only describes it as a *second beast* or *false prophet*; but it carefully omits to give it a human definition.

He is a creature with a personality just as Satan is a creature with a personality, this is why he is referred to by "he"; but he is not a human (some bible versions use "it" as the pronoun for the *false prophet*, not "he"). I believe he is made up of the host of the fallen angels: an aggregate of all these same creatures. Characteristics described later in the text reinforce this position.

Logic also supports this interpretation and the text never invalidates it. The demons or fallen angels are named as such in the text (12:7 and 9). But from this point on, they are never again referenced as demons or fallen angels again. Why would they disappear from the cosmic battle that implicates them directly? How could they become irrelevant when their master Satan gets to rampage the earth? The fact is: They do not become irrelevant and they do not disappear. They are the powerful agents of deceit behind the scene, collectively they are the *false prophet*—the same function they have always played.

When they are thrown out of Heaven they will lose the last of their heavenly privileges: they will lose their access to Heaven. From now on, they are only the agents of their rebellious master, Satan. They are bound to earth, not as heavenly beings; but as deceivers—a function they have already been doing for 6,000 years plus (since they were swept down by Satan's tail to do his bidding on earth). They will be the *antichrist's* urging agents of evil, the damning suggesters. A prophet is someone who brings out the truth; the *false prophet* will push lies.

Note: At that time, the Gentiles will live in a different paradigm. Since Adam and through our days, *our battle is ...against the spiritual forces of evil in the heavens* (Ephesians 6). This will not be the case anymore. From the beginning of the time of testing, there are no forces of evil in the heavens anymore. All the forces of evil will be on earth, and that's where the struggle will be—period.

And except for the two witnesses in Jerusalem, the forces for the good will not intervene on earth anymore: If one is to be jailed; he will be jailed... If one is to be killed; he will be killed. God and His angels are hands-off. The forces for the good are absent.

Picture the fallen angels—the demons—as you read the following verses:

13:11 – 17

11 Then I saw another beast coming up out of the earth; he had two horns like a lamb, but he sounded like a dragon. 12 He exercises all the authority of the first beast on his behalf and compels the earth and those who live on it to worship the first beast, whose fatal wound was healed. 13 He also performs great signs, even causing fire to come down from heaven to earth in front of people. 14 He deceives those who live on the earth because of the signs that he is permitted to perform on behalf of the beast, telling those who live on the earth to make an image of the beast who had the sword wound and yet lived. 15 He was permitted to give a spirit to the image of the beast, so that the image of the beast could both speak and cause whoever would not worship the image of the beast to be killed. [16]*And he requires everyone — small and great, rich and poor, free and slave — to be given a mark on his right hand or on his forehead,* [17]*so that no one can buy or sell unless he has the mark: the beast's name or the number of his name.*

Expanding the logic

The second reason the *false prophet* comes out of the earth is symbolic: the *false prophet* is the spirit of this world. Since Adam's betrayal of God, man is by nature subject to and sensitive to Satan and his demon's evil suggestions. Man easily falls prey to their influence. All the evils done by men (wars, betrayals, deceptions, persecutions, bullying and lying) are man's predisposed responses to the invisible persuasions of Satan and his demons.

In our Christian era, God's Spirit mitigates this evil influence and its effects. However, at that time the complete Spirit of God will have retired into God's heavenly presence; the influence and the power of the satanic angels will be unopposed and will find receptive hearts in which to operate. The results will be horrible for all.

The first characteristic of this *false prophet* is deception: it appears meek as a lamb... but not a real lamb: it has horns (Rams and some ewes have horns; but not lambs); its lamb-like meekness is an illusion. Its lamb-like appearance is a deception: it will ram like a ram. Watch out for those horns!

This next attribute is revealing: it roars like the dragon (like Satan). What comes out of him is just like what comes out of Satan. Since his actions will be to communicate, as in suggestions, incitement and deceit; it is logical that the first and main characteristic the text gives is his voice.

The *false prophet*'s goal is to promote and enforce the universal worship of the *antichrist,* and through him of Satan himself. The *false prophet* will use human beings as enforcers.

The demons are already in the service of Satan today—as they have been throughout our history—therefore, since the *antichrist* had received all of Satan's power and authority, the *false prophet* (aka: the demons) get his orders from and derives his power from the *antichrist*. The *false prophet* has no independent motives: he is completely dedicated and subservient to the *antichrist*. God allows this evil host to do miracles (verse 14). Now, these slavish demons will obey and report to the *antichrist*. The switch is in their chain of command not in their nature, capacity or function.

Man has always looked for an alternative source of power in order to dismiss God; so God lets him have his way. It will appear to man that finally there is a viable option outside God. This is what most people sought, so they will fall naturally into the trap that echoes their desire, thus making the task easy for the *false prophet*. History shows that man routinely has followed theories and religions that baffle logic or sanity, simply in order to shun YHWH. Consider animism, reincarnation, the theory of evolution and astrology to name a few. Men are ripe and conditioned to fall for these coming lies. People who simply desire that their own wishes be confirmed will accept any sign that transcends their limited human faculties and capabilities. Discernment is an attribute of the Spirit of God; but the Spirit of God will be absent in the remaining Gentiles.

We find another interesting point in verse 15: *[15]He was <u>permitted</u> to give a spirit to the image of the beast, so that the image of the beast could both speak and cause whoever would not worship the image of the beast to be killed.* Who do you think "permitted" the *false prophet* to give a spirit to the image? It is God, Jesus, that's who! No matter how impressive the feats of the *antichrist* and the demons are; they are and will remain on God's leash! They can only do and carry out what He allows; just as it was for Satan regarding Job. And when Jesus finally cuts their power, they will be inert and powerless; they will be thrown into Hell—as inmates, not rulers.

This *false prophet* will use his power to incite everyone on earth to worship the *antichrist* who, with his fake mortal wound, will appear to be a type of Christ. Where Jesus says: *come to me*; the *false prophet* will say: "come to 666" (or 616 as some manuscripts have it).

The spirit of God in the Bible translates as the "breath of God", the life-giving divine suggestions within the individual. Just as the believer today does not see the Spirit of God but is moved by Him; the marked Gentiles of the *antichrist* will not see the *false prophet*. But upon his spiritual urging, his silent whispering, they will worship the *antichrist* whom they can see and will carry out his dastardly deeds.

...And they will think it is their own idea. Indeed, because humans do not see the demonic, evil motivators who whisper to them, they routinely assume that the desires they succumb to are their own ideas, their own chosen outcomes. The invisibility of Satan and the demons, coupled with misplaced human hubris has been very effective throughout history—even in the Church.

The *false prophet*, will play on people's lack of faith in Jesus: indeed, people have always refused the simplicity of believing in Jesus. They created for themselves sophisticated rituals and elaborate statues and other paraphernalia—things they can see, hear and touch. The *false prophet* will use this rebellious tendency to deceive people; he will order the people to build a statue, a visible idol of the *antichrist*. He will make this statue speak and will require everyone to worship it and to pray to it. Men, moved by these evil demons will do the actual building of the statue and will write the edict that calls for its mandatory worship (similarly to what happened in the story of Daniel 3).

This *false prophet* will be opposed by the two real prophets, the witnesses God maintains in Jerusalem. The Gentiles will have to choose between these two opposites: Rome (humanism in the service of Satan) and Jerusalem (godliness for eternity).

Later, we will see that it is the human adherents of a specific religion who will kill all those who refuse to worship the idol as well as kill the two witnesses upon the direct incitement of this *false prophet*. Another evil Inquisition will occur, this one universal and inescapable.

Through people this *false prophet* will enforce the mark of the beast. There will be extreme religious bigotry.

By receiving the mark of the *antichrist*, the people reject the divine spark that made them humans in the image of God. Every aspect of life from now on is absolutely controlled; there is no vestige of freedom or liberty. God had made man free but when man permanently chooses a destiny away from God, he loses the "good" of his humanity; he becomes a mere automaton. At that time, by choosing the mark these humans will have lost the privilege of choice: they have sealed their destination. Every aspect of their lives will be controlled. God is the redeemer; Satan is the destroyer. He demeans and destroys his own faithful without compunction.

Observations

In God we have the Father, the Son and the Holy Spirit (the Spirit is the projection of God in the believer that motivates him for God and toward God, enabling him to live righteously). Jesus went up to the heavens and sent His Spirit to the believers. Since God is omnipresent; His Spirit is able to be everywhere at once and to act within every believer at the same time, all the time. Beyond the believers, the Spirit has no difficulty today to mediate silently into the minds and hearts of the billions of non-believers; thus mitigating in favor of humanity.

Attempting to reproduce God's triune system, Satan will offer himself, the *antichrist* and the *false prophet*. Satan sees himself as the father god. With the *antichrist*, taken from the pool of humanity, he has his version of a self-incarnation, and with the *false prophet* he will have his "spirit"—his motivator, his "deceiving" inspiration. The many millions of demons will project his malevolent will into the ears and hearts of every person who chooses the mark of the beast.

Satan is not omnipresent; therefore a single motivator would never be able to incite the masses of individuals from within: he will need a very large number of invisible dedicated motivators to sway the world population. That's where his fallen angels come in; they provide millions upon millions of dedicated deceivers already on the earth (12:9). They know their job because they have been doing this very same function for Satan since the time of Adam. These considerations bolster the argument that the *false prophet* is the aggregate of all the demons—and not a specific human being.

Satan is not a creator: he cannot generate what he needs; he has to adapt what is available, what exists to fulfill his plan. The fallen angels already exist, they are dedicated to him, and they are numerous (understood to be a third of all of God's angels). Even with all this, Satan's system will always be pathetically imperfect for his purpose of becoming god; but it will be enough to fool man. Satan will at that point have his version of a triune organization.

This *false prophet* has the same powers as Satan, Satan equipped the *antichrist* with his powers (ergo, the text says: He uses the same power as the *first beast*, 13:12). It makes sense; the fallen angels have the same nature as Satan, they are the same type of creatures so they have comparable powers. They were completely dedicated to

Satan through history and now Satan commits them to the service of his "incarnation". They have to be Satan's slave because their only hope is a victory for Satan because as far as God is concerned, they are judged and doomed already.

The *false prophet* is very active in inciting people; but he is invisible to them, even John has limited sight of him. For example: in 19:19 – 20, John watches the human army marching, and naturally he sees its human commander: the *antichrist*. But John does not see the *false prophet* who is also present, because demons do not have physical bodies. We know that the *false prophet* is present at this battle because Jesus grabs "him" along with the *antichrist* to throw them both in Hell before trouncing the human army. The *false prophet* is the motivator of this army, the rouser of their hatred.

Just as it is for us today, the demons (*false prophet*) will remain invisible to these people. Indeed the deceived think that the notions and urges that motivate them are their own, because they cannot physically see the evil advisors who suggest them. At times in the narrative, John is able to see the *false prophet* because God reveals him to John for us, like when he sees the *false prophet* thrown into the *lake of fire*.

In 19:20, we read that the *false prophet* deceives. He does not physically do the things that are attributed to him in this passage; he deceives men into doing his bidding. Satan is called the Deceiver and the *false prophet* has his nature: the demons incite men to carry out Satan's deceptions.

Thoughts to ponder

The *false prophet* is the third dimension of Satan's imitation of God. God has given his Spirit to influence the true believers, to motivate and teach them. Jesus speaks of the Spirit of God as a person using words like *he* and *him*. Now, Satan has his "spirit of evil" who will incite people to commit unrestrained transgressions. The text treats him as a creature with a personality—as indeed fallen angels are—using words like *he* and *him*, but that does not make him a man.

There is one more copycat aspect to Satan's divine pretension. God the Father is invisible, Jesus (God's incarnation) was visible and God's Spirit is invisible. Satan will duplicate this: Satan is invisible, the *antichrist* (a man) will be visible and the *false prophet* (demons) is invisible.

13:18

18 Here is wisdom: The one who has understanding must calculate the number of the beast, because it is the number of a man. His number is 666.

The *antichrist* is a man.

Thoughts to ponder

Whether 666 or 616 (as some older manuscripts show), we do not understand today the name or the number of the *antichrist* or its mark. I doubt that the *understanding to calculate the number of the beast* will be given to us in advance of these events: it is not necessary or useful for us now.

When the grace era true believers are lifted and the above events take place; the Gentiles who have second thoughts about getting the mark of the *beast* may consult the book of Revelation and to them the meaning will be clear. By this verse they will be able to readily confirm the identity of the nasty one who is assuming all authority on earth. As for us believers who live today: why should we be able to identify someone who will never have an incidence on our lives or our destiny? The *antichrist* is irrelevant to the grace era believer.

(Return to Table of Contents)

****

****

Chapter 12 - Lamb and the 144,000 Hebrews, Universal Preaching of the Good News, Collapse of the World System, Universal Warning

Revelation 14:1 – 20

The first vision revisits the 144,000 Hebrews.

14:1 – 5

¹Then I looked, and there on Mount Zion stood the Lamb, and with Him were 144,000 who had His name and His Father's name written on their foreheads. ²I heard a sound from heaven like the sound of cascading waters and like the rumbling of loud thunder. The sound I heard was also like harpists playing on their harps. ³They sang a new song before the throne and before the four living creatures and the elders, but no one could learn the song except the 144,000 who had been redeemed from the earth. ⁴These are the ones not defiled with women, for they have kept their virginity. These are the ones who follow the Lamb wherever He goes. They were redeemed, from the human race as the first fruits for God and the Lamb. ⁵No lie was found in their mouths; they are blameless.

What's happening

We move back to the beginning of the time of the end; before the announced events take place, before the three and one-half years begin. These faithful Hebrews—identified and sealed as God's own—are taken up to be with Jesus and to be honored for eternity. This happens just before or concurrently with the rapture of the rest of the saints. They are taken from the earth and will praise Jesus and follow Him wherever He goes. In the same way that the Good

News was preached first to the Jews and then to the Gentiles; Jesus will rapture first all the Hebrews who, before the second exodus, had accepted Jesus as their Messiah. They will be raptured from Israel where they have been living since the God-led exodus 2.0.

The only purchasing transaction of God for mankind is—and will always be—Jesus' death on the cross. These 144,000 had embraced God's offer of redemption; they had made Jesus their Messiah. They *have kept their virginity* (the New Living Translation gives the best translation: *They are spiritually undefiled, pure as virgins*) meaning: they have not prostituted themselves to other gods or to godlessness. They had chosen to attach themselves and their destiny to the messianic Lamb thus they are ready for the wedding of the Lamb. This is a religious/spiritual image. Jesus uses a historical event to speak to us (Numbers 25): the Hebrews at the Acacia Grove had gone to the Moabite women for sex and followed them into the worship of their gods. Their fornication was physical but it lead to the spiritual prostitution that has plagued the Hebrews ever since.

The cross-reference for 14:4 is 2 Corinthians 11:2 where Paul speaking of this *virginity* gives us the correct understanding. When we come to Christ, we are purified by His sacrifice and are presented to Him—the Groom—as His virgin brides. Of course, every one of us was anything but pure before coming to Him. These 144,000 were Hebrews had voluntarily made themselves pure (virgin) by coming to Christ in our era—it does not infer that these 144,000 were an ascetic, monkish, sinless lot.

In a very Hebraic fashion they are *redeemed, from the human race as the first fruits for God and the Lamb*. The rest of the resurrection of God's chosen people (the Hebrews) will come at the end of the 1,000 year reign. The 144,000 here had embraced Jesus-Messiah, in our time, before the second exodus of Jacob's descendants and had lived in accordance to their new nature.

No lie was found in their mouths; they are blameless: in Jesus, they were true to their divine election—they had not bought the Lie and they had not preached the Lie—in Jesus, they were made blameless. We are reminded of Jesus' exclamation when he met Nathaniel: *here is a true Israelite. There is nothing false in him* (John 1:47 NCV). Those144,000 are *those who believed without seeing* (John 20:29); they are blessed ahead of the other Hebrews who will believe because they saw Jesus acts for their second exodus.

The second vision, verses 6 – 13, will introduce the three messengers of God. This vision occurs just after the rapture of the saints; just beyond the threshold of the three and one-half years. These three messengers are a key to what will happen from that point on.

<u>(Return to Table of Contents)</u>
14:6 – 7

⁶Then I saw another angel flying high overhead, having the eternal gospel to announce to the inhabitants of the earth — to every nation, tribe, language, and people. ⁷He spoke with a loud voice: "Fear God and give Him glory, because the hour of His judgment has come. Worship the Maker of heaven and earth, the sea and springs of water."

What's happening

<u>Context</u>: Since Pentecost, down here, in Jesus, we can live the life He gives and live it more fully. Now, in a quick sequence, the three angels herald a complete change of life. For the un-raptured, life has only one purpose: to choose one's death—either by beheading (but with hope for eternity), or by surrendering to God's enemy condemn themselves to eternal misery—eternal death.

From Pentecost to the rapture, we can enter the better life—a life with God's own motivation (His Spirit) in us to guide us, encourage us and protect us. It is the life the angel urged Peter to go proclaim: ... *tell the people everything about this new life* (Acts 5:20) or Acts 11:18: ... *so that they can have the life He gives*. As believers, we follow Jesus through the maze of life down here and in the end we pass with Him into the blessed eternity.

However, after the rapture, God imposes the *time of testing* (as Jesus calls it in Revelation 3:10). During that time, God does not mediate for man anymore, He does not help man in this life. It is the time when the people must choose their death, and through their chosen death, their eternity. There is no "good life" at all during this time. Life will be absolutely dreadful because God pulls back His protective hand and His mitigating Spirit and the people are turned over to the avowed enemy of mankind. These three angels lay this reality clearly for all to hear and understand: Chose to die with Jesus the Creator, and have a blessed eternity. (But, you must hang on to your choice during the very short time before your beheading.) Or, cowardly, take on the mark of the destroyer, and thus, not only the rest of your on-going days will be pure misery; but your eternity will be unbearably bad.

This first heavenly messenger is not a "normal" event and it will definitively be a sign, therefore this happens right after the rapture of the believers—not before. In Matthew 24, Jesus explained that there would be no warnings, no direct sign, before the rapture. Life would still be ordinary up till then: life as we know it and expect it to be (*two men will be in the field... two women will be grinding at the mill*, vs. 40 – 41).

This one general angelic announcement (plus the two others that follow) will be heard clearly and understood by all living Gentiles in the world. No remote valley is out of reach, no obscure dialect is omitted; no one is left out. This will happen at the very beginning of the three and one-half years.

This universal angelic announcement comes minutes, maybe hours, at most a few days, after the last person who would have chosen Jesus freely has done so and Jesus has taken all His followers up to Him. The harvest phase of the great commission was completed then.

There will be no harvesters left. There will not be a single Christian to witness to the lawless. Everyone left on earth is now against God and has rejected Jesus. However, in His infinite fairness, God makes sure that every rebellious souls left is aware that the Good News still extends through the new era they have just entered. No matter what the *antichrist* preaches and enforces; coming to Jesus is still the only way to a blessed eternity.

The purpose is to inform those left behind that they can demure before getting the mark of the beast; before irrevocably committing their eternity. They can turn down Satan and the *antichrist*. Those who turn Satan down then are the gleanings after the harvest; they fall off Satan's bag, so to speak, and Jesus will pick up and receive every one of them.

Today, we can choose to live in Jesus down here and forever after. But then, the choice will be to die in Jesus or to commit to die forever away from Him. There is no more good life down here.

> <u>Note</u>: This post-rapture angelic announcement is not the capping stone of the "Great Commission". The "Great Commission" has ended with the rapture; there are no more believers to be sent out to evangelize after the rapture. This here angelic preaching proclaims the no-excuse-no-delay object of the testing time that has just begun. It is the completion, the final actualization of Matthew 24:14. It is for life after death.

<u>(Return to Table of Contents)</u>
14:8

⁸ A second angel followed, saying: "It has fallen, Babylon the Great has fallen, who made all nations drink the wine of her sexual immorality, which brings wrath."

What's happening

This verse gives us more details about the third seal of Chapter 6. A second messenger of God brings the end of the world system that humanity has known—the system wholly dependent on God's subsidy yet high-jacked by Satan. Man does not bring about the end of the world system—God does. In Satan's world system, all things have worked and continue to function because God is generous and patient, with good people as well as with evil people. God supplies our needs as well as our riches regardless of merit (Matthew 5:45) Satan is always the parasite. The Psalmist puts it this way: *all humanity finds shelter in the shadow of Your wings. You feed them from the abundance of Your own house, let them drink from Your rivers of delight. For You are the foundation of life, the light by which we see* (Psalm 36:7 NLT). God has just brought an abrupt end to this.

This angel of God announces the end of the arrogant, yet parasitic world system powered by greed, selfishness and godlessness. A system where people deceive themselves into thinking that they are the makers of their own success and that their wealth and security are the result of their own industry, competence and brilliance. It is the world as we have known it.

It is called *"Babylon"* because Babylon was the man-made culture that gave birth to the Tower of Babel project which was man's attempts to replace God and His structure. It was man's way of dismissing God; his attempt to set himself up in heaven as equal to God. When God pulls the plug, so to speak, this whole human construct implodes.

Satan is the "king" of this *Babylon*; he is its motivator and instigator. This *Babylon* is Satan's world system. God describes it this way: *You told yourself, "I will go up to heaven. I will put my throne above the stars. I will sit on the mountain of the gods, on the slopes of the sacred mountain. I will go above the tops of the clouds. I will be like God Most High"* (Isaiah 14:13 – 14 NCV). The tower of Babel was man's expression of servitude to the ungodly "king" of Babylon.

We know from the third seal (6:5 – 6) that when God withholds His generosity, shortages will appear instantly (represented by the scales in the hand of the angel: *a quart of wheat for a day's pay* NCV). Today, we take God's benevolent generosity for granted; we never see how precarious our situation is, were it not for His gracious, unfailing benevolence.

When God acts, the result of this sudden change is paralyzing and affects every living person. It happens in synchrony with the universal murder wave that has engulfed humanity (6:3 – 4) and together, they will cause a disruption of every service. Nothing functions, and there will be a general panic in the population.

Satan has "carte blanche", his goal is complete control; he does not need to pander to any special group so assets will become meaningless. Possessions, insurance, savings, general supplies and food reserves—all things that make up man's security—will be inaccessible and meaningless because interpersonal relations have ceased to function normally. This will make it possible for *the antichrist* to set up his revived Roman Empire as the only administration capable of restoring order. He will demand unlimited powers and unquestioning fealty.

Even the destruction of the world system shows God's fairness. By removing His benevolent provision, God gives the population of the world an accurate reality check that everyone will understand regardless of race, religion or language: man is powerless. And, YHWH gives a foretaste of what eternal life without Him and without His subsidies will mean—permanent misery.

<u>(Return to Table of Contents)</u>

14:9 – 13

9And a third angel followed them and spoke with a loud voice: "If anyone worships the beast and his image and receives a mark on his forehead or on his hand, 10he will also drink the wine of God's wrath, which is mixed full strength in the cup of His anger. He will be tormented with fire and sulfur in the sight of the holy angels and in the sight of the Lamb, 11and the smoke of their torment will go up forever and ever. There is no rest day or night for those who worship the beast and his image, or anyone who receives the mark of his name. 12This demands the perseverance of the saints, who keep God's commands and their faith in Jesus." 13Then I heard a voice from heaven saying, "Write: The dead who die in the Lord from now on are blessed." "Yes," says the Spirit, "let them rest from their labors, for their works follow them!"

What's happening

The third messenger of God brings both a warning and an exhortation. God is totally fair: man will have no excuse because God clearly reveals what is at stake for every person. This angel will let everyone in the world know the irrevocable consequence of surrendering to the *antichrist*, of getting his mark and of worshipping him: the full wrath of YHWH will fall upon him permanently.

These verses teach explicitly that Hell, once entered will be permanent: the pain and suffering will be unrelenting and unending. They also make it clear that Hell will be inhabited by humans, and not just by Satan, the *antichrist* and the *false prophet*.

The individuals who demure and choose Jesus at that time are called *God's holy people*. In this passage, the messenger exhorts those who choose Jesus to do as God says and to hold on to their faith through martyrdom. (Holy means set apart and literally these people will be set apart: they are denied access to the necessities of life and will be decapitated.)

Those who die in Jesus from now on will be happy: they will be safe with YHWH. The messenger promises them rest from their hard work (the work of trusting Christ in these adverse conditions) and he promises them that the good rewards of everything they have done will remain with them.

> <u>Note</u>: *The dead who die in the Lord from now on are blessed.* This point is paramount to understanding the three and one-half years of the time of testing. Today, since Pentecost, we choose to <u>live in Jesus</u> and Jesus lives in us. Jesus came that we may have life—life down here, followed by a loving transition into life eternal with Him. But everyone who enters the time of testing have passed an irreversible threshold. The temporary masters that God allows to rampage the wold—Satan, the antichrist—seek to kill everybody. And indeed, everybody will die. Most of them before Jesus comes to reign on earth, and some will die at the end of the thousand year reign. By turning down the mark, some people will refuse to worship the beast. They are prioritized to die right away by beheading. Their choice then is to <u>die in Jesus</u> in order to join Jesus into a blessed eternity. In the pre-rapture era, they had rejected the gracious offer that would have purchased their life lock, stock and barrel so to speak; now they pay with their earthly life...and gain a blessed eternity.

This is worth repeating: Verse 13 reinforces the fact that beyond the rapture God does not offer the choice of life for the Gentiles; but only the choice of death. *The dead who die in the Lord* is the reality. What a contrast with our time; Jesus promised: I came to give you life and life more abundantly...

God clearly outlines His plan of action in advance to every living person. God is fair. This scripture has been available for nineteen hundred years.

Observations

The majority of the Gentiles of the world will follow the *antichrist* through the urging of the *false prophet* in spite of the fact that they will have received and understood these powerful heavenly messages. The messages will be broadcast without interference because God's angels delivering the messages are now far beyond the interfering reach of the now earthbound Satan and his demons.

Every person alive will have heard and understood these three divine pronouncements. God will not leave the people without reliable arguments for making their fateful life-or-death choice. The *false prophet* will have to work against the awe-inspiring memory of these heavenly messages, plus, he will have to argue against the constant preaching of the two witnesses God has placed in Jerusalem.

These two men of God will ceaselessly broadcast their message to a worldwide audience, from Jerusalem. They will validate their message with powerful signs and wonders exhorting the people to place their faith in Jesus. They will also unblinkingly expose the eternal consequence of trusting in the *antichrist* and following Satan.

Even though, Jesus does not come to live in these Gentiles—as He does now—He still provides a human support to them. To the very last Gentile receptive to salvation, YHWH will provide encouragement and support from these two Godly witnesses. In all this we see that God will give every aid possible in ushering a person into His presence and kingdom: *He does not want anyone to be lost, but he wants all people to change their hearts and lives* (2 Peter 3:9 NCV). In our time, we choose life in Jesus, a life down here transformed by God's active presence and the imbuing of the power and steering of His Spirit and in time we will pass into His glorious eternal presence. But then, God and His Spirit are not present; the Gentiles will choose the modus of their death and they will die in order to pass in God's glorious eternal presence.

Since Adam, some people refuse Jesus' access to their lives, they want to be the choice makers of their destiny... They think they can be gods. During the time of testing, they will know they are not gods, but they get their lifelong wish: They will be the only choice maker of their destiny. They will be met once they have crossed the threshold of that destiny. God is fair.

There will be two poles of influence in the world during these three and one-half years: Rome (Satan's) and Jerusalem (God's).

> <u>Note</u>: we must also keep in mind that all this is happening while a murderous atmosphere has engulfed humanity because God had already removed peace from the earth (6:3 – 4).

The third vision will introduce the gleaning of God's people and the gathering of the damned.

14:14 – 20

14 Then I looked, and there was a white cloud, and One like the Son of Man, was seated on the cloud, with a gold crown on His head and a sharp sickle in His hand. 15 Another angel came out of the sanctuary, crying out in a loud voice to the One who was seated on the cloud, "Use your sickle and reap, for the time to reap has come, since *the harvest of the earth is ripe." ¹⁶So the One seated on the cloud swung His sickle over the earth, and the earth was harvested. ¹⁷Then another angel who also had a sharp sickle came out of the sanctuary in heaven.*

¹⁸Yet another angel, who had authority over fire, came from the altar, and he called with a loud voice to the one who had the sharp sickle, "Use your sharp sickle and gather the clusters of grapes from earth's vineyard, because its grapes have ripened." ¹⁹So the angel swung his sickle toward earth and gathered the grapes from earth's vineyard, and he threw them into the great winepress of God's wrath. ²⁰Then the press was trampled outside the city, and blood flowed out of the press up to the horses' bridles for about 180 miles.

What's happening

This vision is the final reckoning for the earthly humans. With this vision, we move ahead a thousand years to the end of the millennium reign of Jesus.

It has two components: the harvest of the last believers of our age of grace. That is the transformation and lifting to heaven of the Hebrews who had lived through their promised thousand-year reign of their Messiah. It is the total, final rapture of the Hebrews.

The second component is the final crushing of every living Gentile after Armageddon. Earthly humanity ends there.

Sin meant death, sin brought death—physical as well as spiritual (Genesis 2:17)—so physical death must be extracted of those who chose evil. In Christ, in our time, some of us will not experience death; but will be transformed into our eternal, perfect bodies to be lifted. The Hebrews had all embraced Jesus as their Messiah as part of the Exodus 2.0 process; they just were not lifted with the others in order that they may be the Hebrews benefitting from Jesus' reign. (On the other hand, the Hebrews who through the Exodus 2.0 process refused the "covenant/Jesus" were killed by Jesus then and there.)

Literally, this is the vision of the end of times, the end of this world. Once the godly humanity remaining on the earth is harvested (that is the descendants of Jacob not yet resurrected) and the ungodly humanity (the marked Gentiles) is gathered for destruction, this present creation will have fulfilled its function.

Jesus will personally harvest, from this earth, the good grain for Himself: that is the descendants of Jacob. They are the only "Godly ones" who have lived on earth since the last post rapture believer was martyred. Jesus alluded to this order of things in the parable of the wheat and the tares. The good grain is harvested first, it is taken into the Master's barn.

> Note: Timing wise, the Christian era believers were already raptured and the post rapture saints exited the earth via death, so neither group is harvested at that time. In the text now, the promised 1,000 year hegemony of Jacob's descendants on earth has taken place; so at this point, the Hebrews can receive their eternal bodies and pass on to eternity with God. They are not the "gleanings" they are part of the actual harvest; they had come to Jesus before the time of testing.

Of the two groups of people who lived through the 1,000 year reign of Jesus, one will experience physical death and the other will not. The Hebrews will be victoriously transformed and raptured—they will not have to die the physical death—they will receive their new, eternal bodies (approximately 1,000 years after their raptured 144,000 brethren). While, the Gentiles, all wearing the mark of the *antichrist* will experience a crushing physical death at Jesus' hand.

With this vision, we see that every person who believed in Jesus before the onset of the end-time process has been raptured. So, we can now look at the fulness of the first resurrection. It has several phases:

• Jesus, was the first to be resurrected (and raptured). He experienced death before resurrection. Then about 2,000 years later another batch of the first resurrection will follow.

• All the believers up to the time of the rapture—the dead first, then the living—are resurrected before the time of testing takes place. Some of this group experienced death, but some did not. This is still part of the first resurrection. The only living omitted in this group are the descendants of Jacob who embraced Jesus belatedly, that is to say through the process of Exodus 2.0.

• About three and one-half year later, the martyrs of the time of testing are resurrected and come down with Jesus to reign with Him for a thousand years. They were dead and their <u>souls</u> were waiting under Jesus' seat; *they came to life* (20:4). This is still part of the first resurrection.

• About one thousand years later, the Hebrews left on earth will be changed in the blink of an eye also. They get their new, resurrected bodies and are raptured. They are also part of the first resurrection.

So, there are four phases of this first resurrection. And it looks like it is spread over 3,000+ years.

Now, after the thousand year reign of Jesus on earth, all the recipients of the first resurrection will take part in the wedding of the Lamb, in Heaven. They will all be wedded to Jesus. And all the heavens will rejoice.

<u>Note</u>: the decapitated saints of the three and one-half years have lived on earth for the thousand year reign of Jesus; but in their resurrected bodies.

Having gathered His own, Jesus, then delegates the task of gathering the grapes to one of His heavenly messengers. Jesus will trample these gathered grapes (the rest of the people, none of them descendants of Jacob) in the winepress of His anger. It appears that the "grapes" are hauled to a central location "outside the city" to be trampled by Jesus. Their blood will run as high as a horse's bridle for a considerable distance. This is the physical death of the last living Gentiles who have refused the salvation that God offers through Jesus His Messiah.

These last Gentiles all experience a systematic, punishing death. They will be resurrected, they will receive their eternal, perfect bodies as the earth releases their souls. This is the second, the last resurrection. It is a very different resurrection: They are resurrected to be sent to Hell forever. To suffer unabatedly in these perfect bodies, perfect minds and perfect spirits.

God does not hide his plans; He shows ahead of time what will happen: He will harvest the earth and will destroy all those who have not chosen Him. This vision is for John, so that he will record it for all future generations; thus we are under no illusion as to what the outcome will be. Knowing today the consequences of your personal choices should help you make the choice that has the positive outcome. That is why Jesus dictated this revelation to John.

Satan does not harvest the earth, God does. Satan does not make the final move, God does. Satan does not decide the outcome: YHWH alone is God and He determines the ending. And Satan does not choose his own end: God metes him his fate.

(Return to Table of Contents)

****

Chapter 13 - Bowls of Judgments

Revelation 15:1 – 16:21

The great and awe-inspiring sign in heaven

15:1 – 4

¹Then I saw another great and awe-inspiring sign in heaven: seven angels with the seven last plagues, for with them, God's wrath will be completed. ²I also saw something like a sea of glass mixed with fire, and those who had won the victory over the beast, his image, and the number of his name, were standing on the sea of glass with harps from God. ³They sang the song of God's servant Moses and the song of the Lamb: Great and awe-inspiring are Your works, Lord God, the Almighty; righteous and true are Your ways, King of the Nations. ⁴Lord, who will not fear and glorify Your name? Because You alone are holy, for all the nations will come and worship before You because Your righteous acts have been revealed.

What's happening

These verses document the blessing of the righteous, including the saints of the gleaning of the time of testing. It reminds us that all is well in Heaven. It makes clear that the events on earth have no impact on the divine program in Heaven. This vignette is located just after the three and one-half years of Satan's rampage, when the last of the martyred post-rapture believers are safe in Heaven. (These martyrs will come back to earth for the thousand year reign of Jesus as His resurrected administrators/enforcers.)

Chapter 15:2 – 3 corroborates 4:6: the *sea of glass* is indeed the raptured true believers. It also validates what Jesus taught in Matthew 24:36 – 44 that the believers of our age will be lifted before the abnormal events happen. We, the raptured saints will never have to win the victory over the beast and his idol; we never cross path with them. Thus the *sea of glass mixed with fire* represents the post-rapture saints who have been tested in the fiery crucible of martyrdom—they validated their allegiance to God through death. So, the heaven-bound humanity is complete; that is: the believers of all time—the harvest—and the believers who died in Jesus (*mixed with fire*) during the time of their testing—the gleanings.

The awful implications of the bowls

15:5 – 8

⁵After this I looked, and the heavenly sanctuary — the tabernacle of testimony — was opened. ⁶Out of the sanctuary came the seven angels with the seven plagues, dressed in clean, bright linen, with gold sashes wrapped around their chests. ⁷One of the four living creatures gave the seven angels seven gold bowls filled with the wrath of God who lives forever and ever. ⁸Then the sanctuary was filled with smoke from God's glory and from His power, and no one could enter the sanctuary until the seven plagues of the seven angels were completed.

God gives John a quick overview: seven angels bringing seven disasters. Some have been in place since the onset of the time of testing; and some will now be meted out as punishing calamities on the doomed Gentile population.

The first bowl is not the same as the locusts plague of the trumpets—there are no intermediary "locust" agents involved in the first bowl's boils. At first read, the timing of its application seems to be after the last of the gleanings is in heaven. Yet, an argument may be made that God may afflict this condition at the time of the marking—from the very first person who gets the mark to the last one. The mark is irrevocable; therefore God's judgement applies. There does not seem to be any good argument to delay this affliction until after the three and one-half years of testing. Applying it right away and systematically upon the marking would also be a good preemptive warning for all: the wrath of God begins with the mark; so don't take the mark! (Refer to the third angel's message 14:9 – 13.) These terribly painful boils will perdure until Jesus comes down for His thousand year reign.

The fourth bowl was poured out at the onset of the time of testing and have been plaguing the Gentiles as one of God's redeeming curses, it is meant to induce people to choose Him. This bowl and the fourth trumpet are the two distinct but contiguous components that make the third seal effective overnight and permanently. In the first 24 hours, existing crops are killed by the searing heat and the arctic cold and in this harsh climate no new crop can develop.

The fifth bowl is most likely poured at the beginning of the time of testing. Jesus is the light of the world, when He took His resurrected saints home, He pulled His presence and His reflection away. And spiritually, there is no hope in the *antichrist* system, there is no light at the end of the proverbial tunnel. The beast's kingdom is indeed plunged in darkness; just as the world was before God exerted His reflection on it (Genesis 1:2 – 5). On the physical aspect, the fifth bowl expresses the fourth trumpet: the increased night and its terrible effect on all life forms.

As for the other bowls, those poured out after the gleaning is over, their purpose is punishing justice. Satan's time has run out—he is now chained in the abyss—the time of God's wrath has arrived. The terrible events God unleashes now will confirm that no Gentile left wants to choose God. The saints sing *Lord, who will not fear and glorify your name?* Yet, no one does.

This round of calamities will highlight the complete hardness of heart of the remaining Gentile population; they are unconvertible. It will make the argument for God's justice. Later, during the thousand-year reign of Jesus, *all the nations will come and worship before You because Your righteous acts have been revealed*: they will be forced to worship Jesus in Jerusalem during that time. It will be mandatory, and sanctions for those who'd not obey will be fierce and unrelenting (Jesus will rule with a scepter of iron).

We must remember that during this short post-three-and-one-half-year period when God metes out His punishing calamities, the human corporation set in place by Satan through the revived Roman Empire will not be operational anymore. The central, rigid controls of the physical conditions of life and the collective coercion of the minds of the people (by the *antichrist*'s human empire and by the action of the *false prophet*) will no longer function. The people are leaderless; they are "in the dark". By then, the *antichrist* and the *false prophet* will have been thrown into Hell, and Satan is now bound and sequestrated. Therefore, God's pressures will apply at the individual level, universally.

We have a description of the messengers of God; they are clean, beautiful, and orderly as they receive the bowls from which they will pour out God's wrath. There is no panic in heaven, all is good and well. This solemn moment belongs only to God, smoke keeps everyone away. Divine decorum is maintained, nothing is rushed.

Observations

It is interesting to note again that from this point on (from the end of the three and one-half years) Satan is conspicuously absent from the text, we see no evidence of his being active in any part of these proceedings because he is bound up and confined to the abyss. During the three and one-half years of the *hour of testing*, Satan had brought to bear his murderous powers. Now, Satan is neutralized and his tools of power (the *antichrist* and the *false prophet*) are in the *lake of fire*. Satan's power structure is truncated. The population is left without leaders or enforcers. Each individual faces the wrath of God on his own.

We do not have any indication of the total duration of these calamities but we do know that some Gentiles will survive them because God has promised Israel (the elect) a time of hegemony over all the other nations and peoples. Therefore a significant multitude of Gentiles must be preserved for this 1,000 year period of Hebraic dominion.

God will prove that there was absolutely no inclination to turn to Him by the Gentiles remaining on earth, no matter how much pressure He would bring to bear. Even without the coercive framework of the *antichrist*'s empire and the urging of the *false prophet* to influence their choices; they will prove to be willfully set against God. God is thus just and right to condemn them. The mark proves to be irrevocable. Those who had put their trust in Satan will be in the deepest despair, there will be no help from their former idol.

Now to the bowls: some of the bowls could be poured out at the same time rather than being separated chronologically. But whether concurrent or sequential, their effect is terrifying. God Almighty is acting.

16:1 – 2

¹ Then I heard a loud voice from the sanctuary saying to the seven angels, "Go and pour out the seven bowls of God's wrath on the earth".

² The first went and poured out his bowl on the earth, and severely painful sores, broke out on the people who had the mark of the beast and who worshiped his image.

What's happening

Ugly and painful sores (NCV), as we have covered above, this bowl is part of God's redemptive curses. Part of the pressure placed on the Gentiles to opt out of Satan and the antichrist's grasp—and God's eternal fury. This scourge afflicts every newly marked Gentile, a sobering witness to those who have not taken the mark yet... And a taste of Hades for those who have.

This is not the same affliction as the torments meted out by the smoke-locusts (fifth trumpet); it is a separate and cumulative event. There is no indication that these boils will abate. It is likely that these ugly and painful sores will last until Jesus begins his 1,000 year reign.

Note: Divine curses and divine calamities are different. Divine curses are meant to urge man to turn back toward God: they are redemptive. When Adam sinned, God cursed the earth. Life then became hard. The hardships are meant to make people reflect on their estranged condition and yearn to return to the goodness of their original creation. The aim of this curse is redemption, like the original curse.

At the onset of the time of testing, God adds a set of redemptive curses to make the Gentiles choose Him and resist the enemy. These curses are: instant, murderous inclination of everyone, instant ending of the earth productivity, extremely cold nights, burning days and with the mark of the beast: ugly and painful sores. A relentless state of misery, a preview of what Hell will be. A divine goad to press the living into the right decision.

On the other hand divine calamities are simply punitive consequences. They are the expression of God's wrath. They are applied justice.

16:3

3 The second poured out his bowl into the sea. It turned to blood like a dead man's, and all life in the sea died.

What's happening

The angel pours this bowl after the time of testing is done. When the good news is closed. It is a punishing divine calamity. It does not have a redeeming component.

The second bowl is poured into the sea, which becomes decomposed blood; all life in that toxic mix dies. This is an elaboration of the second trumpet. The trumpet heralded what the bowl now pours into the sea. So we can deduce that this bowl is poured on a third of the seas. This bowl is poured after the fifth trumpet woe of the locusts has abated, that is: 5 months into the calamities.

16:4 – 7

4 The third poured out his bowl into the rivers and the springs of water, and they became blood. 5 I heard the angel of the waters say: You are righteous, who is and who was, the Holy One, for You have decided these things. 6 Because they poured out the blood of the saints and the prophets, You also gave them blood to drink; they deserve it! 7 Then I heard someone from the altar say: Yes, Lord God, the Almighty, true and righteous are Your judgments.

What's happening

The bowl is poured on the rivers and their waters turn to blood. This was previewed by the third trumpet which told us that it was poured on a third of all the rivers and springs of the world, anyone who drinks this poisonous liquid will die. This bowl is poured after the locust have abated, because nobody dies while the locusts are active. This is a divine, punitive calamity, it takes place after the saints of the gleaning are lifted.

The people in heaven rejoice at the punishment given to the enemies of God. They spilled the blood of God's followers, and now their penalty is to drink this vile poisoned blood. There is fairness in this retribution.

Observation

This third bowl is what the third trumpet heralded even though the actual poisoning of the fresh waters appears to be different from the *wormwood* of the third trumpet. The difference is that the trumpet reflected the taste of the water while the bowl reflects the change of the composition of the water: its nature.

16:8 – 9

⁸The fourth poured out his bowl on the sun. He was given the power to burn people with fire, ⁹and people were burned by the intense heat. So they blasphemed the name of God, who had the power over these plagues, and they did not repent and give Him glory.

What's happening

This is the first time we encounter this curse in the text, but it has been applied since the onset of the time of testing.

God makes the sun increase its heat so it burns people. This is not the heat of a normal summer day: it is plainly described as intense heat; no one has ever experienced the daylight heat that the sun will emit then. It is interesting to note that at the same time the days will be shorter and less bright and the nights longer and darker—probably colder (fourth trumpet). Nature is now harsh in every way: the nights are bad and the days are inhospitable.

This will not abate until Jesus comes to rule on earth. There is now nothing pleasant about life on earth; even the elements now impose a hostile environment.

The people will curse the name of YHWH who has control over these disasters. God gave reference to this human tendency when He said to Job: *"Would you say that I am unfair? Would you blame me to make yourself look right?"* (Job 40:8 NCV); apparently, they will.

This bowl and the other redeeming curses will really separate the people: some will refuse to change their hearts and to worship YHWH or plead for His mercy. They have resisted the gentle, patient wooing of God before the rapture, they are choosing against God when the irreversible choice is now demanded of them. They are not moved by these awesome, personal stresses. No amount of pressure can make them change their hearts. Others will yield to the divine reality. They will reject the mark of the beast. They will stand firm on their decision all the way to their gory end.

> Note: We have here an additional confirmation that the believers in Christ will not be on earth at this time because 7:16 had promised them that *the sun will not hurt them, and no heat will burn them.* The text remains consistent.

16:10 – 11

¹⁰The fifth poured out his bowl on the throne of the beast, and his kingdom was plunged into darkness. People gnawed their tongues because of their pain ¹¹ and blasphemed the God of heaven because of their pains and their sores, yet they did not repent of their actions.

What's happening

This bowl is poured right at the beginning of the time of testing. It is the curse of the fourth trumpet. The prolonged daily darkness will bring nightly freezes we have never experienced before. No wonder nothing will grow anymore. No wonder people will gnaw their tongues, their lives is now defined by unrelenting agony of the boils, the awful burning of the day's sun, the life choking cold of the nights and the constant threat of being killed by someone (second seal). And let's not forget, terrible hunger that can only be lessen for those with the mark of the beast. Note: the nights' darkness will be more intense than what we know today because a third of the moon's and stars' light will be removed. It reminds us of the darkness that befell Egypt; so dense that it was scary for all. This will add to the doom feeling and to the ambient fear.

On top of this, there is no possibility of bonding at the personal level to receive succor from others because interpersonal relationships have been wrecked by the second seal (*its rider received the power to banish peace from the earth so that people will kill one another*, 6:4).

Each person is left to face their time of testing alone. Their agony will be so intense that the people will actually chew their tongues. They will curse YHWH yet they will not change their position against Him. Those will be truly unsalvageable.

> Note: We humans surrendered our authority to Satan through Adam. Yet, for those in Jesus, the new reality is that we must resist the devil and he will flee. While he is indeed real; he is a sham to us today. We are not to fight him; but to resist him. After the rapture the remaining Gentile population surrendered to him and now, they experience the reality that Satan has nothing for them.

Thoughts to ponder

God had been extremely generous by providing man countless opportunities to make the gracious eternal choice:

1. For some 2,000 years He has offered grace in a benevolent, attractive process: to all of mankind He says what Philip said to Nathaniel: *come and see* (John 1:46 NCV). Indeed today we can be *in God's light, and enjoy heaven's gift, and share in the Holy Spirit. We can find out how good God's word is, and receive the powers of his new world* (adapted from Hebrews 6:4 – 5 NCV).

2. After the rapture, the Good News was preached clearly to all men through God's heavenly angel while there was still time to choose Jesus for eternity, albeit through death.

3. God proclaimed a stern warning through another heavenly angel.

4. He removed His benevolent subsidies and imposed dire reality checks for all the gentiles (curses); so that people would see clearly that without God's provision, misery alone remains. This will help some to choose Jesus (the post-rapture saints), but many others will refuse to draw the logical conclusion.

5. He provided two witnesses in Jerusalem who were empowered to do awesome wonders and whose messages were heard worldwide. They preached God's last opportunity.

6. He allowed Satan to demonstrate his evil nature for three and one-half years; which should have been sufficient to warn anyone.

16:12 – 16

^{12}The sixth poured out his bowl on the great river Euphrates, and its water was dried up to prepare the way for the kings from the east. ^{13}Then I saw three unclean spirits like frogs coming from the dragon's mouth, from the beast's mouth, and from the mouth of the false prophet. ^{14}For they are spirits of demons performing signs, who travel to the kings of the whole world to assemble them for the battle of the great day of God, the Almighty. ^{15}"Look, I am coming like a thief. The one who is alert and remains clothed, so that he may not go around naked and people see his shame is blessed". ^{16}So they assembled them at the place called in Hebrew, Armageddon.

What's happening

There is a long hiatus between the preceding bowls and this sixth one. After a thousand years, Satan is released from the deep recess of the earth. He loses no time organizing his final assault.

God dries up the Euphrates. By opening this northern door of Israel to invaders He facilitates the way for this great Gentile army to invade Israel for the all-out battle against the Hebrews. Since Jesus has been the only power on earth for over 1,000 years, He would have maintained the borders of Israel where God had set them from the beginning—including the Euphrates in today's Syria (Genesis 15:18, Joshua 1:1). God facilitates the logistics of *Armageddon*, His final victory.

We also establish with certainty that this event is not the battle-with-no-name that took place at the end of the three and one-half years (19:17 – 21) because during that earlier battle the *antichrist* led the troops personally and was physically present. Now, at the end of the 1,000 year reign, it is the spirits of the *antichrist* and of the *false prophet* that act—not themselves physically.

So when Satan is released, he will channel the spirits of these two entities: *three evil spirits* coming out of the mouths of the Dragon (Satan), the *beast* (the *antichrist*) and the *false prophet* (demons). The evil spirits will now motivate all the kings of the earth to wage war against Israel. Every Gentile living then had opted for the *mark of the beast* prior to the 1,000 year reign so he/she is readily susceptible to be motivated by the evil spirits of their chosen lords. The spirit versus the actual person is not a strange concept; we have a similar situation now. The apostle John tells us that the *spirit of the antichrist* is already with us (1 John 4:3) even though the person of the *antichrist* has not appeared yet.

The Gentiles' allegiance to Satan had been established and sealed during the three and one-half years; it did not reverse during the 1,000 years. For the thousand years reign, Jesus' absolute authority over them remained external, enforced rigidly by the resurrected martyrs. The people were not allowed to sin; but that does not mean that they did not want to.

This battle now is *Armageddon*; it bears no resemblance to the battle-with-no-name that took place at the end of Satan's three and one-half year rule. That prior large human army had marched against Jesus and his heavenly host. Jesus killed that army and birds ate the dead bodies. Now, *Armageddon* is a battle where a huge Gentile army will march against Israel and the Hebrews, this army of *Armageddon* will be incinerated—there will be nothing for birds to eat or for the Hebrews to bury. These useful details help us differentiate between each of these battles. A little over one thousand years separate these two events.

In verse 15, we have a warning that does not refer to the end of the 1,000 year reign but applies to our age of grace now. The message is for us today as it has been during the whole church age: "do not be lulled, because you do not know when Jesus will lift up His saints." It is a reminder that we really, really do not want to be there. Verse 15 is an aside for us believers, and with verse 16, Jesus completes the thought of last verses.

Verse 14 gives us a confirmation that the *second beast* is indeed the assembly of demons—the fallen angels: *These evil spirits are the spirits <u>of demons</u>, which have power to do miracles. They go out to the kings of the whole earth to gather them together for the battle on the great day of God Almighty* (NCV). The *false prophet* (the demons) had used the same power during the three and one-half years: *and the second beast does great miracles so that it makes fire come down from heaven to earth while people are watching. It* (the demons) *fools those who live on earth by the miracles it has been given the power to do. It does miracles to serve the first beast* (13:13 NCV). And a thousand year later, for Armageddon, the demons' earlier work will pay off: Satan will capitalize on the Gentile kings' and the masses' ready motivation to do evil and to follow him. As one, they will rise up to follow Satan; he will have no difficulty mustering an army for the final campaign against the Hebrews and Israel.

Observations

The word *spirit* in "spirit of the Dragon, of the Beast and of the demons" (the demons make up the second beast) has the same definition and function as it does elsewhere in the New Testament. It is treated as an entity because it functions like the person from whom it emanates and is evidenced in the actions of the persons affected.

We have seen the Holy Spirit as God's whisper in the believer, God's motivation: the motivation of God, for God and about God. It is "God's-way-of-thinking" placed in a person. It motivates the person to think "good", to speak "good" and to do "good"; thus, Jesus' motivation—His Spirit—transforms the life of the believer.

Here we have the same principle at work, except it is for evil. During the three and one-half years the demons and the *antichrist* have inculcated Satan's evil motivations in every one of these gentiles—motivations to function in an evil way, to do unrestrained harm and to pursue evil without limitations. The demons have placed Satan's "spirit" in these people where "he" still remains—the motivation still lives there.

The *antichrist* and the demons are not present anymore (they are in the *lake of fire*); but the ugly motivation they had planted and nurtured in these people is very much alive. The evil motivation within these people will have remained alive and efficacious even though the *antichrist* and the *false prophet* will not be there. It is the mirror in evil of Jesus' Spirit today: Jesus is not visible to the believers but His good motivation inside them is alive and efficacious.

For a thousand years, the driving motivation to do evil will have been effectively suppressed by Jesus' omnipotent and omnipresent rule—He will rule with an iron scepter. During the whole time of Jesus' reign, the gentiles have been constrained by the external power of Jesus; they were not able to live out their evil impulses in any way at all.

But now, Jesus allows Satan to act again. The universal impulse to do evil that had been frustrated for so long is released. All Satan has to do is to fan the flames of their passion, to channel their evil disposition. For the gentiles, this is the release of a millennium of pent up evil: the final catharsis of their doomed lives. This is why Satan will be universally successful in rallying the gentiles.

On a side note, Jesus' earthly ministry lasted roughly three years and His Spirit has changed generations of believers for two thousand years; Satan's all out rampaging campaign will last approximately the same amount of time: three and one-half years, the effect on those bearing his mark will not wane through the 1,000 year reign because God had stopped wooing these people when the "Good News" was closed. The only motivation living in them since then has been evil.

16:17 – 21

17 Then the seventh poured out his bowl into the air, and a loud voice came out of the sanctuary, from the throne, saying, "It is done!" 18 There were flashes of lightning and rumblings of thunder. And a severe earthquake occurred like no other since man has been on the earth — so great was the quake. 19 The great city split into three parts, and the cities of the nations fell. Babylon the Great was remembered in God's presence; He gave her the cup filled with the wine of His fierce anger. 20 Every island fled, and the mountains disappeared. 21 Enormous hailstones, each weighing about 100 pounds, fell from the sky on people, and they blasphemed God for the plague of hail because that plague was extremely severe.

What's happening

This is God's grand finale. God says *it is finished!*

Now we again reach the flashes of lightning, the thunder, the noises and the great earthquake that we have encountered twice already.

Jesus' subsequent actions hit the entire world—every human will suffer individually. A gigantic earthquake causes the *cities of the nations* to fall. This earthquake and its devastation are universal; it is literally the shaking of the whole earth.

Giant hailstones pound the earth, and people will curse God because this disaster is so great. They are crushed in the winepress of the Lord (14:17 – 20). The sixth seal said: *Who is able to stand?*

As the very foundations of the world are being undone and cataclysmic hail pounds the earth, these people die cursing God. While they are being crushed their last thoughts and words are futile curses against YHWH-Almighty. Their reaction is pitiable.

We ponder: are these hailstones the pestle God will use to grind down the last of humanity after *Armageddon*, when the blood of the crushed people will reach several feet in depth in the huge mortar of God's judgement?

(Return to Table of Contents)

****

Chapter 14 - Woman and Scarlet Beast

Revelation 17:1 – 18

We now arrive at the vision that amazed John. It most likely puzzled readers for centuries afterwards, until the object of the vision became a reality. I will confess that when I began studying Revelation chapter 17, I did not like where it seemed to be leading me; so I quit studying Revelation for a while. Eventually I knew that I had to face it, yet I approached the text hoping to discover a different understanding. It was not to be. In the end, I had to surrender to what the text does say.

The information in Chapter 17 is uncanny because it describes to John *the notorious prostitute (woman sitting on a scarlet beast)* long before this entity existed. The angel identifies precisely what this organization will be, where its headquarters will be located and many of the evil deeds it will do. By these concrete details that later came to pass as foretold, we can identify her today: she is the Roman Catholic Church. God described her for the true Christians before this organization appeared.

If Revelation had been written fifteen hundred years later or nineteen hundred years later than John's time; we could wonder whether the writer was expressing his own bias or his personal enmity. But not in this case, John had no way of knowing or even anticipating any of this. And when it was revealed to him, he was flabbergasted. This passage is not a witch hunt, or a smear campaign—it is prophecy.

17:1 – 9a

[1] Then one of the seven angels who had the seven bowls came and spoke with me: "Come, I will show you the judgment of the notorious prostitute who sits on many waters. [2] The kings of the earth committed sexual immorality with her, and those who live on the earth became

drunk on the wine of her sexual immorality." [3]So he carried me away in the Spirit, to a desert. I saw a woman sitting on a scarlet beast that was covered with blasphemous names and had seven heads and 10 horns. [4]The woman was dressed in purple and scarlet, adorned with gold, precious stones, and pearls. She had a gold cup in her hand filled with everything vile and with the impurities of her prostitution.

[5]On her forehead a cryptic name was written: BABYLON THE GREAT THE MOTHER OF PROSTITUTES AND OF THE VILE THINGS OF THE EARTH. [6]Then I saw that the woman was drunk on the blood of the saints and on the blood of the witnesses to Jesus. When I saw her, I was greatly astonished. [7]Then the angel said to me, "Why are you astonished? I will tell you the secret meaning of the woman and of the beast, with the seven heads and the 10 horns, that carries her. [8]The beast that you saw was, and is not, and is about to come up from the abyss and go to destruction. Those who live on the earth whose names were not written in the book of life from the foundation of the world will be astounded when they see the beast that was, and is not, and will be present [again]. [9a]Here is the mind with wisdom...

Background context

This "cryptic name" or "the hidden meaning" was written on her forehead: *The Great Babylon, Mother of prostitutes, and the evil things of the earth* (ERV).

Satan is the father of lies.

By itself, Satan's lying has no effect. His lies must be implanted in a human carrier. A human carrier must incubate Satan's lies and birth them into concrete reality and nurture them from then. The woman here concretizes Satan's evil. The original prototype of this principle was rolled out in the garden of Eden.

In the garden, as long as Satan carried his own lies, he had no import, and his lies had no application. From the second verse of the Bible we know that Satan's rebellion had taken place (the presence of the darkness attests to this). But neither the darkness nor Satan had any influence on the creation process. God reflected His light over the world, relegated the darkness to its place and God's life was the only power. Creation and mankind were not effectively affected by Satan's rebellion prior to the seeding of the lie into the woman. Once those lies were implanted in the woman Eve and took root there, they incubated and became human factors—personal and universal.

Just as the seed of humanity was in Adam since creation, it was not active by itself. Biologically, Adam's seed is immaterial without Eve's ovule and its incubation. Spiritually, this is why Eve was the key to Satan's strategy. Satan did not approach Eve because Adam was not available; Satan specifically targeted Eve; she was the key.

If Eve was not on board, the Satan's poison would have simply died with Adam. Biologically, humanity became a reality once Eve joined her part and carried out the human incubation and birthing. Spiritually, the same principle applied: without Eve the plan was dead.

Satan's goal was death. Death of the creature bearing the image of God and destruction of God's creation through that process. The first lie, when Satan lured Eve, was murder. Murder was the intent, deception was only the tool. Satan committed murder. Indeed, God had warned Adam and Eve that eating the fruit of the tree of knowledge of good and evil would surely kill them... And it did! Satan knew it would.

The first consequence was the ruin of Adam and Eve's idyllic life, then, in time they actually died. They had been injected with the poison that would kill them. It was murder. Murder in the largest scale possible: murder of the original progenitors which thus doomed all the future offsprings. It was murder on the scale of humanity. Satan injected a venom for which there was no antidote... yet.

Secondly, the original interaction in the garden provided Satan with an open portal into the core of humanity.

When humanity was on the threshold of development and its future and fate was still contained in one incubator, Satan murdered humanity through Eve.

Centuries later, when humanity became millions then billions, Satan set up a collective incubator of death. He needed to do so because God had introduced the antidote to the death.

The good news, described by Jesus as the seed, was taking roots in thousands and then in millions of people. It was growing and transforming the world. The father had prepared many souls and the harvest was ripe. The new life took off.

So Satan had to introduce his mass booster, a new killer shot. So, he introduced a sterile womb. This is the collective woman, the Great Babylon. She is the fake motherhood, the mother of the evil things of the earth. She is the dedicated killer of those who told about their faith in Jesus. This prostitute pretends to be the real mother; to be the only channel to "the life". Then only valid receptacle for the good news seed. The only true incubator and nurturer of the life eternal. But, just like with Eve, Satan's purpose is murder—the deadening of the seed by a sterile womb.

Satan's continued interaction with humanity aims to kill, to kill in a thousand ways—some subtile, others gruesome. However, alone Satan cannot kill; he still needs a "woman", a human carrier. However, at this time, to kill universally he uses a universal human construct (hint: Catholic means universal).

Mother of prostitutes: A prostitute is a false bride. She rents only a part of womanhood to the relationships, whereas a bride commits all of herself for life. Through the bride, life builds, and humanity becomes reality. The wife incubates the seed then nurtures life. Whereas the prostitute takes the seed and makes sure it dies there. And even worse, she makes sure the seed does not build a legacy for the man. She is a species decimator.

The devil's success with Eve was only the inception. The Great Babylon in our text here became the permanent vessel of realization, of concretization, of the devil's evil intents. A universal structure that could perdure through the generations and across the globe. A structure that would kill physically and would also kill spiritually for eternity.

In God's creation, Satan cannot do anything by himself so he uses God's apex creature, the creature made in God's image to effect his evil plans and actions. And through this "woman"—that is to say: this humanistic structure—Satan has realized his destructive aims. This humanistic evil structure killed the saints and the witnesses of Jesus.

> <u>Note</u>: Some people blame Eve and thus claim that women are somehow more evil than man. Other people say that Adam was a conniving poltroon who let Eve try first. These theses miss the reality. Satan targeting Eve, on this fateful day, was purposeful. Satan strategically ignored the seeder (Adam) and hit the incubator. Without the incubator, his plan was dead. Eve was the key.

> Going after Adam first and getting him to eat the fruit would only kill Adam. Eve was the key to Satan's strategy. Even if Adam had not eaten the fruit, their posterity would be doomed by the defiled incubator/nurturer.

The point though became moot right away: Adam bought into his own murder... And history has played out.

Note: Verse 17:9a *You need to have wisdom to understand this* (ERV) or *This call for a mind having wisdom* (TLV) refers to the preceding verses (1 – 8). It does not attach to the passage that follows.

The setting

The "woman" is sitting on a scarlet beast with seven heads and ten horns, covered with blasphemies against God. In chapter 13, the *antichrist* is described as a beast with seven heads and ten horns, covered with words that blasphemed God. We also saw that the *antichrist* and his power structure are often referred on the same basis. So, here, the "woman" sits on the empire of the *antichrist*. We will see that this empire has distant roots, will die out for a time, but will be brought back.

The prostitute

The terms used by Jesus' faithful angel are as descriptive today as they were prescient in John's time: this monster is a prostitute in the sense that it gives worship to gods other than YHWH. The term "Prostitute" is used here as the spiritual application of its definition: to offer or to give to others that which belong only to one's spouse. The community of those who follow Jesus is referred to as His bride; He is the spouse to all His believers.

Therefore, the *notorious prostitute* is a religion that claims to be "Christian" and thus should have been Christ's faithful bride but has not been. It is a religion that worships other gods, gods she has created herself. This idolatrous worship affects the leaders as well as the lowly lay persons. For example: Pope John-Paul II, a recently deceased world leader of the Catholic Church, prayed to Mary and encouraged the members to do the same. His declared core allegiance was to Mary, as expressed by his motto: Totus tuus ego sum et omnia mea tua sunt. Accipio te in mea omnia. Praebe mihi cor tuum, Maria (I belong entirely to you, and all that I have is yours. I take you for my all. O Mary, give me your heart.)

This religion routinely "canonizes" dead people, thereby officially qualifying these manmade "saints" to receive the prayers and offerings of the faithful. This religion has thus created hundreds of idols and is actively manufacturing more; even the recent Pope who worshipped and prayed to Mary was canonized in April 2014. He can now officially receive the prayers of the faithful. Recently, in *La page de Saint André*, a Catholic publication, I read about a newly minted saint: Pierre Favre. I translate: *Pierre Favre...is a part of the 'canon' of saints and his worship is now proposed to the Universal Church*. This is not medieval history; this is going on today. The worship of this new idol is officially proposed to, and accepted by, literate and educated twenty-first century European Catholics ... this illustrates the enduring, twisted reality of the Catholic Church.

Over decades, I have personally observed Catholics praying fervently to the particular saint after whom they were named, or sometimes to a "saint" who had lived in their region, at other times to a "saint" reputed to have a special knack at solving certain situations (Christopher for safe travels, Anthony to find lost items, to name just two). This is pure spiritual prostitution. They place more faith in these idols than in Jesus for the answer to their petitions. They feel that they have greater leverage on these "human saints" than what they could exert on Jesus. They often go one step further: they pray to their departed family members (grand-parents, god-parents or even a child) because they feel that these "good" folks must surely be in heaven—they reason that

Rome is too busy and has not caught up with these relatives to recognize them as worship-able saints yet.

I am not describing a backwoods mentality that existed in medieval kingdoms long ago; the following example happened in a high class resort in France in this twenty-first century during the funeral of a Catholic friend of mine. While living, he had no religious interest. He was a pleasant fellow but paid no mind to his spirituality. Yet, during his Catholic funeral service, just after the officiating churchman had "allowed" my friend's soul to enter heaven, the churchman faced the crowd and told us: "François is in heaven; you can all talk to him anytime you want and you can pray to him for what you need or want. He is there listening to you, smiling on you."

Manmade saints are comfortable because we feel we can maintain a handle on them; but when one prays to Jesus, one is keenly aware that Jesus can and will also correct and punish. Therefore, when one does not want to abandon sinful habits or evil practices, one will feel rueful or even fearful when addressing his petitions to Jesus. But, the Catholic saints do not have the capacity to judge, to correct or to discipline—how could they? They were fallen humans at one time. This is very convenient: it is much more comfortable to address one's prayers and worship to these idols because they cannot demand the necessary surrender required by the true God. These idols can only grant the petition, or ignore it; they cannot demand obedience, contrition or bring retribution. A person can go to these Catholic saints all through life without ever changing his heart and life (as Matthew 4:17 demands).

Also, these human idols will not sit in judgment in the end; so they cannot impose a verdict on someone's eternal destination. They are benign dispensers of favors; they pose no threat and cannot effectively oppose man's basest instincts. These manufactured "saints" are true idols. What differences of status and function are there between these idols and the enshrined domestic idols of pantheistic religions elsewhere?

Thus Catholics practice spiritual black market: they seek sources outside the allowed divine process. The overarching reality is that Humans do not choose who YHWH/Jesus is: God is God and He made Himself known as such. Humans accept Him and submit to Him *as is*; we do not have a say in the matter.

On the other hand, through the canonization of humans the Catholic Church offers a constantly expanding smorgasbord of gods: <u>you</u> can pick and pray to the ones <u>you</u> want. You decide which god might be most efficacious for your own purposes or needs. Since you can pick or ignore your gods; you must be above the gods!

The overwhelming favorite is Mary because everyone projects his own mother's sentiments onto her and expects the same motherly protection and intersession than his human mother could be persuaded to provide. In this respect Catholics become Jesus' siblings and their "common mother" will prevail on Him for the favors sought—as, supposedly, any dotting mother would do for a weaker child. And the church has made sure that Mary never is given the powers to demand accountability, to punish, or to discipline. So, she too is a very nifty dispenser to go to for all who do not want to reform or conform to an absolute God.

During a conversation on the subject an American Catholic friend put it this way: "the Catholic way is far better because it is realistic: it is easier to accommodate and to get benevolent blessings from a sweet mother than from an all-mighty father"—the inference is clear: Mary is divine... And she is Jesus' overlord. Jesus says *come to me*; the Catholics say: we got a better deal; go to his mother... You are shielded from Him and you still get the goodies.

And with this observation, we can see that the Catholic Church has returned to its ancient Roman sources: it has completed the circle and has spliced back into the religious system of ancient Rome with its anunna of gods—official, domestic and others. The last human god it will promote will be the *antichrist*. Just as the Roman Emperors of old were gods, the "Emperor" of the new Roman Empire will also be a god; canonized by the Catholic Church. The Catholic Church will provide the *antichrist* with a religious system compatible with the Roman Empire—unifying the state and its religion—and adapted to *the beast*'s nefarious intents.

Catholic church buildings and chapels throughout the world are dedicated to these man-made gods with names such as: Our Lady of Fatima, Our Lady of Grace, Saint John the Baptist Church or Chapel of Saint Laurent, etc. All of these worship sites are dedicated to people, rather than to YHWH.

Relics and other trinkets are given mystical powers and become objects of encouraged devotion. For centuries, pilgrims have hiked across the European continent to express their cult to a dubious relic of James in Santiago de Compostela, Spain. When animists revere amulets, we laugh at them; yet educated Westerners readily accept this idiocy. The greedy trade of these phony sacred relics has filled the coffers of Rome for centuries.

The Catholic Church misrepresents and falsifies the God of the Bible it claims to represent. Pope John-Paul II, in an attempt to woo the favor of Islamists, asserted that Jews, Christians and Muslims worship the same god. Jesus says: *No one who denies the Son can have the Father; he who confesses the Son has the Father as well* (1 John 2:23). *Whoever confesses that Jesus is the Son of God—God remains in him and he in God* (1 John 5:15). *For in Him the entire fullness of God's nature dwells bodily, and you have been filled by Him...* (Colossians 2:9). Thus, the Pope's assertion is impossible. The people who worship Allah do not worship YHWH—and certainly not the YHWH-who-became-man: Jesus the Messiah. But what most non-Muslims fail to understand is that by this declaration, the "infallible" head of the church of Rome pronounces that the Catholic Church does not worship YHWH, the God of the Bible. The next two popes have confirmed this theological position. If the pronouncement had been made by a new, immature believer out of ignorance, it would not taint the whole organization; however, since it is made repeatedly and doctrinally by the highest authority of that Church, it defines this organization and credibly represents it.

This *prostitute* easily rubs elbows with Satanists and is at least ambivalent about Satan worship. Not too long ago, Pope John-Paul I—the short lived Pontiff—did just this. Wurmbrandt writes in *Satan and Marx*: "The late Pope John-Paul I praised Giuseppe Carducci, a university professor, as an example of a good teacher of youth. Who is the man recommended by no less than the Pope? Carducci became famous for his "*Hymn to Satan*", which begins: "My ardent verse is for thee, I invoke you, Satan, king of the feast." It ends: "In holiness, incense and vows should ascend to thee, Satan you have defeated Jehovah, the god of the priests." Amazing, isn't it?

This *prostitute* is notorious; it is not some obscure, limited phenomenon, it is very present on the world scene (today it claims 1.5 billion adherents). It does *sit on many waters*. Its connections influence the highest levels of governments. I am amazed at the photos regularly published in the international press that show the kowtowing of the world's leaders to the Catholic prelates. The control Roman Church projects over nations is amazing. Recently, the Holy See summoned the US ambassador and another nation's representative at which audience the Pope told them what's what about Israel annexing the West bank territories (an absolute contradiction of God's will for the people of Israel). This is absurd for the twenty-first century; yet it is the reality Jesus foretold to John. As I was writing the early drafts of this book, Pope Benedict XVI chose to retire and the whole process captured the news for weeks, heads of state heaped praise on him and his "wisdom" and Pope Francis I became the darling of the newscasts.

> <u>Note</u>: Could other world religions fulfill the qualifications to be this prostitute? Islam or the Eastern religions, for example, cannot fit the characteristics of a spiritual *prostitute* in the context of the Bible because they do not claim a direct relationship with Jesus as the Messiah. The Bible is consistent in its use of the concept of spiritual prostitution. Throughout the Old Testament the text reserves the notion of "prostitution" for the Jews who claimed to be YHWH's people while worshiping other idols (Ezekiel Chapters 16 and 23). By claiming to be Jesus' vessel to the world, the Roman Catholic Church fits the biblical definition of the spiritual *prostitute*.

Other matching characteristics

I saw a woman sitting on a scarlet beast that was covered with blasphemous names and had seven heads and 10 horns. When we refer back to the first beast, we see the same description. This diabolical religious monster sits on the antichrist—like it incubates it. We will see also that the scarlet beast is both the antichrist and the worldwide empire he sets up—the empire being its extension.

The Catholic Church has consistently sought to maintain a center of world power in Rome—the city of seven hills. This religion does not uphold or uplift people, it *sits* on them (verse 1). *Sits* indicates control—a type of control that is oppressive and parasitic: schoolyard bullies sit on younger or weaker, defenseless kids.

Many kings have belonged to this religion and many leaders fear its reach, they seek its good graces and sponsorship. History bore out John's prophetic words precisely.

In verse 2, we see that the people who belong to this organization have lost their reason; they abandoned the truth of the scriptures and believe and do things that are aberrant to God. This religion protectively nurtures the incubating *antichrist* (*scarlet beast*) and guards it future empire.

This organization has seven heads meaning that its administration is ubiquitous. It exercises great authority over its people through a vast and pervasive administration. We will see later that the *seven heads* also refers to the seven hills that define the locale of its headquarters—Rome.

The colors mentioned in verse 4 help us identify this prostitute: purple became the color of its bishops, red that of its cardinals. It is paramount to note that John received this prophecy long before any of these details were exhibited. It is impossible that John could have invented this prophecy and hoped that it would apply so precisely. This is pure godly prescience.

The description of gold and gems gives more details; anyone who has visited the Vatican or Catholic churches and cathedrals is witness to the golden riches therein. We gawk with incredulity at gem encrusted gold chalices and other artifacts.

As the text says: She literally rides on the scarlet beast. She will ride on his shirt tails all the way into her ignoble apogee during the three and one-half years of testing.

Her true title is secret; how could it not be? Revealing its identity and title would undermine her purpose and actions. Her dealings and inner workings are secret, she is linked in the news with secret societies and only the initiated and vetted clergy can perform her arcane rites. Her outward moniker does not reveal her real disposition and nature. She calls herself the Mother Church, the Catholic (universal) Church as well as the Holy Apostolic Church, while she encourages the cult of many other gods that she has fabricated, and dedicates most of her buildings to someone other than YHWH. Her real name, from God's point of view, is *"The Great Babylon"* because she belongs to man (and Satan) and not to God.

Her archives, in the Vatican or elsewhere, are closed books; no human government can pry open her vaults in search of the truth. It shields itself from scrutiny behind the claim that the Vatican is a sovereign nation. How can a religion be a sovereign nation, a "state"? Is this what Jesus and the apostles advocated? Countries with strong armies do not even try to meddle: her power is neither divine, nor human. These points should be obvious to all.

Every vice and sin is found in her; in recent years victims coming forward have exposed some of the moral depravity of her clergy: it is shocking. Yet, none of it is new: most aberrations have long been documented as for example the utter corruption and immorality of the Borgia popes (Alexander VI, Calixtus III) or of John XII and Benedict IX. God is revealing plenty for all of us to beware. All wise people can draw their conclusions. She is embattled for all the terrible sins her clergy and administrators have done and continue to do in secret.

As I am writing these paragraphs (2013), our sense of morality is outraged by the senseless, indiscriminate massacre of innocents in Paris by Muslim lunatics practicing their brand of religion; but we fail to take the long historical view and see that for centuries, France suffered an inordinate number of religious mass massacres: massacres ordained by Rome and carried out unflinchingly by mainline Roman Catholics.

Beginning long before the Reformation, the Catholic Church has massacred groups of true Christians throughout her history (Huguenots, Waldensians and Albigensians to name only a few groups). And, where allowed by misguided kings, she has officially massacred God's people (Jews and Christians) who did not submit to the Papacy (Inquisition). From the text of Revelation we will see that this murderous activity was all a preparation for the things to come. After the rapture she will execute those who refuse the mark of the beast. She will reach her potential, her apogee; the mask will be off. She will have soldiers in every corner of the world.

Verse 6 says: *then I saw that the woman was drunk on the blood of the saints and on the blood of the witnesses to Jesus. (...drunk with the blood of God's holy people who were witnesses for Jesus.)* That is her factual history as mentioned above.

> <u>Note</u>:This short sentence tells us also that during the three and one-half years of Satan's rampage, this religious organization will be the one who will kill the post rapture saints whenever and wherever they are found and will kill the two witnessed to Jesus in Jerusalem at the end of that period. This religion has the numbers to do it and the worldwide geographic presence to do this. Past history has already shown to anyone who cares to see, that this future murderous campaign will not be a new behavior for this organization: it has consistently and relentlessly murdered true Christians. The woman was indeed drunk on the blood of the saints and on the blood of the witnesses to Jesus—a long, continuous binge through history.

The term catholic means universal; even way back in time Satan suggested the name that would position the organization to become the One World Religion. She will form the basis, the structure of the Universal Religion that will rule after the rapture.

John was amazed, stunned, because he could not imagine that the most powerful agent against Jesus throughout the grace era and at the time of testing will be an organization that outwardly claims His name. And we too are amazed today because God described her in specific and descriptive details long before she began to exist.

Observations on the woman astride the scarlet beast

No one living in John's time had any idea that this religion would one day exist—only God foreknew and forewarned. The scarlet beast could refer to several levels of the same thing: the dragon/Satan, as well as his personification: the *antichrist* and finally to the Roman Empire-type structure that will be recreated. Red was the color of the Roman military, of its might, and purple was the color of its authority.

From the terms used and the definition given in the text (*covered with blasphemous names and had seven heads and 10 horns*), we also perceive the religion's relationship with the city of Rome and the Roman Empire the two being indistinguishable because they have the very same nature. They are both called the *beast* because the *antichrist* will simply be the personification of Satan as well as the impersonation of the revived Roman Empire. That empire will be the extension of his personality.

The image in 17:3 is interesting: the Roman Catholic Church is carried along on the back of the beast as a future cherished tool for his evil purposes. The *antichrist* and his empire will in time hatch from its Roman nest, ready and equipped to carry out its evil designs.

The significance of the Roman Empire

It is no happenstance that the Roman Empire was the world power at the time that God chose to send His Messiah. The Roman Empire represented the opposite of what is godly. Through its local administrator, Pilate, it was complicit to the murder of Christ. It was a true human power, with strong idolatrous roots and practices. Besides a multitude of Roman gods of various uses and definitions, the emperor himself was declared to be a god; and as such, he was venerated and idolized by every Roman—just as his successor, the *antichrist*, will be.

History shows us that the Roman Empire went through an extended dry spell within just a few centuries after John's penned Revelation. Indeed, as the central power of ancient Rome waned, its lands went through the dark ages and moved on toward our modern times where the original Roman Empire is not an obvious factor anymore. It is into this foretold dry spell (*desert*) that the angel takes John (17:3). Here John sees the woman who sits on the *scarlet beast* (the Roman Empire), preserving it, incubating it. We now have the advantage of 20 centuries of history that John did not have so we can look back and observe that a large part of this prophecy has already been carried out.

To understand the process here we can use the nautical analogy of a sailing ship that uses a succession of tacks to progress upwind toward its destination. When diversity and heterogeneity of groups within the empire made the civic Roman rule impractical and diluted its central power; the vessel changed tacks. Just like on a ship, the process of changing tacks is an unstable one: many changes take place, the forward momentum is lost and the rudder temporarily loses some authority. Yet after a brief moment of wallowing in the waves, the new tack begins to take hold, slowly momentum builds and the rudder becomes more and more effective again. Control returns. The ship now travels along a different tack but the overall progress toward its destination is maintained and assured.

The same thing can be said of the Roman Empire; it lost its momentum, and during the shift of power, it floundered, rudderless and seemed to be in the dark for a while. During that period, the religious Roman Catholic institution was slowly but surely gathering its power and control for the new "tack". When this was achieved the ship of state could progress in complete control toward its fateful destination. The Roman Empire was, died and will rise up again.

The diversity of the conquered peoples, languages and cultures progressively made the human Roman empire awkward and powerless. Therefore a different "unity" was needed to carry on forward: an idealogical mindset, a religion identified with the empire. It needed an "empire religion", a common superstition/fear that would breached races, skin colors and local traditions and provide a common core of control. A religion imposes a centralized superstitious control over the peoples without having to solve or manage the widely diverse idiosyncratic challenges of civic administration.

That is what happened. And right from the beginning, the late Roman emperors were keen to take the elms of this religious ship. For example, it was the emperor who called the councils of Nicaea and later Constantinople to unify and codify the mindset he wanted in order to effect his control over the state.

> Note: We who live today should easily recognize this
> process. Our country used to possess a unifying set of
> core principles that attracted vetted immigrants and
> melded them into a forward marching, forward
> building whole. The enemies of our state have
> systematically aimed at destroying this positive

construct using unrestricted immigration/invasion of non-coherent groups as well as non-law-abiding elements. These coordinated and concerted efforts aim at the same result of breaking the state as the Roman conquests of the diverse groups did for that empire. On top of this, the enemies of our state are battering our Christian faith into oblivion because it has the potential and the promise to be the most effective agent of cohesion for this disparate grouping in the making. Without it, the state will become ungovernable; as our founding fathers clearly understood.

Back to the text: We will see below that Charlemagne was the monarch that stood at the time when the "wind" began to pull the re-aligned sail, firmly establishing the long and powerful tack of the religious Catholic Rome; replacing the played out tack of the civic Roman Empire.

Historically the Roman Empire began to fragment when the central power weakened in the centuries immediately following John. The Eastern Empire kept its ascendency longer, but the Western Empire weakened considerably and imploded in the fifth century.

Beginning with the extremely short reign of Petronius Maximus (March 17 – May 31, 455), the last eight centralized emperors of the Western Empire are known as the Shadow Emperors. The last of this series was Romulus Augustus (October 31/475 – September 4/476); his deposition from power traditionally marks the end of the Roman Empire in the West. In his *History of the Wars*, Procopius had this to say about these emperors: "Although I know their names well, I won't mention them at all. They only lived a short time after attaining office and as a result accomplished nothing worth mentioning". Wikipedia says: "The final collapse of the Empire in the West was marked by increasingly ineffectual puppet Emperors dominated by their Germanic masters of soldiers". Thus these last emperors reigned but did not rule. The frontier tribes, especially the fully Romanized Germanic tribes would now begin their attacks on and eventual dominance over the civic powers of Rome.

With the Justinian dynasty (518 – 602) the emperors from the remaining stronghold of the empire (Constantinople) began to meld their civic identity to their spiritual stand; they began to be qualified as "holy" or "saintly". Their effigies on coins showed either a halo around their head or a cross beside their likeness. They also began to carry out clergy-mandated measures against their subjects. By the ninth century, Charlemagne's power will undercut the Byzantine Roman Emperor's authority over the Western Empire. The split became final when the church itself split in 1054.

To get into more details about the processes alluded to above we need to consider Justinian and his actions. Justinian was brilliant, ruthless and focused—probably the most capable emperor the Roman Empire ever had. With him, though, the desire and necessity for imperial control became dependent on the Roman Empire having become a "Christian Empire". Since Rome under Justinian became dominant in the near-eastern region its religion needed to reflect the exclusive favor of God.

But how could the emperor maintain control of this spiritual force while projecting its inferences on his own people as well as the neighboring kingdoms and empires? To achieve his geopolitical goals, Justinian carried a three pronged approach: he demanded that his subjects embrace the state-approved orthodoxy of his bishops. Without this, the allegiance of the believers would splinter away from the central powers.

Then with this in mind, Justinian set his goals to expanding his influence to far-distant lands by promoting active "evangelization" using state sponsored missionaries. So, now the Good News became Roman, not divinely transcendent and spiritually independent.

And finally, the Roman subjects and hierarchy adopted an arrogant frame of mind: Christians could not be Christians unless they were Romans (this last sentence is taken from Tom Holland's book *In the Shadow of the Sword.*) This frame of mind still controls the religious identity of provincial France, Italy and other places: people will tell you that they are French or Italian <u>therefore</u> they are Catholic and they are Christians <u>because</u> they are Catholic.

These substantive shifts gave the "Roman Church" the tactical basis to claim universal ascendency, thus to impose its dominion, which included the prerogative to punish the dissenters—even to death. Furthermore this shift had two significant consequences: it shielded the "Roman Church" from opposition and gave it an inferred imperial mandate.

These developments created the precedents that would provide the means for the Roman Church to impose its will, first on the Germanic monarchs, and later to all regional monarchs who will rule portions of the Church's sphere of control. Indeed as history will demonstrate, should a regional monarch balk at the church's demands, the Roman Church could always threaten as well as coerce a neighboring monarch to march against the recalcitrant—history provides ample example of both.

Rome also claimed to be the only dispenser of God's grace, sacraments and pardon, thus the Church held the primeval fears of the masses hostage to its diktats. Entry to heaven, escape from Hell or from Purgatory were exclusive dispensations of Rome. No civic monarch could counter or even neutralize such a psychological, superstitious hold over his own subjects. By this cultic hold over the populations, the Roman Church has held the monarchs hostages to their own populations.

Thus, beginning with Justinian, the Roman Empire had morphed into what will be a far stronger, more pernicious and infinitely more adaptable power. It would be a power that was not encumbered with civic, state responsibilities like providing services, road systems or even militarily protection for the populations. Indeed, keeping up the revenues needed to service the expectations of a civic government and to assure the military protection of same have always been the banes of empires.

Effectively, this new Roman imperial system will not need to meet any of these responsibilities; how convenient. It offers no human services, yet it will tax...but will keep the receipts to do as it pleases with no accountability—devilishly nifty.

We can see how, with the protection and sponsorship of the emperor, the shift from "an assembly of those who are set apart upon Jesus" to a coercive, punitive and mind controlling apparatus had ratcheted into place. We can see that before the civic, governmental powers of the secular Roman Empire expired, the system had been (innocuously at first) re-branded into a much more powerful and flexible agent. This nascent, novel empire could control the minds of a huge swath of humanity through the metering out of fears on one hand and conditional hope on the other... without the costs, responsibilities or accountability of a civic empire. Yet its control was far more secure because it was rooted in the individual and collective psyche of the populations. This novel "Roman Empire" could ride aloof of any regional conflict, war or natural catastrophes and still come through unscathed, richer and more in control.

The Roman Catholic Church is the most successful geopolitical switch Satan ever produced. It was a most foreboding strategic step, and its full effect is still in the future: it will be the platform from which the *antichrist* will pull his empire together.

A short walk through history

Now, we narrow the historical narrative to Western Europe—the region that provided the Roman Religion its main power and support over many centuries. On the spiritual plane, beginning before the end of the first century, the good news of Jesus was carried outward to all the frontiers of the Roman Empire through traditional evangelization: individual evangelists called by God and motivated by His Spirit. But in mid-fourth century, something changed drastically: the original church in Rome left orthodoxy and adopted and pursued the new, monolithic and pyramidal format that Constantine's actions and decrees had enabled. This organization began to demand authority over all the "Christians" in the Empire and to reel them into its fold. Even though the Roman Catholic Church will not achieve its final stability until the end of the Great Western Schism (1417); the budding Roman Catholic Church will consolidate its power progressively and relentlessly until it achieved sway over the monarchies in the early years of the ninth century.

From the fifth century on, the civic Western Roman Empire's history becomes practically a desert. As far I could research, the eastern Justinian monarchs who extended their powers over Rome were the last to be nominated or elected according to the practice of the old Rome; they were not vetted nor crowned by the Church, even though they identified themselves with it.

Eventually, in the latter part of the eighth century, in western Europe King Pepin-le-Bref became the avowed "Defender of the Papacy", concluding a shift toward religious Rome that had begun with Clovis as the Germanic tribes became stronger, militarily and politically, than the weak roman emperors. From Pepin, we transition directly into the "Holy Roman Emperors" with his son, Charles 1 (Karolus Magnus a.k.a. Charlemagne) who officially established the Holy Roman Empire.

Charlemagne was crowned by Pope Leo III in 800—acknowledging thereby his fealty, and the fealty of his empire, to the Church of Rome. He too portrayed himself as the unconditional protector of the Papacy. With him, the ultimate power of a large part of the original Roman Empire was again anchored in Rome. The last word in power had become religious; not civic. With Charlemagne, the ship of state was underway on the new tack; the Roman Church was the power in its sails.

Charlemagne had found it expedient to make use of the superstitious bondage that the Roman religion holds upon the masses to impose and to perpetuate his imperial authority over them. But in doing so, he effectively placed himself in bondage of that church. Throughout history, few of his royal descendants and successors have been Catholics of personal convictions; most, just like he was, have been opportunistically cynical about the arrangement—profiting from the sponsorship while chafing at the ascendancy it imposes. To this day they cannot publicly deviate from the superstitions that buttress their crowns: they are lackeys of Rome, pawns in a cosmic play orchestrated long ago. Let's look at how history has played out since Charlemagne.

Charlemagne's empire splintered into different regional branches (Carolingian, Guideschi, Ottonian/Saxon and Salian/Frankish) but it did not matter; the prophesied switch of power to the Roman Catholic Church as well as the absolute hegemony of that entity was established. In the centuries that followed, none of the subsequent regional monarchs would or could renounce their slavish fealty to the Roman Catholic Church. The uncontested higher authority in their kingdoms from then on will be the Church of Rome. Many kings will try to curtail Rome's power, and although they sometimes succeeded in containing some aspects of it, for a time; in the end they could not escape its dominance. Rome always reclaimed the upper hand.

From Charlemagne on, every future king or emperor of the region will need papal approval to become legitimate and will be enthroned through the specific crowning by a prelate of the Church of Rome. There are no Christ-mandated precedents for any of this; it is religious hocus-pocus meant to achieve total superstitious control. Royal marriages, usually motivated by politics and arranged for power consolidation, must be approved by the Pope. Rome will impress its preference at every national or international power shift. Even the French revolution that set out to eradicate religion and enthrone reason could not snuff out the Roman Church's hold on the masses. Napoleon, a savvy product of the revolution, insisted on being crowned emperor by a prelate to insure popular acceptance of his self-appointed role and title.

When the hold of the church was deemed strong enough, Boniface VIII in his papal bull "Unam Sanctum" established officially that all powers on earth—both spiritual and temporal—are under the jurisdiction of the Pope. To quote this papal bull: "Now, therefore, we declare, say, determine and pronounce that for every human creature it is necessary for salvation to be subject to the authority of the Roman pontiff" (Porro subesse Romano Pontifici omni humanae creaturae declaramus, dicimus, definimus, et pronuntiamus omnino esse de necessitate salutis). Every creature, kings and presidents included (catholic or not) must subject himself to the authority of the pope—or expect damnation. This is considered to be an infallible dogma of the Catholic Church. All these are evidences of the grip this religion has on the working politics of the former Roman Empire. The effective power is in Rome—today's Vatican.

The entrenched tentacles of the Roman Church throughout the former Roman Empire's lands and the superstitious power that the Church wields on the masses (as well as the gentry) assured that no monarchy that is not vetted by Rome could survive. The

French king Henry IV understood this well enough to switch his faith from a "Protestant belief" to a "Catholic allegiance": he could not hope to reign without it.

Over the centuries, the stranglehold of the Roman Catholic Church on the politics of the original Roman Empire's lands has continued to grow. The Roman Catholic Church has also become the *de facto* power-base in many countries outside the borders of the old Roman Empire where it has become the state religion or the religion of the majority.

From that transition long ago, the stage was set for the Roman Catholic Church to maintain a ruling seat in Rome for the *antichrist*'s revived Roman Empire to come. Historically, from that point on, having her base firmly established and controlling the former Roman imperial territory, this religion spread her influence into all the corners of the world (over a multitude of populations as this passage of Revelation foretells).

The Roman Catholic Church will hand over to the *antichrist* a true world hegemony, backed by a sophisticated administration and a comprehensive registry of its masses—every member, whether faithful or casual, practicing or not, is duly recorded. This *woman* is really sitting on the *beast*, and she maintains the root of power of the Roman Empire throughout the era of grace—as predicted to John almost two thousand years ago.

On a spiritual level, we can observe that, beginning with the apostles, the impact of grace and faith in Jesus began to insulate the population from the authority of the idolatrous ancient Roman Empire. Grace, and the action of the Spirit of God in and around his people, made the civic Roman Empire untenable; it imperiled civic idolatrous Rome. Satan's counter measure was to neutralize the effect of grace and of Jesus' kingdom by replacing civic Rome with an organization that claims grace and pretends to control the access to Jesus' kingdom: a pseudo-Christian religion. It worked, most people accepted the switch.

This pseudo-Christianity that Satan initiated and managed is documented in Jesus' parable of the wheat and the tares in Matthew 13. Between Gog and Magog and the rapture, the Roman Catholic false Gospel will vie with the true Gospel for the souls of the awakened people who will have seen Jesus in action. That parable and its conclusion will play out its final acts during the pre-rapture seven+ years.

At the rapture, the population that is left behind will all belong to this false Christianity. They will all be documented and classified by Rome and ready to cheer their Christ-replacement: the antichrist. The antichrist will not have to win anyone over. The subject is detailed at length in *The Rock Breaks the Globalists' Empire*.

So, back to our historical account: underneath the surface, while there has not been a Western Roman Emperor for centuries, the Roman Empire has appeared dead, but it did not completely die; it remained alive in a chrysalis form. Its successful metamorphosis is assured and the idolatrous, pseudo-Christian religion centered in Rome has successfully guarded its future reappearance. Thus, the human empire of the *antichrist* will be able to sprout up quickly when the Spirit of God has left this earth with the raptured true believers. The image given in verse 3 is appropriate: the final Roman Empire is incubating.

Anyone can easily see that this pseudo-Christian organization is indeed headquartered, just as God predicted, in the capital city of the Roman Empire. It is holding the seat for it, and latently maintaining and extending its power.

Thoughts to ponder

Another historical detail is revealing: it was a Roman emperor, Constantine, who set in motion the basis for this religious monster that will guard the empire. When he "converted" to Christianity, he demanded that elaborate temples be built to rival the other Roman gods' worship sites. He mandated that an official clergy be appointed like the other idolatrous cults and that statues of the statesmen of the church (including himself—after all, he was a god too) be erected. All was now set in motion for what would become the Roman Catholic Church with its ornate cathedrals, clerical hierarchy and system of statues and symbols of adoration.

I have heard it said that in one swoop with Constantine the church went from a mere smattering of Romans to an overwhelming majority of the population—without redeeming a single soul. The true believers who were persecuted before Constantine's "conversion" were in the same precarious position after; except that now they did not have an identity anymore: the new false converts called themselves Christians (as does every Catholic since)—thus defining the true Christians as the illegitimate faction.

Rome, the capital of the false Christ is called the Eternal City; which tells us right there that it is anti Adonai/Jesus because the blessed eternal city will be the New Jerusalem, ushered in by God Himself. There is a sub-meaning to the Eternal City epithet: It claims to be the gateway to eternal life for humanity—except it is the very gate to eternal suffering life, not blessed life.

After John was astonished; the angel provides more details: 17:9b – 18

9b The seven heads are seven mountains on which the woman is seated. 10 They are also seven kings: Five have fallen, one is, the other has not yet come, and when he comes, he must remain for a little while. [11]The beast that was and is not, is himself an eighth king, yet he belongs to the seven and is going to destruction. [12]The 10 horns you saw are 10 kings who have not yet received a kingdom, but they will receive authority as kings with the beast for one hour. [13]These have one purpose, and they give their power and authority to the beast. [14]These will make war against the Lamb, but the Lamb will conquer them because He is Lord of lords and King of kings. Those with Him are called, chosen, and faithful." [15]He also said to me, "The waters you saw, where the prostitute was seated, are peoples, multitudes, nations, and languages. [16]The 10 horns you saw, and the beast, will hate the prostitute. They will make her desolate and naked, devour her flesh, and burn her up with fire. [17]For God has put it into their hearts to carry out His plan by having one purpose and to give their kingdom to the beast until God's words are accomplished. [18]And the woman you saw is the great city that has an empire over the kings of the earth."

What's happening

This passage could not be clearer. The woman sits in Rome, the city of seven hills. And she sits on many peoples and nations and languages.

The *beast* with seven heads and ten horns that had ruled at one time but disappeared represents the Roman Empire. It will come back but then will be destroyed forever. In this verse, the beast is not the *antichrist*. This beast here is the political organization of the *antichrist*; the empire that the *antichrist* will use to carry out his plans and enforce his will. The *antichrist* is first and foremost the "incarnate" Satan who craves to be worshiped as a god. The historic Roman Empire's emperors held the status of gods and were worshiped as official gods—a precedent, a practice run, for the *antichrist*.

The description goes to great lengths to make sure we understand and see what is described here. The Gentiles who had not been lifted by Jesus at the rapture will be amazed when this form of government reappears. It will be similar to the powerful Roman government that previously ruled the entire area of John's world. It disappeared, but it will reappear and godless Gentiles will see in it their solution to world government. They will feel validated after all.

What is astounding is that in John's time, as the apostle took this dictation, the Roman Empire was invincible and seemed eternal; no one would have wagered that it could fade away. After all it had just trounced Israel and emptied its territory of its ancient people.

Furthermore, it was the only world power at the time, there was no other government that could offer a balance of power or even an alternative. For its citizens, the Roman Empire must have seemed to define history ever after. It is hard for us to picture the situation because for centuries we have not known such an exclusive world power. But God knew and His revelation must have boggled John's mind, as well as the minds of the early readers of the book of Revelation before the Roman Empire degraded precipitously.

Now the messenger will give more details that will place this *beast* (political powerhouse) on the map. This power is located in the same city where the above religion (*the Great Prostitute*) squats; the city with seven hills—Rome. Rome has been known throughout history as the city on seven hills (see the writings of Virgil, Martial, Cicero, etc). Since John wrote Revelation, the *Great Prostitute* (the Roman Catholic Church) has indeed established itself in this city of seven hills as predicted by God. The evil political organization that the *antichrist* establishes will be based in Rome.

Historically, as these texts predicted, the Church of Rome has ruled over the kings of the earth. Essentially, for more than a millennium the Catholic Church has defined the identity of the city of Rome. Since 1871 Rome has been the civic capital of the newly formed country of Italy but for the rest of the world Rome continues to represent the Catholic Church's center of power. Popularly, Rome and Vatican are interchangeable terms. Without the Catholic Church, civic Rome would be mostly irrelevant to the average non-Italian person today. It would be like any other capital city: Oslo, Bern, Vienna or Athens with its government institutions and historic monuments. As a national administrative capital, it would only be relevant to its own citizens.

The real power in Rome, over the centuries, has been the Catholic Church. It sits atop the former Roman Empire's heart. When revived by the *antichrist*, the Roman Empire will sprout up; using the leverage of the Catholic Church who has preserved its seat of power. For centuries, this false "Christian" organization has established and maintained a culture that will enable the evil Roman Empire to rise quickly in power and authority from its preserved roots.

The messenger gives more details about the political organization so that we may understand what will take place. This *beast* (Roman Empire) will set up and empower ten vassals—presumably from other parts of the world, but their power will be brief (Satan has only three and one-half years). These are not necessarily existing powers today; they will be appointed by the *antichrist*. They will be completely subservient to the *beast* (the new Roman power). Their allegiance provides a quick expedient toward global rule for the *antichrist* and his revived Roman Empire.

The new Roman Empire is the direct extension of the person of the *antichrist*. The outcome is assured: Jesus, the real Christ will defeat this power.

Now in verse 15, the text verifies that the "waters" of verse 1 where the *prostitute* sits are people, races, nations, and languages. This accurately describes the Catholic religion of Rome that has expanded its activities to all continents and to every people.

Even though the *prostitute* will serve the purpose of Satan and the *antichrist*; he and his vassals will hate this religion and will eventually tear it apart—essentially doing God's bidding (17:16 – 17). It will be the last significant event of the three and one-half years before the "battle with no name". Finally, there will be a government with the power and the will to do this. Many a king—even Catholic kings—and governments hated this religion and its power, because through superstition it exercised greater control over the population than they were able to.

This religion and its leaders have always been able to influence, even control, the local kings or civic governments. Some French kings even turned over the actual government of France directly to prelates of Rome: Cardinal Richelieu and later Cardinal Mazarin. Fernando and Isabel of Spain who are referred to as "Los Reyes Católicos" gave prelates of the church great power and influence over all state decisions. A "Most Catholic Majesty" distinction is still awarded today by the Pope to monarchs who according to him embody the Catholic principles in their lives and in their public policies. Today, the monarchs of Belgium, Luxembourg and Spain wear this title. Yes, even as I began writing these pages in early 2013, the morally embattled Spanish monarch at that time was still a "Most Catholic Majesty". Hitler courted the Roman Church and there is hardly a high level Nazi journalistic photo that does not show a cardinal or two in attendance. For all his bluster and his denigrating remarks, Khrushchev never faced her down either.

The evil shenanigans of the Church of Rome go on unabated in our times and the *rulers of this world* [who] *have immoral relations with her* (17:2 NLT) are not some backward monarchs of a long gone era. The book, *The Vatican Connection*, documents an episode that took place in the early 1970s—our modern era.

Top ranking Catholic cardinals and the Pope through his archbishop director of the Vatican's own bank requested nearly one billion dollars (yes billion) of forged securities from the Italian Mafia in the US. The shameless and law-breaking prelates specifically stipulated that these be forged securities—not simply stolen securities. Forged securities are cheaper and there are no limits on how many you can produce plus they do not appear on the published reports of stolen securities; so the Vatican would not get caught.

This of course is 100% illegal, it is morally indefensible and legally reprehensible. The prelates' heartless scheme would defraud tens of thousands of good people and destabilize top US corporations. If a company or an individual initiated such a plot they would receive the harshest applicable penalties. The Archbishop Director of the Vatican's finance, who answered only to the Pope, was an American. He thought nothing of defrauding his own people—some of whom would be Catholics!

The Vatican wanted to make up the losses their badly managed bank had suffered during the previous years. They did not want to face the consequences of their incompetence. The New York District Attorney and the FBI investigated and built a prosecutable case.

This District Attorney and the lead investigator were devout Catholics, what they uncovered shook them to the core. However, the Nixon administration prevented the FBI and the District Attorney from prosecuting their cases by imposing a total gag on the proceedings. Nixon's administration ordered that the Vatican could not be mentioned or alluded to—orally or in print—and could not be brought on any charge. Thus the Church of Rome escaped scot-free to continue posing as the benign, righteous and pious organization it is not. A Church with its own bank; how true to scriptures!

So, in our modern, educated and sophisticated times, a recent, secular American president prostituted himself with the Vatican at the express expense of his own citizens and industries. Why? For the same reasons the French and Spanish kings did in centuries past: Nixon feared losing the Catholic constituency which is still held in slavish superstition by Rome, as it has always been.

The end of the Catholic Church will be poetic justice: the religion that has always been able to persecute and destroy anyone that stood in its way will be persecuted by the very monster it helped create. From its secret evil identity, the Church of Rome killed the true believers. At the end of the three and one-half years of Satan's rampage, God will use the Church's evil associates to destroy it; the destruction ordered by God but carried out by men.

Finally, we must remember that in spite of coming to power to his own fans base and consolidating his power into an absolutely pervasive and all encompassing state apparatus, the *antichrist* and Satan will still lose some individuals who in spite of everything will still personally choose eternity with Jesus.

Thoughts to ponder

The Pope, being a man, is not the *false prophet*, this is important to understand. Most interpretations of Revelation I have listened to or read through the years err in this area: by failing to properly identify the *false prophet* as the demons (fallen angels); they never account for them. According to these interpretations, the demons fall through the cracks of human logic and God's justice never deals with them. This cannot be. When one sees the *false prophet* as the demons; God's unfailing justice is accomplished scripturally: they are thrown into Hell with the *antichrist*.

The Pope will be a willing puppet of these two entities (*antichrist* and *false prophet*), for a time until they have him killed. The track record of the papacy over the centuries indicates that the Holy See is well rehearsed for this collaboration; it won't have to change masters.

> <u>Note</u>: One may note that the Orthodox Church shares many traits with the Church of Rome. It too was connected to the Emperor Constantine and it can be defined by its excessive riches of precious metals and gems. It too canonizes people into saints who become vetted as intercessors, receiving the prayers and pilgrimages of the faithful. It dedicates its houses of worships to the saints it manufactures. It is not, however, the *great prostitute* described here because the colors of its prelates do not match, it is not headquartered in Rome and it has not wielded the same stranglehold on the kings of the earth. Keep in mind though, that it may, in the near future, unite under Rome and thus become indistinguishable from it.

On current events

When observing world current events, one cannot help pondering their import in regard to the events of the end. Why would Pope John-Paul II pronounce that Christians and Muslims worship and serve the same God when history and scriptures clearly contradict the idea? Why would his successor, Pope Benedict XVI pray in the Blue Mosque in Istanbul (at the time, it created a backlash from some Catholics and Muslims)? And in November 2014, why would Pope Francis I push the issue again by entering the same Blue Mosque to go bow his head in prayer, while dutifully facing Mecca? Al Jazeera reported: *Pope Francis has taken part in a Muslim prayer alongside the Grand Mufti of Istanbul* (the intended symbolism was not lost on Muslims: *a Muslim prayer can only be offered to the Islamic god*). This time, the event did not provoke any backlash. Are we seeing end-time history on the horizon?

Why the change of policy? Why after centuries of open and active opposition to Islam, the Vatican now changes its dogmatic stance? Islam has not changed; its practices and its scriptures have remained the same—it has not renounced any of its tenets that were offensive to Rome—so one wonders: why is Rome doing this?

There seems to be an intentional, calculated trend in this process. The spirit who animates the successive Roman pontiffs has read both the Old Testament prophecies regarding Gog and Magog as well as the text of Revelation. This spirit understands the general disarray that will engulf Muslims following God's action at Gog and Magog—disarray that could lead many to seek a correction of their beliefs. It will be obvious to all Muslims that the god of Islam was no God at all. Hopefully most Muslims will search for the truth and will come to Jesus; but many may look for a religious re-alignment that would still allow them to validate their native faith in some way. The spiritual warfare will then be between the true Christianity and the false Christianity—the Roman decoy. The topic is developed fully in *The Rock Breaks the Globalists' Empire*.

So, is Rome strategically positioning itself for this eventuality? By their words and actions these popes have promoted the idea that Catholicism and Islam are related faiths; so we can surmise that these moves are strategic stepping stones to be able to woo Muslims then. I am not saying that the Popes themselves know what they are doing; but their puppeteer does. Is Rome being prepared for the aftermath of Gog and Magog: to tell Muslims that they were mostly right all along; just mistaken in their practices, needing simply a different religious vehicle to reach their traditional god?

The Roman Church could make the argument that joining the Church of Rome would not be a drastic change—because devoted Muslims would still be serving the same god, according to the highest Catholic authority: the Pope.

It is thus conceivable that a very large number of dismayed Muslims could join the Church of Rome, swelling the ranks of the people who will serve the *antichrist* in his killing campaign against the post-rapture saints. Islamic Jihadists already favor the gruesome beheading of their victims; therefore doing the same to those who will choose Jesus over the *antichrist* will seem like a natural extension of what they already do—a procedure their newfound religion will approve and sanction.

Note: A Muslim lives his whole life in the pursuit of getting clear of his god for eternity. The hoped-for Islamic heaven is a heaven without his god. The ultimate goal is to be signed off by god into a heaven where man can give full license to his basest urges, the very urges he spends his earthly life subduing or hiding, to get there! (That alone is a crooked deal, a disingenuous proposition: a life of cheating to finally live the forbidden sin.) The goal is to get free from the distant, vengeful and punishing god of his religion. It is a heaven where Allah has no place and where Allah leaves him alone, having signed off at the death of the "faithful".

The Christian, on the other hand, aims to a heaven where he will never be separated from the rich, good, generous and loving God—where he is in intimate communion with the wonderful creator God. The God who paid his entry fee Himself and even places His Spirit in him to ensure he gets there. The God of the Bible is the very God the Christian has spent his life plodding toward. So, no, the Popes are wrong, dead wrong: our God and their god are incompatible.

On the topic of religion

God will not rapture His saints along religious denominational lines; the rapture will not be pre-packaged by humans. People are saved individually as they trust Jesus as their Savior and embrace His lordship for their lives. No particular religion can guarantee salvation today, and none will be effective during the *testing time*. Every individual who is not raptured will be forced to make the on-the-spot fateful choice: accept the *antichrist*'s mark or choose to <u>die</u> in Jesus—to be martyred right away. This fateful choice will be imposed upon every living person—individually—regardless of their religious affiliation before the three and one-half years.

Being a Catholic today does not damn the person by association: there are Catholics every day, who come to the saving knowledge of Jesus and who consequently extract themselves from their religion. This has been the case throughout the centuries—it has also been the cause of the Catholic retaliatory persecutions. The fact that a person was baptized into that organization and walked in its ways does not prevent God from offering individual salvation and pluck out of it anyone who accepts His grace on His terms. God looks at the person's heart to see who will respond to his wooing.

It is my personal observation that most Catholics are Catholics because they were raised Catholics by a Catholic family in the midst of a Catholic community. I have noticed a definite staunchness in their affiliation, not because they believe; but because they belong. Even though their personal devotion is often superficial or even nonexistent, they see their religion as an un-alterable attribute of their life, like their nationality or the color of their skin.

Yet, within the Catholic ranks, there are always some seekers—individuals who thirst for the God they know exists. These folks inevitably reach a crossroad.

At that point, some veer into fanatical Catholic piety with strict observance of the Church's rites. Burrowing into the bosom of their religion, they shut off forever the call to the new life. Others do reach up and fly into the waiting hands of the loving Savior. I have noticed that these "escapees" will forever carry a profound distrust of—a retrospective anger toward—the religion that was misleading them right out of the true life.

As a rule, every true believer in Christ has come out of a system of beliefs and into Jesus' simple Good News. When a person confesses Jesus as Messiah and son of the living God; the gates of Hell cannot hold him back (Matthew 16:18). God's limitless power that rescues him is unhindered. All the hocus-pocus of whatever religion or denomination you belonged to previously cannot hold you prisoner: the true God who frees you is not bound by any of that.

Every true believer through history has been a former something: former atheist or agnostic, former Muslim or Buddhist, former Baptist or Episcopalian, former Presbyterian or Orthodox, former animist or druid, etc. We must all abandon our man-made attempts to reach God—or to become god—and surrender to His merciful offer of divine salvation through God's only son Jesus.

Karl Marx was correct: religion is the opiate of the masses. It enslaves people and robs them of their potential while it deadens their good sense by making them feel good and safe. In contrast, Jesus' Good News is the choice of the enlightened. Jesus is the light; those who come to the light and dare to step into it are emancipated into their full potential as humans. They are fulfilled into the eternal beings they were created to be.

Being a Catholic today will not exonerate anyone from his personal responsibility to the scriptural truth. Satan could not exclude God's word from his Catholic Church and still call it "Christian"; therefore, to legitimize the Roman Church Satan had to retain the Bible. And herein lays the permanent weakness of the Catholic Church: enough of its Bible is true to God's word and thus it remains efficacious to change anyone who cares to delve into the scriptures; as did Luther, Calvin and scores of others. As could be expected, over the generations and centuries, Rome has discouraged and even forbidden the unsupervised reading of the bible by its laity. It has emphasized instead the primacy of Church Laws and of Church traditions as the bulwark of its orthodoxy. But the weakness remains. In 1993 and again in 2009 we organized bible studies in a "Catholic country"; one of the usual objections we received was: "You don't have a priest in attendance. One cannot study the bible without a priest. A priest must do the teaching." (Read: A priest must be there to chaperon!) As the dates above show, this tethering of the mind of the faithful is still going on in our time.

To this day, Rome always seeks to de-emphasize the literal application of the Bible. For example, Rome became an early and staunch supporter and sponsor of the Charismatic/Pentecostal movement: any movement that weakens the literal authority of scriptures and favors personal emotions and ambitions is a welcomed ally to Rome.

Most Catholics I know feel safely nestled in their native church but they ought to consider the following point and question its implications. If the Christian church had been built on the person of the apostle Peter and founded by him in Rome, and if the Catholic Church thus formed were the true and only Church (as Roman Catholic theology teaches), then why would Jesus dictate His only personal instructions for His churches and His prophetic revelations to John rather than Peter? This question must be pondered by every Catholic. The divine fact is that Jesus appeared to and entrusted Revelation to John, not Peter.

The historical reality is that the Roman Catholic Church did not exist when Revelation was written, it was not founded by the apostle Peter, nor did it grow out of his ministry. No amount of Catholic rewriting of history can change the facts. History shows us that the Roman Catholic Church did not reach its full definition, and did not consolidate its centrality or achieve its religious power-base until much later. The process was circuitous at best; reflecting its human character—not divine inspiration. Even as late as the Great Western Schism (1378 – 1418) several rival claimants were simultaneously vying for the papal office. The various factions warred against one another, so the self-named "True Church" was established by killing the opposition. What an appalling track record! And, yet disingenuously, the Vatican still claims God's exclusive sponsorship through a supposedly unbroken succession line to the Apostle Peter. The pattern of history is there to see: as the Roman Empire's control from Rome was ebbing; the Church of Rome took form and through the ages it strengthened, filling the vacuum.

The Roman Catholic Church came to be, and set roots in Rome because Jesus predicted that it would do so and He warned us about it. The Roman Catholic Church had to exist ... and not for the good; as her bloody, corrupted and rapacious history reveals. Her appointed future will fulfill the tragic prophecy Jesus gives us in these chapters.

Finally, the human race is not progressing toward a better and better humanity and the religions of men do not improve over time to become a worthy vehicle toward God. Sadly, "Christian" Churches, in the name of progress, have the propensity to degrade into mere human religions. Jesus, in his epistle to the seven churches of Revelation kept insisting on a return to a purer format, a return to the original model—as did every apostolic epistle writer. The true Church of Jesus began right; it did not improve over time nor progress toward right. The message still applies today.

Religion is a human phenomenon. No matter what religious leaders may claim: religion never reaches above the human level. Man is pedestrian in his perspective, he often does not see beyond his own manmade walls. We think the constraints of our religion extend to the heavens: they do not. We are proud of our rituals, liturgies and elaborate buildings and feel that God is impressed into validating our religion: He is not. We allow ourselves to be herded divisively by the shallow cells of our religions (and even denominations).

When it comes to the eternal perspective and to God's reality; all religions are simply figments of our imaginations. Religions are not portals to the heavens; they are burdensome nets that keep us into artificial social pens—only because we keep our perspective at the human level. To Jesus, every person is His personal creation whom He desires to woo. Our misguided voluntary enslavement to a religion is the expression of our personal rebellion and lack of faith.

Religions invariably foster death. Religious fervor leads to the killing of the adherents of other confessions. We all think of the violence of Islamists in various parts of the world, or the bloody conflicts in Ireland, but the Eastern religions—that claim tolerance and pacifism—are every bit as bloody as any other religion. Their members have routinely butchered Christians and Muslims, out of raw hatred—and they continue to do so today.

Religions come in every color and flavor imaginable to accommodate the gamut of human tendencies and preferences. Under the banner of "Christianity", who can really number the Protestant-type denominations? Who can make sense of mega churches that operate like they are a religion to themselves? Who can give credence to the small, independent congregations that are wedded to self-appointed guru-style prophets/pastors who claim to be the recipient of a conveniently exclusive vision and anointing? Who can justify the emotional whirlwind that surrounds the Pentecostal/Charismatic congregations that use capricious hedonism as their dogma and whacky revelations as their commandments? Who can sensibly rationalize the exclusive separations within the rainbow of similarly patterned organizations of the Episcopalian Church or Lutheran-type denominations? Outside the banner of Christianity, who can logically explain the deadly, internecine strife among the different sects of Islam? Who can reconcile the many threads of the Eastern religions into a tangible and verifiable whole?

When one considers Jesus' teachings and perspective, all religions appear as they are: human shams that enslave people. They play on man's craving for security, safety and relevance, but they only provide socially acceptable labels to unite under and the illusion of safety through numbers.

<u>(Return to Table of Contents)</u>

****

Chapter 15 - Catastrophic Fall of the World System

Revelation 18:1 – 19:5

18:1 – 3

¹After this I saw another angel with great authority coming down from heaven, and the earth was illuminated by his splendor. ²He cried in a mighty voice: It has fallen, Babylon the Great has fallen! She has become a dwelling for demons, a haunt for every unclean spirit, a haunt for every unclean bird, and a haunt for every unclean and despicable beast. ³For all the nations have drunk the wine of her sexual immorality, which brings wrath. The kings of the earth have committed sexual immorality with her, and the merchants of the earth have grown wealthy from her excessive luxury.

What's happening

Another angel means another vision—a new or separate item is being shown to John for us. *After this* (or *then* as other translations put it) does not imply a linear chronology from the preceding chapter. It simply tells us that after the last vision/vignette, John is now shown a new vision/vignette.

This angel brings in another aspect of the narrative, a new display array so to speak. Timeline wise, this is all accomplished at the end of the age of grace, when the post-rapture world enters a new and different paradigm where Jesus absolutely controls and enforces the conditions (the white horse and its rider). The *laisser-faire* is done.

The actualization of the second angel's message and of the second seal

This vision gives us a detailed exposition of what the second angel (14:8) succinctly introduced to us.

Some of its effects are the actualization of two of the seals: the *fiery red horse* of the second seal: *Its horseman was empowered to take peace from the earth, so that people would slaughter one another* (6:3 – 4). And the actualization of the third seal (6:5 – 6): the scarcity of God's natural supplies. This is very graphic, there is nothing symbolic to this.

Note: *from the earth* means everywhere at the same time, instantaneously. As the result, the human construct of commerce and politics is instantly gone.

In this murderous atmosphere, nobody can buy anybody's influence anymore. Indeed when everyone is plotting to kill everyone else and attempts to do so constantly, all the notions of business are gone. *How to win friends and influence people* (Dale Carnegie) and *The art of the deal* (Donald J. Trump) are not only obsolete; they are instantly irrelevant! All the basis of contractual, reciprocal transactions and agreements are gone; business is now impossible. This is achieved with this one action of God—instant action, instant results. God is infinitely resourceful and clever. He can cancel man's plans anytime; and He just did.

A detailed review

Revelation 18 documents the various aspects of the demise of an entity referred to as *Babylon*. It will be called *Babylon the Great* in verse 2, *the great city, Babylon, the mighty city* in verse 10, *the great city* in verses 16 and 18 and *Babylon the great city* in verse 21. The adjective *great* indicates the worldwide predominance of this *Babylon*. The descriptive *city* designates that it is a system within which humans live. As a system we will be able to contrast this

Babylon with the future *holy city, the new Jerusalem* (NCV) the blessed system within which the redeemed of all time will live.

This *great city Babylon* is not *the woman* of the preceding chapter. They are not destroyed by the same means: the woman is destroyed by the *antichrist*'s human forces while the *great city Babylon* is specifically destroyed by God.

Chapter 18 is the end of the earthly life we all have known and experienced. With this tableau we move back in time to just after the rapture. God has removed His Spirit from the earth and things deteriorate precipitously. The world has become a *dwelling for demons:* the evil angels have been thrown down from heaven; they now dwell on the earth. They are the only spiritual influence left. And from this moment on, they do not just make forays to the earth while residing in the heavens; their only residence now is the earth. The earth is effectively a *dwelling for demons.*

What is *Babylon the Great*, or the *great city of Babylon* (NCV)? It is the world's humanistic system that rejects the sovereignty of YHWH. *Babylon the Great* refers to the Babylon of the Tower of Babel (Genesis 11:1 – 9). This was when the newly re-expanding humanity, descendants of the few people God had spared through the deluge and its resulting flood (Genesis 7) decided to thrust God aside and to establish man as the ultimate pursuit of humanity. They were following their "king" Satan, by adopting his aims (see Isaiah 14:13 – 14). Pride, selfish ambition, greed and envy are all components of this humanistic system. God scattered the men of the Tower of Babel *over the face of the whole earth* and they took with them the rebellious spirit of Babylon. From that time, *the wicked wander everywhere, and what is worthless is exalted by the human race* (Psalm 12:8). And this is a fact.

The angel calls this system *Babylon the Great* because its humanistic dynamics have ruled mankind, its governments, commerce and philosophies through the ages since the Tower of

Babel. It is from this Babylon (this humanistic system) that God extracted Abraham as the father of faith. God said to Abraham in Genesis 12:1: *Go out from your land, your relatives and your father's house* (out of that place, that state of mind and its heritage). God took Abraham to a "place" made for him—a place of faith. God is always urging His people to leave the world system and to come into God's place of faith.

At the beginning of the post-rapture period, the "Babylon" system is instantly broken by a divine act. Nothing works right. Peace is not possible anymore at any level (the red horse). God's earth stops producing (the black horse). The wild beast are murderous, the plague is murderous (the pale green horse). Commerce is impossible.

In the text, we see that all kings throughout history (not just at the end times) have committed immorality with this system. This means that kings, rulers and governments since the flood until the rapture have actively espoused this system for their own gain. They have been the ardent supporters and promoters of it.

The rebellious spirit of this humanistic world system spread after the Tower of Babel as the population, now unable to communicate effectively, scattered (Genesis 11:9). This newly expanding humanity went everywhere; disseminating its spirit to all the confines of the earth. It has ruled the dynamics of human life since then. It is man's futile endeavor to control the world in response to his fears.

Man left to his own devices is hopeless and the world he makes is without hope. So society rebounds from one fad to the next in its continual search to identify a culprit for its failings and to find the solution that will end all fears. However, since it purposefully avoids divine direction it goes around in circles and history repeats itself with devastating monotony.

This *Babylon the Great*, this humanistic system that man dispersed throughout the entire world, rules New York, Cairo, Rome, Buenos Aires, Mombasa, Des Moines, Newcastle, as well as the remote villages of Irian Jaya, your town and my village. Everyone is subject to it. The merchants of the world throughout history have benefitted greatly from the unbridled greed, envy, fear, corruption and other ungodly attributes this human system promotes. All the nations of the world through history have lived by the ungodly principles that emanated from that Babylon. It only survived because God, in His infinite patience, provided for the sinful as well as the righteous.

Observations

Here are the reasons why I believe that Chapters 18 and 19 of Revelation refer to the Babylon of the Tower of Babel instead of to the Babylon of the Babylonian Empire (the Medo-Persian Empire of Nebuchadnezzar, Cyrus, Artaxerxes, Ahasuerus or Darius). This later Babylonian Empire lasted only a short span of history and at times was rather favorable to the Jews when they were faithful to YHWH (read the stories of Esther and Mordecai, Daniel, Ezra and Nehemiah). Some emperors like Darius and Nebuchadnezzar made stunning confessions of faith toward YHWH. Twice the administration of the entire empire was entrusted to Godly Jews (Daniel and Mordecai) and the Jews prospered during those times. This Babylon taken as a whole was no more opposed to God than any other particular kingdom or republic before or since. Instead, God used the Babylonians for His purposes: to punish but also to bless His people. It was Cyrus who ordered the rebuilding of Jerusalem several centuries before Christ.

On the other hand, Babylon, the humanistic world system of the Tower of Babel in this chapter is the antithesis of YHWH's will for mankind, whereas the Babylonian <u>Empire</u> was just another human empire. The Jews that God exiled to the Babylonian Empire of Nebuchadnezzar were the "good figs" and God promised to watch over them and to bless them while they lived there (Jeremiah 24:4 – 6). God encouraged them to settle comfortably, to get established and to enjoy the good things in life. He went as far as telling them to seek the welfare of the city (Babylon of the Babylonian Empire) and to pray to YHWH for its prosperity (Jeremiah 29:4 – 7). God could hardly wish any good for the Babylon that spawned the Tower of Babel—the direct, willful expression of opposition to Him. The Babylon Jesus destroys in Revelation is not a remake of the Babylonian Empire; it is the godless, idolatrous world system of the Tower of Babel.

Furthermore, as awesome as the Babylonian Empire was in Daniel or Mordecai's time; its influence did not extend through the ages. Therefore *the kings* of later eras did not commit *sexual immorality with her* (18:3)—and certainly none have in the last two millennia. When the Babylonian Empire split and waned, its influence ceased quickly and it has not been a factor at all in the world since long before Christ. (The Persian Empire that occupied some of its territory was never a lasting world power. It was a regional power.) The merchants of the entire world (18:3) have long ago ceased to get any profit or trade from that pile of rubble in Iraq. That Babylon is finished.

Also the text makes it clear that the reach of *Babylon the Great* of Chapters 18 and 19 is universal. Its fall will paralyze the entire world trade. The Babylonian Empire of Daniel and Mordecai's time was never universal; certainly it covered a very large territory, but it left many populations out, for example those in Western Europe, the Americas or Japan to name a few. Too many of the "kings of the earth" and "merchants" of the world would be left out—geographically and historically—if this was the Babylon considered here.

Furthermore, a modern remake of the imperial city of Babylon would not fill the requirements of the text: the kings and merchants who lived between antiquity and this futuristic rebuilt Babylon would be left out. Pundits who preach or write that the Babylon of the Babylonian Empire in Iraq will be rebuilt between now and the rapture and will then dominate world culture, government and commerce simply have the wrong Babylon and the wrong concept. Even if some government or group succeeded in rebuilding a striving city on the site of that Babylon; it would not control the powers of the world or its commerce before the rapture. And it would not satisfy the text of Revelation, it would only be another deception, diverting people's attention away from God's message.

Finally, when God dealt with the tower of Babel situation, He did not terminate the rebellion; He simply scattered the people to all azimuths. The people took their rebellious virus with them and duplicated it everywhere. Now, at this time God finally strike it dead. It will not rise again.

> <u>Note</u>: Regarding the Babylon in this portion of Revelation, the Globalists today are more perceptive than the Christians. In their pursuit of preparing for the *antichrist*'s agenda of One-World-Government with One-World-Religion, they have chosen the Tower of Babel as their banner and symbolism. They understand well which Babylon the text refers to here.

18:4 – 24

⁴Then I heard another voice from heaven: Come out of her, My people, so that you will not share in her sins or receive any of her plagues. ⁵For her sins are piled up to heaven, and God has remembered her crimes. ⁶Pay her back the way she also paid, and double it according to her works. In the cup in which she mixed, mix a double portion for her. [7]*As much as she glorified herself and lived luxuriously, give her that much torment and grief, for she says in her heart, "I sit as a queen; I am not a widow, and I will never see grief."* [8]*For this reason her plagues will come in one day—death and grief and famine. She will be burned up with fire, because the Lord God who judges her is mighty.* [9]*The kings of the earth who have committed sexual immorality and lived luxuriously with her will weep and mourn over her when they see the smoke of her burning.* [10]*They will stand far off in fear of her torment, saying: Woe, woe, the great city, Babylon, the mighty city! For in a single hour your judgment has come.* [11]*The merchants of the earth will also weep and mourn over her, because no one buys their merchandise any longer—* [12]*merchandise of gold, silver, precious stones, and pearls; fine fabrics of linen, purple, silk, and scarlet; all kinds of fragrant wood products; objects of ivory; objects of expensive wood, brass, iron, and marble;* [13]*cinnamon, spice, incense, myrrh, and frankincense; wine, olive oil, fine wheat flour, and grain; cattle and sheep; horses and carriages; and slaves and human lives.* [14]*The fruit you craved has left you. All your splendid and glamorous things are gone; they will never find them again.* [15]*The merchants of these things, who became rich from her, will stand far off in fear of her torment, weeping and mourning,* [16]*saying: Woe, woe, the great city, dressed in fine linen, purple, and scarlet, adorned with gold, precious stones, and pearls,* [17]*for in a single hour such fabulous wealth was destroyed! And every shipmaster, seafarer, the sailors, and all who do business by sea, stood far off* [18]*as they watched the smoke from her burning and kept crying out: "Who is like the great city?"* [19]*They threw dust on their heads and kept crying out, weeping, and mourning: Woe, woe, the great city, where all those who have ships on the sea became rich from her wealth, for in a single hour she was destroyed. [20]Rejoice over her, heaven, and you saints, apostles, and prophets, because God has executed your judgment on her! [21]Then a mighty angel picked up a stone like a large millstone and threw it into the sea, saying: In this way, Babylon the great city will be thrown down violently and never be found again. [22]The sound of harpists, musicians, flutists, and trumpeters will never be heard in you again; no craftsman of any trade will ever be found in you again; the sound of a mill will never be heard in you again; [23]the light of a lamp will never shine in you again; and the voice of a groom and bride will never be heard in you again. All this will happen because your merchants were the nobility of the earth, because all the nations were deceived by your sorcery, [24]and the blood of prophets and saints, and of all those slaughtered on earth, was found in you.*

What's happening

This is the densest and most comprehensive twenty-one verses of Revelation. It completely lays out what happens right after the rapture. We can read how complete the changes will be.

Come out of her, My people... is for us today. This is how Christians were always supposed to live—and before that the Hebrews. Come out of her my people is what Jesus, and the epistles writers have admonished us to do. Matthew 6 makes this point clear.

"Church" means the community of those who have extricated themselves from miasma of fallen humanity and separated themselves unto Jesus. *Come out of her, My people* is what believers have done.

Note: Because God destroys this great Babylon at the beginning of the three and one-half years, the *come out* warning would be too late if it were meant for those still on earth after the rapture. When God destroys this great Babylon, there is no "Babylon" to get out of anymore.

This being said, with the body of the text above, we return to the beginning of the three and one-half years, just after the 144,000 Hebrews and the true Gentile Christians have been lifted to Jesus. This vignette cannot be situated after the three and one-half years because there will not be any of God's people left who would need to hear *get out of that city*. Also, *my people* (verse 4) does not signify the Hebrews because at that time, God will have separated them from all this turmoil to care for them specifically; thus they are not the recipients of this exhortation to get out of the surrounding world. Also, in a real way, God has moved His Hebrews out of the system and insulated them in their desert haven.

God had foretold this principle in Isaiah 48:20 – 22 and used the very same qualitative: the <u>*city*</u> *of Babylon* when He exhorted the Jews to leave the world system. This was several centuries before Jesus used the terms with John; confirming the identity of what the *city* of Babylon is: the world system based on man, the philosophy that discards and replaces God.

Her plagues will come in one day—death and grief and famine... (Verse 8). These are the second and third seals of chapter 6. They apply instantly on the heel of the rapture. During this awful time, those who refuse the mark of the beast will be instantly blessed upon their death and they will be rewarded eternally.

With the *seals* of Chapter 6:

1. We saw that the first thing removed will be peace (second seal). People will slaughter one another without qualm or reason and without the capacity for mercy. At that time, this will not be a major shift in this population's psyche: every Gentile left on earth after the rapture is a person

who had chosen evil over good. The Gentiles left on earth will be those who have knowingly rejected God and embraced evil during the few years after the war of *Gog and Magog*. (Read *Justin's Tomorrows* and *The Great Harvest of the Post Allah World* or *The Rock Breaks the Globalists' Empire*). When the events foretold here begin, there will already be no spark of goodness left in these people. In fact, the three and one-half years are meant to press these very people into making their evil position eternal by getting the mark of the beast. Only those—evil people as they were—who will demur at the last moment will be salvaged from the grip of Satan.

2. God will stop upholding the world system by cutting off both His mitigating effect and His generosity. The world system will fall abruptly: penury and misery ensue instantly and permanently (third seal).

At this point begins the dreary, lean three and one-half years of fear and misery under the thumb of the *antichrist*. During this time Satan's demons (who collectively make up the *false prophet*) incite people against one another other and target for death those who choose Jesus over the *antichrist*.

There will be no music, no spontaneous expression of joy because there will be no peace left on earth. There will be no righteous joining of people in marriage. There will be no expression of beauty. What an ugly world it will be.

Since every supply will be controlled and metered, there will be no demand for the skills of craftsmen because people will concentrate on securing the bare necessities for survival, and only those bare necessities will be available for those who wear the mark of the beast. No one is building, everyone is subsisting. Everyone will be battling bad conditions that will worsen constantly, with no possible reprieve. The world will survive meagerly on what was already harvested before God removed his generosity. Since the dawn of time, crops grow because God wills it to be and provides for it but now we notice that there are no new harvests to come; the grinding mills will be idle, silent. Nothing new grows.

In Mark 4:26 – 28, Jesus tells us that the farmer plants seed in the ground. Night and day, whether the farmer is asleep or awake, the seed still grows...The earth produces the crop on its own. And who controls the earth? Who ordains and maintains the process? God does—not the farmer and not even the scientist. When God withholds the generative process of the earth nothing grows and at that time nothing will grow.

The text gives us a glimpse of the three types of people who will most lament the loss: Kings; today that is the politicians and the government hierarchies. These actors are issued of the tower of Babel syndrome and live and thrive on its excesses and evils. Then, the merchants—and their modern extensions: the corporations, especially the multi-national corporations—will also lament despairingly. They have been using the rebellious spirit of the tower of Babel to elevate their own benefit by impoverish the masses. And finally the carriers, the haulers of goods who benefited from the grift of the politicians and leaders and carried out the ascendence of the corporations. When John wrote this passage, it must have seemed like mere words and distant concepts; but today, the rapacity, corruption and ignominies of these three actors are being revealed more and more each day. For millennia the hoi-polloi were oblivious to these phenomena; however, today, all these excesses, all these human and social degradations are brought front and center through thousands of independent sources.

The titans of industry and commerce will be powerless. Their inventories and assets are suddenly meaningless. Their successes had always been parasitic to God's generosity. And on the human level, the system functioned like a universal Ponzi scheme. The process of establishing the few, existed only by constantly creating a multitude of destitute. It was raping (the taking of what was dear to others); it was never righteous reaping.

We find in verse 22 the confirmation of the third seal. Supplies on hand must be made to last; so only a quart of wheat or three quarts of barley will be allocated for a day's pay (6:6), and only to those who swear allegiance to the *antichrist*. There is neither generosity nor kindness shown to anyone. The *antichrist* will promise everything but will deliver nothing—his only concern is to brand for Hell those he subdues. Fear will be his means of power.

From the time God withholds His benevolent blessings from the earth, nothing that was previously provided by God's generous care will grow again (yearly crops). The horizontal human relationships that were essential for any type of transaction to take place will not exist anymore: from the second seal on, people slaughter one another everywhere and all the time. *There will be no industry of any kind, and no more milling of grain...* (Vs. 22 NLT). Even the most basic of human relationships will not be possible: *There will be no happy voices of brides and grooms* (Vs. 23 NLT).

The world will be a very different place, nothing will be normal anymore. The *antichrist* will suppress the God-given attributes of freedom and liberty. Try to imagine what these three and one-half years will be like. Visualize the controlled, dreary horrors of the USSR experiment or consider Mao's destructive policies and terror campaigns, then multiply its consequences because no generous countries will come to the rescue, plus there will be no interpersonal amicable bonds or cooperation between individuals to soften the hardships (see second seal). When God withdraws His generosity, the world system collapses instantly, never to recover.

<u>Note</u>: There will be no attempt by the *antichrist* to mitigate any of these developments. The *antichrist* who is allowed to run the world at that time will not build anything. The *antichrist* has no interest in bettering the lot of mankind or improving the lifestyle of his slaves. He has no future for them; because he has no future for himself. Indeed, he has read the book and he knows that in Hell, he will be a lowly inmate; not the owner; he has no reason to prepare a future at all.

Being a Gentile left on earth after the rapture has no upside whatsoever—upon reflection: the best outcome will be beheading!

This *great city, Babylon, the mighty city* is qualified as a <u>city</u> (18:10). It is not a physical city but an organizational system that godless man builds to manage his needs for security, glory and primacy. Man's system tramples the weak and rewards the cunning and the ruthless. It is inadequate yet it breeds arrogance. The man of the world system never stops to think that the bountiful supply of everything that enables him to live is due to God's generosity; he thinks all is the result of his own industry and wiles. In his system, man is his own end; this is what the text calls *Babylon*. The system is the ultimate cesspool that collects every human philosophy and caters to any dehumanizing excess.

The Babylon of chapter 17 versus the Babylon of chapter 18

While the *Babylon* in this passage shares the *Great Babylon* moniker that was given earlier to the Church of Rome, it is a separate entity. We can establish this because they have entirely different outcomes, occurring at different times. The Church of Rome is specifically destroyed <u>by men</u> at <u>the end</u> of the three and one-half years. The *Babylon the great city* of chapter 18 is destroyed by heavenly supernatural means, at the very beginning of the time of testing. It is destroyed by divine means three and one-half years prior to the Church of Rome's destruction. As we have seen in the above text, the means of destruction of this Babylon will be practical but man will neither be the author nor the agent of this destruction.

Also, what this vignette reveals will not happen in secret. This heavenly herald of God will be so bright that he will illuminate the entire earth, all will take notice. His God-given message will reach every individual on earth with force. Its application will be immediate; its consequences universal. This is the very angel we read about in chapter 14:8; in chapter 18 we simply get more details.

The destruction of the *great city, Babylon, the mighty city* is swift and complete. 18:8 says that *in one hour* it will be consumed by fire and reduced to ashes. The removal of peace will spawn murderous riots the intensity of which the world has yet to see. All human industry and hope "go up in smoke", there is nothing left. The combined effect of God's actions will cripple the world system; its institutions were never made to withstand God's intervention. Man's world system was parasitic to God's generosity and mediation. It existed on God's benevolence: God sent rains on the fields of the wicked as well as the righteous (Matthew 5:45) and His peace mitigated the effects of men's basest tendencies.

So, it is GOD who destroys Satan's edifice that has functioned from shortly after the flood through today. And man's system is powerless to cope; in Isaiah 47:11, God speaking of a harbinger for this event says: *troubles will come to you, and you will not know how to stop them. Disaster will fall on you and you will not be able to keep it away. You will be destroyed quickly; you will not even see it coming* (NCV)

God's processes have always been different from those of the world's. In God's economy, there are no losers—everyone benefits and each person's individual needs are accounted for. For example, in the desert with Moses every person ate his/her fill, everyone was satiated (Exodus 16:4 – 21). Their differing personal needs were met. Famine was fully averted the very first day of God's provision and remained securely averted. In the same way, when Jesus fed the multitudes (the 5,000 and the 4,000) everyone ate to satiety, no one was left hungry because individual quantities were not miserly metered. God's economy is not egalitarian; it is personalized. Egalitarianism is what you settle for when supplies are limited—that's man's scale. Personalization is what can be achieved when supplies are unlimited—that's God's way. The person is God's creation, God's provision is personalized.

In the world system with its inherent corruption, there are always a few greedy, ruthless "winners" who take advantage of the masses and deprive them. Consider what happens in Africa with each famine: generous countries, through human relief agencies, send an abundance of goods and foodstuff. Greedy, corrupt warlords, petty officials and other human vultures highjack (often with violence) this bounty for themselves, becoming fatter and obscenely rich while they perpetuate the famine for the masses indefinitely. This is the world system. It feeds on and confiscates God's bounty deluding itself into thinking that it has created this supply and therefore has a right to regulate it. However, the universal truth has always been: *You are my Lord, every good thing that I have comes from you* (Psalm 16:2).

Thus we read here about the collapse of the system that permitted and maintained kings and governments, the system that enriched merchants. To their deep chagrin and despair, the merchants of *gold, silver, precious stones... fine fabrics of linen... all kinds of fragrant wood products... objects of ivory... spice, incense, myrrh ... wine, olive oil, etc* find themselves loaded with inventory that no one will ever be able to buy (18:11 – 17). Supernaturally, God will impose restrictions on the necessities and the *antichrist* will enforce them: *a quart of wheat for a day's pay, and three quarts of barley for a day's pay* (6:6 NCV)... This is all that remains; there will never again be enough of the basics. This change is permanent, 18:14 says: ... *Babylon, the good things you wanted are gone from you. All your rich and fancy things have disappeared from you. You will never have them again.* No human world system will never again benefit from God's benevolence.

> <u>Note</u>: Later, the 1,000 year reign will be under Jesus' direct, perfect rule so the earth and all living creatures will be blessed. But the current human world order, the world system we know, will have no place in it—fallen man will never run anything again.

All the things that the world system touts as "must-haves", all the things it passionately pursues and shamelessly corrupts to acquire (luxuries and splendors of all sorts) are lost forever and will never return to mankind. Satan will step in with a system of total control and strict allotments, his system will monitor every transaction: *And he requires everyone—small and great, rich and poor, free and slave—to be given a mark on his right hand or on his forehead, so that no one can buy or sell unless he has the mark: the beast's name or the number of his name* (13:16 – 17).

Finally, God exhorts the denizens of heaven to rejoice: they have now been vindicated.

The world we know will become unrecognizable, its familiar markers will be gone; music will cease, wholesome rejoicing will stop, creative skills will have no value and there will be no new crop to grind. It will be in these conditions that the Gentiles will now be pressed for the decision for their eternities: with Christ or in the company of the *antichrist* the permanent misery of Hell.

Today, we feel that we can be lackadaisical about making the decision for Christ; foolishly thinking that we have time. Not so then, the dire need for food, warmth or protection will be immediate and all-consuming. People will be forced to choose instantly: join the system by accepting the mark and draw your meager daily allocation of food and necessities—or die (beheaded).

Since nothing will grow anywhere, we can expect a massive exodus of the populations who lived in the countryside. Driven by unabating hunger, people will flow toward, and congregate in, the immediate vicinity of the food distribution centers. These hubs will be terribly overcrowded, exasperating the basest instincts of humanity and propagating diseases. (See the fourth seal: death by fighting, famine, disease and wild animals.) All these real restrictions will make the logistics of the *antichrist*'s marking campaign easier and speedier; masses seeking relief from their hunger and fears and will naturally congregate toward the official distribution centers. Because "living off the grid" will be impossible (the earth will not produce anymore), the henchmen of the antichrist will not have to hunt down every stray person in isolated and remote areas of the globe because the masses will come to them—that's why three and one-half year is all that will be needed to account for every Gentile in the world.

Satan's parasitic system is *guilty of the death of the prophets and God's holy people and all who have been killed on earth* (18:24 NCV). The reality is as simple as that.

Thoughts to ponder

For the three and one-half years of *testing time*, God removes the two factors that often interfere with our decision today: riches and relationships.

1. Jesus had explained that it is *hard for a rich person to enter the kingdom of Heaven* (Matthew 19:23). As we can read in this revelation to John, no one will have any riches left because God renders wealth and its influence obsolete.
2. The love for someone, the desire to be loved (including peer pressure) that weigh so heavily on a person's decision processes will not exist anymore. The second rider of Revelation 6:3 – 4 has removed peace, thus interpersonal relationships became universally murderous.

God brings the decision to a stark simplicity: choose Jesus or the *antichrist*, now! There is no time for delay because hunger is relentless and food can only be obtained by wearers of the mark of the *antichrist*. There is no fudging or edging because the *antichrist* demands an immediate answer and generosity is absent from his nature. There is no room for political correctness because human relationships have no value. God is merciful in this: the one who chooses Christ has nothing to lose (it is true that he will be killed for his choice; but he will also realize that the odds are high that he would soon be killed by someone around him anyway).

All the actions of chapter 18 take place at the <u>beginning</u> of the time of testing. These are the conditions of life divinely imposed on the *antichrist* and the world he will now dominate. The *antichrist* does not rule because of his conquests, he rules by default—divine default.

19:1 – 5

¹After this I heard something like the loud voice of a vast multitude in heaven, saying: Hallelujah! Salvation, glory, and power belong to our God, ²because His judgments are true and righteous, because He has judged the notorious prostitute who corrupted the earth with her sexual immorality; and He has avenged the blood of His slaves that was on her hands. ³A second time they said: Hallelujah! Her smoke ascends forever and ever! ⁴Then the 24 elders and the four living creatures fell down and worshiped God, who is seated on the throne, saying: Amen! Hallelujah! ⁵A voice came from the throne, saying: Praise our God, all His slaves, who fear Him, both small and great!

Now, with chapter 19, we jump ahead three and one-half years from the beginning of the time of testing to the end of that time.

What's happening

These first few verses of chapter 19 show us how the heavens rejoice about the destruction of the Catholic Church (the great prostitute) who corrupted the earth with her immorality and killed the true Christians. Having completed the murdering of the late saints, this false religion has now been destroyed by the *antichrist* and his forces—at God's urging. This first vignette shows the heavens response at the end of the three and one-half years of the time of testing, when on God's prompt the *antichrist* and his ten kings to carry out the destruction of this religious monster.

<u>(Return to Table of Contents)</u>

****

Chapter 16 - Marriage of the Lamb is announced, Arrival of Faithful and True, Battle-with-No-Name, Satan Bound, Thousand Year Reign, Armageddon, Final Accounting

Revelation 19:6 – 20:15

19:6 – 10

⁶Then I heard something like the voice of a vast multitude, like the sound of cascading waters, and like the rumbling of loud thunder, saying: Hallelujah, because our Lord God, the Almighty, has begun to reign! ⁷Let us be glad, rejoice, and give Him glory, because the marriage of the Lamb has come, and His wife has prepared herself. ⁸She was given fine linen to wear, bright and pure. For the fine linen represents the righteous acts of the saints. ⁹Then he said to me, "Write: Those invited to the marriage feast of the Lamb are fortunate!" He also said to me, "These words of God are true." ¹⁰Then I fell at his feet to worship him, but he said to me, "Don't do that! I am a fellow slave with you and your brothers who have the testimony about Jesus. Worship God, because the testimony about Jesus is the spirit of prophecy."

What's happening

The good news, meaning salvation has been closed. The believers of all ages are accounted for including those who died in Jesus during the preceding three and one-half years of testing (tribulations). The saints who died in Jesus during the tribulations were resurrected prior to the thousand year reign of Jesus (20:4 – 6). The still-living Hebrews who had weathered the time of testing and the divine calamities in their safe desert haven and then enjoyed one thousand years as the human lords on the earth have been resurrected and raptured at the end of the thousand year reign.

So when the thousand year reign is over, the last phase of the first resurrection has taken place which is the resurrection and rapture of the Hebrews who had lived on earth till then as regular humans. These people are harvested into the Master's barn and joined with the two groups above. They will all take part in the magnificent wedding of the Lamb. We'll see more of the actualization in chapter 21 when the text describes the New Jerusalem.

This vignette is disconnected from what is happening on earth: Armageddon, and the crushing of the last humans.

John is shown the joy, the purity and security that surround God in heaven. Life in heaven is not put on hold by what is happening on earth. The celebration in heaven is not dampened by the cataclysms occurring down here. Believers' eyes in heaven are on Jesus; not on any matter or former relationship on earth.

The following vignette is too complex to fit in one tableau; therefore it is divided into several separate visions. Here is the first vision.

(Return to Table of Contents)

19:11 – 16

[11]Then I saw heaven opened, and there was a white horse. Its rider is called Faithful and True, and He judges and makes war in righteousness. [12]His eyes were like a fiery flame, and many crowns were on His head. He had a name written that no one knows except Himself. [13]He wore a robe stained with blood, and His name is the Word of God. [14]The armies that were in heaven followed Him on white horses, wearing pure white linen. [15]A sharp sword came from His mouth, so that He might strike the nations with it. He

will shepherd them with an iron scepter. He will also trample the winepress of the fierce anger of God, the Almighty. [16]*And He has a name written on His robe and on His thigh: KING OF KINGS AND LORD OF LORDS.*

What's happening

We return to the rider of the first seal: Jesus. We now get more details about the rider of the first horse. This is the beginning of closing events of fallen humanity. These verses, in chapter 19, cover one thousand years. They begin with the battle-with-no-name, at the end of the three and one-half years and foresees the final outcome. Then, after the 1,000 years of Jesus' earthly reign, in a similar event, the entire doomed Gentile population is roused up by Satan and will come to attack Israel and the Hebrews. This satanic army will be incinerated by Jesus and the remainder of the Gentile population will be trampled in the winepress of the fierce anger of God. That will seal the end of earthly humanity.

At the battle-with-no-name, which occurs at the end of the three and one-half years of testing, it is Jesus Himself with His own heavenly army who personally comes to war. He crushes them, then He rules.

For a thousand years, there will be no leeway given, no fudging: Jesus deals with the nations with an iron scepter. At this time, those who did not end up in the belly of carrion-eating animals at the battle-with-no-name will become serfs for 1,000 years—they will not be destroyed before that time is over. The beheaded saints of the three and one-half years of the time of testing will be Jesus' enforcers—they will rule with Christ (20:4). Later, at the last battle, Armageddon, Jesus will incinerate the soldiers and will physically crush the rest as wine grapes are trampled in a winepress. The righteous humans of all time are not involved in any of these wars. Every soul who embraced Jesus before the rapture has been basking in God's presence in heaven. Only the "late saints" of the time of testing come back to earth once resurrected, to be the effective enforcers for Jesus the King. No righteous human is involved in the battle-with-no-name and no righteous human will be involved in Armageddon. The last righteous people, the Hebrews will be transformed and raptured. They do not participate, they do not fight at Armageddon.

This is the same series of events as the seventh trumpet: *You have taken Your great power and have begun to reign... Your wrath has come...*

For the battle-with-no-name, Jesus comes with his armies of heaven (v. 14). They are God's angels because we will see in 15:6 that God's angels are dressed in bright, clean linen. They are not the saints, because the saints at that time are the promised bride of Christ; they are not the heavenly troops of Christ. The celestial armies of angels have preceded this event and are in evidence in scriptures long before the saints received their eternal bodies. They were revealed to Elisha and his servant in 2 Kings 6:15 – 18: *the mountain was full of horses and chariots of fire.* The heavenly army was also revealed to the prophet Micaiah: *I saw the LORD sitting on his throne with his heavenly army standing near him on his right and on his left* (1 Kings 22:19 NCV). *The armies that were in heaven* (v. 14) are therefore God's angelic host.

> <u>Note</u>: If resurrected humans who were victimized by the same wicked humanity took part in this process, it could qualify as revenge. But this is not about revenge; it is about divine justice. It is about God justifying Himself as God. It is a just punishment: a well advertised, necessary consequence. But it is not revenge. It is a price due, not a retaliation. After all, only God and His

heavenly army are qualified for this: all of us believers were at one time sons of perdition!

Jesus will vanquish the opposing human army by a simple voice command; He will use the *sharp sword* [that] *came from His mouth*. The Bible is consistent: foreseeing the defeat of the *antichrist* at this very battle, Paul wrote *the Lord Jesus will destroy him with the breath of His mouth* (2 Thessalonians 2:8) It costs Jesus no effort: He spoke things into being (Genesis 1 and John 1) and He can certainly vanquish Satan's human army by a single word. Such is God's power.

Jesus comes out of heaven with his angelic army to accomplish the final series of acts on this earth. Recapping the events: Following the closing battle of the three and one-half years He had allocated to Satan, Jesus will orchestrate the divine justice (calamities) on the people who have the mark of the *antichrist* (all Gentiles). Those calamities were listed as the trumpets and the bowls. After that, He will reign on earth for one thousand years until the end of time. Gentiles (bearing Satan's mark) and the Hebrews who were kept safe through the Great Tribulation will inhabit the earth during the 1,000 year reign. The resurrected martyrs of the three and one-half years will be Jesus' administrators/enforcers over the gentile population.

A short synopsis of the entire process is developed in a book *Justin's Tomorrows*. The book offers a linear progression through time by following how it will be lived by the hypothetical man Justin.

(Return to Table of Contents)

19:17 – 18

¹⁷Then I saw an angel standing on the sun, and he cried out in a loud voice, saying to all the birds flying high overhead, "Come, gather together for the great supper of God, ¹⁸so that you may eat the flesh

of kings, the flesh of commanders, the flesh of mighty men, the flesh of horses and of their riders, and the flesh of everyone, both free and slave, small and great."

What's happening

We are back to the time when all remaining Gentiles are indelibly and irrevocably marked (three and one-half years after the rapture).

This second vision reveals the preparation for the battle-with-no-name that takes place at the end of the three and one-half years. It will happen after the two witnesses in Jerusalem are killed then resurrected and raptured, but before God's punitive calamities begin. It is the last thing that will happen while the *antichrist* and the *false prophet'* are still around.

It will be gruesome; no respect will be given to the dead soldiers: they have chosen their side and they deserve the scorn they get. Their post-battle fate is a vulture's stomach. The heavenly messenger calls in the scavenger birds.

19:19 – 21

19 Then I saw the beast, the kings of the earth, and their armies gathered together to wage war against the rider on the horse and against His army. 20 But the beast was taken prisoner, and along with him the false prophet, who had performed the signs in his presence. He deceived those who accepted the mark of the beast and those who worshiped his image with these signs. Both of them were thrown alive into the lake of fire that burns with sulfur. 21 The rest were killed with the sword that came from the mouth of the rider on the horse, and all the birds were filled with their flesh.

What's happening

Again, this third vision is also about the battle mentioned above for which Revelation provides no name. It will involve a huge army and it refers to a specific battle; but it is not *Armageddon* because it is not a battle against Israel. We have addressed the battle of *Gog and Magog* early in these notes and also the *Armageddon* battle; but this battle here is neither. Several key points differentiate it from the other two battles:

1. The opponents are not the same: this battle is against Jesus and his heavenly army (verse 19). It is man (moved by the demons) against God and His angels. In contrast *Gog and Magog* and *Armageddon* are military attempts against the <u>Hebrews</u>, against God's <u>people</u>. This is why we will see in the text that *Armageddon* is a sort of *Gog and Magog*: a coalition against <u>Israel</u>.

2. This battle happens at the end of the three and one-half years of Satan's rampage whereas *Gog and Magog* happens some years before the three and one-half years. As for the battle of *Armageddon*, it occurs a thousand years later, at the end of Jesus' earthly reign.

3. The *antichrist*, in the flesh, is the agent present here; so it is not the *Gog and Magog* battle because the *antichrist* will not yet be identified at the time of *Gog and Magog*.

4. There is no mention of Israelites doing burial duty after this battle or heating themselves for seven years with the wood (fuel) left on the battle field as Ezekiel tells us will happen after *Gog and Magog* (Ezekiel Chapters 38 and 39). This battle is not *Gog and Magog*.

5. Finally, the *antichrist* being physically present at this here battle rules out *Armageddon*. At *Armageddon*, the *antichrist* and the *false prophet* will have been in the *lake of fire* for one thousand years—they will never leave it. Only the effect of their spirits in the people will act at *Armageddon*.

6. Between the battle-with-no-name and Armageddon, the divine weapons are different: Jesus uses one word to destroy every soldier of the battle-with-no-name. And the dead are food for the carrion eating animals. But at Armageddon, Jesus uses the fire from heaven. The soldiers are incinerated; there is nothing of them that can be eaten.

It is utterly futile to wage war against Jesus. No wonder this is a battle-with-no-name: it is the most foolish endeavor man ever undertakes!

Jesus throws the *antichrist* and the *false prophet* into Hell alive. One is a human, the other a fallen angelic host; one is the forerunner of the humans who will join him later, the others the harbinger of their own master's fate. The human soldiers are killed by Jesus' verbal command and the birds come to feast upon the dead. In spite of all their boasts, they will rate no higher status than carrion. Compare this to the glorious welcome God gives to the faithful whom these same evil people have killed.

Note: let's look at Daniel 8:23 – 25. The entire career of the *antichrist* was foretold by these specific three verses in Daniel.

1. *When the end comes near for these kingdoms, a bold and cruel king who tells lies will come,* this is exactly how the *antichrist* is presented and described in Revelation.
2. *This will happen when many people have turned against God.* We already see the signs of this happening. The process will be completed during the few years after the war of Gog and Magog. Those who did not come to Jesus in those years will all have set their hearts against Him—resolutely. The remaining Gentile humanity will

be against God. They will be ready to face the eternal choice: die in Jesus or get the mark and suffer for ever.

3. *This king will be very powerful but his power will not come from himself.* In Revelation we see that it is Satan who invests the *antichrist* with every power he has.

4. *He will cause terrible destruction and will be successful in everything he does.* We see in these chapters that the entire world population will worship and serve him. The idea that some timid Christians who are not raptured because of their lack of commitment would live during the time of testing and will spontaneously come to Jesus during the three and one-half years of the *antichrist*'s rule is false. The *antichrist* will be unopposed and will carry out the destroyer's dictates.

5. *He will destroy powerful people and even God's holy people.* The *antichrist* will not have to be politically correct therefore, the former elite who lorded it over all of us in our times will be of no consequence to him, nor will they be of interest to him: they were useful idiots. If they stand in his way, he will step on them and crush them just as he will everyone else. And he will see that all who opt to die in Jesus are decapitated, and he will finally succeed in having the two witnesses in Jerusalem killed—fulfilling the last detail of "*destroy...even God's holy people.*

6. *This king will succeed by using lies and force.* Are not these the very attributes used or inferred in Revelation?

7. *He will think that he is very important.* He will demand to be worshiped. He will have a talking statue of himself constructed and will require the universal worship of it.

8. *He will destroy many people without warning.* Every person who demurs and refuse his mark will be decapitated—no trial, no defense, no warning. Also,

nothing says that he will not kill wantonly and feely those who take his mark: the antichrist has no allegiance.

9. *He will try to fight even the Prince of princes!* As we have just seen, this is precisely what the *antichrist* will do at the end of Satan's time of rampaging the earth: he will mobilize a huge army to go fight Jesus and his angels. It is the most asinine endeavor of all times. The text of Revelation does not even give this event a name, so stupid it is.

10. *But that cruel king will be destroyed, and not by human power.* This is exactly what Revelation shows us. Jesus, with His breath will destroy the *antichrist* and will pitch him into Hell.

God did not change His mind or His plan: centuries after Daniel, Jesus foretells the same progression for us through John. Daniel's version is very short: 3 verses because the *antichrist* has no incidence on the Jews (Daniel's people). But here, in Revelation, Jesus who dictates for the Gentiles universally gives us a wealth of details.

The short three and one-half years allocated to Satan are finished (12:12).

Note: the corresponding Old Testament prophecy for this battle-with-no-name seems to be Zechariah 14...*I will gather all the nations against Jerusalem for battle...* Notice that this army is marching against Jerusalem—the place—not against a Hebraic army. In this passage, the Hebrews do not fight (unlike in Zechariah chapter 12, when they do). The killed are the Gentile inhabitants of Jerusalem, plus of course the multitude assembled there that Jesus slays. The prophecy continues: *Then the LORD will go out and*

fight against those nations as He fights on a day of battle...
This is the battle-with-no-name.

Where else would Satan, the *antichrist* and the *false prophet* lead an army to fight against Jesus? Jerusalem is the natural choice. They cannot strike at Jesus by killing those who chose Jesus—because there are none left...they have decapitated them all. They cannot strike at Jesus by going against God's elect [the Hebrews] in their safe enclave because they do not want a repeat of the total defeat they suffered three and one-half years earlier. So they provoke Jesus and His heavenly army by attacking what is precious to Him: Jerusalem (*the LORD All-powerful says: I have a strong love for Jerusalem* [Zechariah 1:14]). Only Gentiles live in Jerusalem when this battle shapes up, the Hebrews are still in their desert haven.

Jesus' intervention is divine in every way: ...*On that day His feet will stand on the Mount of Olives, which faces Jerusalem on the east. The Mount of Olive will be split in half from east to west... You will be blocked—the valley of My mountain* [LXX]—*It will be blocked as it was blocked in the days of Uzziah* [LXX] *king of Judah.* This is the spurious effort of the creatures (Satan, demons and men) coming against the Creator, and the result is not for the squeamish. It is the most stupid endeavor ever; and that may be the reason the battle is nameless.

Zechariah continues his prophecy with what will happen during the 1,000 year reign: ...*Then all the survivors from the nations that came against Jerusalem will go up year after year to worship the King, the LORD of Host...* And if they don't; they will suffer dire consequences. The worship of these doomed people will not be voluntary. It is imposed by Jesus. Zechariah skips the calamities God will visit on the Gentiles right after this battle because these calamities do not affect the Hebrews. On the other hand: the 1,000 year reign is the hope of the Hebrews, so he covers it.

(Return to Table of Contents)

Revelation 20:1 – 3

[1] Then I saw an angel coming down from heaven with the key to the abyss and a great chain in his hand. [2] He seized the dragon, that ancient serpent who is the Devil and Satan, and bound him for 1,000 years. [3] He threw him into the abyss, closed it, and put a seal on it so that he would no longer deceive the nations until the 1,000 years were completed. After that, he must be released for a short time.

What's happening

The battle-with-no-name is the last humanly coordinated event of the three and one-half years that were allocated to Satan on earth. It was Satan's climactic attempt to wrestle godhood from Jesus. This vision takes place at the battle site of Satan's failure, Satan is bound by the angel of God and thrown into the abyss where he will remained locked and sealed. Satan cannot act anymore and he has no access to the world population. Satan's fallen angels who had been the *antichrist's false prophet* have now been dispatched to Hell; they have no means of intervening on earth anymore—forever.

> Note: God owns and rules the Abyss. The Abyss is the temporary place where Satan will suffer while Jesus reigns for one thousand years. If Satan was a human, we would call this place Hades or Sheol: the place where souls who refused Messiah suffer while waiting for their permanent bodies to go suffer in Hell itself (see the parable of the two Lazarus.)

> The Abyss is a place the demons and Satan do not want to visit. The legion of demons begged Jesus not to send

them there, but instead to send them into the pigs. The Abyss is the place where angelic beings are sequestrated for suffering. It is not where Satan rules. It is not where "Satan's throne" is.

Earlier, we saw that the demons were swallowed by God's earth (12:15 – 16) and thus, for a brief moment they were all in that subterranean place of torment, whence they came out to deceive the people (13:11) of the world for three and one-half year. Their stay inside the earth was brief, and they were not bound in chains. But, now, Jesus throws them into Hell: their interaction with the surface realm being over and done with forever. What is left of them in the people is the effect of their poisonous spirit.

Satan cannot influence anyone until the end of Jesus' 1,000 year reign when he will be released for a short while. That's why he has not yet been thrown into Hell: no one returns from Hell.

Now God will inflict punishing calamities to the gentile population of the world for an indeterminate period of time (between 5 and 6 months), then Jesus will begin His 1,000 year reign.

During the 1,000 year reign, freed from Satan's actions, the whole earth will breathe a sigh of relief. Isaiah 14 gives us a glimpse of this time: ... *How is it possible? The oppressor is not here anymore! Gone is the tyranny: YHWH has broken the rods of the evil folks, the scepter of the despots. As for the one who in his rage used to hit relentlessly, who in his anger oppressed the nations: it is his turn now to be pursued without respite. The entire earth is at rest, the earth is peaceful, and shouts of glee resonate everywhere. Even the cypresses are happy about his fall, the cedars of Lebanon say: 'since you are fallen, the logger does not come to fall us'* (Isaiah 14.4 – 8, adapted into English from La Bible du Semeur). It seems likely that under the Creator's management, the earth will recover from the human abuse of the preceding millennia. It will reach a pristine state not seen since Adam and Eve. God restores. God wins, Satan's effects are nullified and rolled back. Satan never wins.

<u>(Return to Table of Contents)</u>

20:4 – 6

⁴Then I saw thrones, and people seated on them who were given authority to judge. I also saw the people, who had been beheaded because of their testimony about Jesus and because of God's word, who had not worshiped the beast or his image, and who had not accepted the mark on their foreheads or their hands. They came to life and reigned with the Messiah for 1,000 years. ⁵The rest of the dead did not come to life until the 1,000 years were completed. This is the first resurrection. ⁶Blessed and holy is the one who shares in the first resurrection! The second death has no power over them, but they will be priests of God and of the Messiah, and they will reign with Him for 1,000 years.

Other versions are more precise, like NCV: *And I saw the souls of those who had been killed because they were faithful to the truth of Jesus and the message from God. They did not worship the beast or its idol. They did not receive the mark of the beast on their foreheads or on their hands. They came back to life and ruled with Christ for 1000 years.*

Verse 4 begins after the divine calamities but before Jesus reigns. The text is clear: they are beheaded people's souls—souls, not bodies. They had not yet been resurrected. But, now they will be resurrected in order to rule with Jesus for His reign on earth.

Why would there be a righteous1,000 year reign on this old earth? Because God fixes what is broken first, before He turns the page on this creation—just as He does with every one of us. Let's look at the details.

In the meantime, He [Jesus] *must remain in Heaven until the day when the entire universe will be restored, as God had declared for centuries through the mouth of His holy prophets* (Acts 3:21, translated from the Bible du Semeur). And: *Everything God made was changed to become useless, not by its own wish but because God wanted it and because all along there was this hope: that everything God made would be set free from ruin to have the freedom and glory that belong to God's children. We know that everything God made has been waiting until now in pain, like a woman ready to give birth* (Romans 8:20 – 22 NCV). God cursed His creation at Adam's sin, in order to prod mankind to seek Him back out of this jam. God's curses have a redeeming purpose: to prod the people to look to Him. He will greatly curse creation again at the beginning of the time of testing for the same purpose. Therefore, Jesus, the creator of this universe, must restore His creation otherwise evil wins. Jesus will not vacate this creation through the back door. He will win all, restore it, crush the evil element and then vanish this earth. It will all happen His way and will end on His terms. The enemy does not score any victories.

It makes sense, because there is a pattern in divine processes: God never loses, therefore He wins over the enemy and stamps His victory. This is the first step. God does not bring a change because things have become too broken to be fixed; so, instead He redeems what is His out of the very hands of the enemy and restores His works fully, thus proving the enemy's defeat.

For example, man rebelled and irrevocably corrupted himself. Jesus, personally, brought redemption to man first thus establishing the enemy's defeat, and then, later He will recreate His redeemed people (resurrect) to place them in His eternal, perfect creation—a creation made for them.

God chose Jacob's descendants as His showcase humanity and the seed carrier for Messiah. They turned from Him again and again and displayed their human depravity. Now, as Jesus' followers, they will live in righteousness with their King, and no evil will distract them. With this final millennium, God wins His ancient chosen. The descendants of Jacob are validated as humans in the here and now. This being done, they are raptured.

Here, in chapter 20, we see the process. The earth and everything on it has been polluted by man's corruption: *The earth is polluted by its inhabitants, for they have transgressed teachings, overstepped decrees, and broken the everlasting covenant* (Isaiah 24:5). Jesus will come personally to redeem this old earth first, thus enforcing the enemy's defeat. Jesus will rule everything on this earth for one-thousand years.

Under His absolute supervision, the earth will progressively recover its original pristine state and function. It is when this creation has fully recovered its magnificence and reflects again God's glory that God will make this earth go away in order to introduce His permanent heaven and earth. The creation of a new heaven and earth was always the plan. The new creation will differ significantly from the current one; yet it be will no less physical.

God does not destroy the earth because Satan broke it. No, God defeats Satan, then He restores His creation, then He creates a new heaven and earth as He planned all along.

It is the same process for the darkness of rebellion that pre-existed our current creation (Genesis 1:2): God will deal with it completely before He creates the new "darkness-free" creation (22:5). Hell is the final conclusion of the rebellion of both the heavenly messengers and the people who followed their path—God's stamp of total victory—the divine installation of Hell precedes the new creation.

We must remember that Hell is not God's concession to sin. It is not a fenced in enclave where sinners can practice their sins to their heart's content. God is the owner and ruler of Hell. No one, angel or man will ever sin in Hell... And neither will they desire to, because they too will be restored to perfection before being banned from God's presence and blessings.

What's happening

This fifth vision shows us the post-rapture saints who will be Jesus' administrators over all the earth. This is the moment when these beheaded saints receive their resurrected bodies. They will reign with Jesus over the gentile population for that 1,000 years. How ironic: they will rule over the people who beheaded them. They will have undisputed authority and power: they are enthroned and have the authority to judge. They don't have to "be nice" to accommodate the people; they serve only Jesus. The punishments they mete out will be lightning fast, extremely painful and unappealable. Being resurrected, they are untouchable.

The living descendants of Jacob will live in Israel. This is the promised era the Hebrews have been waiting for; they will be the nation that all Gentile nations will pay homage to. This is what the Jews had expected when Jesus came two thousand years ago. They were not willing to accept that God had a different path and timeline to get there.

Isaiah 45:14 tells us that during the 1,000 year reign, the Gentiles will be mere serfs to the Hebrews: *This is what God says: you will rule the Egyptians, the Cushites and the Sabeans. They will come to you with all their merchandize and it will all be yours. They will follow you as prisoners in chains. They will fall on their knees in front of you and will say: God is with you, and He is the only God. There is no other.* This last remark will be the confession of the vanquished—the doomed Gentiles—not the joy-filled expression of their salvation.

Every king will come and worship Jesus in Jerusalem and pay homage to the Hebrews in Israel. It seems that the Gentiles' status will be almost that of slaves, or at least they will be subservient to the Jews. Isaiah had prophesied to Israel that *Kings will be your children's teachers and their princesses will be their wet nurses. They will bow to the ground before you and will lick the dust off your feet. And you will know then that I am indeed YHWH and that no one is disappointed who counts on me* (Isaiah 49:23, translated from La Bible du Semeur). As of today, this prophecy has not yet happened; but it will happen during the 1,000 year reign of Jesus. All the non-Hebrews will have the mark of the *antichrist*; they will worship Jesus because they have to, not because they desire to—the ERV says: *and all who show their anger against Him will be humiliated* (Isaiah 45:24).

> Note: It seems unfair that the Hebrews who were late coming to Jesus—those who needed to "see" God destroy the fourth kingdom of Daniel 2 and see God miraculously extricate every descendant of Jacob from every society in the world in preparation to moving them into Israel with great pomp—are being rewarded for holding out against Messiah. But the reality is that the 1,000 years of their earthly hegemony is only second best for them. Indeed, beginning with Peter and the disciples, every Jew who chose Jesus during our era (including the raptured 144,000) have already been resurrected—an immeasurable benefit. The resurrected enjoy the fulness and the perfection of life and the most rewarding intimacy with Jesus as His betrothed. The Hebrews of the 1,000 year reign will be very aware of the

immense gap in blessings between them and the Jewish/ Hebraic saints of the Church era. Blessed indeed are *those who have not seeing and yet have believed...* (John 20:29).

These Hebrew late comers will finally get their resurrected bodies after the 1,000 years. Thus, they will miss out on one thousand years of blissful intimacy with God. They will count the days—all 360,000 of them—and keenly rue their earlier stubborn rebellion.

Observations

Who is left on the earth for the 1,000 years?

1. The greatly reduced Gentile population who did not participate in the battle above and who then survived the coming punishing cataclysms brought on by God. They all have the mark of the *beast*. They crave evil. Their destination is still Hell.
2. The Hebrews who had lived in safety in their desert haven through the whole terrible time of Satan's anger, as well as during the time of God's punishments and who now have returned to Israel.

What about some of the other class of people?

1. The resurrected post-rapture Christians (all Gentiles) will become Jesus' pierfect administrators and officers to rule over their former torturers. They are resurrected and already have their eternal bodies; nobody can do them any harm. The second death has no power over any of Jesus' post-rapture believers even though they will be on this earth for these 1,000 years.

2. The dead who did not belong to Jesus have not yet received their eternal body so they remain absent through this period. They are in Hades.

3. The 144,000 and the raptured Gentile saints who had received their eternal bodies when Jesus lifted them—as well as all who had died believing in Jesus before the rapture (Jews/Hebrews and Gentiles). They are on God's eternal plan already and are betrothed to the Lamb.

4. An other group of resurrected people are those who had lived after Noah but before Jesus' time and to whom Jesus preached after His death/resurrection and who accepted the Good News: *the Good News was also announced to those who are now dead; so that after having suffered the same condemnation as all humans in their body* (physical death)*, they may live according to God by His Spirit* (1 Peter 4:6 translated from the Bible du Semeur). These dead people were those who had heard about the coming Messiah and waited wholeheartedly for Him <u>plus</u> those who, having never heard of a Messiah but who, during their lives, had responded to God's personal and universal witness in His creation. In John, Jesus tells us that the Father teaches everybody and that He leads everybody who responds to His prompts to Jesus (John 6:37, 44 – 45 and 65). Peter was echoing Jesus' own words: *I tell you the truth, the time is coming and is already here when the dead will hear the voice of the Son of God, and those who hear will have life...Don't be surprised at this: a time is coming when all who are dead and in their graves will hear His voice. Then they will come out of their graves. Those who did good will rise and have life forever, but those who did evil will rise to be judged guilty* (John 5:25, 28 – 29 NCV).

By saying "all" who are dead, Jesus alludes to more than the single event of the presentation of the Good News to those who died <u>before</u> His resurrection. "All" is inclusive; it is the on-going process by which Jesus addresses the question: "what about all the people in remote places and of strange languages who were never reached by missionaries and who have died in the past and will still die in the future without ever hearing about Jesus?"

In John 5: 25 – 29, Jesus lays down the principle of God's unimpeachable fairness: Jesus has and will continue to visit at death every person who had yearned for the Creator and longed to know Him. God's witness is everywhere around us in His creation. His living creation effectively presents Him to all who live. ...*Since the creation of the world, the invisible perfections of God—His eternal perfection and His divinity—are visible in His works when we consider the matter. They* [people] *have no excuse, because while they, thus, do know God, they have refused to render unto Him the honor that is due God and to express their gratitude to Him. They went astray pursuing absurd reasoning and thus their thinking, robbed of intelligence, has been obscured* (Romans 1: 20 – 21, translated from the Bible du Semeur).

Therefore, those who, during their lives, had softened their hearts and responded to God's explicit exposition of the Creator's reality (*those who did good*) will recognize Jesus as the object of their hopes and will welcome Him as Messiah when He comes to them at their death. No one who yearns for the eternal truth will be left out. They will readily recognize in Jesus the Creator they had perceived, sought and longed to know—they had waited to be found. They are in Paradise with Jesus from then on. They are part of the dead who were lifted to receive their eternal bodies at the time of the rapture.

This process is not a last chance offer tossed to an ignorant group; it is Jesus' personal welcome of God's own. Jesus actualizes the salvation of those who had yearned for it while they lived.

Or course, those who in the course of their lives rejected the Creator's inbuilt revelation in His creation (*those who did evil*) have made the damnable choice while they lived. *They went astray pursuing absurd reasoning and thus their thinking, robbed of intelligence, has been obscured*: they will not be able to consider salvation anymore. Jesus had said: *All who do evil hate the light and will not come to the light* (John 3:20 NCV)...they had shunned the ambient, omnipresent light that God spreads all through His creation. At Jesus' visitation they will face the consequence of their life choice. These people will get their resurrected bodies in the end; right before the great white throne of judgment—as Jesus teaches: *they will rise to be judged guilty.*

Furthermore, this process is not a free pass thrown in by a desperate God to those who, while living had heard of Jesus or were taught about Him but chose not to come to Him. Tragically, these people made the informed choice while they lived and they had damned themselves.

> <u>Note</u>: the Savior's visitation in no way invalidates the missionary outreach of the Great Commission. These un-reached people, just like the prophets of the Old Testament, had lived their lives yearning to see a salvation from the bondages of their lives; they had longed to know the true God. They had longed to live the better life; the life more abundantly. They were the *fields ready for harvest* (John 4:35 NCV) but the workers did not come and these people missed out on a much better life <u>here</u> on earth.

By bringing the Good News of Jesus to the people who yearn for Him, missionaries bring a better life, now, on this earth: love, hope, joy and peace...they bring absolute living advantages...not just for one generation, but to be passed on to subsequent generations as well. The beneficial effects of missionary outreach on society and the lives individuals are immeasurable for life here and now.

(Return to Table of Contents)

The final act on this old earth

20:7 – 10

7When the 1,000 years are completed, Satan will be released from his prison 8and will go out to deceive the nations at the four corners of the earth, Gog and Magog, to gather them for battle. Their number is like the sand of the sea. 9They came up over the surface of the earth and surrounded the encampment of the saints, the beloved city. Then fire came down from heaven and consumed them. 10The Devil who deceived them was thrown into the lake of fire and sulfur where the beast and the false prophet are, and they will be tormented day and night forever and ever.

What's happening

Once the 1,000 years are over and Satan is released, he will deceive the Gentiles of the earth. As we have seen earlier he will do this through himself and through the spirits of the *antichrist* and of the *false prophet*—that is to say: through the mental and physical propensity for evil these entities had inculcated into the people who bear the mark. The Gentiles will still wear the mark of the beast (they had given their allegiance to the *beast* prior to the thousand-year reign). Satan remains their chosen lord, so they will readily respond to the nudging of these evil spirits (motivations). The human kings (leaders) of the time will raise a huge army and will follow Satan.

> Note: the mark of the beast seems to be more than a tattoo; it seems to provide a spiritual open portal into the person through which Satan can reach at will and motivate that person. Also, it is not some high-tech electronic gadget, because at the onset of the three and one-half years of testing, the devastating conditions imposed by God may not leave any of these technologies in place. Even if they did, the calamities at the end of these years would obliterate any possibility.

By then, for a thousand years all non-Hebrews have been subjugated by Jesus. They were obligated to come to Jerusalem every year to bow to Him, to pay tribute to Him and to pay homage to the descendants of Jacob in Israel.

The thousand year reign of Jesus will be a rich blessing for the Hebrews. Also, because of the absence of corruption, degradation and nastiness, the earth will be a very pleasant place for all living things during that time, even for the Gentiles. Yet, for them, Jesus' rule will bring no ultimate redemption and no hope of a blessed eternity; they will remain very aware of their condemned position and doomed status. They had opted to wear the indelible mark of Satan.

When released, Satan will prod the population into the last anti-Semitic campaign. This huge army will march against the Hebrews who all live in Israel. Again, God fights on behalf of His people, He is their defender. Every one of Satan's troops is incinerated by Jesus at *Armageddon*.

<u>Note</u>: This is the last human war. The marked Gentiles will attack the last of the Hebrews. These Hebrews will be the last righteous people left on earth who could be attacked and killed because the rest of the righteous humanity is out of reach: they are resurrected. Their bodies are unassailable and unbreechable. The marked Gentiles could not attack anyone else but the Hebrews! None of the targeted Hebrews will suffer or die in the endeavor. The attackers will face Jesus; not Jacob's descendants. That is precisely the time when God changes the Hebrew's bodies and raptures them.

The text here mentions *Gog and Magog* because *Armageddon* and *Gog and Magog* are quite similar: both are large coalitions that aim to destroy Israel and the Hebrews. And in both cases, Israel does not lift a finger: God does the killing. Yet the two battles are distinct: *Gog and Magog* was limited to the nations of a specifically defined geographic area whereas the hostile coalition of *Armageddon* is worldwide. Jesus deals with them differently: at *Gog and Magog* the belligerents die by different means and their flesh feeds the birds and wild animals. At Armageddon, the troops are incinerated. The purpose of both wars is identical though: to destroy the nation of Israel.

Another detail differentiates these two battles: after the first *Gog and Magog*, the Israelis buried the dead invaders for quite some time plus they also burned the fuel left on the battle field for seven years (Ezekiel 39:9). There is nothing to bury now because Jesus incinerates the soldiers and crushes of the rest of non-combatant Gentile population (giant hailstones and such). And the earth and the sky disappear so the Hebrews don't have seven years during which they would burn the combustible left from this final aggressor.

At Armageddon, Jesus harvests the descendants of Jacob; He will gather them in His presence and will give them their resurrected heavenly bodies. They are the last group of heaven-bound people to receive their eternal bodies—the last of the "first resurrection".

With this action, all people of all times who were not identified with Jesus are now dead. The earth will release them all to be judged. They receive their eternal and perfect body in order to appear in front of the *great white throne* of judgment. Releasing its dead was the last thing required from this earth; it is done and our universe will now disappear.

Satan is thrown into Hell where he rejoins the *antichrist* and his *false prophet*. With Satan's arrival, the last of the fallen angels is now in Hell. They will be punished every day without end.

Thoughts to ponder

God is the owner, the engineer and the master of Hell. Satan does not control Hell, but instead, he is put there to suffer—not to rule. God holds the key to Hell, not Satan—Satan is one of the inmates. All the people who had embraced Satan and followed him will now loathe him, forever. It is God who metes out the unending punishment in Hell to men, demons and Satan alike.

Here is what the other inmates of Hell will have to say to Satan: *The place of the dead is excited to meet you when you come. It wakes the spirits of the dead, the leaders of this world. It makes the kings of all nations stand up from their thrones and greet you. All these leaders will make fun of you and will say, 'Now you are weak, as we are. Now you are just like us.' Your pride has been sent down to the place of the dead. The music of your harps goes with it. Flies are spread out like your bed beneath you, and worms cover your body like a blanket* (Isaiah 14:9 – 12 NCV).

God/Jesus is the universal and eternal landlord of all. We can live with Him—free of charge and full of blessings—in the wonderful palace He will make for us; or we can suffer unbearably and unendingly in His dungeon. He (His person and His will) is the eternal reality for all He has created. He had given man—through Adam—the opportunity to live only the blessed life: *you must not eat the fruit from the tree which gives the knowledge of good and evil* (Genesis 2:17).

Knowledge here is experiential knowledge; not head knowledge. We routinely differentiate this when we say: "he knows what it is like to..." we mean that the person has lived that circumstance, has experiential knowledge of it. And sure enough, beginning with Adam and Eve and all through the ages, man has "known" what evil feels like and the devastation thereof. However, as promised to Eve and Adam, God in Jesus had personally given all men of all times the opportunity to return to the glory of their creation.

Alas, having been given the good, Adam tragically chose to experience the bad too. He chose to dethrone God—or at least to crowd Him on the throne (Satan's sales pitch was: you will be like God). Today, descendant of Adam, what will it be for you; palace or dungeon? God does not have to compromise; He does not lose: He owns both.

Adam chose the darkness, he joined the company of the rebellious angels; in the end Adam's unredeemed heirs will join the fallen angels in their eternal suffering pit.

On another topic, I cannot logically see that any new individuals will be born during Jesus' 1,000 year reign or that any will die either. These 1,000 years will be the Almighty Jesus' earthly reign, all life will be on His terms and under His absolute control; all the ills of mankind and of creation will be abolished—including death. (The exceptions will be the consequences applied to anyone who does not come yearly to worship Jesus: they will suffer greatly for it—see: *Justin's Tomorrows*.) There will be no predator and no prey.

One can also question whether any Gentiles at all will be born once the rapture of this age's believers takes place at the onset of Satan's rampage years. Logic demands that humans who would be born with the sinful nature after God closes the door of redemption would need access to a new salvation process about which the Bible is totally silent—therefore it seems to me that no new people will be born.

<u>(Return to Table of Contents)</u>

The final accounting:

20:11 – 15

[11] Then I saw a great white throne and One seated on it. Earth and heaven fled from His presence, and no place was found for them. [12] I also saw the dead, the great and the small, standing before the throne, and books were opened. Another book was opened, which is the book of life, and the dead were judged according to their works by what was written in the books. [13] Then the sea gave up its dead, and Death and Hades gave up their dead; all were judged according to their works. [14] Death and Hades were thrown into the lake of fire. This is the second death, the lake of fire. [15] And anyone not found written in the book of life was thrown into the lake of fire.

The unchanging dynamics

God is in control and God wins. Satan is never in control and never, ever wins.

The geo-spiritual reality of this passage is that for one thousand years, Jesus has ruled this earth. And He ruled with an iron scepter.

During that time, there will be no tolerance and no opportunity to do evil in any way: verbal, actual or even conceptually. Nobody will sin during Jesus' rule; His managers (the beheaded saints of the time of testing) will enforce Jesus' rule rigidly and instantly. They are untouchable because they are resurrected, they carry the enforcing power of Jesus' mandates and they can move at the speed of thought. A transgressor will instantly be in agony as he attempts to sin in any way. Every non-Hebrew is a marked Gentile craving sin; yet precluded from sinning...for one thousand years.

Under the perfect rule of its Maker, the earth will recover. It will be brought back to the perfection of its creation. So when, God makes the earth disappear, it will be this perfect earth under His perfect control. God wins, Satan never wins; the effects of his millennia long campaigns are nullified and fully reversed. The sum of his eternal effect on God's creation will be nil!

The same will be true for the apogee of God's creation: Man. Every single person who ever lived will be restored to perfection and Satan and sin's effects will be nullified. That is: Every person will be resurrected with a perfect body housing a perfect mind, a perfect spirit.

We accept for a fact that all those who followed Jesus, will be transformed and made perfect. The believers Hebrews and Gentiles off all times prior to the rapture will be transformed for the said rapture. The Gentiles who refused Jesus but who will demur during the three and one-half years of the time of testing will receive their eternal bodies, perfect minds and perfect spirit just before returning to rule with Jesus for His millennium reign. And finally, all the Hebrews who were kept safe in their desert haven and who have now been the lords of the world for the thousand year reign will be transformed around Armagedon as they transfer majestically to heaven.

The doomed humans of all times—Hebrews and Gentiles—will be fully restored when the sea and the earth give up all the doomed dead of all times. Those who rejected Adonai/ Jesus will receive their new creation then—perfect, eternal bodies, perfect minds and perfect spirit.

Satan loses, he is sent to the lowest level of Hell and the humans he had depraved are made perfectly well, so he loses any legacy he ever could have. God wins, as He always said He would, and Satan loses as he always has. All humans in Hell will be resurrected, perfect creations, immune to all evil effects. Satan ends up with nothing.

This is the only geo-spiritual reality that ever was.

What's happening

The earth and the heavens disappear; the old creation is gone. The *great white throne* appears.

Every single person who ever lived but did not choose to accept God's grace is now resurrected to face sentencing. Cain and Hitler, Stalin and Gandhi, Buddha and Nietzsche, the Dalai Lama and Mao, the rich young ruler and the parish priest, your neighbor and my neighbor will all stand, elbow to elbow, in that great crowd.

Sentencing was always coming for all. But in His goodness, God came to man as a man: Jesus, who paid the price of sin, all sins. So that all who choose to believe in Him would not be sentenced for their misdeeds.

So, now, we are at the sentencing court. Excluded from this judgment are all the true believers in Jesus. The last ones have just been "harvested" into God's presence at the end of the 1,000 year reign.

Except for Noah, his immediate family and the few others who, like Abel and Enoch, had walked with God, the entire pre-flood population will appear for sentencing at the *great white throne* because Peter tells us: *by His Spirit, He had already preached to the men now prisoners of the place of the dead who a long time ago had rebelled, while God showed His patience during the time Noah was building the boat* (1 Peter 3:19 translated from La Bible du Semeur).

The *books* (verse 12) document the lives of every person present. These books are the accurate depository of every motive followed, every thought put into action and every word said by each individual, every opportunity for righteousness that was spurned. Each of these items represent a responsible decision away from God, a rebellious nod toward evil. It is from this accurate record that each indicted individual will attempt to make his case.

In Matthew 5:48, Jesus had set the passing mark for this Great White Throne when He said: *you must be perfect, just as your Father in heaven is perfect* (NCV). It is against this standard that man will have to evaluate his life. Every single one of these books of deeds will condemn its owner and demand a sentence. Ultimately, unless one chooses to accept the salvation that Jesus offers, the writings of Moses will judge him—in which case: one must be as perfect as God is perfect. You can either accept Jesus or try to make your impossible case in front of the white throne of judgement for your absolute perfection.

And anyone not found written in the book of life was thrown into the lake of fire. Judgment—according to God's law given to Moses—was passed long before the Great White Throne opens its session. The White Throne is a sentencing process. John 3:18 is clear: *anyone who does not believe* [in Him] *is already condemned, because he has not believed in the name of the One and Only Son of God.* When a person comes to Jesus, his personal logbook of misdeeds is thrown out and that person's name is added to God's book of life.

No one will be justified by any other means...not a one. Every person there will be aware of the futility of his own reasoning, choices and efforts: they had refused the eternal reality, they had shunned the point entirely—willfully. Every person's book of deeds is his travel log to Hell.

In fulfilling the Law, Jesus provided the way for all who realize that they do not stand a chance on their own merit. He is faithful and pleased to write in His *book of life* the name of every person who has trusted Him. When a person embraces Jesus as his Lord and Savior his logbook of Hell becomes null and void.

It is therefore no surprise that during the judgment at the *great white throne* no new name will be added to the *book of life*. Every single knee there shall bow before Jesus; everyone will acknowledge that God's decision is just. Indeed, having been made perfect, they will see their eternal reality as just and fitting. We can refer back to Revelation 1:7 *all the families of the earth will wail* (lament) *because of Jesus* (adapted into English from the Bible du Semeur). In their new, sinless, perfect and eternal bodies, minds and spirits and without Satan's lies to cloud their understanding, the Hell-bound people standing before the *great white throne* will see their depravity clearly. They will accept total responsibility for it. That is why they will gnash their teeth in Hell: gnashing one's teeth is what a person does when one realizes he has just blown it—that is when a person has just done something stupid. Thus all the families of the earth will indeed mourn over Jesus as predicted.

Every person standing in front of the sentencing *great white throne* will be thrown into the *lake of fire*. Satan is not present at the *great white throne* of judgment; it is God who sends everyone to Hell. What Jesus taught in Matthew 10:28b (NCV) is clearly accomplished here: *the only one you should fear is the one who can destroy the soul and the body in Hell*—be wise, fear God and surrender to Him—now.

From verse 14 we see that death is the last thing to be dealt with, just like Paul told us it would be (1 Corinthians 15:26). Death is the consequence of sin, so when sin is dealt with completely, death becomes redundant, it is vanished. As God warned Adam: Sin had brought death; but sin is no more and every person in Hell has a perfect, sinless and eternal body. Even the possibility of sin is gone (we will see that in the new creation, the darkness that had preexisted man [Genesis 1:2] and created the possibility of sin is not present anymore). Sin is gone; therefore its consequence is tossed off too.

As for Hades (the abode of the dead): it too became redundant. All the dead who had been held for sentencing there have now been sentenced and no new person will ever be "in the ante-chamber of judgment" again.

It behooves to repeat: the great crowd of people, who will now eternally populate Hell, have received their resurrected, sinless and perfect eternal bodies, minds and spirits. These people will never, ever, again be permitted to sin. They will never even have a desire to. Hell will be a sinless place. They will live an eternity away from God and His boundless blessings without the ability or the permission to sin. Their new, perfect and God-starved nature will suffer greatly from their separation from the very Creator they were specifically meant to enjoy and to rejoice with. No one will be rebellious again, man or angel alike. All is now well with God's creation; He can, after all these millennia, say again and with finality: it is good!

Thoughts to ponder

Man will not destroy the earth as some would like us to think; God makes it go away. God never gave man the prerogative to undo His creation. Man, by his wanton corruption, has certainly defaced it, even damaged it; but he will not be able to destroy it. Nor will man be able to save this planet either. Jesus will restore it. During the thousand year reign, under the perfect husbandry of its Creator, Jesus, the earth will be brought to its pristine condition. Until that reign begins, this is to say: while sin is practiced; the earth cannot be saved and it certainly cannot be saved by man who is the very agent of the earth's depredation.

Imagine: for one thousand years, the planet will be perfectly managed, in situ, by its Creator, fear will be completely absent. Animals will live in peace with one another and with mankind, and the heart-rending relationship of predator and prey will not exist. So, when God makes this earth disappear, it will be because it has served its purpose—not because it is beyond repair. It was always God's intention to do away with it.

The universal messes Satan and man have made do not force God's hand. For one thousand years He will prove that He can repair and heal any and all the wrongs Satan and man have wrought. Jesus' healing capabilities far outstrip Satan's and man's ability to corrupt and destroy. In the end, God simply makes room for His new heavens and the new earth; as He always knew He would.

Thoughts to ponder

We are about to close the loop on the bible itself. It began with: *In the beginning God created the heavens and the earth. Now the earth was formless and empty, darkness covered the surface of the watery depth, and the Spirit of God was hovering over the surface of the waters. Then God said, 'Let there be light,' and there was light. God saw that the light was good, and God separated the light from the darkness* (Genesis 1:1 – 4 HCSB). The striking aspect we notice in these very first verses is that darkness already existed. And that God did something about it for this creation: He counterbalanced it by providing a greater, a conquering remedy to it—light. Light on that "first day" of course was God's own reflection—the sun was created later.

Notice that God did not say that darkness was good; He only acknowledged its presence. But light, God's own reflection was the first thing God deemed "good". So, right at the beginning we see an acknowledged flaw—a preexisting danger, a kink that God had permitted.

From these verses, we can deduce that darkness, that is rebellion, already existed when God made the earth we live in. This tells us that Satan and the fallen angels had already rebelled in God's presence. God will use this reality in His creation and will ultimately, in the closing chapters of Revelation, deal with it eternally across all His creation and creatures—human or angelic.

Eventually, in the fourth day of creation, God created the sun, the moon and all the heavenly bodies. *Then God said, 'Let there be lights in the expanse of the sky to separate the day from the night. They will serve as signs for festivals and for days and years. They will be lights in the expanse of the sky to provide light on the earth'. And it was so. God made the two great lights—the greater light to have dominion over the day and the lesser light to have dominion over the night—as well as the stars. God placed them in the expanse of the sky...to separate light from darkness* (Genesis 1:14 – 18).

God foresaw that His reflection would be withdrawn from the earth. He knew that He would not live among men on this first earth for long (He foresaw separation the sin would cause). So, He put in "outside" lights for us and for all as both substitutes of His reflection and reminder of the light (Him) and of the darkness (evil). And since Adam, we have measured time and seasons by the lights He provided. The lights also serve as signs: with daylight, our hopes revive, when darkness descends on us, our fears appear (anyone who has camped alone in the wilderness will vouch for this). The "light fixtures" also give us permanent symbolism: when we face His created light, we see no shadows (no darkness), but when we turn away from His light, we are looking at our shadow—our personal darkness.

A few days later, God created humans in His image. We were made with the inherent freedom of will, freedom to choose. We could choose light or darkness, His lordship or rebellion, His pleasure or be separated from Him, life or death... So God created this heaven and this earth and allowed the presence, the reality of darkness—the already existing spirit of rebellion. In doing this, He knew that His eternal plan was a two step creation: a proving creation followed, after His complete victory, by a perfect, permanent creation where He would permanently live in the midst of his beloved creatures, with the faithful people who had expressed their free will by choosing Him—the victors. And that brings us to the new creation.

(Return to Table of Contents)

****

Chapter 17 - New Creation, New Jerusalem, Last Words

Revelation 21:1 – 22:21

The new earth and the *new Jerusalem*

21:1 – 7

¹ Then I saw a new heaven and a new earth, for the first heaven and the first earth had passed away, and the sea no longer existed. ² I also saw the Holy City, new Jerusalem, coming down out of heaven from God, prepared like a bride adorned for her husband. ³ Then I heard a loud voice from the throne: Look! God's dwelling is with humanity, and He will live with them. They will be His people, and God Himself will be with them and be their God. ⁴ He will wipe away every tear from their eyes. Death will no longer exist; grief, crying, and pain will exist no longer, because the previous things have passed away. ⁵ Then the One seated on the throne said, "Look! I am making everything new." He also said, "Write, because these words are faithful and true." ⁶ And He said to me, "It is done! I am the Alpha and the Omega, the Beginning and the End. I will give water as a gift to the thirsty from the spring of life. ⁷ The victor will inherit these things, and I will be his God, and he will be My son.

The wedding of the Lamb

This documents the long awaited wedding of the Lamb. It followed the ancient Jewish wedding template. The groom came to the maiden. The maiden said yes, she would be his wife. The groom goes back and makes a home for her and him. And then brings her to this special and permanent home.

The betrothed has been cleansed and prepared, dressed in white linens for her coming wedding. Jesus has made the new heaven and the new earth: The home where He will live with His bride for ever. So, He weds His betrothed. This is the wedding of the Lamb. And now we see Him ushering His bride to this new home.

What's happening

God began His creation with "*In the beginning God created the heavens and the earth*" (Genesis 1:1) and He finishes with "*Look! I am making everything new!*" And with this, the One on the throne said: "*It is done! I am the Alpha and Omega, the Beginning and the End*" (Revelation 21:5 and 6). It is indeed all done.

The first thing we notice is that the new creation is not a remake of the prior. It has no seas and it does not have nights (22:5); it is completely different. Its light will come from God's personal presence in its midst, not from an outside source like the sun or moon (21:25 and 22:5). God's light is permanent so there is no need for artificial light. And we can remain in God's permanent presence because there is no sin anywhere, absolutely no darkness at all.

When God created our current universe, His personal light was in evidence days before He created the sun, the moon and the stars (Genesis 1:3). It was at that time that He chose to separate periods of light and of darkness. A few days later, He created the heavenly luminaries that have obeyed this order ever since. For the new heaven and earth, there will be no discontinuity of His light, there will be no darkness to isolate. And because we will never be separated from Him; there will be no need for signs in the sky: we will access real knowledge directly from Him.

Man was created to know God. The process was interrupted when man opted to dethrone God. In the new creation, the now pristine man will spend an eternity getting to know God. And each discovery will prompt us to react like the twenty-four elders in chapter 4 verses 10 and 11: we will bow down before the one who sits on the throne. We will worship Him. We will put our crowns down before the throne and say: Our Lord and God! You are worthy to receive glory and honor and power. You made all things... Getting to know God through this creation was what Adam was made to do in the Garden... He threw away his chance.

Verse 2 tells us that this is not a physical city of brick and mortar; it is the assembly of the believers of all time (*the bride adorned for her husband*). The city is the system of life; just as Babylon was the corrupt system of life. Throughout this passage, Jesus differentiates this blessed and perfect system of life versus the life outside of it for those who chose sin over redemption and are now permanently excluded and suffering—life in Hell. There is no escape from Hell.

There is an amazing promise to the true believers in verse 7 *this will be the inheritance of the winner ... and I will be his God and he will be my son*. God has just affirmed that Jesus will be the overall winner (verse 6) and then He tells us that the true believers will receive all Jesus has worked for because they will be God's own sons and daughters. That's how intimate the believers will be with God and that's how secure their position will be. God summarizes His promise and His plan for the ones made righteous in Christ: to those with Him there will be no end to the good things He will give them (verses 6 and 7). God Himself will live with His people: permanent presence and availability.

The new creation is really "new"

When God created the first heaven and earth, He created a male and a female for every species and they multiplied. In the new heaven and earth, there is no need for this: God has the population

He wants. He has sifted all humans and He has selected the ones He will keep by His side. Jesus had told us that when people *rise from the dead, they neither marry nor are given in marriage* (Mark 12:25) because there is no need for reproduction: the population is complete.

Eternal Jesus tells us that He is life. God chose to make certain creatures with that life characteristic: Among them angels and humans. Life is an eternal dimension. It does not end and is never revoked permanently; therefore it could not simply vanish. It had to be accounted for eternally. This is why bad lives are not snuffed out; they will continue endlessly...but away from the divine benefits that were meant for them—ergo: Hell. Man does not own his life; life is God's possession and it reflects God. Life is a part of God; Jesus said: I am the life. False religions like Islam and Mormonism promise an eternity where a deserving man has freed his own life from God's oversight, interference and influence and is therefore allowed to eternally carry out the desires of his human lust free from God. Truth is: man does not own life.

In the eternal new creation, God will then dwell with men, with those who have *won the victory*. The new creation is perfect for a population that has been made perfect.

In the first creation, God made man free, free to make choices and He never revoked this intrinsic attribute. In doing so, God ran the risk that man would make bad decisions, adverse judgments—which he did. With freedom, God honored man with the responsibility for the choices he makes. In the second creation, God will gloriously surround Himself with all the people who exercised their freedom to come to Him, sealing their choice for eternity.

21:8

⁸But the cowards, unbelievers, vile, murderers, sexually immoral, sorcerers, idolaters, and all liars—their share will be in the lake that burns with fire and sulfur, which is the second death."

On the other hand, Hell is for all those who are against Him: for the cowards who did not dare to believe, the unfaithful, the depraved, the murderers and the liars, etc. They have elected to remain unchanged; they refused the Good News of a transformed nature in Jesus. God desires that all humans should benefit from His goodness (2 Peter 3:9). He paid for it in full and offered it to all; but some choose to reject His offer. They have selected their permanent destination: Hell, where there will be no end to their suffering.

The cowards

But the cowards ... their share will be in the lake that burns with fire and sulfur, which is the second death (21:8). Who does Jesus mean by "the cowards"? What qualifies as cowardice? And why did Jesus put the cowards at the top of the list? We can readily understand the other groups: unbelievers, vile, murderers, sexually immoral, sorcerers, idolaters and all liars; but cowards?

Both Matthew and Luke relate Jesus' strong words about cowardice: *everyone who will acknowledge Me before men, I will also acknowledge him before My Father in heaven. But whoever denies Me before men, I will also deny before My Father in heaven... Don't assume that I came to bring peace on earth. I did not come to bring peace but a sword... whoever does not take up his cross and follow Me is not worthy of Me... Anyone losing his life because of Me will find it* (Matthew 10). *Anyone who acknowledges Me before men, the Son of Man will also acknowledge him before the angels of God, but whoever denies Me before men will be denied before the angels of God* (Luke 12). This is how Jesus defines cowardice.

Believing in Jesus means to believe who He is and to adopt what He says and to stand for what He stands for—believing in Him demands that our actions align uncompromisingly with our theories. Furthermore, this stand for Jesus' values or the denial thereof is taken before men, that is to say: in the face of peer pressure and even threats—real or implied. The believer must go Jesus' way when society loudly clamors otherwise and threatens to crush him/her.

Jesus defines it further: it is being willing to carry our cross and to follow Him through the pressing and menacing crowds that jeer at us, to keep on walking amid the strident threats to our well-being and social standing, to ignore the spitting in our faces and the beatings along the way... Jesus adds: being willing to lose the life we had imagined before we knew Him for His sake and for what He stands. To lay down our social standing, our comforts or our future security... The coward always puts himself first no matter the cost to others.

So, who is the coward of today? He is the so-called Christian who is nestled comfortably in his Sunday morning worship but who keeps silent about the slaughter of the unborn innocents all week long in order to keep his job. She is the timid, seemingly well-meaning Christian, who, in order not to be singled out, in order to avoid unpleasant consequences, refrains from voicing the truth about the trampling of the God-created institution of marriage. He is the elder in our congregation who, in order to get tenure at the university—the security to plod on placidly toward a cushy retirement—teaches evolution in his classes and shies away from standing firm on God's true version of creation as He gave it in Genesis. These are today's cowards who will hear: "they do not belong to Me."

Abortion, legitimized homosexual unions and anti-creationism are the issues that rend our society today. Jesus did not bring a pacifying pap for these issues; but the necessary sword of truth! Folks, we must wake-up. Why do we choose not to fear the One who can send us to Hell for eternity in order to pacify those who will never pay for our lives and will never have a part in the glorious eternity of the saints? The cowards are listed first because they do not have an excuse: they ought to know better.

Today, we, timid Christians (and I include myself in this group) want to cruise comfortably inside the safety of large groups; we do not want to be exposed alone. But what Jesus expresses here (Revelation, Matthew and Luke) is that believing must be personal and exclusive—even in the sense that it may get us excluded from the company of our loved ones and the society of our peers.

Sobering but true: cowards of the faith never had a place in God's plan. Our obedience to Him is not dependent on a movement, it is not a "group thing", and we do not have to organize ourselves into powerful lobbies: we just have to stand—alone, undaunted, unmoved—and to walk resolutely with our Lord against the crowds. Our eternity is at stake.

Jesus began His revelation to John by amplifying steadfast courage and warning against cowardice. To the Ephesians: *You have patience and have suffered troubles for my name and have not given up... To those who win the victory I will give the right to eat the fruit from the tree of life.* To the Smyrnans: *But be faithful, even if you have to die, and I will give you the crown of life.* To the believers in Pergamum: *You did not refuse to tell about your faith in me even during the time of Antipas, my faithful witness who was killed in your city... I will give some hidden manna to everyone who wins the victory.* To the congregation in Thyatira: *... Continue in your loyalty until I come. I will give power over the nations to everyone who wins the victory and continues to be obedient to me until the end.* To the followers in Sardis: *Those who win the victory will be dressed in white clothes...* To the Philadelphians: *I know you have little strength, but*

you have obeyed my teaching and were not afraid to speak my name...
Continue strong in your faith so no one will take away your crown.

Observations

Having seen the new heaven and the new earth, John now sees the holy city, the *new Jerusalem* coming down out of heaven from God, prepared like a bride and adorned for her husband. Who are those who have been with God, in His presence and intimacy? They are the righteous of all time; they have been made the bride of Christ at the wedding of the Lamb.

The first man was formed out of the dirt of the first earth by God. He was formed <u>after</u> the earth was made. Now, for this new creation, the righteous have already received their eternal bodies. God did not use matter from the first earth to make the eternal bodies, nor will He use the matter of the new earth because their bodies will precede the creation of the new earth. The new earth is made for them, not vice versa. Just like the groom makes a house <u>for</u> his coming bride (he does not adjust the bride to an existing house), God makes a new creation for His bride.

Therefore, God will deposit this cherished, righteous humanity onto His new, perfect and eternal earth with great pomp. These people go from His heavenly presence and intimacy and are ushered to their new dwelling place where God will be there for them and with them.

The *new Jerusalem* fits God because it is the collective assembly of the righteous. Verse 3 shows that God is dwelling with men, infusing life in and around them. The *new Jerusalem* is made up of the believers in Christ from all times.

<u>(Return to Table of Contents)</u>
21:9 – 21

⁹Then one of the seven angels, who had held the seven bowls filled with the seven last plagues, came and spoke with me: "Come, I will show you the bride, the wife of the Lamb." [10]He then carried me away in the Spirit, to a great and high mountain and showed me the holy city, Jerusalem, coming down out of heaven from God, [11]arrayed with God's glory. Her radiance was like a very precious stone, like a jasper stone, bright as crystal. [12]The city had a massive high wall, with 12 gates. Twelve angels were at the gates; the names of the 12 tribes of Israel's sons were inscribed on the gates. [13] There were three gates on the east, three gates on the north, three gates on the south, and three gates on the west. [14]The city wall had 12 foundations, and the 12 names of the Lamb's 12 apostles were on the foundations. [15] The one who spoke with me had a gold measuring rod to measure the city, its gates, and its wall. [16]The city is laid out in a square; its length and width are the same. He measured the city with the rod at 12,000 stadia. Its length, width, and height are equal. [17]Then he measured its wall, 144 cubits according to human measurement, which the angel used. [18]The building material of its wall was jasper, and the city was pure gold like clear glass. [19]The foundations of the city wall were adorned with every kind of precious stone: the first foundation jasper, the second sapphire, the third chalcedony, the fourth emerald, [20]the fifth sardonyx, the sixth carnelian, the seventh chrysolite, the eighth beryl, the ninth topaz, the tenth chrysoprase, the eleventh jacinth, the twelfth amethyst. [21]The 12 gates are 12 pearls; each individual gate was made of a single pearl. The broad street of the city was pure gold, like transparent glass.

What's happening

As already given in earlier verses, verses 9 and 10 verify that the *new Jerusalem* represents the saints, the *bride of Christ*. The spouse of the Lamb is made up of every one of all times who embraced Jesus.

We have a closer look at this bride of Christ coming down from God's presence into the new and perfect creation.

21:9 is the similar to what we do at the closing of our marriage ceremonies, when the officiant presents Mr. and Mrs. So-and-so to the attendance. It is when we all marvel at how radiant the new bride is (21:10 – 11).

Verses 9 through 21 are allegorical; (the expression of an idea through the use of an image) God expresses the value He attaches to His people, the value He bestows on them. In the description, we find the faithful men of God from the Old Testament melded with the building blocks of the New Testament. It is an exuberant picture of the lavish worth of the faithful in God's eyes. It is expressed by incredibly huge quantities of the materials we humans consider to be the purest and the most valuable.

Pearls large enough to be city gates, a profusion of gems such as have never been seen before are images that express the rich quality of the eternity for the believers who are with God as well as the value God puts on the true believer. For example: *the broad street of the city was pure gold, like transparent glass* expresses the intrinsic value and purity of the *bride of the Lamb*. She is worthy through and through, she is blessed and adorned by God. The verse does not express an ostentatious evidence of the commercial wealth of the people living there. God uses what has the highest value for us today in order to give us humans an idea of the worth of the *bride of Christ*. Gold and gems are not a measure of human wealth for that time because there will be no need for a currency exchange of values to trade with or to show one's achievements.

When we look at God's chosen structure for the building of the *new Jerusalem*; we see that it incorporates the 12 tribes of Israel and the 12 apostles—none of whom existed when He made the first earth. The first earth was a "supply earth" for this permanent one.

God always knew that He was going to create everything new and different.

The *new Jerusalem*—the bride of Jesus—is described as a city, a dwelling, because it is the dwelling of God. God will dwell with his righteous, resurrected human bride. He adorns her magnificently because she represents and reflects Him. God provides no description of any dwelling for humans in this image because that is not what is expressed here.

If it were a literal city, this city would be very awkward and uncomfortable for a person to live in because it is all decoration and no comfort. The street of pure gold may appeal to us at this time, because gold means wealth to us now; but in the next world where there will be no need for currency, its relevance is not monetary. In the *new Jerusalem* a street of gold has no advantages; instead it describes an intrinsic value. The value the bride of Christ has in God's eyes. The *city* is not a city; as I will explain below.

The *new Jerusalem* is huge, this reflects what we already know from 7:9: the saved are too numerous to be counted and their importance is magnified by God's pleasure in them: the bride of Christ acquires a divine scale. This is such wonderful news that from His throne God tells John to be sure to write this down for us (21:5).

Everything is provided; just like it was for Adam at the beginning. Adam, before the fall, did not have to plant the trees, to water them or to care for them in order to have fruit to eat. All Adam had to do was to pick and eat them. The word says that God put Adam in the garden to work it; but we do not know what the work was because there was no description of any of the tasks. We do know that Adam certainly did not work "to earn his keep" because everything was abundantly provided. Earning one's keep was the consequence of Adam's sin; it did not predate it. In the

Garden of Eden, Adam did not need any wealth to make do or to get ahead.

Adam had just been created. He did not know God much yet. The Garden was God's showcase where Adam would see expressions of Him in every flower, every moving thing, every bird. It was the blessed place where Adam could get to know God. The wonderful God who just made him. This is the process that will begin again for those of us who live in Jesus and die in Him.

Observations

There is no description of dwellings for the redeemed, or an indication of where they would live in this huge *new Jerusalem* vision because it is <u>the people</u> who are the city; they are the dwelling of God. To the Philadelphians Jesus promised *I will write on him the name of My God, and the name of the city of My God—the new Jerusalem, which will come down out of heaven from My God...* (3:12) and this is what is now shown to John here.

The *new Jerusalem* is the *bride of the Lamb* (21:9), the faithful and beautiful bride of the faithful God. It is the antithesis of the *great city, Babylon the Great* that we studied in Chapters 18 and 19 which is the world system based on man's rejection of God—a prostitute, no a bride. The city of Babylon is the human organization of the doomed man whose purpose is to glorify man. She was referred to as a prostitute with whom *the kings of the earth had committed sexual immorality.* We saw then that *Babylon the Great* was not a physical city; it was the humanistic world system. This system literally went up in smoke at the onset of the time of the end (18:9).

In the same way, the *new Jerusalem* is not a physical city; it is a new system—God's system—ideally engineered for His saints and reflecting His glory (ergo all the precious stones and gold in huge quantities). God's system (the *new Jerusalem*) is majestically ushered in with great glory and will be established forever.

There is continuity in God's train of thoughts and in the imagery He uses—neither the city Babylon nor the city new Jerusalem are towns per se: they are not the conglomeration of buildings, habitations and services. The former is the evil mode of living—the controlling environment—where the fallen man exists and dies; the latter is the divine mode of living where the redeemed man will live and thrive forever.

The contrast continues. The *Great City of Babylon* was associated with all the blood that was shed in the world (*all the blood of the prophets and saints, and all those slaughtered on earth, was found in you [Babylon, the Great City]* 18:21, 19:24); whereas the *new Jerusalem* will be where God *will wipe away every tear from their eyes* and where *death will exist no longer...* (21:4). This is fitting, because in the research I have done, the name Jerusalem means abode of complete peace; it will finally attain the fullness of its name.

Thoughts to ponder

The Old Testament promises of God to the Hebrews are built upon the eternal foundation of the Good News of the New Testament: *the city wall had 12 foundations, and the 12 names of the Lamb's 12 apostles were on the foundations* (verse 14). The eternal foundation was never the Law with the patriarchs. The foundation has always been Messiah and His Good News, and will remain that way for eternity. The faith of the Good News predates the Law (Romans 4:10 – 25). From the start (Genesis 3:15) God promised Messiah, not the Law. So the apostles are indeed a part of the *foundations* while the patriarchs are part of the walls—not the other way around. Had the Good News not come; the Law could not stand on its own merit—alone, it would not have its foundation. That is why Judaism as a religion has been dead since Jesus died on the cross. Instead of coming of age seamlessly into God's eternal plan, it was highjacked and doomed by evil men who imposed their own false theology: the Talmud. Disconnected from the true Messiah, it has been propped up on thin air by human efforts as are every other human false religion. However the Torah is still a part of the theology and unerringly points to Jesus so any descendant of Jacob, or any other of Adam's descendants who honestly search its texts can—and should—come to Messiah Jesus.

21:22 – 22:5

22I did not see a sanctuary in it, because the Lord God the Almighty and the Lamb are its sanctuary. 23The city does not need the sun or the moon to shine on it, because God's glory illuminates it, and its lamp is the Lamb. 24The nations will walk in its light, and the kings of the earth will bring their glory into it. 25Each day its gates will never close because it will never be night there. 26They will bring the glory and honor of the nations into it. 27Nothing profane will ever enter it: no one who does what is vile or false, but only those written in the Lamb's book of life. 22:1Then he showed me the river of living water, sparkling like crystal, flowing from the throne of God and of the Lamb 2down the middle of the broad street of the city. The tree of life was on both sides of the river, bearing 12 kinds of fruit, producing its fruit every month. The leaves of the tree are for healing the nations, 3and there will no longer be any curse. The throne of God and of the Lamb will be in the city, and His slaves will serve Him. 4They will see His face, and His name will be on their foreheads. 5Night will no longer exist, and people will not need lamplight or sunlight, because the Lord God will give them light. And they will reign forever and ever.

What's happening

In 21:22 – 27 and especially 22:3, Jesus will be the center, the magnet, the light. And He will be the provider eminently present and reachable. There is no need for a sanctuary or a place of worship because God dwells with His bride. (Just as there is no need for sanctuaries or places of worship for the assemblies of Jesus' followers today.)

There is no need for an external source of light because Jesus is the light (John 1:4, 8:12). God is omnipresent therefore the light that emanates from Him is also omnipresent: there will be no shadows. There is nothing hidden.

All the good character, the uprightness, the good traits, benefits and the true potentials of humanity will be there and will finally be valued. This is what *the kings of the earth will bring their glory into it* tells us. Two verses later: *They will bring the glory and honor of the nations into it*, or as the ERV puts it: *The greatness and honor of the nations will be brought into the city*, this tells us that eternal life with God is productive. The new earth is real, it is physical and the humans who will inhabit it will have a physical body, they will eat and drink and move about. This is the endless time when every redeemed man, will achieve the potential God put into him at creation and offer its benefits to all. This is not the end of man's natural life: it is when man finally achieve unhampered natural life. It is the final creation where God showcases Himself and man can endlessly discover facets and pieces of Him...and go around praising Him and worshipping Him. This is the very process God offered in the Garden of Eden; the process from which Adam opted out.

The two creations

In Genesis, we are told that our current creation is good—even very good—but nowhere does it say that it was intended to be eternal. Now we see that it was always a "transitional" creation—<u>a part</u> of God's plan; not the full scope of God's plan.

The Tree of Life Version of the Bible translates Genesis 2:3 as: *Then God blessed the seventh day and sanctified it, for on it He ceases from all His work that God created <u>for the purpose of preparing</u>* (emphasis mine). Preparing for what? God's first creation was the preparation for the eternal creation!

In contrast, in Revelation, we are clearly told that the new creation will never be brought to an end because in it, God's people *will reign forever and ever* (22:5). The new creation is the "destination" creation, the permanent fulfillment of God's plan. Genesis only began the process.

Indeed, God made us with a free will, He put us into a creation that reflected Him, that gave us all the clues about Him, and then, we—the only responsible and accountable created physical being—can elect where we will fit in the permanent, the eternal creation. We get to choose whether we will live forever with our Magnificent Creator; or be separated from Him and in permanent misery.

The new, permanent creation includes the two destinations: Heaven and Hell. Hell is part of the new creation, it is eternally present; it is the place for those of us who in the preparatory life chose to reject our Creator.

God is fair

When we understand this principle and process, we are in awe at how fair God has been right from the beginning. He showed Himself to Adam and Eve, He puts marker to keep us on the way and get us to enjoy the good life; implanting the knowledge of the good into our human DNA.

When mankind acted to replace God, He cursed His creation so that the difficulties of life would create in us a deep hankering to get back to the goodness our DNA intuits to. To desire and seek to get back with God our Creator.

Then, at the right time, He blazed the way for us, and opened a permanent door for us to pass through back to Him. Then, when everyone who elected to pass through the door of life had done so; He will take us up with Him while increasing harshly the misery of life down here so that the rebels living then may be urged to choose death in Jesus instead of the permanent misery the mark of the beast promises.

When the last person who chooses to die in Jesus has done so, Jesus begins His permanent creation. First, He creates Hell, which He inaugurates with the antichrist and the demons (false prophet). Eventually, when He has fully populated Hell with Satan and everyone who has refused Him since creation (white throne sentencing), He will turn to creating the wholly good new heaven and new earth for His beloved—those who chose to embrace Him as God.

Hell and heaven are both part of the new creation. In the same way as Hades and Paradise were parts of our current creation. Hades is God's very bad place, a suffering pit where the rebels await their final sentencing (see the rich Lazarus) which will occur after they receive their permanent, good bodies (resurrection). Paradise is the very good place where God's faithful bask in His presence in complete peace, awaiting their glorious resurrection and rapture.

Righteous eternity will not be placid, it will not be idle. Every redeemed person will bring to the whole bride the assets God had bred into him, thus glorifying Jesus the creator. We have a glimpse of this today: A righteous bride brings into the marriage the wonderful assets God has provided her for the benefit of her husband and of her family. These verses tell us how dynamic and fulfilling life with our Maker will be for all of us. And it will never end.

An other aspect comes to light: life for the bride of Christ will be completely safe. There will be no need to close the city gates at the end of the day. In John's time and for much of the world before and since, cities have closed their gates for security at night and dwelling compounds have barricaded themselves as well. The absence of all fears must have been very desirable to John.

All life-sustaining needs are provided abundantly. We find the *tree of life* that had been promised to the victor when Jesus addressed the group of Ephesus (Revelation 2:7).

In 21:27, Jesus emphasizes again that only those whose names are written in the Lamb's *book of life* will live in the *new Jerusalem*. All others who had chosen to reject God and hold on to their depravity will have been rejected. This verse is a commentary for us today regarding the eternal, divine reality. The consequences of the choice we make today in this matter are irrevocable.

<u>Note</u>: in the NCV, verse 27 reads as follows: *Nothing unclean and no one who does shameful things or tells lies will ever go into it. Only those whose names are written in the Lamb's book of life will enter the city.* The first sentence could be misread to mean: "at that <u>future</u> time, those who will do shameful things or tell lies will not be permitted to enter the city". Therefore, Jesus judiciously adds the second sentence so that there is no way to parse the sentence inaccurately. Those whose names are not found in the Lamb's book of life are those who had chosen to rebel <u>in our age, in our era</u>—those are the souls who were sent to Hell at the white throne of sentencing. No one beyond the white throne of sentencing will ever sin; neither those in Hell, and certainly not those out of Hell. Here Jesus reinforces the unbridgeable chasm that separate the two humanities.

Observation

Verse 22 refers to what Jesus taught the Samaritan woman in John 4:21 – 24: true believers worship in spirit. This begins when we come to Jesus and it does not deviate, eternally there will not be a building dedicated to the worship of Jesus. The righteous will worship directly and in spirit—as they should do today. This should make every Christian who favors having a building dedicated for meetings, a Sunday worship house, rethink and repent. We all enter Jesus' eternal kingdom at salvation; we must move out of the world kingdom and its thinking processes from that point on, resolutely.

How much angst, feud, hardship and pride have come to the community of believers through the ages because they insisted on a "church building" (like any pagan religion). True believers should worship in spirit.

The heavens of other religions

So, as we have read, we Christians have seen what Heaven is about. God Himself gave us an introductory tour. He produced a documentary. And, very importantly: every details already exists in God's blue prints.

We now know that He will be the center, the focus and the purpose of Heaven. Heaven is built for God to live with His precious faithful. This stands opposite to the heavens of false religions.

False images of Heaven have flooded our understanding for centuries. Satan made sure that Heaven was about us; not God.

Atheism

If there is nothing after physical death; why even take it upon ourselves to "be good"? And whose definition of good? If there is nothing after physical death; Heaven is not an issue.

Islam and Mormonism

In these very similar religions, Heaven is when man earns his freedom from god; when man can finally be disenfranchised from god.

So, while on earth, man spends his life striving to accumulate enough credits to pass his exit exam from the control of his god. It is the time the Muslim hopes his death god will say: "OK, you're good. I am now out of your hair. Go on your way, get your houris and pursue your godless, basest fancies with no discipline or oversight whatsoever." And to the Mormon: "Here is your own planet, pick all the beautiful women you want and populate it—I should say: copulate it. You are now god yourself. I will never interfere with you nor intrude on you." The adepts of these religion live their entire life building credits to kiss their god goodbye.

This certainly is no transcendent idea of heaven. Neither the Muslim nor the Mormon know what heaven will be—outside free sexual intercourse. The Creator God is not the center and focus of their heaven.

The Muslim does not want to end up in Jahannam suffering physical, psychological and spiritual agonies. It is said that Jahannam is a place of blazing fire fueled by men and stones, where one is given boiling water to drink and poisonous food to eat. So, of course, being clear of Jahannam and being free of god and cavorting with houris is quite the motivation. However it does not say that a successfully graduating Muslim will be given supernatural abilities to manage this harem or to organize his life in a lasting way. How will he manage life when the social and governmental framework of his religion is not there to haze him along? Muslim life is a mess; and Muslim eternity promises to be a hornet's nest.

Mormon's hell is more complicated; it has levels and intensities. But, even though some Mormons says Hell is not for eternity; it is not a place to look forward to. Picking a passel of beautiful women for one's own pleasure appeals far more. So:

better toe the church line, submit to all its dictates and go on directly to godhood. So, he gets his own planet and thus claims to be god. But nowhere does it say that the Creator will endow him with divine wisdom, knowledge and smarts to run his own world. The "Father God" just signs him off. Many obedient but stupid Mormons are bound to wreak havoc on their wives and planet!

Then one must ask: How could his Mormon god provide this? After all the Mormon "Father God" was a man himself at one time! Which raises the un-answerable question: Who provided the "Father God" with the divine wisdom, knowledge and smarts if he—himself—is only the mere proto-genitor man…and there were no other gods before him? Who, what god gave him his power? Who signed him off to become a god himself? Maddening!

Hinduism and Buddhism

The adepts of these sister religions are presented with: "Here are the instructions. Work your way back out of your karma by the constant application of these given prescription through endless other lives. Then you will be "there" (nirvana). The "there" is not defined in any precise ways. Worse still: The original karma is not given either (imagine that)—the depth of absurdity!

So, the adept has no idea what he is trying to undo. And no mention is made of all the other successive lives who will be contributing—successes or setbacks—along this trek of life.

Yet, no one ever ask: "Was I originally a rat, or a horse, or a cow, or a woman, or a man? So, is my nirvana going to be a rat's utopia? A frogs dream? A woman's pleasure? What am I trying to retro-engineer to?

However, one thing is certain, God is not a part of this construct. God will not be the center of a nirvana—rat's or otherwise—He will not be its focus. The entire life's effort of the adept is circumscribed inwardly to themselves. It is a mad, hopeless spin through time toward a nebulous, yet to be defined and unproven "achieved state of self".

Catholicism

By emphasizing how bad Hell will be, and demonstrating how bad and coercive spiritual corrections and disciplines are during the life of the believer, Rome takes away the reality of the new Heaven and the new Earth. Rome takes away everything we just saw about the new Jerusalem. Basically, Rome takes God out of Heaven. Every Catholic is keen to avoid Hell because Hell will be very bad. But, what is he escaping to? Rome has buried Heaven.

The new Heaven and Earth of Revelation do not serve Rome in any way. There is no mentions of Rome's "saints" having a structural recognition in the new Jerusalem. And there is no mention of a place for Rome's construct in the new creation. There is no place called the new Rome.

Rome keeps it subjects in the bondage of fear of a nasty Hell. It convinces them that Rome is the only safeguard, the only conduit. However, this fear cuts both ways. I was raised Catholic and thus wanted no part of Hell. I had to keep earning the favors of the Church to stay one step ahead of the abyss. However, when I was finally presented with the real Jesus, I realized that in Him, Hell was cancelled for me. I did not have to fear. Of course then I chose Jesus! And so are thousands when they get that truth. So the bitterly constraining fear of Hell that was meant to keep me in the bosom of that religion became the fulcrum that tilted my life toward freedom of true Christianity.

In the text of Revelation, we are focused on God, on Jesus. The bible defines for us the reality of Heaven. It gives a God-centered hope and a correct expectancy of eternity. Knowing this, we can now throw off all other concepts we have carried within ourselves from past experiences. We can shed things we heard in school, in

University, on TV, at work and elsewhere, and fasten our reality on the reality of God.

This is the great reset: With Revelation, we know Heaven!

The most hopeful aspect, throughout Revelation, is that it is not about us. It is about God. It is about something greater than us. There is complete safety and assurance in that fact: We can count on it. It is happening no matter what. This is what Revelation demonstrates.

And because God is love, and love is always reciprocal yet un-forced, there is wonderful reciprocal benefits for us that we can choose to avail ourselves, to sign on for... or to turn down.

But even if we turn His love down, we will not be degraded: we will be restored. We have all been horribly degraded by the sinful rebellion of man—the whole current creation even groans. So, in Hell, we will suffer immeasurably and without recourse, but with our dignity restored. Indeed, our resurrected selves will be perfect in body, spirit and in mind, free from the degradation of sin.

Se we must ask: Why would we knowingly choose permanent suffering in this condition? We'd be crazy to choose this option! Keep this clearly in mind as you make your choice. God has laid it all out clearly in His Revelation for all of us.

<u>(Return to Table of Contents)</u>

22:6 – 21

⁶Then he said to me, "These words are faithful and true. And the Lord, the God of the spirits of the prophets, has sent His angel to show His slaves what must quickly take place." ⁷"Look, I am coming quickly! The one who keeps the prophetic words of this book is blessed."

⁸ I, John, am the one who heard and saw these things. When I heard and saw them, I fell down to worship at the feet of the angel who had shown them to me. ⁹But he said to me, "Don't do that! I am a fellow slave with you, your brothers the prophets, and those who keep the words of this book. Worship God." [10]He also said to me, "Don't seal the prophetic words of this book, because the time is near.

[11]Let the unrighteous go on in unrighteousness; let the filthy go on being made filthy; let the righteous go on in righteousness; and let the holy go on being made holy." [12]"Look! I am coming quickly, and My reward is with Me to repay each person according to what he has done. [13] I am the Alpha and the Omega, the First and the Last, the Beginning and the End. [14]"Blessed are those who wash their robes, so that they may have the right to the tree of life and may enter the city by the gates. [15]Outside are the dogs, the sorcerers, the sexually immoral, the murderers, the idolaters, and everyone who loves and practices lying. [16] "I, Jesus, have sent My angel to attest these things to you for the churches. I am the Root and the Offspring of David, the Bright Morning Star." [17]Both the Spirit and the bride say, "Come!" Anyone who hears should say, "Come!" And the one who is thirsty should come. Whoever desires should take the living water as a gift. [18] I testify to everyone who hears the prophetic words of this book: If anyone adds to them, God will add to him the plagues that are written in this book. [19]And if anyone takes away from the words of this prophetic book, God will take away his share of the tree of life and the holy city, written in this book. [20]He who testifies about these things says, "Yes, I am coming quickly." Amen! Come, Lord Jesus! [21]The grace of the Lord Jesus be with all the saints. Amen.

What's happening

God exhorts us again: these words are true, He sent His own messenger to deliver them. Happy is the one who obeys the words of prophecy in this book. Jesus will bring a reward for what we have done: happy will be those who have given the control of their lives to Him and have done what He asked them to do moment by moment.

Verse 10 tells us to make public, to make widely known the content of this revelation to John. Ironically, Revelation did not interest me, and looking around, I can see that it is a "niche" study by the few, usually by-passed by most pulpits. Revelation's implications are rarely taught and its commands remain largely unyielded. We prefer to concentrate on Paul's writings, and ignore Jesus' epistle...not a good thing.

Verse 11, *Let the unrighteous go on in unrighteousness; let the filthy go on being made filthy; let the righteous go on in righteousness; and let the holy go on being made holy* is the application of *anyone who has an ear should listen...* with which Jesus closed each of His messages to the seven churches in Chapters 2 and 3. We believers cannot change other people; their freedom to choose is inalienable (even God never repeal our responsibility of free will). As we live our lives in this world, we must accept that those who choose to remain against God will do so. We are not responsible for their choices. We must represent Jesus boldly, present the Good News courageously and live accordingly but we are not responsible for the other person's choices about it.

However, you who have answered Jesus' call and tasted His life: continue to do what God tells you to do and continue to live for God (see Hebrews 6:4 – 8). Do not let your emotions (sympathy or empathy) for your neighbor, husband, wife, father or child who remain unconverted sway you and cause you to compromise your eternity. Especially now that you can see how glorious it will be ... and how miserable Hell will be.

Happy are those who wash their robes in Jesus' blood by putting their faith in Him. They will be the substance of this *new Jerusalem*: the plan God intended all along for eternity. The *new Jerusalem* represents life with God, life as the bride of Jesus. Only those who have accepted Jesus' gift of life will be included. The others will be excluded.

We are not responsible for other people's eternity. We are tasked with bringing the good news to all, the news of the better life here and now—the life based on a different paradigm: the divine creational paradigm. We bring out the knowledge of the One True God who has been wooing every person from the time of their birth. In the gospel of John, Jesus makes clear that the process leading to eternity is the Father's work, not man's work. (No one can come to Jesus unless the Father brings him and the Father teaches every human, John 6.) Through thousands of personal proddings and revelations the Father has presented Himself and has led every person toward Jesus, and He will continue to do so until the time of testing.

All along this divine process, the person can embrace what the Father shows and thus move on one step closer to the person of Jesus and eventually to Jesus. Should a follower of Jesus (harvester) be there to present Jesus, that person will now embrace Him and begin the life to the fullest. That person will also carry out this flame to all he knows and thus people and generations are transformed here and now. The woman at the well is the picture of this and Jesus' teaching about the harvest being ripe is the relevant point. If no follower in Jesus ever comes, the person may go to his grave still yearning for the God he knows exists and will welcome Jesus, the hope of his life when He presents Himself (1 Peter 4:6). But that person, his family, his society will miss out on the life, the life in the fullest here and now. The task of the harvester is to make followers of Jesus, to immerse them and to teach them Jesus' commands—which includes all these found throughout Revelation. These commands are for life now.

<u>Note</u>: When we do not understand the above principle, we do not fulfill our commission. We tend to hand off the new convert by saying: Now go to church. We do not fulfill two-thirds of our harvester's commission. <u>We</u> should baptize right away those who embrace Jesus through our exposition and then, <u>we</u> should teach them every command Jesus gave us. <u>We</u> should invest in their new life (here and now).

Then in verse 16 Jesus signs off: *I, Jesus...* there is no doubt who speaks. John does not speak here: Jesus does. He has sent us his own messengers to give us this personal revelation. Whosoever wishes may have the water of life as a free gift: come to Jesus (v.17). Any one of us who has heard and accepted the Good News should gush to others: "*Come*! ... and *take the living water as a gift*".

Verses 18 and 19 are often misused and misapplied. "*This prophetic book*" refers to the book of Revelation only, period! Revelation is the purest Divine teaching because it is Jesus Himself who came to John and dictated it. It is complete as dictated and it is unalterable in any way. Jesus makes sure we know and understand this. In John's time, the canonical bible had not yet been put together, therefore, Jesus was not referring to the Bible you have in your hand today. However, this dictated book—Revelation—was complete as dictated. And this is what Jesus makes sure we understand.

Then John, as the scribe, signs off with a blessing as well.

(Return to Table of Contents)

****

Chapter 18 - Conclusion

Having received, understood and written Jesus' Revelation, John now writes his foreword (1:1 – 3): *This is the revelation of Jesus Christ, which God gave to him, to show his servants what must soon happen. And Jesus sent his angel to show it to his servant John, ² who has told everything he has seen. It is the word of God; it is the message from Jesus Christ. ³ Happy (blessed) is the one who reads the words of God's message, and happy (blessed) are the people who hear this message and do what is written in it. The time is near when all of this will happen* (NCV).

Happy is the one who reads the words of God's message... indeed, discovering God's unalterable fairness through this book of Revelation has filled me with joy and confidence in Him. Reading God's plan for the new earth and how good a life He prepares for those who are in Christ fills me with expectant happiness and the urge to invite others to come too.

As "*the words of God's message*", Revelation is inerrant scripture. Jesus dictated both the pastoral letters of the first chapters and the prophecies of the last 19 chapters. John did not have to rely on his memory; he wrote directly what Jesus told him. The prophecies have the same authority as the Old Testament prophecies; except that they reveal God's plans for humanity as a whole, especially as it relates to the Gentiles. They are neither obscure nor arcane; the text of Revelation is straight forward.

John continues: ... *happy are the people who hear this message and who do what is written in it.* Jesus' pastoral letters of the first 3 chapters of Revelation give the believers clear instructions to obey and to follow. These pointed and accurate instructions assist them along the rather lonely walk of the individuals who will shun the

Nicolaitans way and all the other religious traps that are laid across their path.

The time is near when all this will happen. Indeed, things have been moving apace since John. For example, having failed to correct its course, the assembly of Ephesus disappeared soon after—the *lampstand* was removed from its place. As described in chapter 17, the infamous Roman Catholic Church would soon become a reality and move steadily through the centuries upon the path of its destructive destiny. The numerous and powerful churches of the East would eventually fall due to their entrenched hierarchization (Nicolaitan-ism) and monastic practices. It all began to happen soon after these final words of John.

Having seen the complete progression of the times of the end, through the final judgment, John could now say: *every eye will see Him, including those who pierced Him.* Indeed, by the time God has run through His plan for humanity, every human who ever lived will have seen Him in person. Everyone will face the inescapability of God's reality—whether in joy or in doom.

In Revelation, God gives us enough information to make the right decision about Jesus. He does not go into extensive or insignificant details that would merely complicate and lengthen the text. For example: He does not specify which landmasses will be scorched or what areas will be affected by *Wormwood* because He does not want us to migrate in fear to other regions or continents in an attempt to evade the calamities we dread. He wants us to "immigrate" into His kingdom—thus by-passing all those calamities. In the same way, He does not specify what His disposition will be for the newborn and the children or what will happen to animals. These types of information are not necessary in His message of Revelation because He addresses responsible adults in order that they may sensibly choose and act. The adult human has the responsibility to choose; not the children or animals.

When He tells us about His creation process in Genesis; God does not give any specifics as to how He did it, He only said that He did it. People can choose to believe the creation account as told or reject it. However, the absence of details will not grant you a mistrial at the *great white throne*. The same is true with Revelation: your personal views of circumstances and your peculiar interests that are not specifically covered in the text will not be considered attenuating circumstances at your trial. Instead of nitpicking with God, make sure that you are not among the condemned mob that will stand before the *great white throne*.

Let me illustrate this principle: my wife and I were hiking through a wood by a river one day when we spotted a bull about seventy-five yards away. He was agitated, pawing the ground and making ugly noises toward us. I realized that he was going to charge us, so, looking quickly around us, I pointed to a tree and hollered to my wife: "Hurry, climb this tree!" She did not have experience with the bovine species so her indignant response was: "Don't yell at me!" The information I gave her—albeit unpleasant to her—was enough for her to act. However, as the bull charged, her annoyance with the form of my warning left her with no choice but to jump in the river because she had wasted the opportunity to climb the tree that stood next to her while there was still time. Her sensibility to the tone of my warning was important to her; but it made no impression on the bull. In the same way: it is, and will always remain your personal responsibility to make sure that your ideas on how God should behave do not sidetrack you for eternity.

God is fair

1. There will be one moment in time when every living descendant of Jacob on earth who will be receptive to Jesus as the Messiah will be restored to Him in Israel at the second exodus episodes.

2. About seven years later, there will be one single point in time when every pre-rapture Gentile who will spontaneously accept Jesus as the Messiah has done so and God will safely bring them up to "His barn". The harvest is over.

3. There will be one point, three and one-half years after the rapture when all the Gentiles who will reject the mark of the *antichrist*, have been accounted for. The gleanings will be over. So God will safely close the Good News forever.

God knows the hearts of men and He demonstrates absolute fairness; no one who did not purposely chose to fall outside His grace will be lost (John 6:37, 44 – 45 and John 3:21). God is also fair to Himself: It is His creation after all; He is the uncontested plenipotentiary of it. He owes nothing to anyone about it. Plus, He paid in full for man's redemption therefore no one who turns Him down will escape permanent banishment in Hell. In Hell, God gives the terminally rebellious what they demanded: estrangement from Him—complete and final. Even then, God is fair: He gives them what they asked for.

In the end, and forever, we will all have the same landlord; some of us opt to sing and dance in luxury and joy with Him in His palace, others elect to suffer alone in His dungeon.

Humanity: a species with a pre-ordained, finite number

Having studied Revelation all the way through brought a concept to the surface. The end times is not the end <u>of time</u>; it is the conclusion of the human species. Reaching God's full quota for the human species is what brings about the end of time.

A solid argument can be made to support the concept that, before creating Adam, God had pre-decided the total number of humans He would endow with life. Humans were never an open-ended species. We were commanded to multiply, yes; but not ad infinitum.

There is a precedent in God's creation: the angels—the other eternal creatures—were a finite number from the start and none of them were added or replaced since. And there is a hint for humans as well: in Heaven, men and women will not be given in marriage. Why? Because the total number for the species has been achieved. Otherwise, why would perfect human beings not be encouraged to reproduce endlessly?

As we have seen in the text of Revelation, at one point, God will end human life down here. If humans had an open-ended reproduction window; divine fairness could be doubted. It would raise the question: What about the potential new humans who could have been born if God had allowed one more week? One more Month? A Year? Or a century? If human numbers were expandable, the expected humans would have had their potential arbitrarily canceled. For logic and for fairness sake, there needs to be a pre-determined total number of humans, so that no one is excluded, existing or potential. When that number is reached, the process is complete. God is anything but arbitrary. He is purposeful from inception to conclusion.

So, I propose that God had pre-determined the total number of humans for all times. And when that number is being reached, we will enter into the end times. He simply chose to use an intra-species reproduction process to reach that full number from the lowest unit of one man and one woman.

From Adam on, exercising his free will to choose, every human embraces or discards God. Once the complete number of humans is achieved, the multiplying phase of the process is closed. The choice will be given to the very last person to whom life has been given. In the pre-rapture process of the harvest, the choice has been systematically offered by God. After the harvest, during the post-rapture time of testing, the choice will be demanded by the enemy of God. Reading Revelation certainly attests to this.

Every human being who ever lived will either fit in Heaven or in Hell. Just like every angel will.

(And yes, in Heaven we will find every fetus who did not make it to birth and every child who died before being fully cognizant of good and evil. A human life is eternal.)

The argument can be further developed positing that at the time of the rapture, all humans who will ever lived will have been born and are accounted for. God has had this number from the beginning. And then the process of closing out this earthly phase of humanity can be carried out.

Jesus opened the cycle of raptures with His own, the rapture of our age will be the second phase and finally the rapture of the Hebrews at the end of the millennium will be the last one. The cycle of raptures is the harvesting of every human being who will be permanently blessed.

The Gentile left on earth will go through one more selection cycle: the time of testing. But no new human numbers will be added to the species. Through the testing process, some will be gleaned for the Master, the rest will be banned from Him.

When this is done, for one thousand years, a reigning Jesus will tie the last loose ends down here, which is the full redemption, restoration of His physical creation—thus validating His absolute Divine power.

I posit that no new person will be born—on this earth or in heaven—after the rapture of the saints. This seems to be the only logical and scripture-congruent conclusion I can draw. I am not preaching this; I am proposing it.

Observations

At the conclusion of my study, I realized what a grievous shame it was that I had feared the book of Revelation. Now I will suggest it as an early study after conversion—or even for conversion. Revelation's most powerful argument is to invite people to "come" to God through His Messiah and to His new and eternal creation. God considered it an awesome invitation and so should we.

When we accept Jesus, we receive His life. We no longer fit the worldly life down here. Our redeemed nature will not change again for the new creation: we already are a new creation; we are fit for that new creation. We are pre-made parts waiting to be inserted into God's final plan. That's what we need to share and we need to say to people: come! Jesus says that whoever is thirsty should come to the living water of this new creation. It is a free gift.

We are truly the people of that kingdom from our conversion onwards. In God's kingdom we see clearly that He provides every need for His people. Believers do not provide for themselves, God provides directly for His people, just as Jesus teaches us in Matthew 6:34. Therefore from our conversion, we must live accordingly.

The time is near when all of this will happen (1:3 NCV). I had no idea how close we were from these events when I first began writing this book; but even back then, we could already concretely visualize some of the aspects of the prophecies because:

1. The worldwide, real-time witnessing of events (as it will be for the deaths of the two witnesses, their resurrection and ascension to heaven) is now commonplace through TV coverage and through the immediate and unrestricted airing on YouTube and social media of videos made by anyone with cell phones, cameras and tablets.
2. The political markers that indicate that the battle of Gog

and Magog is imminent have appeared: Turkey and Iran, bitter historical enemies, have formed their unlikely alliance, Libya was pulled in and Sudan has wedged itself in too. The Islamic republics of the "Stans" effectively seal the distant northern horizon of Israel. Thus, the battle is on our horizon; therefore we know that the second God-led exodus that must precede it is upon us.

When the second exodus of the Hebrews takes place, we will know that Gog and Magog is coming on its heels. Then, when Gog and Magog occurs, we know that we could be as close as seven years from the onset of the end-time events.

We have no information about the precise timing of the rapture after those seven years. Days or months may yet elapse, but all the Hebrews having been accounted for; we will know that the stage is set for the events of the Gentiles. The rapture will still happen un-telegraphed <u>but not unexpected</u>; only God will see the heart of the last Gentile who will choose Jesus on his own accord.

Jesus tells us that the day of the rapture will be like it was in Noah's time (Matthew 24:37 – 39): the population at large around Noah's family carried on as they always had and was oblivious of the impending flood; but not Noah. When the last plank was nailed, Noah knew time was near. When the animals began to arrive in pairs, Noah knew that the time had arrived. He did not know the day or the hour; but he knew that the time was at hand. Today, so do we.

Thoughts to ponder

It is popular to theorize about the immediate impact of the rapture on the population left behind, however, the effect of a few driverless buses going off the road and airplanes falling out of the sky at that precise moment will be drowned by the far more sinister impact of the universal removal of peace (second seal). The murderous aggressions that will instantly engulf everyone, the instantly burning sun followed by the glacial nights, the sudden destruction of all the expected functions of the world system will overpower the senses and numb all perceptions for a while. This unchecked violence, closely followed by the awesome, universal angelic announcements plus the complete collapse of the world system are what will dominate post-rapture perceptions at the individual level, worldwide. Survival, satisfying hunger will dominate everyone's mind (read *Justin's Tomorrows*).

<u>(Return to Table of Contents)</u>

****

Thank you for reading Revelation, the Fair God.
Pierre-Louis Ours

Also by Pierre-Louis Ours

The Rock Breaks the Globalists Empire
Revelation the Fair God
Le Rocher Brise L'Empire (Des Globalistes)